D1313903

STUDY GUIDE

for Stiglitz and Boadway's

Principles of Microeconomics

and the Canadian Economy

Second Edition

ALAN HARRISON
McMaster University

LAWRENCE W. MARTIN
Michigan State University

W · W · NORTON & COMPANY · NEW YORK · LONDON

Copyright © 1997, 1994, 1993 by W. W. Norton & Company, Inc.

All rights reserved

Second edition

Printed in the United States of America

ISBN 0-393-97056-6 (pbk.)

W. W. Norton & Company, Inc., 500 Fifth Avenue, New York, N.Y. 10110
http://www.wwnorton.com

W. W. Norton & Company, Ltd., 10 Coptic Street, London WC1A 1PU

3 4 5 6 7 8 9 0

PREFACE

This Study Guide is designed to help you understand the material in Joseph Stiglitz and Robin Boadway's *Principles of Microeconomics and the Canadian Economy*. Each chapter in this volume corresponds to the equivalently numbered chapter in the main text.

There are three parts to each Study Guide chapter. The first part contains a *Chapter Review* and sections on *Essential Concepts* and *Behind the Essential Concepts*.

The second part provides a self-test, with three sorts of questions, plus answers to every question. There are true-or-false questions, multiple-choice questions, and completion questions. Attempting the self-test after reading each chapter of *Principles of Microeconomics and the Canadian Economy* and the first part of the associated chapter in the Study Guide should help you to determine how well you understand the material.

The final part of each chapter is entitled *Doing Economics: Tools and Practice Problems*, which is designed to teach you the basic skills of economics. The exercises are sets of related problems, and working through them will help you to apply what you have learned. For each type of problem, there is a *Tool Kit* that gives step-by-step instructions, followed by a worked problem and several practice problems. Again, answers are provided in all cases.

Alan Harrison would like to thank Jeannine Holmes for her valuable help with the preparation of this edition of the Study Guide. The authors alone are responsible for any errors that remain, but there would have been many more had it not been for Jeannine's diligence.

We hope you find the Study Guide helpful to your understanding of the material in Stiglitz and Boadway's *Principles of Microeconomics and the Canadian Economy*, and we hope that you enjoy studying microeconomics. If you or your instructor have comments on, or suggestions for improvement to, this Study Guide, please send them to Alan Harrison (Department of Economics, McMaster University, Hamilton, Ontario L8S 4M4; e-mail: SGCAN@elgar. economics.mcmaster.ca).

Good luck with your economics course.

CONTENTS

Part One

Introduction

Chapter 1

THE AUTOMOBILE AND ECONOMICS

Chapter Review

The story of the automobile is a rich one, introducing as it does the principal ideas of economics. The dominant idea is that economics is about the choices made by the three major groups of participants: individuals or households, firms, and government. These choices control the allocation of resources, another central concern of economics. The automobile story also highlights the three markets on which this book focuses: product, labour, and capital. The chapter closes with a discussion of economists' use of models and theories to describe the economy and the sources of disagreement among economists. This chapter sets the stage for the introduction of the basic economic model in Chapter 2.

ESSENTIAL CONCEPTS

1. The brief history of the automobile given here illustrates the broad and varied subject matter of economics and many of the important themes of this book. We see the importance of investors and entrepreneurs and the risks they face, and the central roles of research, technological advance, and patents. The problem of incentives appears both in the conflicting interests of Henry Ford and his investors and in the effect of high wages on his workers.

The upheavals caused by oil price increases in the 1970s and the influx of competition from foreign producers show us how the Canadian economy now functions in the world economy. Finally, a large and growing government presence has mandated environmental and safety regulations and provided protection against foreign competition. Indeed, in the United States, it has even supplied money to bail out a major producer.

2. Economics studies how **choices** are made by individuals, firms, governments, and other organizations and how those choices determine the allocation of resources. **Scarcity,** the fact that there are not enough resources to satisfy all wants, requires that choices must be made by individuals and by the economy as a whole. The fundamental questions that an economy must answer are the following:

   a. What is produced, and in what quantities?
   b. How are these goods produced?
   c. For whom are these goods produced?
   d. Who makes economic decisions, and by what process?

3. The Canadian economy is a mixed one that relies primarily on private decisions to answer the four basic economic questions. **Markets,** which exist wherever and whenever exchanges occur, influence the choices of in-

dividuals and firms, but government also plays a prominent role. The government sets the legal structure within which market forces operate. It also regulates private activity, collects taxes, produces some goods and services, and provides support for the elderly, the poor, and others.

4. Trade takes place between individuals and firms in three major markets: the **product market,** the **labour market,** and the **capital market.** Figure 1.1 sketches the interactions. Notice that in general, individuals buy goods and services from firms; they also supply labour and funds for investment to firms.

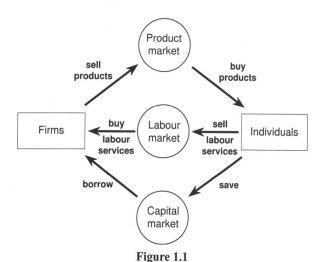

Figure 1.1

5. There are two broad branches in economics. **Microeconomics** studies the product, labour, and capital markets, focusing on the behaviour of individuals, households, firms, and other organizations that make up the economy. **Macroeconomics** looks at the performance of the economy as a whole and at such aggregate measures as unemployment, inflation, growth, and the balance of trade.

6. Economics uses models and theories, which are sets of assumptions and conclusions, to understand and predict the behaviour of the economy. Economists want to discover and interpret relationships among economic variables and especially to distinguish where there is causation and where there is only correlation.

7. Economists are frequently asked to give advice regarding public policy. Sometimes they disagree. When they do, it is usually because they hold different views about either the appropriate theoretical model of the economy or the effects that a policy will have.

BEHIND THE ESSENTIAL CONCEPTS

1. In this book you will learn many economic theories and models. Models and theories are simplified representations of the vast and complex economic world. The way that a model is made simple and workable is through as-

sumptions. We assume that only certain factors are relevant to the problem at hand. Then we derive conclusions from the assumptions and test the model by comparing its predictions with what we know of the world.

You need to do two different things with the models that you will come across in your study of economics. First, you must understand how the model works—specifically, what is assumed and how the conclusions follow. The second task is to evaluate how well the model explains what it is supposed to explain. As you read the many arguments and pieces of evidence, keep in mind how they fit with the model's basic assumptions and conclusions.

2. Economic **variables** are measurable, and they change. The price of potatoes is an economic variable; so is the rate of unemployment. We look for two types of relationships among these variables. First, we are interested in whether certain economic variables move together. For example, workers who have received more years of education are usually paid higher incomes. Levels of schooling and wages are **correlated.** But we are also interested in whether a change in one variable **causes** a change in another variable. Specifically, does more education cause higher wages (perhaps by raising workers' productivity)? Before economists make conclusions, they require a sound model that shows how a change in an economic variable was caused and also some evidence that the model's assumptions are appropriate and that its predictions proved accurate.

3. **Positive economics** focuses on questions about how the economy works. What does it do, and why does it do it? **Normative economics,** on the other hand, typically asks what should be done. Keep in mind, however, that normative economics cannot prescribe which value to hold; it describes the appropriate policy given the value.

4. Microeconomics and macroeconomics are two ways of looking at the economy. Microeconomics looks from the bottom up; it starts with the behaviour of individuals and firms and builds to an understanding of markets and the economy as a whole. Macroeconomics, on the other hand, is a top-down look, beginning with a description of the performance of aggregate economic variables and then constructing explanations. Micro- and macroeconomics must fit together. The models that explain how individuals, firms, and markets work must be consistent with the models that we use to describe the economy as a whole.

SELF-TEST

True or False

1. Henry Ford patented the internal combustion engine.

2. Henry Ford paid his workers especially high wages because he wanted them to earn enough to buy his cars.

3. Patents give exclusive rights to market an innovation for a limited period of time.

4. The import restrictions negotiated by the U.S. and Canadian governments on exports of Japanese automobiles raised the Canadian price of both automobiles built in Canada and those imported from Japan.

5. The Canada-U.S. Auto Pact requires that all automobiles produced in Canada be sold in Canada.

6. Economics studies how individuals, firms, governments, and other organizations make choices and how those choices determine the allocation of the economy's resources.

7. The four basic questions concerning how economies function are: what is produced and in what quantities, how are the goods produced, for whom are they produced, and who makes the decisions?

8. Most resource allocation decisions in Canada are made by the different levels of government.

9. In centrally planned economies, most decisions are made by the government.

10. The three major markets are the product, labour, and insurance markets.

11. Microeconomics focuses on the behaviour of the economy as a whole.

12. Macroeconomics studies the behaviour of firms, households, and individuals.

13. If two economic variables are correlated, there may not be a systematic relationship between them; if there is a sytematic relationship between them, they are correlated.

14. When two variables are correlated, it is because changes in one cause changes in the other.

15. Normative economics deals with questions concerning how the economy actually works.

Multiple Choice

1. The price of the original Model T Ford, when it was first introduced in 1909, was _____ U.S. dollars:

    a. 250
    b. 360
    c. 440
    d. 900
    e. 1,500

2. A patent on a new product:

    a. gives the inventor exclusive rights to sell his idea but not the product.
    b. gives the inventor exclusive rights to produce and market the product.
    c. discourages innovative activity.
    d. ensures that there will be adequate competition for the new product.
    e. prevents the inventor from charging too high a price for the product.

3. Today, there are three North American automobile manufacturers. In 1903, there were:

    a. fewer than 10.

    b. between 10 and 25.
    c. between 25 and 75.
    d. between 75 and 100.
    e. over 100.

4. The North American automobile industry was more heavily affected than the automobile industries in Europe and Japan by the increase in oil prices in 1973 that resulted from the restrictions on supply introduced by the Organization of Petroleum Exporting Countries (OPEC) because:

    a. gasoline taxes were higher in North America.
    b. the Europeans and the Japanese preferred the bigger North American cars.
    c. OPEC sold oil to Europe and Japan at discount prices.
    d. North Americans switched to smaller European and Japanese cars.
    e. North America had no domestic supply of oil.

5. In the 1980s, the Canadian and U.S. governments negotiated limitations on exports of Japanese automobiles to North America. This led to:

    a. higher prices of both North American and Japanese cars.
    b. higher prices of Japanese cars and lower prices of North American cars.
    c. an increase in exports of Japanese automobiles to North America.
    d. lower prices of Japanese cars and higher prices of North American cars.
    e. lower prices of both North American and Japanese cars.

6. In the 1980s, the Canadian and U.S. governments negotiated limitations on exports of Japanese automobiles to North America. This led to:

    a. higher prices of Japanese cars and lower prices of North American cars.
    b. the production of North American manufacturers' automobiles in Japan.
    c. the takeover of North American automobile manufacturers by Japanese firms.
    d. the production of Japanese manufacturers' automobiles in North America.
    e. lower prices of Japanese cars and higher prices of North American cars.

7. The Canada-U.S. Auto Pact:

    a. was superseded by the Canada-U.S. Free Trade Agreement.
    b. came into force after the Canada-U.S. Free Trade Agreement.
    c. remained unchanged by the Canada-U.S. and North American Free Trade Agreements.
    d. came into force after the North American Free Trade Agreement.
    e. was superseded by the North American Free Trade Agreement.

8. Because resources are scarce:

    a. the poor have no choices to make.

b. choices must be made.
c. all except the rich must make choices.
d. they must not be used.
e. governments must allocate resources.

9. All of the following, except one, are the fundamental questions concerning how economies function. Which is the odd one out?

a. What is produced, and in what quantities?
b. How are the goods produced?
c. For whom are they produced?
d. Who makes the decisions?
e. Is the economy efficient?

10. In a market economy, the four basic questions are answered by:

a. faceless bureaucrats.
b. the government and individuals.
c. individuals and firms.
d. firms and the government.
e. faceless corporations.

11. In Canada, the government's role includes all of the following except one. Which is the odd one out?

a. ownership of the means of production
b. setting certain prices
c. imposing taxes and subsidies
d. provision of certain goods
e. determination of the legal structure

12. In market economies, goods are consumed by those who:

a. need them but cannot afford them.
b. work the hardest.
c. can afford them and do not want them.
d. most deserve them.
e. want them and can afford them.

13. The market economy revolves around trades in the:

a. labour, foreign exchange, and stock markets.
b. product, labour, and stock markets.
c. foreign exchange, labour, and capital markets.
d. capital, product, and labour markets.
e. stock, foreign exchange, and capital markets.

14. In the labour market, households:

a. are buyers and firms are sellers.
b. and firms are both buyers.
c. are sellers and firms are buyers.
d. and firms are both sellers.
e. and firms are neither buyers nor sellers.

15. When economists talk about the capital market, they mean the market for:

a. loanable funds.
b. inputs in production.
c. capital goods.
d. plant and machinery.
e. physical plant.

16. Macroeconomics studies the behaviour of:

a. firms.
b. individuals.
c. households.
d. the economy.
e. workers.

17. A set of assumptions, or hypotheses, and the conclusions derived from those assumptions is called:

a. a theory.
b. a variable.
c. a social science.
d. correlation.
e. verification.

18. Consider the statement: "Women who work outside the home tend to have a lower-than-average wage if they have a higher-than-average number of children." This is an example of:

a. normative economics.
b. a prediction.
c. correlation.
d. causation.
e. a theory.

19. Which of the following is an example of positive economics?

a. The government should stimulate the economy to end the recession.
b. The output lost by the policy of keeping the interest rate high to protect the exchange rate was too high a price to pay.
c. The interest rate should be lowered to encourage investment.
d. There is no point defending the exchange rate by keeping the interest rate high if it causes unemployment.
e. The government cannot lower the interest rate without reducing the exchange rate.

20. Which of the following is an example of normative economics?

a. If investment were higher, this would stimulate the economy.
b. A recession is defined as two quarters of negative growth.
c. The government cannot lower the interest rate without reducing the exchange rate.
d. The interest rate should be lowered to encourage investment.
e. A reduction in the interest rate encourages investment.

Completion

1. Exchanges take place in _____.

2. In a _____ economy, some decisions are made by government and others by markets.

3. All the institutions involved in borrowing and lending money make up the _____ market.

4. The behaviour of the economy as a whole, and espe-

cially of certain aggregate measures such as unemployment and inflation, is called _____.

5. The branch of economics that focuses on firms, households, and individuals and studies product, labour, and capital markets is called _____.

6. The statement that crime rates are higher in low-income areas is an example of _____.

7. If it were established that poverty leads to crime, this would be an example of _____.

8. Economists use _____, which are sets of assumptions, conclusions, and data, to study the economy and evaluate the consequences of various policies.

9. _____ economics rests on value judgments; _____ economics describes how the economy behaves.

10. The four basic questions that economists ask about the economy are (1) what is produced and in what quantities, (2) _____, (3) for whom are they produced, and (4) who makes the decisions?

Answers to Self-Test

True or False

1. f	4. t	7. t	10. f	13. t
2. f	5. f	8. f	11. f	14. f
3. t	6. t	9. t	12. f	15. f

Multiple Choice

1. d	6. d	11. a	16. d
2. b	7. c	12. e	17. a
3. e	8. b	13. d	18. c
4. d	9. e	14. c	19. e
5. a	10. c	15. a	20. d

Completion

1. markets
2. mixed
3. capital
4. macroeconomics
5. microeconomics
6. correlation
7. causation
8. theories or models
9. Normative; positive
10. how are these goods produced

Chapter 2

THINKING LIKE AN ECONOMIST

Chapter Review

The concept of scarcity discussed in Chapter 1 implies that choices must be made. This chapter begins to explain how economists think about choice, and how choices are influenced and coordinated by markets. A basic economic assumption is that of rational choice, which simply says that people select the alternative they prefer most from among all those that are available. The alternatives available to any particular firm or individual, of course, depend upon the choices made by other firms and individuals. All these rational choices must somehow fit together, and markets serve the function of coordinating them. How they do so is the subject of Chapters 3 through 5.

ESSENTIAL CONCEPTS

1. The **basic economic model** includes three elements: individuals, firms, and markets. Economic decisions such as what and how much of each type of good to produce, how to produce them, what kind of career to pursue, and how to spend one's earnings are made by **rational, self-interested individuals** and **rational, profit-maximizing firms. Markets** serve the economic role of coordinating these decisions.

2. The basic economic model assumes that markets are **perfectly competitive.** In competitive markets, there are many consumers and firms, and each is small relative to the size of the overall market. One key feature of perfect competition is that any firm charging more than the going price will lose all its customers. Without any ability to influence the market price, the firm is a **price taker.** (Later in this book, we will encounter monopolists and other types of **price makers,** who have the power to charge higher prices without losing all their customers.)

3. Private **property rights** play an important role in the basic model. They include the right to use resources in certain ways and the right to sell them in markets. These two aspects of property rights provide incentives to use resources efficiently and to transfer resources to their most valuable use. Inefficiencies can arise when property rights are ill-defined, restricted, or completely absent.

4. When compensation is tied to performance, people have strong incentives to work hard and be productive, but those who are more fortunate and successful also will earn higher incomes. On the other hand, distributing the output more equally undermines incentives. This **incentive-equality trade-off** is one of the basic questions facing societies: how should the tax and welfare system

be constructed to balance the competing ends of providing strong incentives and promoting equality?

5. **Scarcity** implies that not everyone who desires a good or resource can have it. There is an allocation problem. In market economies, goods are allocated to the highest bidder. Another solution to the allocation problem is to **ration**. Rationing schemes include queues, lotteries, coupons, and rationing by government regulation. Unless supplemented by markets, rationing schemes are likely to lead to inefficiencies.

6. The basic economic model assumes that decisions are made rationally: individuals and firms balance the benefits and costs of their decisions. Economists see rational decision making as a two-step process. First, find which alternatives are feasible. This step is the construction of the **opportunity set**. Next, select the best alternative from those within the opportunity set.

7. The chapter presents three types of opportunity sets. The **budget constraint** shows what combinations of goods can be consumed with a limited amount of money. The **time constraint** indicates alternative uses of limited time. Finally, the **production possibilities curve** depicts the combinations of goods that a firm or an entire economy can produce given its limited resources and the quality of the available technology.

8. The best alternatives in an opportunity set lie along the outer edge. This is because people prefer more goods to fewer. Operating on the outer edge also implies that there will be a **trade-off**: more of one good or activity means less of another. For example, on the budget constraint, consuming more of one good means that less money is available to spend on another good. On the time constraint, if an individual devotes more time to one activity, there is less time available for other endeavours. A society that chooses to produce more of one good must settle for lower production of other goods.

9. The **opportunity cost** of a good or activity is the option forgone. The opportunity cost of consuming more of one good is consuming less of some alternative good. The opportunity cost of an activity is the other endeavour that would have been, but now cannot be, undertaken. The opportunity cost of producing one good is the necessarily lower production of another.

10. The opportunity cost, not the price, is the proper measure of the economic cost of any choice. For example, in addition to the ultimate purchase price, the opportunity cost of buying an automobile includes the time and expense devoted to investigating alternatives, searching for the best deal, and negotiating the terms.

11. Opportunity costs are measured in total and at the margin. When a firm is deciding where to locate its plant, it compares the **total costs** at each location. When a firm is considering how large a plant to build, it looks at the costs of increasing or decreasing the size. These are the **marginal costs**, the costs of a little bit more or a little bit less.

BEHIND THE ESSENTIAL CONCEPTS

1. The basic competitive model introduced in this chapter is critical to your understanding of economics. It will be expanded and applied in all the chapters that follow, but you should master the concepts given in this chapter: rational individuals choose the best combinations of goods along their budget constraints, firms maximize profits, and trading takes place in competitive markets, where each individual and firm is a price taker.

2. The opportunity set itself shows all the alternatives that are available. Because more is generally preferred to less, however, economists focus on the outer boundary of the opportunity set. For example, Figure 2.1 shows an opportunity set for an agricultural firm that must divide its resources between growing corn and growing wheat. The entire shaded area shows all the combinations that are possible. The economist's attention is drawn to the outer edge, the production possibilities curve, because to choose a combination inside (such as point A) would be inefficient.

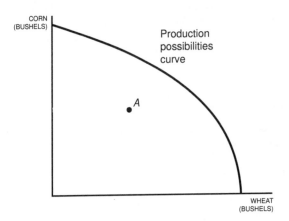

Figure 2.1

3. The terms "opportunity set," "budget constraint," "trade-off," and "opportunity cost" are related, but they are distinct, and you should take care to understand each one. Figure 2.2 shows the opportunity set for a student who consumes hamburgers and pizzas. The **opportunity set** shows all the combinations of hamburgers and pizzas that are affordable. Points A and B are affordable; they lie within the opportunity set, but have the critical characteristic of lying along its outer edge, which is the budget constraint. The trade-off is that more hamburgers mean fewer pizzas. If Joe chooses B rather than A, he eats another pizza and exactly two fewer hamburgers. The trade-off between any two points measures the opportunity cost. In this case, the opportunity cost of this extra pizza is the two forgone burgers. When the outer edge of the opportunity set is a straight line, the trade-offs will be the same all along the line; when it is a curve, the trade-offs will change.

4. Opportunity costs are forgone alternatives—not money, not time, and not resources. For example, if you spend

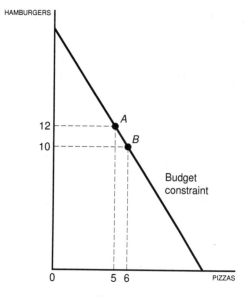

Figure 2.2

one hour in class tomorrow, the opportunity cost of attending that class is not the hour itself. That hour will pass whether you go to the class or not. The opportunity cost is what you would have done with that hour. It is the activity you give up. Strictly speaking, the opportunity cost of buying a book for $20 is not the money, but what would have been purchased with the $20 if it had not been spent on the book.

5. **Sunk costs**, outlays that cannot be recovered, are not opportunity costs. Because these expenditures are not affected by the choice of any alternative, they do not represent the opportunity cost of any alternative. For example, suppose that you sign a one-year lease on an apartment and are forbidden to sublet it. When you consider whether to stay in town for the summer or travel abroad, the rent you owe your landlord is irrelevant. You cannot do anything about it. Regardless of which alternative you choose, you must pay the rent. The rent is a sunk cost, not an opportunity cost.

6. Be clear about the difference between total costs and marginal costs. Marginal costs are the costs of a little more or a little less of some activity. Before considering going into business, you evaluate the total opportunity costs of the enterprise—all the costs of setting up the plant, designing and producing the product, and locating the market. When you are considering whether to produce another unit of output, however, it is the marginal opportunity cost that is important. The marginal cost of producing a little bit more is just the added cost incurred when producing more with the plant already set up, the product designed, and the market found.

7. The principle of **diminishing returns** explains what happens if more and more of one input is added to the production process when the amount of another input is fixed. Output rises but by successively smaller amounts. For example, suppose more workers are hired to pick apples in an orchard. The addition of each worker increases the total number of apples picked, but the increase in ap-

ples picked gets smaller as the number of workers already picking apples increases. It is not that the new workers are any worse at picking apples, just that the orchard gets more crowded, and there are fewer trees per worker, so picking becomes more difficult. Equivalently, the opportunity cost of successive increases in output—the marginal cost—increases with total output.

SELF-TEST

True or False

1. The basic model of economics seeks to explain why people want what they want.

2. In the basic competitive model, firms maximize profits.

3. Inequality is generally greater when society is organized to provide stronger incentives to perform efficiently.

4. If a firm is a price taker, any increase in the price it charges will mean that it loses all its customers.

5. Both the right to use a resource in certain ways and the right to transfer that resource are important aspects of private property rights.

6. Common ownership of property is the reason for diminishing returns.

7. A legal entitlement—that is, the right to use a resource in certain ways—often prevents the resource from going to its highest valued use.

8. Lotteries are an inefficient means of allocating resources because they do not allocate goods to the highest bidder.

9. Rationing by queues wastes the time spent waiting in line.

10. The opportunity set includes only the best available alternative.

11. The production possibilities curve shows the boundary of the opportunity set.

12. The principle of diminishing returns says that as more units of any input are added to a production process, total output eventually falls.

13. If an economy is not using its resources in the most productive way, economists say that there is inefficiency.

14. Sunk costs should not be included in opportunity costs.

15. If one pizza sells for $8 but two pizzas can be purchased for $12, the marginal cost of the second pizza is $6.

Multiple Choice

1. Which of the following is not part of the basic competitive model of the economy?

   a. the assumption of rational choice
   b. assumptions about the behaviour of consumers
   c. assumptions about the behaviour of firms
   d. assumptions about the behaviour of government
   e. assumptions about markets

2. Individuals and firms in the economy must make choices because of:

   a. diminishing returns.
   b. rationality.
   c. scarcity.
   d. tastes.
   e. property rights.

3. The assumptions of rational choice on the part of consumers means they:

   a. act in their own self-interest.
   b. act to further the interests of society.
   c. never make mistakes.
   d. choose inputs and output to maximize profit.
   e. all make the same decisions.

4. In the basic model of perfect competition, firms:

   a. and consumers are price makers.
   b. are price takers and consumers are price makers.
   c. and consumers are neither price makers nor price takers.
   d. are price makers and consumers are price takers.
   e. and consumers are price takers.

5. In the basic model of perfect competition, the economy is efficient; this means that:

   a. government must be involved.
   b. scarcity is eliminated.
   c. resources are not wasted.
   d. choice is unnecessary.
   e. individual behaviour is irrelevant.

6. In the basic model of perfect competition, the economy is efficient. All of the following statements, except one, are an implication of efficiency. Which is the odd one out?

   a. It is not possible to produce more of one good without producing less of another.
   b. Scarcity is eliminated.
   c. All mutually beneficial trades have been made.
   d. Resources are not wasted.
   e. It is not possible to make anyone better off without making someone else worse off.

7. Which of the following most completely describes what is required for incentives that ensure the efficient working of a market economy?

   a. prices and property rights
   b. prices but not property rights
   c. neither prices nor property rights
   d. property rights but not prices
   e. rights and property prices

8. If a firm changes from paying commissions on total sales to paying each member of its sales staff a fixed salary, this is likely to:

   a. increase incentives for its sales staff and increase the inequality in earnings among the sales staff.
   b. increase incentives for its sales staff and reduce the inequality in earnings among the sales staff.
   c. have no effect on incentives for its sales staff or on the inequality in earnings among the sales staff.
   d. reduce incentives for its sales staff and increase the inequality in earnings among the sales staff.
   e. reduce incentives for its sales staff and reduce the inequality in earnings among the sales staff.

9. The decline of fish stocks on the Grand Banks off the coast of Newfoundland is a consequence of:

   a. well-defined property rights.
   b. restricted property rights.
   c. entitlement as a property right.
   d. ill-defined property rights.
   e. unrestricted property rights.

10. When a property right is a legal entitlement:

   a. not all mutually beneficial trades are made.
   b. the assumption of rational choice is inappropriate in the case of the owner.
   c. the competitive economy is efficient.
   d. incentives are appropriate for efficient resource allocation.
   e. a market exists in which entitlements are traded.

11. All of the following are methods by which resources can be allocated. Which is efficient?

   a. queuing
   b. lotteries
   c. nontradable coupons
   d. government regulation
   e. prices

12. Fred has $10 to spend on baseball cards and hamburgers. The price of baseball cards is $.50 per pack. Hamburgers sell at a price of $1 each. Which of the following possibilities is not in Fred's opportunity set?

   a. 10 hamburgers and 0 packs of baseball cards
   b. 5 hamburgers and 10 packs of baseball cards
   c. 4 hamburgers and 14 packs of baseball cards
   d. 2 hamburgers and 16 packs of baseball cards
   e. 1 hamburger and 18 packs of baseball cards

13. Each month, Maria's parents give her an allowance, which she spends on CDs and audio tapes. CDs cost $20 each and audio tapes cost $10. Which of the following is correct?

   a. The opportunity cost of a CD is an audio tape.
   b. The opportunity cost of a CD is two audio tapes.
   c. The opportunity cost of an audio tape is two CDs.
   d. The opportunity cost of a CD is half of an audio tape.
   e. We need to know Maria's income to determine the opportunity cost.

14. The production possibilities curve shows the combinations of:

   a. goods a society can produce, given the quantities of inputs available.
   b. goods an individual can buy, given the prices of the goods and the individual's income.
   c. inputs required to produce a given quantity of a commodity.
   d. activities an individual can undertake in a limited time, given the cost in time of each.

e. consumption and leisure available to an individual, for different amounts of time worked.

15. Jean spends an hour shopping. She buys one sweater for $30. The opportunity cost of the sweater is:

   a. the next-best use of the hour.
   b. the next-best use of $30.
   c. a pair of pants.
   d. the next-best use of $30 and one hour.
   e. none of the above

16. Renting an apartment, Jorge signs a lease promising to pay $400 each month for one year. An upright citizen, Jorge would never dream of breaking the lease, even if he had to move away and could not occupy the apartment, and the apartment owner has included a clause in the lease that prevents Jorge from subletting the apartment. The rent therefore represents an example of:

   a. an opportunity set.
   b. a sunk cost.
   c. diminishing returns.
   d. rationing.
   e. a time constraint.

17. The cereal manufacturer has a new deal on Nature's Crunch Cereal. A box sells for $2.55, but each box comes with a coupon worth $.50 off the purchase price of the next box you buy. The marginal cost of the first box you buy is:

   a. $3.05.
   b. $2.55.
   c. $2.05.
   d. $1.55.
   e. $.50.

18. The cereal manufacturer has a new deal on Nature's Crunch Cereal. A box sells for $2.55, but each box comes with a coupon worth $.50 off the purchase price of the next box you buy. The marginal cost of the second box you buy is:

   a. $3.05.
   b. $2.55.
   c. $2.05.
   d. $1.55.
   e. $.50.

19. Fred is considering renting an apartment. A nice one-bedroom apartment rents for $400, and an equally attractive two-bedroom apartment can be had for $500. The $100 difference is:

   a. the opportunity cost of the two-bedroom apartment.
   b. the marginal cost of the second bedroom.
   c. an example of diminishing returns.
   d. the marginal cost of the apartment.
   e. an example of non-price rationing.

20. The Canadian government has invested billions of dollars of taxpayers' money in the Hibernia oil field off the coast of Newfoundland. Discussions of continued financial support often include reference to the money that has already been spent. The money already spent is:

   a. a marginal cost; as such, it is irrelevant to a discussion of continued support.
   b. a marginal cost; as such, it is relevant to a discussion of continued support.
   c. an opportunity cost; as such, it is relevant to a discussion of continued support.
   d. a sunk cost; as such, it is relevant to a discussion of continued support.
   e. a sunk cost; as such, it is irrelevant to a discussion of continued support.

Completion

1. Economists assume that people make choices _____, taking into consideration the costs and benefits of their alternatives.

2. A market with large numbers of buyers and sellers, each of whom cannot influence the price, is an example of _____.

3. The right of an owner of a resource to use it in certain ways and to sell it is called a _____.

4. Allocating goods and services by some means other than selling to the highest bidder is called _____.

5. The collection of all available opportunities is called the _____.

6. _____ limit choices.

7. The amounts of goods a firm or society can produce from a given amount of resources are its _____.

8. The idea that as more units of an input are used in a production process, each successive unit adds less to output is an example of the principle of _____.

9. The fact that more time spent studying means less time available for other activities illustrates a _____.

10. An expenditure that cannot be recovered is a _____ cost.

Answers to Self-Test

True or False

1. f	4. t	7. t	10. f	13. t
2. t	5. t	8. t	11. t	14. t
3. t	6. f	9. t	12. f	15. f

Multiple Choice

1. d	6. b	11. e	16. b
2. c	7. a	12. c	17. b
3. a	8. e	13. b	18. c
4. e	9. d	14. a	19. b
5. c	10. a	15. d	20. e

Completion

1. rationally
2. perfect competition
3. property right
4. rationing
5. opportunity set
6. Constraints
7. production possibilities
8. diminishing returns

9. trade-off
10. sunk

Doing Economics: Tools and Practice Problems

For the problem sets in this section, we reach into the economist's tool box for five important techniques, each of which will reappear throughout the remainder of the book. Three relate to the opportunity set: budget and time constraints, for which the outer edge of the opportunity set is a straight line; multiple constraints involving, for example, limits on both time and money; and production possibilities curves, which can be straight lines but are more often curved. The remaining two techniques relate to costs: the distinction between sunk and opportunity costs, and the use of marginal analysis to balance costs and benefits.

The simplest type of opportunity set has an outer boundary that is a straight line. Tool Kit 2.1 shows you how to construct these opportunity sets.

Tool Kit 2.1: Plotting the Straight-Line Opportunity Set

Examples of straight-line opportunity sets include budget constraints, time constraints, and production possibilities curves under conditions of constant returns. The budget constraint indicates which combinations of goods can be purchased with the consumer's budget. To plot it, you need to know the size of this budget and the prices of the goods. The time constraint indicates which combinations of time-consuming activities can be undertaken with a limited amount of time. To plot it, you need to know the amount of time the consumer has available to allocate and the time requirements of each activity. The production possibilities curve indicates which combinations of goods can be produced with a limited amount of inputs. To plot it, you need to know the amounts of the inputs, and the details of the technology by which inputs are transformed into output.

Follow this procedure to plot straight-line opportunity sets.

Step one: Draw a set of coordinate axes. Label the horizontal axis as the quantity of one good or activity and the vertical axis as the quantity of the other good or activity.

Step two: Calculate the maximum quantity of the good or activity measured on the horizontal axis. Plot this quantity along the horizontal axis.

Step three: Calculate the maximum quantity of the good or activity measured on the vertical axis. Plot this quantity along the vertical axis.

Step four: Draw a line segment connecting the two

points. This line segment is the relevant part of the opportunity set.

Step five: The slope is the opportunity cost of a unit of

the good or activity on the horizontal axis, measured in units of the good or activity on the vertical axis. In the case of the budget constraint, it is called the relative price, the price of the good measured on the horizontal axis divided by the price of the good measured on the vertical axis.

1. (Worked problem: budget constraint) Diana has an entertainment budget of $200 each month. She enjoys lunches with friends and going to the movies. The price of a typical lunch is $10. Movie tickets are $5 each. Construct her opportunity set.

Step-by-step solution

Step one: Draw coordinate axes and label the horizontal one "Lunches" and the vertical one "Movies." (There is no rule as to which good goes where. It would be fine if lunches were measured on the vertical axis and movies on the horizontal.)

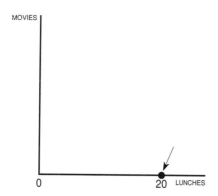

Step two: Calculate the maximum quantity of lunches. This number is $200/$10 = 20 lunches. Plot this quantity along the horizontal axis.

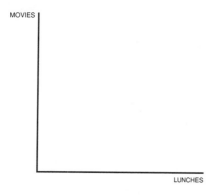

Step three: Calculate the maximum quantity of movies. This number is $200/$5 = 40 movie tickets. Plot this quantity along the vertical axis.

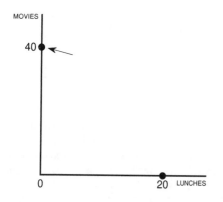

Step four: Draw a line segment connecting these two points. This line segment is the budget constraint.

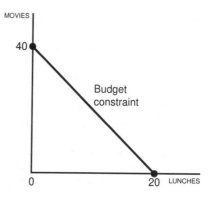

Step five: The slope of the budget constraint is 40/20 = 2. The price ratio is $10/$5 = 2. (Strictly speaking, these slopes are negative, but we follow the practice of dropping the negative sign as long as there is no confusion.)

2. (Practice problem: budget constraint) Velma Thomas must pay for both prescription medicine and nursing care for her elderly father. Each bottle of pills costs her $40, and the price of nursing care is $100 per day. She has been able to scrape together $1,000 each month for these expenses. Construct her opportunity set, going through all five steps.

3. (Practice problem: budget constraint) Construct the following opportunity sets.

    a. Clothing budget per year = $900; price of suits = $300; price of shoes = $90.
    b. Food budget = $200 per week; price of restaurant meals = $20; price of in-home meals = $5.
    c. University expense budget = $1,200 per term; price of books = $50; price of courses = $200.
    d. Annual provincial transportation department budget = $100,000; cost of fixing potholes = $200; cost of replacing road signs = $500.

4. (Worked problem: time constraint) Ahmed likes to visit his invalid father across town. Each visit, including transportation and time with Dad, takes 3 hours. Another of Ahmed's favourite activities is his tango lessons. These are given downstairs in his apartment building and take only an hour each. With work and night school, Ahmed has only 15 hours each week to divide between visiting his father and tango lessons. Construct his opportunity set.

Step-by-step solution

Step one: The time constraint works very much like the budget constraint. Plot coordinate axes and label the horizontal one "Visits" and the vertical one "Lessons."

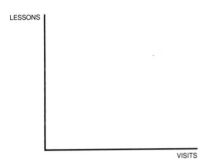

Step two: Calculate the maximum number of visits to his father. This number is 15/3 = 5 visits. Plot this quantity along the horizontal axis.

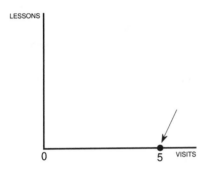

Step three: Calculate the maximum number of tango lessons. This number is 15/1 = 15 lessons. Plot this quantity along the vertical axis.

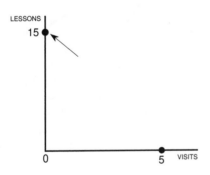

Step four: Draw a line segment connecting these two points. This line segment is the time constraint.

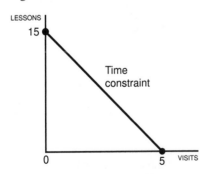

Step five: The slope of the time constraint is 15/5 = 3, which means Ahmed must forgo three tango lessons every time he visits his father.

5. (Practice problem: time constraint) Michael Terranova has 2 hours to make his house as clean as possible. The place needs vacuuming and dusting. He can dust one piece of furniture in 10 minutes. Each room takes 20 minutes to vacuum. Plot his time constraint.

6. (Practice problem: time constraint) Construct the following opportunity sets.

   a. Total time available = 6 hours; time required to iron each shirt = 15 minutes; time required to iron each dress = 30 minutes.

   b. Total time available = 20 days; time required to study each chapter = 1/2 day; time required to write book reports = 2 days.

   c. Total time available = 40 hours; time required to counsel each disturbed teenager = 2 hours; time required to attend each meeting = 1 hour.

   d. Total time available = 8 hours; time required to visit each client = 4 hours; time required to telephone each client = 10 minutes.

7. (Worked problem: production possibilities curve) First, assume that there is one resource, which can be used in the production of either of two goods, and that there are no diminishing returns. In this case, the production possibilities curve is a straight line, and we treat it just as we did the budget and time constraints.

   There are 25 farm workers employed at a vegetable farm. Each worker can pick 4 bushels of cucumbers an hour. Alternatively, each worker can pick 1 bushel of peppers an hour. Each worker can work 8 hours a day. Plot the daily production possibilities curve.

Step-by-step solution

Step one: Plot coordinate axes and label the horizontal one "Cucumbers" (measured in bushels) and the vertical one "Peppers."

Step two: Calculate the maximum number of cucumbers that can be picked each day. This number is 25 (workers) × 8 (hours) × 4 (bushels an hour) = 800 bushels of cucumbers. Plot this number along the horizontal axis.

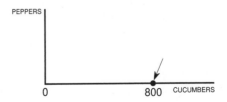

Step three: Calculate the maximum number of peppers that can be picked each day. This number is 25 (workers) × 8 (hours) × 1 (bushel an hour) = 200 bushels of peppers. Plot this number along the vertical axis.

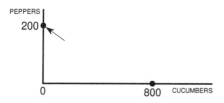

Step four: Draw a line segment connecting these two points. This line segment is the production possibilities curve.

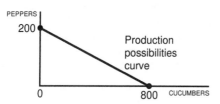

Step five: The slope is 200/800 = 1/4, which means that the opportunity cost of 1 bushel of cucumbers is 1/4 bushel of peppers.

8. (Practice problem: production possibilities curve) Coach Hun has four assistant coaches. They make recruiting visits and also run clinics for local youth. Each can make 32 recruiting visits a week. Alternatively, each can run 8 clinics in a week. Plot the production possibilities curve.

9. (Practice problem: production possibilities curve) Construct the following opportunity sets.

   a. Total amount of land available = 10 hectares of land; output of corn per hectare = 2,000 bushels; output of wheat per hectare = 1,000 bushels.

   b. Total amount of labour available = 40 hours; output of donuts per hour = 150; output of sweet rolls per hour = 50.

   c. Total amount of floor space available = 1,000 square metres; sales of women's sportswear per square metre = $500; sales of housewares per square metre = $200.

   d. Total amount of fuel available = 5,000 litres; kilometres per litre for tank travel = 3; kilometres per litre for armoured personnel carriers = 9.

MULTIPLE CONTRAINTS

Individuals often face more than one constraint. For example, many activities cost money and take time. This means the opportunity set includes only those alternatives that meet both constraints. Having the time to do something is no good if you do not also have the money. Tool Kit 2.2 shows you how to combine multiple constraints into a single opportunity set. Notice how the resulting boundary of the opportunity set is convex when viewed from the origin.

Tool Kit 2.2: Plotting Multiple Constraints

To plot the opportunity set when more than one constraint applies, follow this three-step procedure.

Step one: Plot the first constraint. (For example, this might be the budget constraint.)

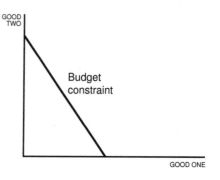

Step two: Plot the second constraint. (For example, this might be the time constraint.)

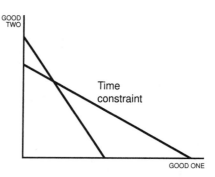

Step three: Darken the section of each constraint that lies under the other constraint. This is the outer edge of the opportunity set. Points on the section of each line that are not darkened meet one constraint but not both.

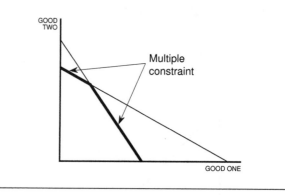

---

10. (Worked problem: multiple constraints) Out of work for six months, Donna feels that it is time to start looking for a job. Her father (gently) suggests that she apply in person to several of the retail stores on the west side of town. Each store application would require $5 in out-of-pocket expenses for transportation and dry

cleaning. (She realizes that only those who wear clean clothes stand any chance of receiving an offer.) Each trip would require 5 hours.

Donna's mother (not so gently) says that she should mail letters of application to a wide variety of potential employers. Each letter of application would require only $1 in mailing and copying costs and 1/2 hour of time.

Donna can devote 30 hours and $50 dollars each week to her job search campaign. Plot her opportunity set.

Step-by-step solution

Step one: Follow the procedure for plotting her budget constraint. Label the horizontal axis "Personal applications" and the vertical one "Mail applications" Your answer should look like this.

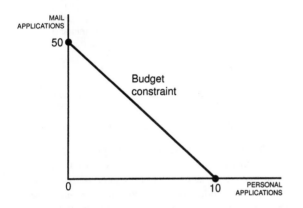

Step two: Follow the procedure for plotting her time constraint. Your answer should look like this.

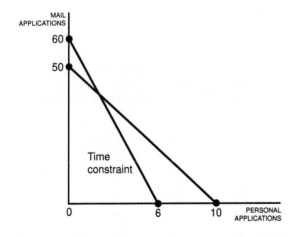

Step three: Darken the section of each constraint that lies under the other constraint. Notice that between points *A* and *B* on the diagram, it is the budget constraint that is binding, but between *B* and *C,* the time constraint is the limiting one.

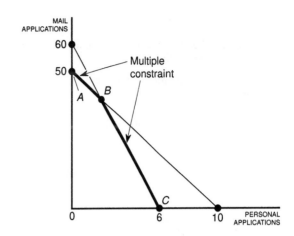

11. (Practice problem: multiple constraints) Harold's leaf-raking business is taking off. He has so many jobs to do that he is thinking of renting a leaf blower. This would cost him $20 per day. With a leaf blower, he could clean 10 lawns each day. He can only do 4 each day with his trusty rake, which costs nothing. Harold works 7 days each week, but has only $100 to spend. Plot his opportunity set for the 7-day week. (Hint: The axes should be labelled as lawns cleaned with a leaf blower and lawns raked by hand.)

12. (Practice problem: multiple constraints) The maintenance department at Alberti Van and Storage has 8 mechanic-hours to tune truck engines and replace the mufflers. It takes 1 hour to tune an engine and 1/2 hour to replace the muffler. In addition, the parts budget is only $100, the parts required to tune an engine cost $10, and each muffler costs $20. Construct the department's opportunity set.

13. (Practice problem: multiple constraints) Lamont tests swimming pools and cleans locker rooms for local country clubs. He has 20 hours available, and it takes him 1 hour to test each pool and 1/2 hour to clean each locker room. He has a budget of $50 to spend. It costs him $10 to test each pool and $1 to clean each locker room. Construct his opportunity set.

PRODUCTION POSSIBILITIES CURVES

Usually, production possibilities curves are bowed out. This can arise for either of two reasons. First, it is often the case that not all units of an input are equally well suited to production of a particular good. As more of the good is produced, the economy has to use units of the input that are less and less well suited to the good's production. Second, when the quantity of a particular input is fixed, the concept of diminishing returns applies. As more and more units of the input are used in combination with the fixed input, successive increases in output get smaller and smaller.

Tool Kit 2.3 shows you how to plot production possibilities curves that are bowed out.

Tool Kit 2.3: Plotting the Production
Possibilities Curve

Follow this five-step procedure to plot the production possibilities curve.

Step one: Draw and label a set of coordinate axes.

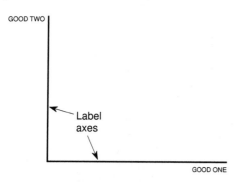

Step two: Calculate the total amount of the good measured on the horizontal axis that can be produced if all the resource is used. Plot this quantity along the horizontal axis.

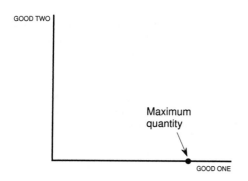

Step three: Calculate the total amount of the good measured on the vertical axis that can be produced if all the resource is used. Plot this quantity along the vertical axis.

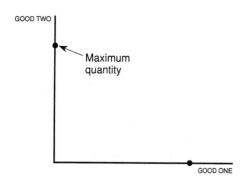

Step four: Calculate and plot several other feasible

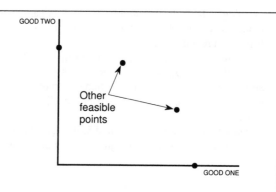

combinations.

Step five: Draw a smooth curve connecting these

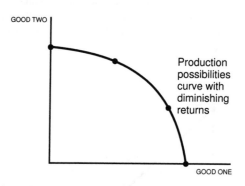

points. This curve is the production possibilities curve.

The absolute value of the slope of the curve measures the marginal opportunity cost of the good on the horizontal axis, in terms of units of the good on the vertical axis. As production of good one increases, the curve gets steeper; this means the opportunity cost of good one is rising.

14. (Worked problem: production possibilities curve) Iatrogenesis, a medical laboratory, employs 4 lab technicians. The table below shows output per day for various numbers of lab technicians.

Technicians doing cultures	Throat cultures	Technicians doing vaccines	Vaccines
1	50	1	20
2	90	2	35
3	120	3	45
4	140	4	50

Plot the production possibilities curve for Iatrogenesis.

Step-by-step solution

Step one: Draw coordinate axes. Label the horizontal one "Throat cultures" and the vertical one "Vaccines."

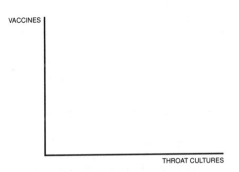

Step two: Calculate the maximum number of throat cultures. If all 4 technicians do throat cultures, the number is 140. Plot this number.

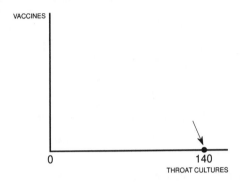

Step three: Calculate the maximum number of vaccines. If all 4 technicians do vaccines, the number is 50. Plot this number.

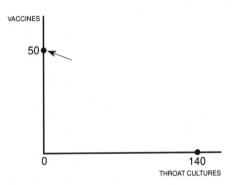

Step four: Calculate several other feasible points. For example, if 1 technician does throat cultures, then 3 can do vaccines. Reading off the table, we see that the combination produced is 50 throat cultures and 45 vaccines. Similarly, if 2 do throat cultures and 2 do vaccines, the outputs are 90 throat cultures and 35 vaccines. Another feasible combination is 120 cultures and 20 vaccines. Plot these points.

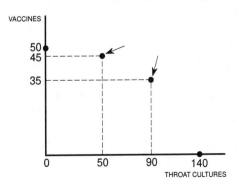

Step five: Draw the production possibilities curve through the points that have been plotted.

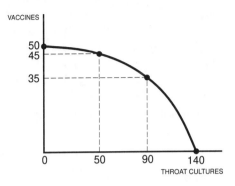

Step six: Observe that, as expected, the slope gets steeper as the number of throat cultures is increased.

15. (Practice problem: production possibilities curve) Mulroney Memorial University has a crime problem. Members of the criminal element have stolen many bicycles and a great deal of stereo equipment. To address this crime wave, the campus police has hired 5 new officers. The following table gives the expected number of thefts for various assignments for these new officers.

New police officers assigned to bicycle duty	Reduction in bicycle thefts	New police officers assigned to dorm patrol	Reduction in thefts of stereo equipment
1	25	1	10
2	45	2	18
3	60	3	25
4	70	4	31
5	75	5	36

Plot the production possibilities curve.

16. (Practice problem: production possibilities curve) Movaway Company has employed 4 maintenance inspectors for their fleet of trucks and forklifts. The following table shows how assigning inspectors leads to fewer breakdowns.

Inspectors assigned to check trucks	Reduced number of truck breakdowns	Inspectors assigned to check forklifts	Reduced number of forklift breakdowns
1	5	1	3
2	9	2	5
3	12	3	6
4	14	4	6

Plot Movaway's production possibilities curve.

17. (Practice problem: production possibilities curve) The Golden Bear vegetable farm (located on erstwhile corn-growing land in Alberta) has 800 tonnes of fertilizer. The following table shows how the outputs of endive and bib lettuce are expected to respond to different amounts of fertilizer.

Fertilizer used on endive crop (tonnes)	Output of endive (bushels)	Fertilizer used on lettuce crop (tonnes)	Output of bib lettuce (bushels)
0	1,400	0	2,000
200	2,400	200	3,400
400	3,200	400	4,200
600	3,600	600	4,700
800	4,000	800	5,000

Plot the farm's production possibilities curve.

SUNK COSTS

Rational individuals make choices by carefully weighing the benefits and opportunity costs of the alternatives open to them. Expenditures that have been incurred and cannot be recovered should not be included in any calculation of opportunity cost. Only forgone alternatives are relevant. Tool Kit 2.4 shows you how to distinguish opportunity costs from sunk costs.

Tool Kit 2.4: Distinguishing Opportunity Costs and Sunk Costs

Opportunity costs are forgone alternatives. To find the opportunity cost of an action, it is necessary to see what is changed by undertaking that action rather than its alternative. Follow this four-step procedure.

Step one: To find the opportunity cost of an action, first specify the next-best alternative. This is what would be done if the action in question were not chosen.

Step two: Calculate the total cost for the action and its alternative.

Step three: Calculate the opportunity cost. Subtract the cost for the alternative from the cost for the action. This difference is the opportunity cost of the action.

Step four: Calculate the sunk costs. Any costs that are the same for both the chosen action and its alternative are sunk costs.

---

18. (Worked problem: opportunity costs and sunk costs) Bruce Peninsula Airlines is studying the question of when to cancel flights for its Toronto to Tobermory route. Flying nearly empty planes seems like bad business. The company wants to know the opportunity cost of going ahead with a scheduled round-trip flight. There are two scheduled flights each day. Here are some relevant cost data.

Salaries of crew	$ 1,000 per day
Fuel	$ 400 per round trip
Mortgage on plane	$ 100 per day
Landing fees	$ 50 in Tobermory
	$ 100 in Toronto
Other in-flight costs	$ 100 per round trip

Calculate the opportunity cost of each round trip.

Step-by-step solution

Step one: The next-best alternative to going ahead with the scheduled round-trip flight is not flying.

Step two: Calculate the total cost for going ahead with the flight and cancelling it. If the flight is made, the expenditures are all those listed above. If the flight is cancelled, the company saves on fuel, landing fees, and other in-flight costs. The salaries of the crew and the mortgage must be paid whether the flight goes ahead or not.

Expenditures if flight is not cancelled

= $1,000 + $400 + $100 + $50 + $100 + $100 = $1,750.

Expenditures if flight is cancelled = $1,000 + $100 = $1,100.

Step three: Calculate the opportunity cost of the flight: $1,750 − $1,100 = $650.

Step four: Calculate the sunk costs. The remaining $1,100 for salaries and mortgage are sunk costs. Whether or not the flight is cancelled, these cannot be recovered.

19. (Practice problem: opportunity costs and sunk costs) Often during the summer term, courses are scheduled but cancelled at Mulroney Memorial University's downtown education building. In order to see whether this is a good policy, the administration needs to know the opportunity cost of going ahead with a scheduled course offering. Here are some cost data.

Compensation for instructor	$4,000
Air conditioning and lighting	$1,000
Custodial services	$2,000
Property taxes	$2,500

Each course requires one room. Any rooms not used for summer courses can be rented to local groups for $1,200 for the summer term.

a. Find the opportunity cost of offering a course.
b. How much are sunk costs?

20. (Practice problem: opportunity costs and sunk costs) The Bank of Canada is downsizing. It is considering offering early retirement to 8 bureaucrats. Each is 2 years from regular retirement age. (For simplicity, ignore discounting the second year's dollars in this problem.)

Salaries	$50,000 each (per year)
Fringe benefits	$20,000 each (per year)
Office space for all 8	$10,000 annually (lease signed for 1 more year)
Pension benefit	$20,000 each if retired (per year)

a. If the 8 bureaucrats do receive early retirement, what is the opportunity cost?
b. How much are sunk costs?

MARGINAL COST AND MARGINAL BENEFIT

Rational individuals always consider the benefits and costs of any action. Once they decide to do anything, they are faced with the question of how much of it to do. Answering this question involves looking at the benefit and cost of a little more or a little less, that is, the marginal benefit and marginal cost. Tool Kit 2.5 shows you how to calculate the marginal benefit and marginal cost of an economic decision.

Tool Kit 2.5: Using Marginal Benefits and Marginal Costs

To determine how much of any activity to do, follow this four-step procedure.

Step one: Identify the objective of the activity and the benefit and cost of various levels of the activity.

Step two: Calculate the marginal benefit. This is the extra gain from a little bit more of the activity.

Step three: Calculate the marginal cost. This is the extra cost from a little bit more of the activity.

Step four: Choose the level of the activity for which the marginal benefit equals the marginal cost.

---

21. (Worked problem: marginal cost and marginal benefit) A new inoculation against Honduran flu has just been discovered. Presently, 55 people die from the disease each year. The new inoculation will save lives, but unfortunately, it is not completely safe. Some of the recipients of the shots will die from adverse reactions. The projected effects of the inoculation are given in Table 2.1.

Table 2.1

Percent of population inoculated	Deaths due to the disease	Deaths due to the inoculations
0	55	0
10	45	0
20	36	1
30	28	2
40	21	3
50	15	5
60	10	8
70	6	12
80	3	17
90	1	23
100	0	30

How much of the population should be inoculated?

Step-by-step solution

Step one: Identify the objective, benefit, and cost. The objective is to minimize total deaths from the disease and the inoculations, and the problem is to choose the percentage of the population to inoculate. The benefit is reduced deaths caused by the disease, and the cost is the deaths caused by the shots.

Step two: Calculate the marginal benefit. The first 10 percent of the population inoculated reduces deaths caused by the disease from 55 to 45. The marginal benefit of the first 10 percent is 10. From the second 10 percent (increasing the percentage from 10 to 20), the marginal benefit is $45 - 36 = 9$. The schedule of the marginal benefit is given in Table 2.2.

Table 2.2

Percent of population	Marginal benefit
10	10
20	9
30	8
40	7
50	6
60	5
70	4
80	3
90	2
100	1

Step three: Calculate the marginal cost. Inoculating the first 10 percent causes no deaths. The second 10 percent (increasing the percent of the population getting the shots from 10 to 20 percent) causes 1 death. The schedule for the marginal cost is shown in Table 2.3.

Table 2.3

Percent of population	Marginal cost
10	0
20	1
30	1
40	1
50	2
60	3
70	4
80	5
90	6
100	7

Step four: Choose the level of inoculation percentage for which marginal benefit equals marginal cost. The percentage of the population to inoculate is 70. To see why this is correct, notice that inoculating 10 percent of the population saves 10 lives (marginal benefit = 10) and causes no deaths (marginal cost = 0). The net savings in lives is 10. Increasing the percentage to 20 percent saves 9 lives at a cost of 1 death. The net savings is 8 lives. Continuing as long as deaths do not exceed lives saved gives 70 percent. Notice that increasing the percentage to 80 percent saves fewer people (marginal benefit = 3) than it kills (marginal cost = 5). This is a bad idea. We should stop at 70 percent. (Note: Given the objective of minimizing the total number of deaths, stopping at 60 percent is just as good as stopping at 70 percent. By moving from 60 percent to 70 percent, four more

people will die from the disease, but four fewer will die because of the inoculation, so the total number of deaths is no
different than if 60 percent of the population were inoculated. This is an inevitable consequence of applying the rule
that the marginal benefit must equal the marginal cost in a
discrete problem.)

22. (Practice problem: marginal cost and marginal benefit)
The transportation department has 10 workers fixing
potholes. It is considering allocating some of these
workers to reprogramming traffic lights. Each activity
saves travel time for commuters, and this is the objective of the transportation department. Table 2.4 gives
the time savings of each activity as the number of
workers assigned to it varies. Remember that if a worker is assigned to reprogramming lights, he cannot fix
potholes.

Table 2.4

Workers assigned to reprogramming	Total time saved	Workers assigned to fix potholes	Total time saved
1	100	1	125
2	190	2	225
3	270	3	305
4	340	4	365
5	400	5	415
6	450	6	455
7	490	7	485
8	520	8	510
9	540	9	530
10	550	10	540

How should the workers be assigned? (Hint: Let the
number of workers assigned to reprogramming be the
activity. What is the cost of assigning these workers?)

23. (Practice problem: marginal cost and marginal benefit) Bugout pesticide kills insects that eat lettuce
leaves. Currently 11 leaves per head are eaten by the
insects. In the right concentrations, Bugout can be effective. On the other hand, there are side effects.
When the concentration is too great, leaves fall off
the lettuce head. Table 2.5 shows the relationship between concentrations of Bugout, leaves eaten, and
leaves fallen. What concentration should the manufacturer recommend?

Table 2.5

Concentration (parts per million)	Leaves eaten per head	Leaves fallen per head
1	7	0
2	4	1
3	2	3
4	1	6
5	0	10
6	0	15

Answers to Problems

2.

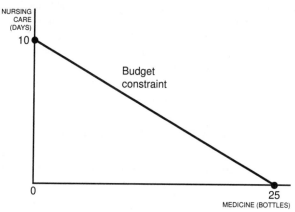

3.

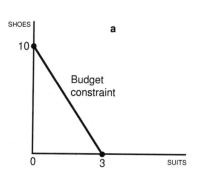

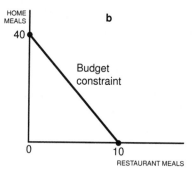

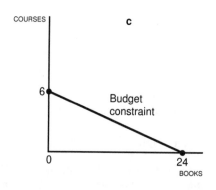

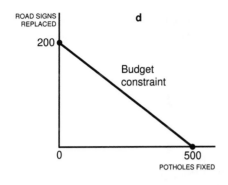

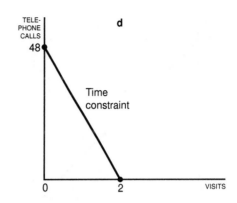

5.

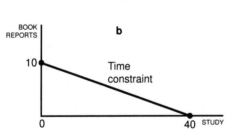

6.

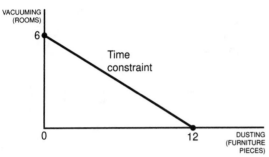

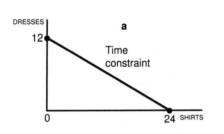

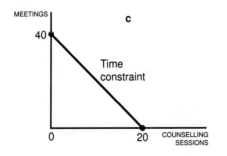

8.

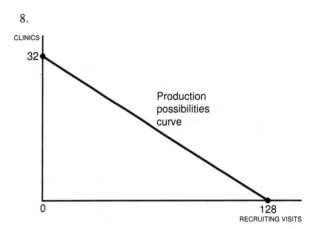

9.

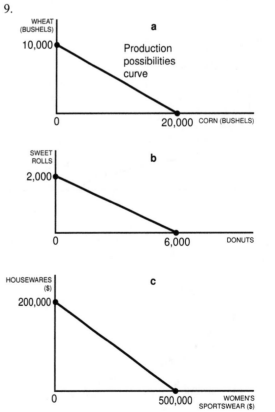

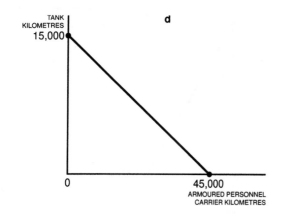

d

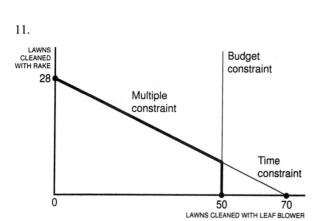

11.

12.

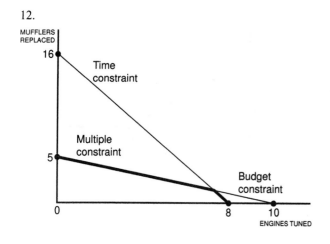

13.

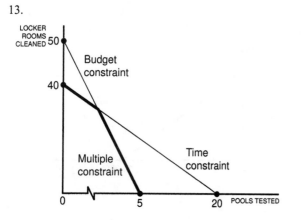

15.

Reduction in bicycle thefts	Reduction in thefts of stereo equipment
0	36
25	31
45	25
60	18
70	10
75	0

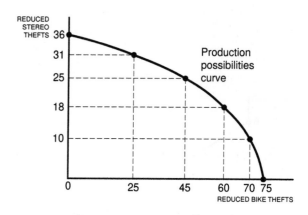

16.

Reduced number of truck breakdowns	Reduced number of forklift breakdowns
0	6
5	6
9	5
12	3
14	0

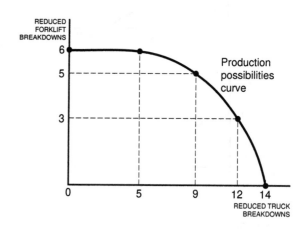

17.

Endive (bushels)	Lettuce (bushels)
1,400	5,000
2,400	4,700
3,200	4,200
3,600	3,400
4,000	2,000

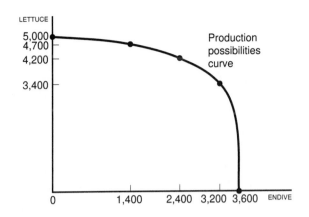

19.

	Costs of holding class	Costs of cancelling class
Compensation for instructor	$4,000	0
Air conditioning and lighting	$1,000	$1,000
Custodial services	$2,000	$2,000
Property taxes	$2,500	$2,500
Rent	0	– $1,200
Total	**$9,500**	**$4,300**

a. Opportunity cost = $9,500 – $4,300 = $5,200.
b. Sunk cost = $4,300.

20.

	Cost of early retirements	Cost of retaining bureaucrats
Salaries	0	$50,000 × 8 × 2
Fringe benefits	0	$20,000 × 8 × 2
Office space for all 8	$ 10,000	$20,000
Pension benefit	$ 20,000 × 8 × 2	0
Total	**$330,000**	**$1,140,000**

a. Opportunity cost = $1,140,000 – $330,000 = $810,000.
b. Sunk costs = $330,000.

22. The marginal benefit of assigning a worker to reprogram the lights is the time saved; the marginal cost is the time lost because the worker was not assigned to fix potholes.

Workers assigned to reprogramming	Marginal benefit	Marginal cost
1	100	10
2	90	20
3	80	25
4	70	30
5	60	40
6	50	50
7	40	60
8	30	80
9	20	100
10	10	125

Assign 6 to reprogramming and 4 to fixing potholes.

23. The benefit of recommending higher concentrations of pesticides is the reduction in leaves eaten; the cost is the loss of the leaves that fall off.

Concentration of pesticide	Marginal benefit	Marginal cost
1	4	0
2	3	1
3	2	2
4	1	3
5	1	4
6	0	5

The manufacturer should recommend a concentration of 3 ppm.

TRADE

Chapter Review

Chapter 3 takes up the key feature of markets: exchange. The fundamental aspect of market-based economies is voluntary trade. By definition, voluntary trade is mutually beneficial; it creates a surplus for both buyer and seller. If this were not true, the trade would not take place! An important insight of trade theory is the principle of comparative advantage, which shows how individuals and countries can specialize in production and thereby increase the gains they receive from trade. Economists emphasize these gains from trade and see little sense in protectionist arguments that trade between countries should be limited. The next two chapters will show how markets help realize some of the potential gains from trade.

ESSENTIAL CONCEPTS

1. Voluntary trade between rational individuals is **mutually beneficial;** it is good for both buyer and seller. Naturally, the buyer would like a lower price, and the seller prefers a higher price. Both might also benefit from better information. Nevertheless, the fact that the exchange takes place implies that given the information each has at the time of the transaction, both judge that they are better off trading than not trading.

2. Trade between individuals within a country and trade between individuals in different countries take place in markets. The three broad classes of markets are the product, labour, and capital markets. These three markets are all integrated internationally; this has led to a high degree of economic interdependence among nations.

3. Trade is many sided, or multilateral. A typical person sells labour to an employer and uses the wages earned both to purchase goods and services from many other firms and to save for future consumption. Similarly, a country may import more from some trading partners and export very little to those countries. With other trading partners, the country may export more than it imports. A country may also buy more goods and services than it sells abroad, and make up the difference by borrowing in capital markets or sending its workers to foreign labour markets.

4. The principle of **comparative advantage** says that individuals and countries will specialize in those goods that they are relatively more efficient in producing. To be relatively efficient means to have a lower opportunity cost. Countries will have comparative advantages in different goods. Each can import certain goods from abroad for a

lower opportunity cost than it would incur producing them at home. Similarly, each can export to foreign countries those goods for which it has a comparative advantage.

5. Comparative advantage leads to **specialization** in trade, but specialization itself increases productivity and further lowers opportunity costs. First, individuals and countries grow more efficient at their specialties through practice. Second, producing for others allows a larger scale of operations, more **division of labour** into separate tasks, and more specialization. Finally, specialization creates conditions in which invention and innovation flourish.

6. Different countries and individuals have comparative advantages in different activities. Reasons for a comparative advantage can include natural endowments such as climate (for a country) or manual dexterity (for a tailor), human or physical capital, knowledge, and experience. These factors may be gifts of nature, or they may be the result of investment, experience, education, training, or other past actions.

7. **Protectionism** is the idea that the economy needs safeguarding against the perceived harmful effects of trade. Proponents of protectionism use many arguments; chief among them are the loss of domestic jobs, the vulnerability to foreign influences, the unfair trade practices of foreign governments, trade imbalances, and the potential damage to weak economies. To economists, none of these arguments is convincing.

BEHIND THE ESSENTIAL CONCEPTS

1. An exchange creates and divides a surplus. The surplus is the difference between the value to the seller of what is traded and its value to the buyer. If there is no surplus, the exchange does not take place; the seller simply refuses to trade if he thinks the good is worth more than the buyer is willing to pay. The division of the surplus is another matter. Both the buyer and seller will receive some of the surplus. This is what economists mean when they say that trade is mutually beneficial: each party receives some of the surplus. The buyer pays somewhat less than the maximum she is willing to pay, and the seller receives somewhat more than the minimum he is willing to accept. Of course, whatever the division of the surplus, each would prefer to receive more.

2. When individuals trade, both buyer and seller gain. Each is better off with the trade than he or she would be if the trade did not take place. Likewise, countries also gain from trade. Trade allows specialization on the basis of comparative advantage, and countries benefit from more goods and services. But although each country as a whole gains from trade, not every individual in each country is better off. Some businesses lose out to foreign competition, and some workers lose jobs. Other businesses gain new markets, and new jobs are created. Thus, international trade creates both gains and losses, but overall, the gains outweigh the losses.

3. The problem with protectionism is that it looks only at the losers from international trade. Tariffs, quotas, and other protectionist policies can, at least temporarily, protect the losers, but only by limiting the trade. Limiting the trade means limiting the gains as well as the losses. Because the gains from trade exceed the losses, protectionism can only make matters worse for the economy as a whole.

4. To gain a better understanding of comparative advantage, it helps to distinguish it from **absolute advantage.** Country A has an absolute advantage over country B in the production of a particular good if country A can produce a unit of the good with fewer units of inputs than country B. Comparative advantage, on the other hand, pertains to opportunity cost. As we have seen, the opportunity cost is not the inputs used in production; rather, it is the alternative use of those inputs. Thus, a country has the comparative advantage in the production of a good if it has the lower opportunity cost.

For instance, assume that only labour is required to produce tomatoes or bookcases. Workers in country A can produce a carload of tomatoes in 40 hours, while the same number of workers in country B require 80 hours. Country A has an absolute advantage in producing tomatoes. To determine comparative advantage, however, we must look at how productive those workers are elsewhere in the economy. If 40 hours of labour in country A produce 2 bookcases, but 80 hours in country B produce only 1, then country B has a comparative advantage in tomatoes. Why? Because producing a carload of tomatoes in country A costs 2 bookcases, but producing a carload of tomatoes in country B costs only 1 bookcase. So the opportunity cost of a carload of tomatoes in country B is lower than in country A by 1 bookcase.

SELF-TEST

True or False

1. Unless the gain from trade is divided equally between buyer and seller, an exchange cannot be mutually beneficial.

2. The difference between what a consumer pays for something and what she is willing to pay is called her producer surplus.

3. Nearly a third of all goods and services purchased in Canada are imported.

4. If one party to a trade enjoys no consumer surplus from the trade, there is no gain from the trade.

5. With multilateral trade, imports from a particular country may not equal exports to that country.

6. The country that can produce a unit of a good with the least amount of labour is said to have a comparative advantage in the production of that good.

7. Trade on the basis of comparative advantage leads to complete specialization.

8. The marginal rate of transformation measures how many units of one commodity have to be sacrificed to produce one more unit of another commodity.

9. If two countries have different marginal rates of transformation, there can be no mutually beneficial trade between the two countries.

10. When a country has an absolute advantage in a good, it will always specialize in that good.

11. Specialization allows division of labour.

12. The extent of the division of labour is limited by the size of the market.

13. Comparative advantage is determined by the endowment of natural resources, human and physical capital, knowledge, and the experience that comes from specialization.

14. Opposition to trade between nations is called protectionism.

15. Although trade benefits the country as a whole, many individuals may lose from trade in a particular product.

Multiple Choice

1. A voluntary trade between a buyer and a seller benefits:

   a. the buyer or the seller, but never both.
   b. both the buyer and the seller.
   c. neither the buyer nor the seller.
   d. only the seller.
   e. only the buyer.

2. The gains from a voluntary trade between a buyer and seller:

   a. are nonexistent.
   b. accrue entirely to the buyer.
   c. accrue to both the buyer and the seller.
   d. accrue entirely to the seller.
   e. are actually losses.

3. When economists argue that both parties involved in a voluntary trade benefit from the exchange, they are assuming:

   a. that the gains are divided equally between buyer and seller.
   b. that both parties place the same value on the traded good.
   c. that both parties desire the same price.
   d. that both parties are well informed.
   e. none of the above

4. Emile is willing to pay $2.25 for a fancy loaf of bread. Mario's bakery can produce the loaf at a marginal cost of $1. Mario sells Emile the loaf for $1.75. Emile's consumer surplus is:

   a. $1.25.
   b. $1.
   c. $.75.
   d. $.50.
   e. $.25.

5. Emile is willing to pay $2.25 for a fancy loaf of bread. Mario's bakery can produce the loaf for a marginal cost of $1. Mario sells Emile the loaf for $1.75. Mario's producer surplus is:

   a. $1.25.
   b. $1.
   c. $.75.
   d. $.50.
   e. $.25.

6. The argument that a trade is mutually beneficial applies:

   a. only to individuals.
   b. only to firms.
   c. only to countries.
   d. to individuals and firms but not to countries.
   e. to individuals, firms, and countries.

7. Of all goods and services sold in Canada, the proportion that is imported is about:

   a. four-fifths.
   b. three-quarters.
   c. one-half.
   d. one-third.
   e. one-quarter.

8. The proportion of all goods and services produced in Canada that is exported is about:

   a. one-quarter.
   b. one-third.
   c. one-half.
   d. three-quarters.
   e. four-fifths.

9. If Japan buys oil from Saudi Arabia, Saudi Arabia buys grain from Canada, and Canada buys cars and TVs from Japan, this is an example of:

   a. multilateral trade.
   b. bilateral trade.
   c. absolute advantage.
   d. protectionism.
   e. diminishing returns.

10. If Canada has a comparative advantage in the production of wheat relative to Japan, then:

   a. fewer resources are required to produce wheat in Canada than in Japan.
   b. Canada also has an absolute advantage in the production of wheat.
   c. the opportunity cost of producing wheat is lower in Canada than in Japan.
   d. Japan has an absolute advantage in the production of another commodity.
   e. there is no potential for mutally beneficial trade between Canada and Japan.

11. If Canada has an absolute advantage in the production of wheat relative to Japan, then:

   a. fewer resources are required to produce wheat in Canada than in Japan.
   b. Canada also has a comparative advantage in the production of wheat.
   c. the opportunity cost of producing wheat is lower in Canada than in Japan.
   d. Japan has an absolute advantage in the production of another commodity.
   e. there is no potential for mutually beneficial trade between Canada and Japan.

12. The trade-off between two commodities along the production possibilities curve is called:

    a. specialization.
    b. the principle of diminishing returns.
    c. comparative advantage.
    d. the marginal rate of transformation.
    e. absolute advantage.

13. Suppose that in Canada, increasing wheat output by 1,000 tonnes would require a reduction in steel output of 500 tonnes, but in the United States, increasing wheat output by 1,000 tonnes would require reducing steel output by 1,000 tonnes. Then we can infer that:

    a. Canada has a comparative advantage in the production of steel.
    b. Canada has an absolute advantage in the production of wheat.
    c. the United States has an absolute advantage in the production of steel.
    d. Canada has an absolute advantage in the production of steel.
    e. Canada has a comparative advantage in the production of wheat.

14. Suppose that in Canada, increasing wheat output by 1,000 tonnes would require a reduction in steel output of 500 tonnes, but in the United States, increasing wheat output by 1,000 tonnes would require reducing steel output by 1,000 tonnes. Then we can infer that:

    a. the opportunity cost of wheat is lower in Canada than in the United States.
    b. the United States has an absolute advantage in the production of steel.
    c. the United States has a comparative advantage in the production of wheat.
    d. Canada has an absolute advantage in the production of steel.
    e. the opportunity cost of steel is lower in Canada than in the United States.

15. Suppose that in Canada, increasing wheat output by 1,000 tonnes would require a reduction in steel output of 500 tonnes, but in the United States, increasing wheat output by 1,000 tonnes would require reducing steel output by 1,000 tonnes. Then we can infer that:

    a. the United States has a comparative advantage in the production of wheat.
    b. Canada will benefit by exporting wheat to the United States in exchange for imports of steel from the United States.
    c. the opportunity cost of wheat is lower in the United States than in Canada.
    d. Canada will benefit by exporting steel to the United States in exchange for imports of wheat from the United States.
    e. Canada has a comparative advantage in the production of steel.

16. All of the following, except one, are reasons why specialization increases productivity. Which is the odd one out?

    a. Specialization allows workers to become more efficient by repeating the same tasks.
    b. Specialization saves time needed to switch from one task to another.
    c. Specialization results in more repetitive tasks.
    d. Specialization allows larger-scale production which means greater efficiency.
    e. Specialization allows the assignment of tasks to those who have comparative advantage.

17. Which of the following is not a determinant of comparative advantage?

    a. natural endowments
    b. acquired endowments
    c. superior knowledge
    d. protectionism
    e. specialization

18. When economists argue that both countries involved in a voluntary trade benefit from the exchange, they mean:

    a. all individuals and firms in both countries benefit.
    b. all individuals and firms in at least one country benefit.
    c. some individuals and firms in both countries benefit and the gains exceed the losses.
    d. some individuals and firms in both countries benefit and the losses exceed the gains.
    e. none of the above

19. The North American Free Trade Agreement lowered trade barriers among which of the following countries?

    a. all countries in North America and Central America
    b. the United States, Canada, and Mexico
    c. all countries in North America and the Caribbean
    d. the United States, Canada, and Chile
    e. all countries in North and South America

20. Those who advocate barriers to free trade between countries are said to favour:

    a. protectionism.
    b. diminishing returns.
    c. multilateral trade.
    d. bilateral trade.
    e. specialization.

Completion

1. The difference between what a person is willing to pay for an item and what she has to pay is a gain from trade, or _____.

2. If a country is relatively more efficient at producing a good than its trading partners, then that country is said to have a _____ in the production of that good.

3. If a country can produce a commodity using fewer inputs than another country, that country is said to have the _____ in the production of that good.

4. Trade between two individuals or countries is called _____ trade.

5. The trade-off between the production of two commodities is called the _____.

6. A country specializes in commodities in which it has the _____.

7. Specialization allows _____ of labour.

8. _____, such as location, natural resources, and climate are bases of comparative advantage.

9. Acquired endowments, such as physical and human _____, represent other sources of comparative advantage.

10. The doctrine that the economy of a country is injured by trade is called _____.

Answers to Self-Test

True or False

1. f	4. f	7. f	10. f	13. t
2. f	5. t	8. t	11. t	14. t
3. t	6. f	9. f	12. t	15. t

Multiple Choice

1. b	6. e	11. a	16. c
2. c	7. d	12. d	17. d
3. e	8. b	13. e	18. e
4. d	9. a	14. a	19. b
5. c	10. c	15. b	20. a

Completion

1. surplus
2. comparative advantage
3. absolute advantage
4. bilateral
5. marginal rate of transformation
6. comparative advantage
7. division
8. Natural endowments
9. capital
10. protectionism

Doing Economics: Tools and Practice Problems

This chapter introduces comparative advantage, a very important concept. The principle of comparative advantage illustrates how individuals, firms, and countries can benefit by specializing in performing tasks or producing goods and trading with each other. This problem set will help you to identify comparative advantage and to see why comparative advantage determines the division of labour and the pattern of trade. You will also study the gains from trade when they proceed according to comparative advantage. Finally, you will use the idea of comparative advantage to construct the production possibilities curve for the case in which resources differ.

COMPARATIVE ADVANTAGE

A country has a comparative advantage in a good when its opportunity cost of producing that good is lower than the opportunity cost in another country. It will increase production of the good and export it in exchange for goods in which other countries have the comparative advantage. Tool Kit 3.1 shows you how to use the production possibilities curve to calculate opportunity cost, identify comparative advantage, and thereby determine the pattern of production and trade.

Tool Kit 3.1: Identifying Comparative Advantage

When a country or individual has a comparative advantage in performing some task or producing some good, that country or individual is relatively more efficient, which means that the country or individual has the lower opportunity cost. The following procedure shows you how to identify comparative advantage and predict the pattern of trade. It is written for the case of two-country trade.

Step one: Plot the production possibilities curve for each country. Be sure to be consistent and measure units of the same good along the horizontal axis in each case.

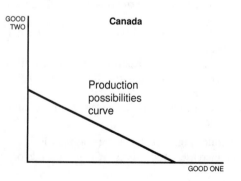

Step two: The slope of the production possibilities curve is the opportunity cost of the good on the horizontal axis, and it indicates the trade-off. The flatter slope implies a comparative advantage for producing the good on the horizontal axis.

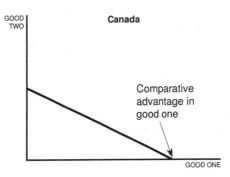

Step three: The steeper slope indicates a comparative advantage in the production of the good on the vertical axis.

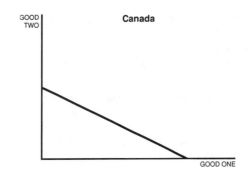

Step four: In a system of free trade, each country will produce more of the good in which it has a comparative advantage, and the relative price will lie somewhere between the opportunity costs of the two countries.

1. (Worked problem: comparative advantage) Workers in Canada and Italy can produce shoes and computers. The annual productivity of the workers in each country is given in the table below.

Country	Computers	Shoes
Canada	5,000	10,000
Italy	2,000	5,000

a. Which country has a comparative advantage in computers? in shoes?
b. Predict the pattern of trade.
c. Indicate the range of possible relative prices that would bring about this pattern of trade.

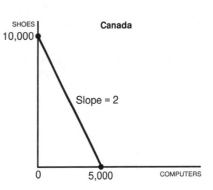

Step-by-step solution

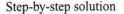

Step one (a): Plot the production possibilities curves. Measure computers on the horizontal axis.

Step two: The production possibilities curve for Canada has the flatter slope; therefore, Canada has a comparative advantage in the production of computers.

Step three: The production possibilities curve for Italy is steeper, and Italy has a comparative advantage in shoes.

Step four (b and c): Italy will trade shoes for Canadian computers. The relative price must lie between 2 shoes per computer (the Canadian opportunity cost) and 2.5 shoes per computer (the Italian opportunity cost).

2. (Practice problem: comparative advantage) Workers in Nigeria and neighbouring Niger produce textiles and sorghum. The productivities of each are given in the table below.

Country	Textiles (bales)	Sorghum (bushels)
Nigeria	100	500
Niger	50	400

   a. Which country has a comparative advantage in textiles? in sorghum?
   b. Predict the pattern of trade.
   c. Indicate the range of possible relative prices that would bring about this pattern of trade.

3. (Practice problem: comparative advantage) For each of the following, determine which country has a comparative advantage in each good, predict the pattern of trade, and indicate the range of possible relative prices consistent with this pattern of trade.

a.

Country	Fish	Wheat (bushels)
Greece	60	80
Poland	35	70

b.

Country	Heart bypass operations	Auto parts (containers)
United States	5,000	10,000
Canada	3,000	9,000

c.

Country	Scrap steel (tonnes)	Finished steel (tonnes)
Thailand	20	20
Laos	10	2

d.

Country	Wine (barrels)	Wool (bales)
Portugal	2	2
Great Britain	4	8

GAINS FROM TRADE

When countries trade, there is mutual gain in the sense that their opportunity sets expand beyond their production possibilities curves. To exploit the potential of trade, production and trade must be organized according to comparative advantage. Tool Kit 3.2 shows you how both trading partners can gain from trade.

Tool Kit 3.2: Showing the Gains from Trade

   When the pattern of trade is based upon comparative advantage, both countries can gain. Specifically, they each can consume a bundle of goods that lies beyond their own production possibilities curve. The following steps show how this is possible.

Step one: Draw the production possibilities curve for each country, identify the country with a comparative advantage in each good, and identify the trade-offs for each country.

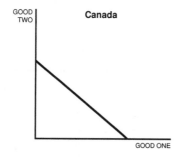
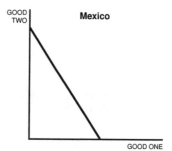

Step two: Choose a relative price between the trade-offs. This implies a line that is steeper than the flatter curve and flatter than the steeper curve.

Step three: For the country with the comparative advantage in the horizontal-axis good, label the horizontal intercept *A* and draw a line segment from *A* with a slope equal to (–) the relative price. This line segment shows the bundles of goods that the country can consume by trading at the given relative price.

Step four: For the country with the comparative advantage in the vertical-axis good, label the vertical intercept *A* and draw a line segment from *A* with a slope equal to (−) the relative price. This line segment shows the bundles of goods that this country can consume by trading at the given relative price.

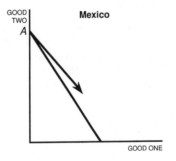

Step five: Pick a pair of consistent points, where Canada's exports equal Mexico's imports, one on each line segment, and show how each country can benefit from trade.

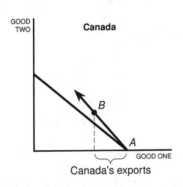

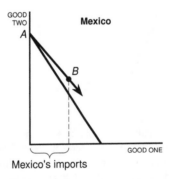

4. (Worked problem: gains from trade) This problem builds upon problem #1. Show that Italy and Canada can benefit by trading on the basis of comparative advantage.

Step-by-step solution

Step one: Identify the country with a comparative advantage in each good and the trade-offs for each country. Canada has a comparative advantage in computers, and the trade-off is 2 shoes per computer. Italy has a comparative advantage in shoes, and the trade-off is 2.5 shoes per computer.

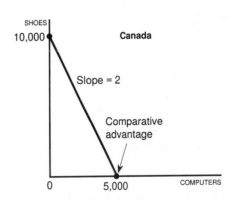

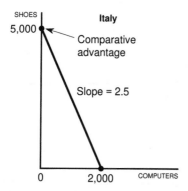

Step two: Choose a relative price between the trade-offs. Let's choose 2.25 shoes per computer.

Step three: For the country with the comparative advantage in computers, which is Canada, label the horizontal intercept *A* and draw a line segment from *A* with a slope equal to –2.25. This line segment shows the bundles of goods that Canada can consume by trading at the given relative price.

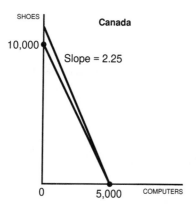

Step four: For the country with the comparative advantage in shoes, which is Italy, label the vertical intercept *A* and draw a line segment from *A* with a slope equal to –2.25. This line segment shows the bundles of goods that Italy can consume by trading at the given relative price.

Step five: Pick a pair of consistent points, one on each line segment, and show how each country can benefit from trade.

Let Canada produce 4,000 computers for domestic consumption. This leaves 1,000 for trade. At a relative price of 2.25 shoes, the 1,000 computers trade for 2,250 shoes. Plot the point (2,250, 4,000) and label it *B*. Italy must then produce 2,250 shoes for trade. This leaves 2,750 shoes for domestic consumption. The 2,250 shoes trade for 1,000 computers. Plot the point (1,000, 2,750) and label it *B*. At this point, Canada exports 1,000 computers and imports 2,250 shoes, while Italy imports 1,000 computers and exports 2,250 shoes. Trade is balanced, and each country consumes beyond its production possibilities curve.

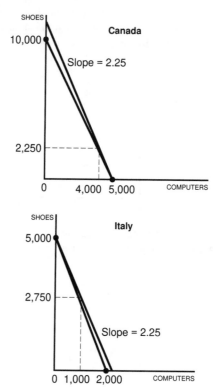

5. (Practice problem: gains from trade) This problem builds upon problem #2. Show that workers in Nigeria and Niger can benefit by trading according to comparative advantage.

Production Possibilities and Comparative Advantage

Free trade assigns to each country the task of producing those goods in which it has a comparative advantage. The same is true for trade between individuals. To see why this is efficient, we consider the joint production possibilities curve in the case in which there are two or more different types of resources that can be used in the production of two goods. To do this efficiently, it is necessary to assign resources to produce the good in which each has a comparative advantage. Tool Kit 3.3 shows you how to do this. Compare the shape of the production possibilities, with the opportunity sets in Chapter 2 when there were multiple constraints or diminishing returns.

Tool Kit 3.3: Plotting the Production Possibilities
Curve When Resources Are Different

When resources differ in their productivity, plotting
the production possibilities curve requires that the resources be assigned to produce goods according to the
principle of comparative advantage. Follow these six
steps to see how this is done.

Step one: Draw a set of coordinate axes. Label the horizontal axis as the quantity of one good and the vertical axis as the quantity of the other good.

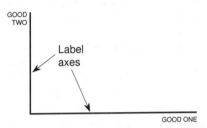

Step two: Calculate the maximum quantities of each
good that can be produced. Plot the quantity along the
vertical axis and label the point *B*. Plot the quantity
along the horizontal axis and label this point *A*.

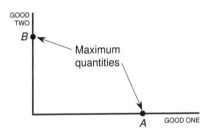

Step three: Identify the resource with the comparative
advantage for each good.

Step four: Choose the resource with the comparative
advantage in the horizontal-axis good and assign it to
produce this good, while keeping the other resource
producing the vertical-axis good. Calculate the total
quantities produced, and plot this point. Label it *C*.

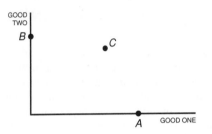

Step five: Connect the points *BCA* with line segments.
This is the production possibilities curve.

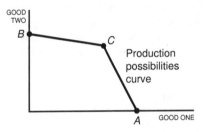

Step six: Verify that the absolute value of the slope is
increasing. Because the slope measures the opportunity cost of the horizontal-axis good, this means that the
opportunity cost is increasing.

6. (Worked problem: production possibilities curve) Harrigan and her daughter have formed a two-person firm to
handle business incorporations and real estate transactions. The hours required for each type of task are given
below. Each works 48 hours every week.

Lawyer	Hours required to perform each incorporation	Hours required to complete each transaction
Harrigan	4	8
Daughter	8	24

Plot their weekly production possibilities curve.

Step-by-step solution

Step one: Draw and label a set of coordinate axes. Put real
estate transactions on the horizontal axis and incorporations
on the vertical.

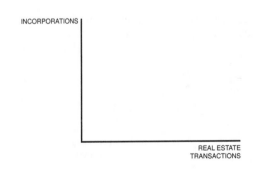

Step two: Calculate the maximum number of incorporations
they can do in a week. For Harrigan, this number is 48/4 =
12; for her daughter, it is 48/8 = 6. The pair can complete 18
incorporations. Plot this point along the vertical axis, and label it *A*. Concerning real estate transactions, Harrigan can
do 48/8 = 6; her daughter, 48/24 = 2. The pair can do 8. Plot
this point along the horizontal axis, and label it *B*.

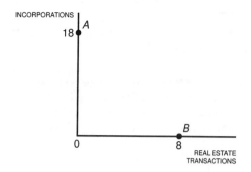

Step three: Identify the resource with the comparative advantage for each good. Since it takes Harrigan 8 hours to complete each real estate transaction but only 4 to do an incorporation, each real estate transaction requires enough time to do 2 incorporations. The opportunity cost of a real estate transaction for Harrigan is, then, 2 incorporations. By the same argument, the opportunity cost for her daughter is 24/8 = 3 incorporations; thus, Harrigan has the comparative advantage in real estate transactions, while her daughter has the comparative advantage in incorporations.

Step four: We assign to Harrigan the task of real estate transactions, leaving her daughter to do the incorporations. With this assignment, they can do 6 incorporations and 6 real estate transactions (see step two). Plot this point, and label it *C*.

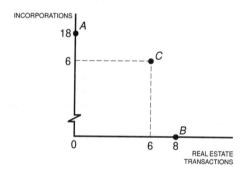

Step five: Draw line segments connecting the points. This is the production possibilities curve.

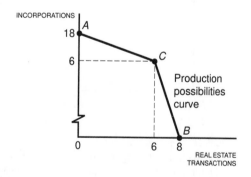

Step six: Note that between *A* and *C* the slope is 2, but between *C* and *B* the slope increases to 3. The shape of the production possibilities curve thus indicates diminishing returns.

7. (Practice problem: production possibilities curve) A farmer has 3 hectares of land. Owing to various characteristics of the land, his ability to produce his two cash crops (corn and soybeans) differs on each hectare. The technology of production is given in the table below.

Maximum outputs of each crop per hectare (bushels)

	Hectare #1	Hectare #2	Hectare #3
Corn	200	200	100
Soybeans	400	200	50

These figures represent the maximum output of each crop, assuming that only one crop is grown on the hectare. That is, hectare #1 can produce either 200 bushels of corn or 400 bushels of soybeans. Of course, the farmer can also divide the hectare into one part corn and one part soybeans. For example, he can grow 100 bushels of corn and 200 bushels of soybeans on hectare #1. Plot the production possibilities curve.

8. (Practice problem: production possibilities curve) Plot the following production possibilities curves.

a. Maximum harvest of each type of fish per trawler (tonnes)

	Trawler #1	Trawler #2	Trawler #3
Salmon	2	3	4
Tuna	2	6	6

b. Maximum amounts of pollutants removed (parts per million [ppm])

	Smokestack scrubbers	Coal treatment
Sulphur	100	50
Particulates	500	100

Answers to Problems

2. a. Nigeria has a comparative advantage in textiles. Niger has a comparative advantage in sorghum.
 b. Nigeria will trade its textiles for sorghum from Niger.
 c. The relative price will lie between 8 and 5 bushels of sorghum per bale of textiles.
3. a. Greece has a comparative advantage in fish. Poland has a comparative advantage in wheat. Greece will trade its fish for Polish wheat. The relative price will lie between 4/3 and 2 bushels of wheat per fish.
 b. The United States has a comparative advantage in heart bypass operations, and Canada in auto parts. The United States will trade heart bypass operations for Canadian auto parts. The relative price will lie between 2 and 3 containers of auto parts per operation.
 c. Thailand has a comparative advantage in finished steel, Laos in scrap steel. Thailand will trade its finished steel for Laotian scrap steel. The relative price will lie between 1 and 5 tonnes of scrap steel per tonne of finished steel.

d. Portugal has a comparative advantage in wine, Great Britain in wool. British wool will be traded for Portuguese wine. The relative price will lie between 1 and 2 bales of wool per barrel of wine.

5. Choose, for example, 6 bushels of sorghum per bale of textiles as the relative price. Nigeria can produce 100 bales of textiles and trade 20 to Niger for 120 bushels of sorghum. The point (80, 120) lies outside its production possibilities curve. Niger can produce 400 bushels of sorghum and trade 120 bushels to Nigeria for 20 bales of textiles. The point (20, 280) lies outside its production possibilities curve.

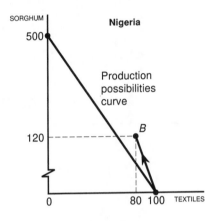

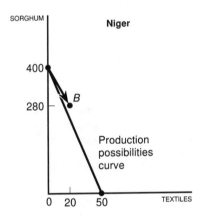

7.

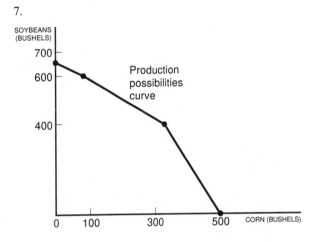

8.

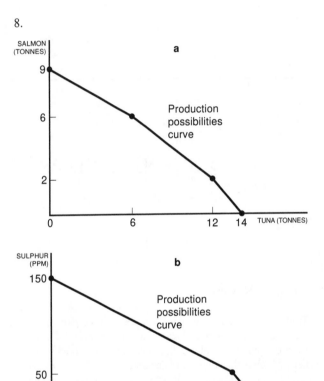

DEMAND, SUPPLY, AND PRICE

Chapter Review

Trade, the markets in which it occurs, and the gains it provides for both buyers and sellers are all important concepts from Chapter 3. Chapter 4 discusses the basic model of markets, which is the supply and demand model. The focus is on prices and quantities—how they are determined and how they change when other factors change. Chapter 5 then applies the supply and demand model to major areas of concern to economists: what happens to the quantity demanded or supplied when prices change, and what happens when prices cannot adjust, because, for example, the government has set price floors or ceilings.

ESSENTIAL CONCEPTS

1. Consumers **demand** goods and services. They are willing and able to pay, and given a price, they will buy a certain quantity. Several factors influence demand, but the most important is **price**. As the price falls, people buy more of the good or service; as the price rises, they purchase less. The entire relationship between the price and the quantity that a person buys is called the individual **demand curve.**

2. Adding all the individual demand curves gives the **market demand curve.** For every price, ask how much each individual will buy. Add these quantities. The result is the market demand curve, which shows the total amount of the good that will be purchased by all individuals at each price.

3. Firms **supply** goods and services. They are willing and able to produce and sell the good, and at a given price, they will sell a certain quantity. Several factors influence the supply, but the most important is price. As the price rises, producers will supply more; as the price falls, producers will supply less. The entire relationship between the price and the quantity that the producer will sell is called the individual **supply curve.**

4. Adding all the individual supply curves gives the **market supply curve.** For every price, ask how much each producer will sell. Add these quantities. The result is the market supply curve, which shows how much of the good will be sold by all producers at each price.

5. The price at which consumers want to buy exactly the quantity that firms want to sell is the **equilibrium price.** This quantity, which is the same for demand and supply, is the **equilibrium quantity.** It is an equilibrium because there are no forces that would cause it to change.

6. If the price is higher than the equilibrium price, firms want to sell more than consumers want to buy. There is **excess supply.** Unable to sell all their goods, many firms compete, by lowering prices, to attract more consumers. Similarly, if the price is lower than the equilibrium price, consumers want to buy more than firms want to sell. There is **excess demand.** Seeing the glut of consumers, firms raise their prices. In sum, if the price is above equilibrium, it falls; if it is below equilibrium, it rises. When the quantity consumers want to buy exactly equals the quantity firms want to sell, there are no forces tending to increase or lower the price. Price is at rest, at its equilibrium level.

7. Many factors affect the demand and supply. For demand, these factors include changes in income, prices of substitutes and complements, the composition of the population, and people's tastes. This is only a partial list. A change in any one of these factors—or in anything else that affects the willingness to pay for the good—**shifts** the entire demand curve, and a new equilibrium must be found.

   Supply is affected by changes in technology and input price—more generally, anything that causes costs to change. Again, a change in any one of these factors shifts the supply curve and leads to a new equilibrium.

BEHIND THE ESSENTIAL CONCEPTS

1. The demand curve is the entire range, or schedule, that indicates how many units of the good will be purchased at each price. At a given price, this number is called the quantity demanded. In diagrams of demand curves, the quantity demanded is measured along the horizontal axis. To find the quantity demanded, simply read it off the demand curve at the current price. Economists are sometimes sloppy and say "change in demand" without being clear whether they mean a shift in the demand curve or a change in the quantity demanded. The latter is brought about by a change in price, and it involves only a movement along the same demand curve. To guard against confusion in stressful situations (like tests!), say "demand curve" when you refer to the entire schedule of prices and quantities and "quantity demanded" when you want to indicate the number of goods purchased.

2. It is very important to understand why the market demand curve is drawn as it is. When the price rises, the market quantity demanded falls for two reasons. First, each individual buys less. The principle of substitution says that other available goods and services can serve as alternatives, and at higher prices, people switch to consume these substitutes. Second, some individuals find the price to be too high altogether, and they leave the market completely. When the price falls, the opposite happens. People substitute away from other goods and buy more of the one with the lower price. Furthermore, the lower price attracts new consumers to the market.

3. The market supply curve slopes upwards. This means that as the price rises, more is offered for sale. Again,

there are two reasons. First, firms are willing to sell more at higher prices. Second, higher prices attract new firms into the market.

4. Other factors that shift the demand curve include consumer income, tastes, prices of substitutes and complements, and the composition of the population. The supply curve shifts with changes in technology or input prices. These factors are the most common causes of shifts, but anything that affects the willingness and ability to pay for goods shifts the demand curve, and anything that affects costs shifts the supply curve. For example, if it rains in April, the supply of crops may increase, and the demand for umbrellas may also increase.

5. Successful supply and demand analysis proceeds in four steps:
   a. Start with an equilibrium.
   b. Figure out which curve shifts.
   c. Shift the curve and find the new equilibrium.
   d. Compare the price and quantity at the original and new equilibria.

   Be careful to avoid a common pitfall. Suppose you are asked to show the effect of a change in tastes that shifts demand to the right. The failing student's analysis goes like this: "Demand shifts to the right; this increases quantity and price, but the increase in price leads producers to want to supply more, so the supply also shifts to the right." What is wrong with this answer? Stop before the "but." True, the demand shift does raise price and quantity, but that is the end of the story. The increase in price does lead producers to want to supply more. As they supply more, there is a movement along the supply curve, but not a shift. Changes in the price of a good *never shift* the demand curve for that good or the supply curve for that good; rather, changes in the price of a good cause a *movement* along the demand curve or supply curve. There is more discussion on this point, with lots of practice problems, in the "Doing Economics" section of this chapter.

SELF-TEST

True or False

1. Prices provide incentives to help the economy use resources efficiently.

2. As the price falls, the quantity demanded decreases.

3. The market demand curve is the sum of the prices of each individual demand curve.

4. The individual demand curve is an example of an equilibrium relationship.

5. One reason why the supply curve slopes upwards is that at higher prices, more firms enter the market.

6. In equilibrium, there is neither excess demand nor excess supply.

7. If the price is above the equilibrium price, consumers can buy as much as they are willing to buy.

8. If the price is below the equilibrium price, sellers cannot sell as much as they are willing to sell.

9. The law of supply and demand says that the equilibrium price will be that price at which the quantity demanded equals the quantity supplied.

10. The individual supply curve is an example of an identity.

11. The price of diamonds is higher than the price of water because diamonds have a higher value in use.

12. A change in a consumer's income will shift her demand curve.

13. A change in the price of a good will shift its market demand curve to the right.

14. An increase in the price of butter will shift the demand curve for margarine to the right.

15. A decrease in the price of butter will shift the demand curve for bread to the left.

Multiple Choice

1. When the forces of demand and supply operate freely, prices:

   a. rise when there is excess supply.
   b. signal scarcity.
   c. rise without limit.
   d. are uninformative.
   e. fall when there is excess demand.

2. Demand curves are _____; this means that the quantity demanded _____ when the price falls.

   a. downward-sloping; falls
   b. downward-sloping; is unchanged
   c. upward-sloping; falls
   d. upward-sloping; rises
   e. downward-sloping; rises

3. Market demand is the:

   a. vertical sum of the individual demand curves.
   b. horizontal sum of the individual demand curves.
   c. sum of the prices paid for the different quantities demanded.
   d. sum of the prices paid by all individuals.
   e. total expenditure by all individuals in the market.

4. As the price falls, the quantity demanded increases along the market demand curve. Two possible explanations are:
   I. Existing consumers buy more.
   II. There are more consumers buying.
   Which of the following is appropriate?

   a. I is an explanation; II is not.
   b. I is not an explanation; II is.
   c. I and II are both explanations.
   d. Neither I nor II is an explanation.
   e. I and II are both explanations, but if one applies, the other does not.

5. Which of the following will shift the market demand curve to the left?

   a. an increase in income
   b. an increase in the price of a substitute
   c. a reduction in price
   d. an increase in the price of a complement
   e. an increase in price

6. Supply curves are _____; this means that the quantity supplied _____ when the price falls.

   a. downward-sloping; rises
   b. downward-sloping; falls
   c. downward-sloping; is unchanged
   d. upward-sloping; falls
   e. upward-sloping; rises

7. Market supply is the:

   a. sum of the prices at the different quantities demanded.
   b. vertical sum of the firms' supply curves.
   c. sum of the prices paid by all individuals.
   d. horizontal sum of the firms' supply curves.
   e. total expenditure by all individuals in the market.

8. As the price rises, the quantity supplied increases along an individual supply curve because:

   a. the higher price gives the firm an incentive to sell more.
   b. new firms enter the market and total supply increases.
   c. individuals want to buy more when the price rises.
   d. the demand curve is downward-sloping.
   e. none of the above

9. As the prices rises, the quantity supplied increases along the market supply curve because:
   I. Existing firms want to sell more.
   II. There are more firms selling.
   Which of the following is appropriate?

   a. I is an explanation; II is not.
   b. I is not an explanation; II is.
   c. Neither I nor II is an explanation.
   d. I and II are both explanations.
   e. I and II are both explanations, but if one applies, the other does not.

10. Which of the following will shift the market supply curve to the right?

   a. a reduction in price
   b. a technological improvement
   c. a reduction in the availability of credit
   d. an increase in an input price
   e. an increase in price

11. All of the following, except one, cause shifts in the market demand curve. Which is the odd one out?

   a. a change in income
   b. a change in the price of a substitute
   c. a change in tastes
   d. a change in the price of a complement
   e. technological change

12. Changes in the price of all except one of the following will shift either the demand curve for CDs or the supply curve of CDs. Which is the odd one out?

a. labour
b. capital
c. CDs
d. audio tapes
e. CD players

13. If the market price is below its equilibrium level, then there:

 a. is excess demand and upward pressure on the price.
 b. is excess supply and upward pressure on the price.
 c. are no forces operating to change the price.
 d. is excess supply and downward pressure on the price.
 e. is excess demand and downward pressure on the price.

14. If the market price is above its equilibrium level, then there:

 a. is excess demand and upward pressure on the price.
 b. is excess supply and upward pressure on the price.
 c. are no forces operating to change the price.
 d. is excess supply and downward pressure on the price.
 e. is excess demand and downward pressure on the price.

15. If the market price is at its equilibrium level, then there:

 a. is excess demand and upward pressure on the price.
 b. is excess supply and upward pressure on the price.
 c. are no forces operating to change the price.
 d. is excess supply and downward pressure on the price.
 e. is excess demand and downward pressure on the price.

16. If the price of margarine increases, the equilibrium price of butter will increase. The higher price of butter is the result of:

 a. a shift of the demand curve, which leads to a movement along the supply curve.
 b. a shift of the demand curve, together with a shift of the supply curve.
 c. neither a shift nor a movement in either the demand or the supply curve.
 d. a movement along the demand curve, together with a movement along the supply curve.
 e. a shift of the supply curve, which leads to a movement along the demand curve.

17. A recent regulation requires tuna fishing companies to use nets that allow dolphins to escape. These nets also allow some tuna to escape. This regulation shifts the:

 a. supply of tuna to the right and causes a decrease in the price of tuna.
 b. demand for tuna to the left and causes an increase in the price of tuna.
 c. supply of tuna and the demand for tuna to the left.
 d. demand for tuna to the right and causes a decrease in the price of tuna.
 e. supply of tuna to the left and causes an increase in the price of tuna.

18. The scare in Europe about mad cow disease:

 a. shifted the demand curve for beef to the right and lowered the price of beef.
 b. shifted the demand curve for beef to the left and lowered the price of beef.
 c. resulted in a movement down the demand curve for beef and lowered the price of beef.
 d. shifted the supply curve for beef to the left and raised the price of beef.
 e. shifted the supply curve for beef to the right and raised the price of beef.

19. The law of supply and demand states that:

 a. supply curves are upward-sloping.
 b. demand curves are downward-sloping
 c. increases in income shift the demand curve to the right.
 d. increases in input prices shift the supply curve to the left.
 e. when a market is out of equilibrium, forces operate to restore equilibrium.

20. In his explanation of why diamonds are more expensive than water, even though water is more important to life, Adam Smith stated that it was because:

 a. diamonds are luxuries and water is a necessity.
 b. the prices reflect value in exchange rather than value in use.
 c. prices are not a reflection of value.
 d. the prices reflect value in use rather than value in exchange.
 e. the market tends to undervalue important commodities.

Completion

1. If the price of a good or service falls, the quantity demanded _____.

2. If the price of a good or service falls, the quantity supplied _____.

3. The quantity of a good or service purchased at each price is given by the _____.

4. The quantity of a good or service offered for sale at each price is given by the _____.

5. In an economic equilibrium, there are no forces for _____.

6. The law of supply and demand says that at the equilibrium price, the _____ equals the _____.

7. The statement that market supply equals market demand is an example of an _____.

8. The statement that market supply is the total of all individual supplies is an example of an _____.

9. An increase in the price of a good leads to a _____ its demand curve.

10. A change in technology leads to a _____ the supply curve.

Answers to Self-Test

True or False

1. t	4. f	7. t	10. f	13. f
2. f	5. t	8. f	11. f	14. t
3. f	6. t	9. t	12. t	15. f

Multiple Choice

1. b	6. d	11. e	16. a
2. e	7. d	12. c	17. e
3. b	8. a	13. a	18. b
4. c	9. d	14. d	19. e
5. d	10. b	15. c	20. b

Completion

1. increases
2. falls
3. demand curve
4. supply curve
5. change
6. quantity demanded, quantity supplied
7. equilibrium relationship
8. identity
9. movement along
10. shift of

Doing Economics: Tools and Practice Problems

Three techniques receive attention in this section. The first technique shows how to add individual demand and individual supply curves to get market demand and market supply curves. The next technique involves finding the equilibrium price and quantity, where the market clears. Finally, some general instructions about supply and demand analysis are given and developed in several problems. Each of these techniques is fundamental and will appear repeatedly throughout this book.

MARKET DEMAND AND MARKET SUPPLY

When the price of a good falls, consumers want to buy more units of the good and firms want to sell fewer units of the good. We say there have been movements along the market demand and supply curves. The market curves are found by adding all the individual demand and supply curves, which are the behavioural relationships indicating each consumer's quantity demanded and each firm's quantity supplied at each price. Tool Kit 4.1 shows you how to calculate the market demand and supply curves from the individual relationships.

Tool Kit 4.1: Calculating Market Demand and Supply

The market demand curve is the sum, at each price, of the quantities demanded by each individual. The market supply curve is the sum, at each price, of all the quantities supplied by each firm. Follow these steps to obtain a market demand or market supply curve.

Step one: Make two columns. Label the left-hand column "Price" and the right-hand column "Quantity."

Price	Quantity

Step two: Choose the highest price at which goods are demanded. Enter this in the first row of the price column.

Price	Quantity
p_1	

Step three: If you are calculating a market demand curve, determine how many units of the good each individual will purchase at that price; that is, determine each individual's quantity demanded. (If you are calculating a market supply curve, determine each firm's quantity supplied.) Add these quantities. Enter the total in the first row of the quantity column.

Price	Quantity
p_1	$Q_1 = Q_a + Q_b + Q_c + \cdots$

Step four: Choose the second highest price, and continue the process.

1. (Worked problem: market demand) The individual demands of Jason and Sheila for economics tutoring are given in Table 4.1. Calculate the market demand. (Jason and Sheila are the only two individuals in this market.)

Table 4.1

Jason		Sheila	
Price	Quantity	Price	Quantity
$10	6	$10	4
$ 8	8	$ 8	5
$ 6	10	$ 6	6
$ 4	12	$ 4	7

Step-by-step solution

Step one: Make and label two columns.

Price	Quantity

Step two: Choose the highest price. This is $10. Enter this in the first row under price.

Price	Quantity
$10	

Step three: Find the market quantity. Jason would buy 6; Sheila would buy 4. The total is 6 + 4 = 10. Enter 10 in the corresponding quantity column.

Price	Quantity
$10	10

Step four: Repeat the process. The next lower price is $8. Jason would buy 8; Sheila would buy 5. The total is 8 + 5 = 13. Enter $8 and 13 in the appropriate columns.

Price	Quantity
$10	10
$ 8	13

Continue. The entire market demand is given below.

Price	Quantity
$10	10
$ 8	13
$ 6	16
$ 4	19

2. (Practice problem: market demand) Gorman's tomatoes are purchased by pizza sauce makers, by submarine sandwich shops, and by vegetable canners. The demands for each are given in Table 4.2. Find the market demand.

Table 4.2

Pizza sauce		Submarine shops		Vegetable canners	
Price	Quantity (bushels)	Price	Quantity (bushels)	Price	Quantity (bushels)
$5	25	$5	5	$5	55
$4	35	$4	6	$4	75
$3	40	$3	7	$3	100
$2	50	$2	7	$2	150
$1	80	$1	7	$1	250

3. (Practice problem: market supply) The technique for finding the market supply curve is the same as for the market demand. Simply sum the quantities supplied at each price. There are three law firms that will draw up partnership contracts in the town of Pullman. Their individual supply curves are given in Table 4.3. Find the market supply curve.

Table 4.3

Jones		Jones and Jones		Jones, Jones, and Jones	
Price	Quantity	Price	Quantity	Price	Quantity
$200	0	$200	6	$200	4
$220	0	$220	8	$220	8
$240	0	$240	12	$240	10
$260	8	$260	24	$260	11

EQUILIBRIUM

When the market is in equilibrium, quantity demanded equals quantity supplied. We say the market clears. The price that clears the market is the equilibrium price, which is the price at which consumers want to buy exactly the quantity firms want to supply. Tool Kit 4.2 shows you how to find this equilibrium.

Tool Kit 4.2: Finding the Equilibrium
Price and Quantity

The equilibrium price in the demand and supply model is the price at which the buyers want to buy exactly the quantity that sellers want to sell. In other words, the quantity demanded equals the quantity supplied. The equilibrium quantity in the market is just this quantity. Follow these steps to find the equilibrium in a market.

Step one: Choose a price. Find the quantity demanded at that price and the quantity supplied.

Step two: If the quantity demanded equals the quantity supplied, the price is the equilibrium. Stop.

Step three: If the quantity demanded exceeds the quantity supplied, there is a shortage. Choose a higher price and repeat step one. If the quantity demanded is less than the quantity supplied, there is a surplus. Choose a lower price and repeat step one.

Step four: Continue until the equilibrium price is found.

---

4. (Worked problem: equilibrium price and quantity) The supply curve and demand curve for cinder blocks are given in Table 4.4. The quantity column indicates the number of blocks sold in one year.

Table 4.4

Demand		Supply	
Price	Quantity	Price	Quantity
$2.00	50,000	$2.00	200,000
$1.50	70,000	$1.50	160,000
$1.00	100,000	$1.00	100,000
$0.75	150,000	$0.75	50,000
$0.50	250,000	$0.50	0

a. Find the equilibrium price and quantity.
b. If the price is $1.50, is the market in equilibrium? Will there be a surplus or a shortage? If so, what is the size of the surplus or shortage? What will happen to the price? Why?
c. If the price is $0.75, is the market in equilibrium? Will there be a surplus or a shortage? If so, what is the size of the surplus or shortage? What will happen to the price? Why?

Step-by-step solution

Step one (a): Choose a price. At a price of, say, $2.00, the quantity demanded is 50,000 and the quantity supplied is 200,000.

Step two: The quantities are not equal.

Step three: There is a surplus. The equilibrium price will be lower.

Step four: Continue. Try other prices until the quantity supplied equals the quantity demanded. The equilibrium price is $1.00, where the quantity equals 100,000. We can now see the answers to parts b and c.

Step five (b): If the price is $1.50, the quantity demanded is 70,000, and it is less than the quantity supplied, which is 160,000. There is a surplus, or excess supply, of 90,000 (160,000 − 70,000). The price will fall because producers will be unable to sell all that they want.

Step six (*c*): If the price is $0.75, the quantity demanded is 150,000, and it is greater than the quantity supplied, which is 50,000. There is a shortage, or excess demand, of 100,000 (150,000 − 50,000). The price will rise because producers will see that buyers are unable to buy all that they want.

5. (Practice problem: equilibrium price and quantity) The demand curve and supply curve in the market for billboard space adjacent to a highway are given in Table 4.5. The price is the monthly rental price. The quantity column shows numbers of billboards.

Table 4.5

Demand		Supply	
Price	Quantity	Price	Quantity
$100	5	$100	25
$ 80	8	$ 80	21
$ 60	11	$ 60	16
$ 40	14	$ 40	14
$ 20	22	$ 20	3

a. Find the equilibrium price and quantity.
b. If the price is $20, is the market in equilibrium? Will there be a surplus or a shortage? If so, what is the size of the surplus or shortage? What will happen to the price? Why?
c. If the price is $80, is the market in equilibrium? Will there be a surplus or a shortage? If so, what is the size of the surplus or shortage? What will happen to the price? Why?

6. (Practice problem: equilibrium price and quantity) Find the equilibrium price and quantity in each of the following markets.

a. The supply and demand curves for new soles (shoe repair) are given in Table 4.6.

Table 4.6

Demand		Supply	
Price	Quantity	Price	Quantity
$35	17	$35	53
$30	21	$30	37
$25	25	$25	25
$20	30	$20	15
$15	35	$15	0

b. The supply and demand curves for seat cushions are given in Table 4.7.

Table 4.7

Demand		Supply	
$8	4	$8	32
$7	8	$7	28
$6	12	$6	22
$5	16	$5	19
$4	17	$4	17

SUPPLY AND DEMAND

The model of supply and demand is probably the most useful technique in microeconomics. Economists use it to study how markets are affected by changes in, for example, tastes, technology, and government programmes of one form or another. The model offers a wealth of insight into the workings of the economy. Tool Kit 4.3 shows you how to put the model of supply and demand to work.

Tool Kit 4.3: Using Supply and Demand

Supply and demand analysis provides excellent answers to questions of the following form: "What is the effect of a change in _____ on the market for _____?" You are well on your way to success as a student of economics if you follow this procedure carefully when answering such questions.

Step one: Begin with an equilibrium in the relevant market. Label the horizontal axis as the quantity of the good or service and the vertical axis as the price. Draw a demand and a supply curve and label them *D* and *S*, respectively.

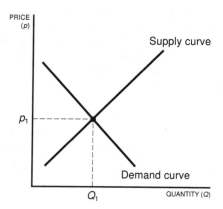

Step two: Determine the answers to the following questions. Does the change shift the demand curve, and if so, how? Does the change shift the supply curve, and if so, how?

Step three: Shift the appropriate curve in the appropriate direction.

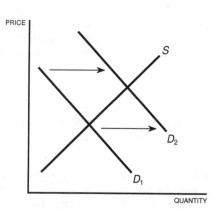

Step four: Find the new equilibrium, and compare it with the original one.

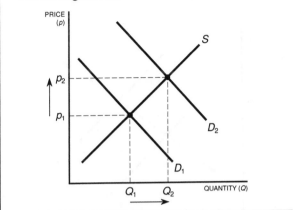

7. (Worked problem: using supply and demand) In response to concern about the fumes emitted by dry cleaning establishments, regulations have been issued requiring expensive filtering systems. How will this regulation affect the dry cleaning market?

Step-by-step solution

Step one: Start with an equilibrium.

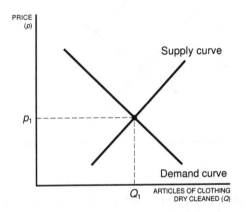

Step two: Figure out which curve shifts. The mandated filtering systems increase the dry cleaning firm's costs, and so shift the supply to the left.

Step three: Shift the curve.

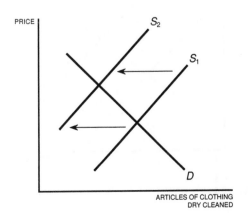

Step four: Find the new equilibrium and compare. The effect of the regulation is to raise the price and lower the quantity of clothes dry cleaned.

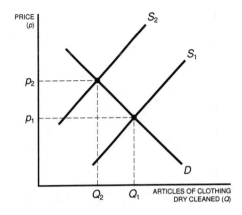

8. (Practice problem: using supply and demand) As the oil market comes to the realization that Kuwait's production will not return to prewar levels, the price of oil has increased by $4 per barrel. Explain the effect of this oil price increase on the market for natural gas.

9. (Practice problem: using supply and demand) For each of the following, show the effects on price and quantity. Draw the diagrams and follow the procedure.

a. An increase in income
b. A decrease in income
c. An increase in the price of a substitute
d. A decrease in the price of a substitute
e. An increase in the price of a complement
f. A decrease in the price of a complement
g. An increase in the price of an input
h. A decrease in the price of an input
i. An improvement in technology

Answers to Problems

2.
Price	Quantity (bushels)
$5	85
$4	116
$3	147
$2	207
$1	337

3.
Price	Quantity
$200	10
$220	16
$240	22
$260	43

5. a. Equilibrium price = $40; quantity = 14.
   b. If the price is $20, there is a shortage of 22 − 3 = 19. The price will be driven up.
   c. If the price is $80, there is a surplus of 21 − 8 = 13. The price will be driven down.

6. a. Price = $25; quantity = 25.
   b. Price = $4; quantity = 17.

8. Oil and natural gas are substitutes, and therefore the demand curve shifts to the right, the price increases, and the quantity increases.

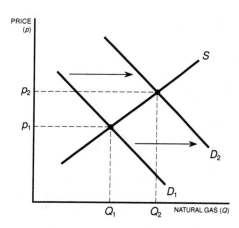

9. *a.* Demand shifts to the right; this drives the price up and increases the quantity.

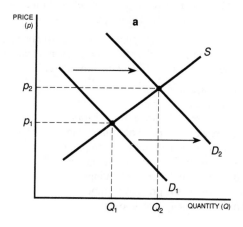

b. Demand shifts to the left; this drives the price down and decreases the quantity.

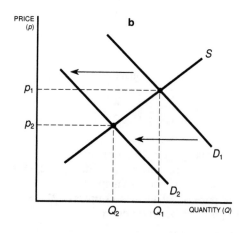

c. Demand shifts to the right; this drives the price up and increases the quantity.

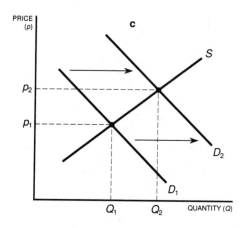

d. Demand shifts to the left; this drives the price down and decreases the quantity.

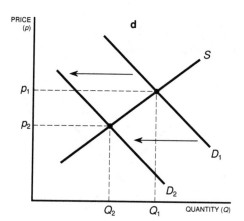

e. Demand shifts to the left; this drives the price down and decreases the quantity.

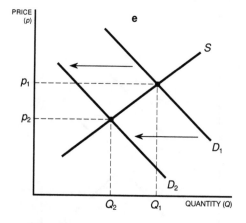

f. Demand shifts to the right; this drives the price up
    and increases the quantity.

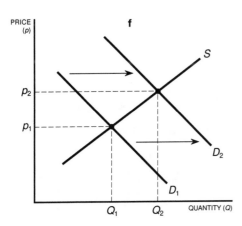

h. Supply shifts to the right; this decreases the price
    but increases the quantity.

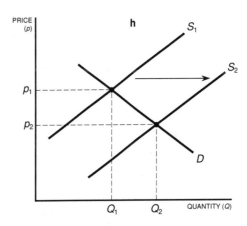

g. Supply shifts to the left; this increases the price but
    decreases the quantity.

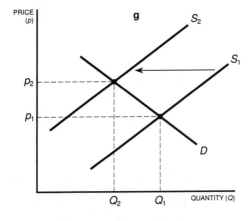

i. Supply shifts to the right; this decreases the price
    but increases the quantity.

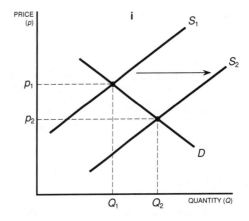

Chapter 5

USING DEMAND AND SUPPLY

Chapter Review

The model of demand and supply introduced in Chapter 4 is one of the most useful in all the social sciences. The ideas of demand and supply form the basis of all economic study, and will be used throughout this text. This chapter develops the model in more detail and introduces the concept of elasticity. Elasticity is best thought of as "sensitivity." The price elasticity of demand, for instance, measures the sensitivity of the quantity demanded to a change in price. The chapter then applies the model to the study of the effects of taxes and price controls.

ESSENTIAL CONCEPTS

1. When price falls, quantity demanded increases. If the demand curve is steep, the increase in quantity is smaller than it would be if the curve were flat. Although it might seem natural to measure how the quantity responds to price changes by the slope of the demand curve, economists employ the concept of **elasticity.** They do so because elasticity will produce the same measure no matter what units are used. The **price elasticity of demand** is the percentage change in the quantity demanded brought about by a 1 percent change in price.

2. If the percentage change in quantity demanded in response to a 1 percent change in price is less than 1 percent, quantity demanded is not very sensitive to price changes and demand is said to be **inelastic**. In this case, revenue changes in the same direction as price: if the price goes up, sales will go down but revenue, which is just price multiplied by the quantity demanded, will rise. If the percentage change in the quantity demanded is greater than 1 percent, demand is said to be **elastic**. In this case, revenue will move in the opposite direction to price, so a price reduction will increase revenue.

3. The **price elasticity of supply** is the percentage change in the quantity supplied brought about by a 1 percent change in price. It is the basic measure of the sensitivity of the quantity supplied to changes in price.

4. The price elasticity of demand is greater when there are close substitutes available. Both the price elasticity of demand and the price elasticity of supply are greater in the long run because individuals and firms have more time to find substitutes and make adjustments.

5. When the demand curve shifts, there is a movement along the supply curve. Usually equilibrium price and equilibrium quantity both change. Which changes more is determined by the price elasticity of supply. If supply is relatively elastic, for example, most of the adjustment

will be in the equilibrium quantity, and there will be only a relatively small change in the equilibrium price. Similarly, if the supply curve shifts, the relative impact on equilibrium price and quantity will depend on the price elasticity of demand.

6. The economic effects of a tax are seen by focusing on the market affected by the tax. For example, a tax on the sale of gasoline shifts the supply curve up (vertically) by the amount of the tax, raises consumer prices, and reduces the quantity of gasoline sold. Except in a case where demand is perfectly inelastic or supply is perfectly elastic, the increase in consumer price is less than the amount of the tax. This means that producers are able to pass on only part of the tax to their customers and must bear some of the burden themselves.

7. **Price ceilings,** when set below the market-clearing price, lead to shortages, which means that the quantity demanded exceeds the quantity supplied. **Price floors,** when set above the market-clearing price, result in surpluses; in this case, the quantity demanded is less than the quantity supplied. In each case, the quantity actually exchanged is less than it is at the market-clearing price.

BEHIND THE ESSENTIAL CONCEPTS

1. The concept of elasticity appears many times throughout the text, and is worth mastering. Suppose that price falls by 1 percent. We know that quantity will increase as consumers substitute towards the lower price, but by how much? The price elasticity provides the answer. It is the percentage change in quantity brought about by a 1 percent change in price.

2. The relationship between elasticity and total revenue is very important. Total revenue is just price multiplied by quantity. If the price of a bicycle is $200 and there are 20 sold, then total revenue is $200 × 2 = $4,000. When price falls, total revenue is pushed down because each unit sells for less money; however, total revenue is pushed up because more units are sold. Whether on balance total revenue rises or falls depends on the elasticity. Table 5.1 helps to keep the relationship between elasticity and total revenue straight.

Table 5.1

If price rises:
   total revenue *falls* if the price elasticity of demand is greater than 1 (elastic).
   total revenue *rises* if the price elasticity of demand is less than 1 (inelastic).
   total revenue *does not change* if the price elasticity of demand equals 1 (unitary elasticity).

If price falls:
   total revenue *rises* if the price elasticity of demand is greater than 1 (elastic).
   total revenue *falls* if the price elasticity of demand is less than 1 (inelastic).
   total revenue *does not change* if the price elasticity of demand equals 1 (unitary elasticity).

3. What makes the demand for some goods (like motor boats) elastic, while the demand for others (like milk) is inelastic? The most important factor is the availability of substitutes. The **principle of substitution** says that consumers will look for substitutes when the price rises. If there are close substitutes available, then finding substitutes will be easy and consumers will switch. If close substitutes are not available, the consumers are more likely to swallow the price increase and continue purchasing the good.

4. Suppose that the government levies a tax on the supply of hotel rooms. Who pays the tax? While it is natural to think that the hotel pays the tax because it actually writes the cheque to the government, when you look at the issue through the lens of supply and demand, you see the value of economics. The tax increases the hotel's costs, and therefore it shifts the supply curve up and raises the price. Because they must pay higher prices for hotel rooms, consumers pay some of the tax.

5. Price ceilings only make a difference if they are set below the market-clearing price (where the supply and demand curves intersect). A price ceiling set above the market-clearing price has no effect. Similarly, a price floor set below the market-clearing price does not do anything.

6. Price floors and ceilings also affect the quantity traded in the market. If there is a price ceiling, then the quantity demanded exceeds the quantity supplied. The supply is the short side of the market, and although consumers would like to buy more of the good, the quantity traded is what producers are willing to sell. This is shown in panel A of Figure 5.1. With price floors, the opposite is true. The demand is the short side of the market, and the quantity traded equals the amount that consumers are willing to buy, as shown in panel B. In each case, we say that the short side of the market determines the actual quantity traded, and the actual quantity traded is less than the market-clearing quantity.

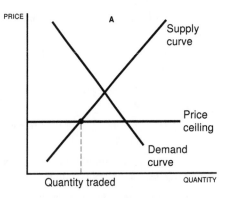

Figure 5.1

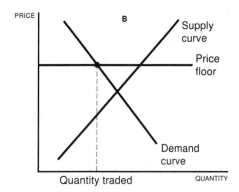

Figure 5.1

SELF-TEST

True or False

1. The price elasticity of demand is greater for goods and services that have better close substitutes.

2. The price elasticity of demand is always constant along the demand curve.

3. If demand is price elastic, revenue increases when price falls.

4. A horizontal demand curve is perfectly elastic.

5. A vertical supply curve is perfectly inelastic.

6. If the supply curve is unitary elastic, then total revenue is constant as price changes.

7. If the supply curve is upward-sloping, a rightward shift in the demand curve increases the equilibrium price and the equilibrium quantity.

8. If the demand curve is downward-sloping, a rightward shift in the supply curve increases the equilibrium price and the equilibrium quantity.

9. When the demand curve is very elastic, relatively more of a tax on the production of some good or service will be borne by producers.

10. A tax on the sale of beer shifts the supply curve vertically by the amount of the tax.

11. When prices are sticky, shortages and surpluses can result in the short run.

12. A price ceiling set above the equilibrium price will have no effect on the market.

13. A price ceiling set below the equilibrium price will have no effect on the market.

14. A price floor set above the equilibrium price in the milk market will lead to a surplus of milk.

15. If the supply of labour is perfectly inelastic, a minimum wage set above the equilibrium wage will not result in any unemployment.

Multiple Choice

1. The price elasticity of demand for a good is likely to be:

   a. more elastic when there are fewer close substitutes for the good.
   b. less elastic when it is easier to find substitutes for the good.
   c. more elastic when there are no close substitutes for the good.
   d. less elastic when there are more close substitutes for the good.
   e. more elastic when there are more close substitutes for the good.

2. Suppose that the price of ice cream falls by 10 percent and the quantity demanded rises by 20 percent. The demand for ice cream:

   a. has a price elasticity of demand of 2.
   b. is price-inelastic.
   c. has a price elasticity of demand of 1.
   d. has unitary price elasticity.
   e. has a price elasticity of demand of 0.5.

3. If the price elasticity of demand for milk is 1/3 and price rises by 30 percent, the quantity demanded:

   a. rises by 10 percent.
   b. falls by 10 percent.
   c. does not change.
   d. falls by 90 percent.
   e. rises by 90 percent.

4. An increase of 10 percent in the price of cheese:

   a. raises revenue by 10 percent when demand is price-elastic.
   b. raises revenue when demand has unitary price elasticity.
   c. lowers revenue when demand is price-elastic.
   d. lowers revenue when demand has unitary price elasticity.
   e. lowers revenue by 10 percent when demand is price-elastic.

5. If the price elasticity of demand for pasta is 0.7, demand for pasta:

   a. is perfectly elastic.
   b. is relatively elastic.
   c. has unitary elasticity.
   d. is relatively inelastic.
   e. is perfectly inelastic.

6. Which of the following statements is correct?

   a. The price elasticity of demand is constant along a straight-line demand curve.
   b. Demand is more price-elastic in the short run than in the long run.
   c. If total revenue rises when price increases, demand is relatively inelastic.
   d. A demand curve with unitary price elasticity has a slope of unity.
   e. If total revenue does not change when price changes, demand is perfectly inelastic.

7. If the demand curve is horizontal, then the price elasticity of demand is:

    a. equal to 0.
    b. greater than 0 but less than 1.
    c. equal to 1.
    d. greater than 1 but less than infinity.
    e. infinite.

8. If we were to compare the price elasticities of demand for broccoli and for all green vegetables, we would expect that:

    a. the price elasticity of demand for broccoli would be smaller than the elasticity of demand for all green vegetables.
    b. the price elasticity of demand for broccoli would be greater than the elasticity of demand for all green vegetables.
    c. the price elasticity of demand for broccoli would be the same as the elasticity of demand for all green vegetables, because broccoli is a green vegetable.
    d. the price elasticity of demand for broccoli could be greater or smaller than the elasticity of demand for all green vegetables.
    e. they would both be greater than the price elasticity of demand for lettuce.

9. If the price elasticity of supply for shoes is 2 and price rises by 30 percent, the quantity supplied:

    a. falls by 15 percent.
    b. rises by 15 percent.
    c. does not change.
    d. rises by 60 percent.
    e. falls by 60 percent.

10. If the price elasticity of supply for bread is 1.5, the supply of bread:

    a. is perfectly elastic.
    b. is relatively elastic.
    c. has unitary elasticity.
    d. is relatively inelastic.
    e. is perfectly inelastic.

11. If the supply curve is vertical, the price elasticity of supply is:

    a. equal to 0.
    b. greater than 0 but less than 1.
    c. equal to 1.
    d. greater than 1 but less than infinity.
    e. infinite.

12. Compared with its short-run value, the long-run price elasticity of supply is:

    a. smaller; this means that in response to a shift in demand, in the long run the change in equilibrium quantity is larger and the change in equilibrium price is smaller than in the short run.
    b. greater; this means that in response to a shift in demand, in the long run the change in equilibrium quantity is smaller and the change in equilibrium price is larger than in the short run.
    c. greater; this means that in response to a shift in demand, in the long run the changes in both equilibri-

um quantity and equilibrium price are larger than in the short run.

    d. greater; this means that in response to a shift in demand, in the long run the change in equilibrium quantity is larger and the change in equilibrium price is smaller than in the short run.
    e. smaller; this means that in response to a shift in demand, in the long run the change in equilibrium quantity is smaller and the change in equilibrium price is larger than in the short run.

13. If the supply curve is perfectly price-elastic, a rightward shift of the demand curve:

    a. increases both equilibrium quantity and equilibrium price.
    b. increases equilibrium price but leaves equilibrium quantity unchanged.
    c. increases equilibrium quantity but leaves equilibrium price unchanged.
    d. decreases equilibrium quantity but leaves equilibrium price unchanged.
    e. decreases both equilibrium quantity and equilibrium price.

14. Assume the price elasticity of demand for tires is 1.5, and the supply curve is upward-sloping. If a tax of $1 per tire is levied, then the price paid by consumers will:

    a. remain unchanged.
    b. increase by less than $1.
    c. increase by exactly $1.
    d. increase by more than $1 but less than $1.50.
    e. increase by exactly $1.50.

15. For a given upward-sloping supply curve, the proportion of a tax borne by consumers is:

    a. larger, the lower the price elasticity of demand is.
    b. one-half when the price elasticity of demand is unity.
    c. larger, the higher the price elasticity of demand is.
    d. zero when the price elasticity of demand is zero.
    e. smaller, the lower the price elasticity of demand is.

16. When supply of a good is perfectly price-elastic, a tax of $1 per unit levied on that good:

    a. raises the price paid by consumers by less than $1.
    b. has no effect on the price paid by consumers.
    c. raises the price paid by consumers by more than $1.
    d. lowers the price received by suppliers by exactly $1.
    e. raises the price paid by consumers by exactly $1.

17. All of the following, except one, are true of taxes levied on goods. Which is the odd one out?

    a. If the purpose of the taxes is to raise revenue, they should be levied on goods that are relatively price-inelastic.
    b. If the purpose of the taxes is to discourage consumption, they should be levied on goods that are relatively price-elastic.
    c. When the purpose of the taxes is to raise revenue, they tend to redistribute income towards low-income households.
    d. When the purpose of the taxes is to discourage consumption, they tend to be levied on goods that are

consumed proportionately less by low-income households.

   e. When the purpose of the taxes is to raise revenue, they tend to be levied on goods that are consumed proportionately more by low-income households.

18. A price ceiling (e.g., a controlled rent) set below the equilibrium price will _____; a price ceiling set above the equilibrium price will _____.

   a. create a surplus; have no effect
   b. have no effect; create a surplus
   c. lead to a price increase; lead to a price decrease
   d. create a shortage; have no effect
   e. have no effect; create a shortage

19. A price floor (e.g., a minimum wage) set below the equilibrium price will _____; a price floor set above the equilibrium price will _____.

   a. create a surplus; have no effect
   b. have no effect; create a surplus
   c. lead to a price increase; lead to a price decrease
   d. create a shortage; have no effect
   e. have no effect; create a shortage

20. All of the following, except one, are true of rent controls. Which is the odd one out?

   a. They create a shortage of rental accommodation and make it difficult to find vacant apartments.
   b. They create a greater shortage of rental accommodation the longer they are in effect.
   c. They keep rents artificially low for those who already have or can find apartments.
   d. They discourage people from giving up rental accommodation and thereby restrict labour mobility.
   e. Their harmful effects are soon recognized by governments, which quickly remove them.

Completion

1. The percentage change in the quantity demanded as a result of a 1 percent price change is called the _____.

2. Price changes have no effect on revenue if the price elasticity of demand is _____.

3. If the price elasticity of demand lies between 0 and 1, then we say that demand is relatively _____.

4. A horizontal demand curve indicates that demand is _____.

5. If the supply curve is vertical, then the price elasticity of supply equals _____.

6. A $.50-per-litre tax on the production of gasoline can normally be expected to raise price by _____.

7. If demand is relatively inelastic, most of the tax is borne by _____.

8. A price ceiling set below the equilibrium price will create a _____.

9. A price floor set above the equilibrium price will create a _____.

10. The minimum wage is an example of a _____.

Answers to Self-Test

True or False

1. t	4. t	7. t	10. t	13. f
2. f	5. t	8. f	11. t	14. t
3. t	6. f	9. t	12. t	15. f

Multiple Choice

1. e	6. c	11. a	16. e
2. a	7. e	12. d	17. c
3. b	8. b	13. c	18. d
4. c	9. d	14. b	19. b
5. d	10. b	15. a	20. e

Completion

1   price elasticity of demand
2   1
3   inelastic
4   perfectly elastic
5   zero
6   less than $.50
7   consumers
8   shortage
9   surplus
10 price floor

Doing Economics: Tools and Practice Problems

Three techniques receive attention in this section. You will first learn how to calculate elasticity, then how to measure the effects of taxes, and finally how to analyze the effects of price controls.

ELASTICITY

When price changes, by how much does the quantity demanded or the quantity supplied change? The answer is provided by the elasticity, which measures the responsiveness of quantity to price changes. Tool Kit 5.1 shows you one method for calculating elasticity. The problems that follow focus on the elasticity of demand, and also illustrate the relationship between the elasticity of demand and revenue.

Tool Kit 5.1: Calculating Elasticity

Follow these steps to calculate elasticity.

Step one: To find the elasticity between two points on the demand or supply curve, let p_1 and Q_1 be the price and quantity at the first point, and let p_2 and Q_2 be the price and quantity at the second point.

Step two: Substitute the prices and quantities into the formula

elasticity $= (Q_1 - Q_2)(p_1 + p_2)/(Q_1 + Q_2)(p_1 - p_2)$.

---

1. (Worked problem: calculating elasticity) The demand curve for bulletin boards is given below.

Price	Quantity
$35	800
$30	1,000
$25	1,200
$20	1,300

a. Calculate total revenue for each price.
b. Calculate the price elasticity of demand between $35 and $30, between $30 and $25, and between $25 and $20. Does elasticity change along this demand curve?
c. Verify the relationship between elasticity and total revenue.

Step-by-step solution

Step one (a): Total revenue at $35 is $800 \times \$35 = \$28,000$. Total revenue at $30 is $1,000 \times \$30 = \$30,000$. Continue, and enter the numbers in the table.

Price	Quantity	Total revenue
$35	800	$28,000
$30	1,000	$30,000
$25	1,200	$30,000
$20	1,300	$26,000

Step two (b): Let $\$35 = p_1$, $800 = Q_1$, $\$30 = p_2$, and $1,000 = Q_2$. Substituting into the formula gives

elasticity $= (35 + 30)(1,000 - 800)/(800 + 1,000)(35 - 30)$
$= 1.44$, which is elastic.

Step three: Between $30 and $25,

elasticity $= (30 + 25)(1,200 - 1,000)/(1,000 + 1,200)(30 - 25)$
$= 1$, which is unitary elastic.

Step four: Between $25 and $20,

elasticity $= (25 + 20)(1,300 - 1,200)/(1,200 + 1,300)(25 - 20)$
$= 0.36$, which is inelastic.

Clearly, the elasticity is not constant. The demand curve is less elastic at lower prices.

Step five (c): Between $35 and $30, where the demand is elastic, total revenue rises from $28,000 to $30,000 as price falls. Between $30 and $25, where the demand is unitary elastic, total revenue is constant at $30,000 as the price falls. Between $25 and $20, where the demand is inelastic, total revenue falls from $30,000 to $26,000 as the price falls. Check Table 5.1 to verify that these numbers are consistent with the general relationship between price elasticity of demand and total revenue.

2. (Practice problem: calculating elasticity) The demand curve for bookends is given below.

Price	Quantity
$10	70
$ 8	90
$ 6	120
$ 4	130

a. Calculate total revenue for each price.
b. Calculate the price elasticity of demand between each of the adjacent prices. Does elasticity change along this demand?
c. Verify the relationship between elasticity and total revenue.

3. (Practice problem: calculating elasticity) For each of the following, calculate the total revenue for each price and the price elasticity for each price change, and verify the relationship between elasticity and total revenue.

a.

Price	Quantity
$12	6
$10	8
$ 8	10
$ 6	12

b.

Price	Quantity
$100	80
$ 80	85
$ 60	90
$ 40	95

c.

Price	Quantity
$9	10
$8	14
$7	18
$6	22

TAX INCIDENCE

The incidence of a tax refers to its impact on the price paid by the consumer and the price received by the firm. The model of demand and supply can be used to determine the incidence of a tax. The model demonstrates that, more often than not, the burden of a tax does not fall only on the person or firm that initially pays it. In fact, unless the demand curve or the supply curve is perfectly elastic or perfectly inelastic, consumers and firms share the burden of the tax. Tool Kit 5.2 shows you how to calculate the incidence of a tax. It also demonstrates how taxes reduce output and why it does not matter who initially pays the tax.

Tool Kit 5.2: Using Supply and Demand for Tax Incidence

This procedure uses the model of demand and supply to analyze the effects of a tax on a good. Follow the steps to see how consumers and firms share the burden of a tax.

Step one: Start with an equilibrium in the relevant market.

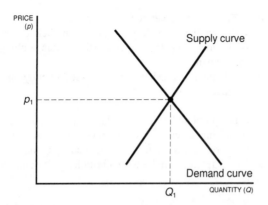

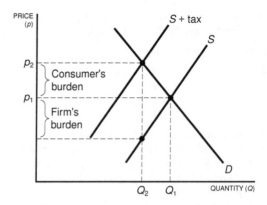

Step two: Identify whether consumers or firms must initially pay the tax.

Step three: If the firms must pay the tax, shift the supply curve up (vertically) by exactly the amount of the tax. (If the consumers must pay the tax, shift the demand curve down by exactly the amount of the tax.)

Consumers' burden = new equilibrium price
– original equilibrium price.

Firms' burden = original equilibrium price
– new equilibrium price + tax.

If the consumers initially pay the tax, use the following formulas to calculate tax incidence.

Consumers' burden = new equilibrium price + tax
– original equilibrium price.

Firms' burden = original equilibrium price
– new equilibrium price.

Step six: Verify that if either the demand curve or the supply curve is perfectly elastic, the burden of the tax is not shared. If demand is perfectly elastic, firms finish up paying the whole of the tax. If supply is perfectly elastic, consumers pay the tax.

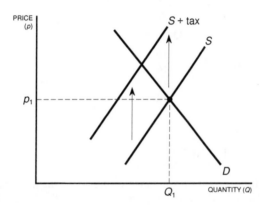

Step four: Find the new equilibrium.

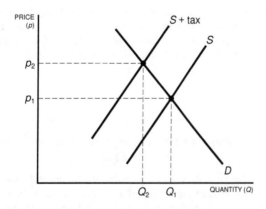

Step five: Determine the economic incidence of the tax. If the firms initially pay the tax, use the following formulas to calculate economic incidence.

4. (Worked problem: tax incidence) The demand curve and supply curve for two-bedroom apartments in Halifax are given in Table 5.2.

Table 5.2

Demand		Supply	
Price	*Quantity*	*Price*	*Quantity*
$800	100	$800	500
$750	200	$750	500
$700	300	$700	450
$650	400	$650	400
$600	500	$600	300

a. Find the equilibrium price and quantity.
b. Suppose that landlords are required to pay a tax of $100 per apartment to the city government. Use supply and demand analysis to determine the incidence of the tax.
c. Now suppose that rather than being paid by the landlords, the tax must be paid by the tenants. Use supply and demand analysis to determine the incidence of the tax.
d. Does it matter who pays the tax?

Step-by-step solution

Step one (a): Find the no-tax equilibrium. When the price is $650, the market clears with 400 apartments rented. This is the answer to part a.

Step two (b): Identify whether the landlords or tenants must pay the tax. For part b, the landlords pay the tax.

Step three: Because the tax is paid by the landlords, the supply curve shifts up by $100, the amount of the tax. The new supply curve is found by adding $100 to the price column, as in Table 5.3.

Table 5.3

Supply	
Price	Quantity
$900	500
$850	500
$800	450
$750	400
$700	300

Step four: Find the new equilibrium. The market clears at a price of $700 and a quantity of 300.

Step five: Determine the economic incidence of the tax.

Tenants' burden = new equilibrium price
  − original equilibrium price
  = $700 − $650 = $50.
Landlords' burden = original equilibrium price
  − new equilibrium price + tax
  = $650 − $700 + $100 = $50.

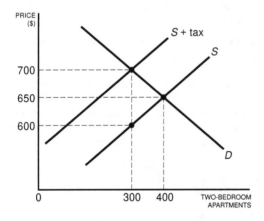

Step six (c): To answer part c, we repeat the procedure for the case where the demander must pay the tax.

Step seven (this repeats *step one*): The original no-tax equilibrium is the same with the price equal to $650 and 400 apartments rented.

Step eight (two): In this case, the tenants pay the tax.

Step nine (three): We shift the demand curve down by $100. The new demand curve is given in Table 5.4.

Table 5.4

Demand	
Price	Quantity
$700	100
$650	200
$600	300
$550	400
$500	500

Step ten (four): The market clears at a price of $600 and a quantity of 300.

Step eleven (five): We determine the incidence as follows.

Tenants' burden = new equilibrium price
  + tax − original equilibrium price
  = $600 + $100 − $650 = $50.
Landlords' burden = original equilibrium price
  − new equilibrium price
  = $650 − $600 = $50.

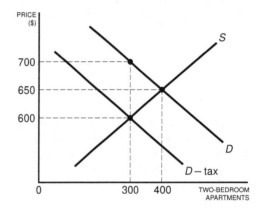

Step twelve (d): It does not matter who pays the tax! In either situation, the total amount that tenants pay is $700, the net amount that landlords receive is $600, and the equilibrium quantity is 300. The diagrams illustrate the solution.

5. (Practice problem: tax incidence) The demand curve and supply curve for unskilled labour are given in Table 5.5.

Table 5.5

Demand		Supply	
Wage	Quantity	Wage	Quantity
$6.50	1,000	$6.50	1,900
$6.00	1,200	$6.00	1,800
$5.50	1,400	$5.50	1,700
$5.00	1,600	$5.00	1,600
$4.50	1,800	$4.50	1,500
$4.00	2,000	$4.00	1,400

a. Find the equilibrium wage and quantity hired.
b. Consider the effect of the unemployment insurance

tax. Suppose that it equals $1.50 per hour and is paid by the employers (they are the demanders in this market). Use supply and demand analysis to determine the incidence of this tax.

c. Now suppose that rather than being paid by the employers, the tax must be paid by the workers. Use supply and demand analysis to determine the incidence of this tax.

d. Does it matter who pays the tax?

PRICE CONTROLS

The model of demand and supply can be used to determine the effects of price controls. The control (if it is effective) will change the price without shifting either the demand curve or the supply curve. The price is therefore away from equilibrium, and the short side of the market (the lesser of the quantity demanded and the quantity supplied) determines the quantity traded. Surpluses or shortages occur. Tool Kit 5.3 shows you how a price control affects a market and how to determine whether there will be a shortage or a surplus.

Tool Kit 5.3: Using Supply and Demand for Price Controls

This procedure uses the model of demand and supply to analyze the effects of a price control. Follow the steps to see how shortages and surpluses occur when prices are set away from the equilibrium.

Step one: Start with a market-clearing equilibrium.

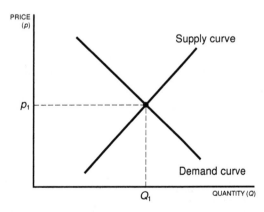

Step two: Identify the controlled price, and decide whether it is a floor or a ceiling.

Step three: Find the new equilibrium price. If it is a price floor set below the market-clearing price or a price ceiling set above the market-clearing price, then the equilibrium is the market-clearing one found in step one. If it is a price floor set above the market-clearing price or a price ceiling set below market clearing, then the controlled price is the equilibrium price.

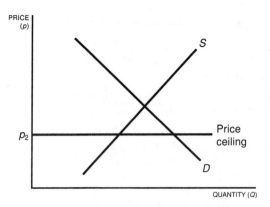

Step four: Determine the shortage or surplus. For a price ceiling set below the market-clearing price, there is a shortage:

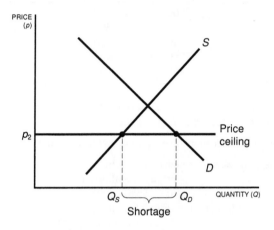

shortage = quantity demanded – quantity supplied.

For a price floor set above the market-clearing price, there is a surplus:

surplus = quantity supplied – quantity demanded.

---

6. (Worked problem: price controls) Dental bills in Toothache City rose again last year. The City Council is considering a bill to place a ceiling on fees that dentists can charge for teeth cleaning. The supply curve and demand curve for teeth cleanings are given in Table 5.6.

Table 5.6

Demand		Supply	
Price	*Quantity*	*Price*	*Quantity*
$65	100	$65	190
$60	120	$60	180
$55	140	$55	170
$50	160	$50	160
$45	180	$45	150
$40	200	$40	140

a. Find the equilibrium price and quantity for teeth cleanings in Toothache City.

b. The City Council passes a price ceiling ordinance, setting the maximum price at $40 per cleaning. Use supply and demand analysis to determine the effects of the price control.

Step-by-step solution

Step one (a): Find the equilibrium price and quantity. The market clears at a price of $50 and quantity equal to 160.

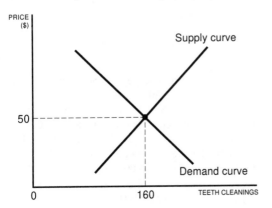

Step two (b): Identify the controlled price and whether it is a floor or a ceiling. The price control is a price ceiling set at $40.

Step three: Determine the new equilibrium price. The ceiling is below the market-clearing price; therefore, the new price is equal to the ceiling price of $40.

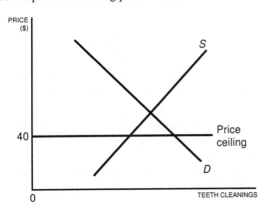

Step four: Determine the shortage or surplus. When the price is $40, the quantity demanded is 200 and the quantity supplied is 140. Although consumers would like more, there are only 140 cleanings actually performed. This results in a shortage of 200 − 140 = 60 teeth cleanings. The diagram illustrates the solution.

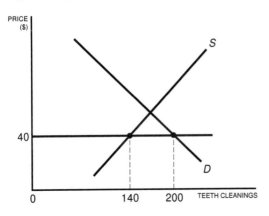

7. (Practice problem: price controls) The legislature in the state of Canute is considering price ceilings on automobile insurance premiums. The supply curve and demand curve for automobile insurance policies ($250 deductible on liability, no collision) are given in Table 5.7.

Table 5.7

Demand		Supply	
Price	Quantity	Price	Quantity
$800	1,000	$800	1,800
$750	1,100	$750	1,500
$700	1,200	$700	1,200
$650	1,400	$650	900
$600	1,600	$600	600

  a. Find the equilibrium price and quantity.
  b. Suppose that a price ceiling of $650 is imposed. Use supply and demand analysis to determine the effects of the price control.

8. (Practice problem: price controls) Fearful of a restless urban population, Corporal Thug, the new supreme ruler of Costa Guano, attempts to mollify the masses with a wage increase. Thug mandates that employers must pay at least $8 per day. The supply and demand curves for urban labour are given in Table 5.8.

Table 5.8

Demand		Supply	
Wage	Quantity	Wage	Quantity
$8.50	400	$8.50	4,000
$8.00	600	$8.00	3,200
$7.50	700	$7.50	2,600
$7.00	800	$7.00	2,200
$6.50	900	$6.50	1,800
$6.00	1,000	$6.00	1,000

  a. Find the quantity demanded, the quantity supplied, and the size of the surplus or shortage, if any.
  b. Democracy comes to Costa Guano! Corporal Thug is overthrown and the minimum wage repealed. Use supply and demand analysis to determine the effects of removing the price control.

Answers to Problems

2. *a.*

Price	Quantity	Revenue
$10	70	$700
$ 8	90	$720
$ 6	120	$720
$ 4	130	$520

  b. Between $10 and $8,

$$\text{elasticity} = (10 + 8)(90 - 70)/(10 - 8)(90 + 70)$$
$$= 1.125.$$

Between $8 and $6,
elasticity = (8 + 6)(120 − 90)/(8 − 6)(120 + 90)
= 1.
Between $6 and $4,
elasticity = (6 + 4)(130 − 120)/(6 − 4)(130 + 120)
= 0.2.

c. When elasticity is 1.125, the demand curve is elastic, and total revenue rises from $700 to $720 as price falls. When elasticity is 1, the demand curve is unitary elastic, and total revenue remains constant at $720 as price falls. Finally, when elasticity is 0.2, the demand curve is inelastic, and total revenue falls from $720 to $520 as price falls.

3. In the following tables, the number in the elasticity column corresponding to each price refers to the elasticity over the interval between that price and the next highest price.

a.
Price	Quantity	Total revenue	Elasticity
$12	6	$72	
$10	8	$80	1.57
$ 8	10	$80	1.00
$ 6	12	$72	0.64

b.
Price	Quantity	Total revenue	Elasticity
$100	80	$8,000	
$ 80	85	$6,800	0.26
$ 60	90	$5,400	0.20
$ 40	95	$3,800	0.14

c.
Price	Quantity	Total revenue	Elasticity
$9	10	$ 90	
$8	14	$112	2.430
$7	18	$126	1.875
$6	22	$132	1.300

5. a.   Wage = $5; quantity = 1,600.
   b.   The new supply curve is given in Table 5.9.

Table 5.9

Supply	
Wage	Quantity
$8.00	1,900
$7.50	1,800
$7.00	1,700
$6.50	1,600
$6.00	1,500
$5.50	1,400

The new equilibrium wage = $5.50; quantity = 1,400.
Firms' burden = $5.50 − $5.00 = $.50;
workers' burden = $5.00 + $1.50 − $5.50 = $1.00.

c. The new demand curve is given in Table 5.10.
The new equilibrium wage = $4.00; quantity = 1,400.
Firms' burden = $4.00 + $1.50 − $5.00 = $.50; workers' burden = $5.00 − $4.00 = $1.00.

Table 5.10

Demand	
Wage	Quantity
$5.00	1,000
$4.50	1,200
$4.00	1,400
$3.50	1,600
$3.00	1,800
$2.50	2,000

d. No. The firms' burden, workers' burden, and equilibrium quantity are the same in each case.

7. a. Price = $700; quantity = 1,200.
   b. Price = $650; quantity demanded = 1,400; quantity supplied = 900; shortage = 1,400 − 900 = 500.

8. a. Wage = $8.00; quantity demanded = 600; quantity supplied = 3,200; surplus = 3,200 − 600 = 2,600.
   b. Price = $600; quantity = 1,000.

Part Two

Perfect Markets

Chapter 6

THE CONSUMPTION DECISION

Chapter Review

The detailed study of microeconomics, the branch of economics that focuses on the behaviour of individuals and firms and builds to an understanding of markets, begins in this chapter and continues throughout Parts Two and Three of the text. The basic competitive model of the private economy developed here is one you'll use throughout this course. Chapters 6 to 10 build on this model; they explore first the decisions individuals make—how much to consume, work, save, and invest—and then the decisions firms make—what and how much to produce and by what method. The entire model is put together in Chapter 11.

ESSENTIAL CONCEPTS

1. The consumer's decisions about how much of each good to purchase—that is, the consumer's demand for each good—are made in a two-step procedure. First, the consumer finds how much can be consumed given the amount of money available. This step is the construction of the **opportunity set,** the outer edge of which is the **budget constraint.** Second, the consumer chooses the

best alternative along the budget constraint. Figure 6.1 depicts a budget constraint.

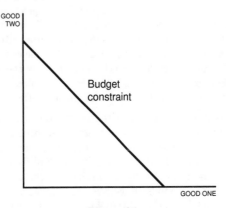

Figure 6.1

2. The budget constraint shows how much of each good can be purchased with the money available. The **slope** of the budget constraint is the **relative price** of the good measured on the horizontal axis—the price of the good on the horizontal axis measured in terms of the good on the vertical axis. This relative price indicates the **trade-**

off: how much of one good must be forgone to consume one more unit of the other.

3. The benefit or utility that a consumer derives from a good is measured by how much the consumer is willing to pay. Consumers focus on the margin (the next unit) and continue to purchase more of the good until the *marginal benefit equals the price.*

4. When income increases, the budget constraint shifts outwards, but its slope does not change. When income decreases, the budget constraint shifts inwards. For most goods, consumption of a good increases as income increases, and decreases as income decreases. These are called **normal goods.** In the case of a few goods, consumption may increase as income decreases, and decrease as income increases. These are called **inferior goods.** The **income elasticity of demand** measures the sensitivity of consumption to changes in income. It is positive for normal goods and negative for inferior goods.

5. If the income elasticity is greater than 1, this indicates a good on which the consumer spends a larger proportion of income as income rises. Such a good is called a **luxury.** If the income elasticity is positive but less than 1, the consumer spends a smaller fraction of income on the good as income rises. Such a good is called a **necessity.**

6. When price changes, the budget constraint rotates. If the price of the good on the horizontal axis increases, the constraint pivots inwards on its vertical intercept and becomes steeper. If the price falls, the constraint pivots outwards on its vertical intercept and becomes flatter. If the price of the good on the vertical axis changes, the constraint pivots on its horizontal intercept; it becomes steeper when the price falls (because the relative price of the good on the horizontal axis has risen) and flatter when the price rises.

7. Price changes cause substitution and income effects. Suppose the price of a good rises. Because the good is relatively more expensive, the principle of substitution says that consumers will shift some of their consumption to other goods. This change is the **substitution effect.** At the same time, because the price is higher, the consumer's purchasing power is lower. This causes the consumer to buy less if the good is normal but more if the good is inferior. This change is the **income effect.**

8. **Utility** is the term economists use for the benefits that individuals receive for consuming goods. As people consume more of a particular good, they get smaller increments of utility. In other words, there is **diminishing marginal utility.** When the consumer has chosen the best bundle of goods, the consumer's utility is maximized and the marginal utility of each good equals its price.

9. **Consumer surplus** equals the difference between what the consumer is willing to pay for goods and the price (what the consumer has to pay). Figure 6.2 shows a demand curve for apples, which also represents what the consumer is willing to pay for apples. When the price is $.25, the consumer purchases 8 apples per week. The

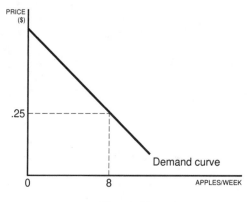

Figure 6.2

consumer surplus, shown as the area between the demand curve and the price, measures the consumer's gain from trade.

BEHIND THE ESSENTIAL CONCEPTS

1. The budget constraint shows which combinations of quantities of goods are affordable. If you know the prices of goods and an individual's income, you can draw that individual's budget constraint. People who have the same income and must pay the same prices have the same budget constraint. As price changes, each individual's budget constraint changes in the same way. The budget constraint indicates opportunities; it says nothing about the value that the consumer places on the goods. Individual tastes only come into the picture when the actual choices are made.

2. The slope of the budget line depends only on prices, not on income. Therefore, changes in income cannot change the slope of the budget line. Changes in income bring about a parallel shift in the budget constraint. Price changes, on the other hand, do change the slope. The budget constraint rotates when price changes.

3. Economists measure the responsiveness of quantity demanded to income changes by using the income elasticity of demand. Elasticities are relative percentage changes. The income elasticity equals the percentage that the quantity demanded changes when income changes by 1 percent.

4. The distinction between substitution and income effects is important, and it will reappear in other chapters. Income effects are small in the consumption decision. To see why, suppose the price of milk falls by 10 percent. If you were previously spending $30 per month on milk, you can now buy as much milk as before for only $27. This makes you better off by $3, and the income effect of the price change is the impact on your milk consumption of this extra $3 of income, which is hardly likely to represent a significant change in your consumption. The substitution effect is more important. It is your response to the change in the relative price, and a 10 percent re-

duction in the price changes the price of milk relative to other goods by 10 percent, which is a significant change.

5. The basic economic model says that individuals balance the benefits and costs of their decisions. It emphasizes choice at the margin, for the next unit of a good or service. Individuals continue buying until the marginal benefit equals the marginal cost. For the consumer, the marginal benefit (called the marginal utility) is just how much the consumer is willing to pay for another unit. The marginal cost is the price. When marginal utility equals price, the consumer has realized all the possible gains from the purchase of the good.

6. There are two important diagrams in this chapter: the budget constraint and the demand curve. Although each is downward sloping, they should not be confused. The budget constraint drawn in Figure 6.1 shows the combination of goods that a person can afford. Quantities of goods are measured on each axis. The demand curve drawn in Figure 6.2 shows how much of *one* good will be purchased at each price. The quantity of the good is measured on the horizontal axis, and the price is measured on the vertical axis.

SELF-TEST

True or False

1. The budget constraint indicates that the amount spent on goods cannot exceed disposable income.

2. The slope of the budget constraint shows the trade-off between two goods.

3. Income determines the slope of the budget constraint.

4. The amount that an individual is willing to pay for coffee is called the marginal utility of coffee.

5. The amount that an individual is willing to pay for an extra cup of coffee is called the marginal utility of coffee.

6. A rational individual will increase consumption of a good until the marginal utility equals the price.

7. When income increases, the budget constraint rotates and becomes flatter.

8. When income increases, the consumer demands more of inferior goods.

9. If an individual spends a smaller proportion of income on a good as her income rises, the good is a luxury.

10. If the income elasticity is less than zero, then the good is an inferior good.

11. The long-run income elasticity of demand is greater than the short-run income elasticity of demand.

12. The benefits of consumption are called utility.

13. The difference between what the consumer is willing to pay for a good and what he has to pay is called the marginal utility.

14. When the price of a good falls, the substitution effect encourages more consumption of that good.

15. When the price of a normal good falls, the income effect encourages more consumption of that good.

Multiple Choice

1. All of the following, except one, are true statements about the budget constraint. Which is the odd one out?

   a. Points inside the constraint indicate unattainable combinations of goods.
   b. The slope of the constraint is determined by the relative price of the good that is measured on the horizontal axis.
   c. The constraint is the consumer's opportunity set.
   d. The slope of the constraint measures the consumer's trade-off.
   e. A change in income causes a parallel shift of the constraint.

2. Suppose that the price of a movie ticket is $5 and the price of a pizza is $10. The trade-off between the two goods is:

   a. half a movie ticket for one pizza.
   b. two movie tickets for one pizza.
   c. two pizzas for one movie ticket.
   d. ten pizzas for one movie ticket.
   e. none of the above

3. Each month, Mona's parents give her an allowance. She is not allowed to borrow money, and any of her allowance that is left at the end of the month is deducted from her next month's allowance, so she does not bother to save. Mona spends all her allowance on CDs and audio tapes. If her parents increase her allowance, her budget constraint (which is drawn with CDs on the horizontal axis):

   a. shifts inwards parallel to the original budget constraint.
   b. pivots outwards on the vertical intercept.
   c. is unaffected.
   d. pivots inwards on the horizontal intercept.
   e. shifts outwards parallel to the original budget constraint.

4. Each month, Mona's parents give her an allowance. She is not allowed to borrow money, and any of her allowance that is left at the end of the month is deducted from her next month's allowance, so she does not bother to save. Mona spends all her allowance on CDs and audio tapes. If the price of audio tapes rises, her budget constraint (which is drawn with CDs on the horizontal axis):

   a. shifts inwards parallel to the original budget constraint.
   b. pivots outwards on the vertical intercept.
   c. is unaffected.
   d. pivots inwards on the horizontal intercept.
   e. shifts outwards parallel to the original budget constraint.

5. Each month, Mona's parents give her an allowance. She is not allowed to borrow money, and any of her allowance that is left at the end of the month is deducted

from her next month's allowance, so she does not bother to save. Mona spends all her allowance on CDs and audio tapes. If the price of CDs falls, her budget constraint (which is drawn with CDs on the horizontal axis):

a. shifts inwards parallel to the original budget constraint.
b. pivots outwards on the vertical intercept.
c. is unaffected.
d. pivots inwards on the horizontal intercept.
e. shifts outwards parallel to the original budget constraint.

6. Each month, Mona's parents give her an allowance. Mona spends all her allowance on CDs, which cost $20, and audio tapes, which cost $10. The absolute value of the slope of her budget constraint:

a. cannot be determined without knowing the amount of Mona's allowance.
b. is equal to 0.5; this means the constraint has been drawn with audio tapes on the vertical axis.
c. is equal to 2; this means the constraint has been drawn with CDs on the vertical axis.
d. is equal to 2; this means the constraint has been drawn with CDs on the horizontal axis.
e. cannot be determined without knowing Mona's price elasticity of demand.

7. The income elasticity of demand is the percentage change in:

a. quantity demanded resulting from a 1 percent change in price.
b. price resulting from a 1 percent change in quantity demanded.
c. quantity demanded resulting from a 1 percent change in income.
d. income resulting from a 1 percent change in quantity demanded.
e. price resulting from a 1 percent change in quantity supplied.

8. If the share of income that Vanessa spends on CDs rises as her income increases, then the income elasticity of demand is:

a. greater than 1; this means that economists classify CDs as a luxury for Vanessa.
b. greater than 0 but less than 1; this means that economists classify CDs as a necessity for Vanessa.
c. less than 0; this means that economists classify CDs as an inferior good for Vanessa.
d. greater than 0 but less than 1; this means that economists classify CDs as a luxury for Vanessa.
e. greater than 1; this means that economists classify CDs as a necessity for Vanessa.

9. If Vanessa buys fewer CDs when her income increases, then the income elasticity of demand is:

a. greater than 1; this means that economists classify CDs as a luxury for Vanessa.
b. greater than 0 but less than 1; this means that economists classify CDs as a necessity for Vanessa.
c. less than 0; this means that economists classify CDs as an inferior good for Vanessa.
d. greater than 0 but less than 1; this means that economists classify CDs as a luxury for Vanessa.
e. greater than 1; this means that economists classify CDs as a necessity for Vanessa.

10. Vanessa spends a large proportion of her allowance on her favourite type of candy bar. When the price falls, the substitution effect of the price change is:

a. Vanessa's response to the fall in the relative price of candy bars, and the income effect is her response to the reduction in her purchasing power.
b. Vanessa's response to the rise in the relative price of candy bars, and the income effect is her response to the increase in her purchasing power.
c. determined by Vanessa's price elasticity of demand for the candy bars.
d. Vanessa's response to the rise in the relative price of candy bars, and the income effect is her response to the reduction in her purchasing power.
e. Vanessa's response to the fall in the relative price of candy bars, and the income effect is her response to the increase in her purchasing power.

11. Vanessa spends a large proportion of her allowance on her favourite type of candy bar. When the price falls, the substitution effect of the price change encourages her to buy:

a. fewer candy bars.
b. more candy bars.
c. fewer candy bars only if the candy bars are an inferior good.
d. more candy bars only if the candy bars are a normal good.
e. fewer candy bars only if her income elasticity for the candy bars is between 0 and 1.

12. Vanessa spends a large proportion of her allowance on her favourite type of candy bar. When the price falls, the income effect of the price change encourages her to buy:

a. fewer candy bars.
b. more candy bars.
c. fewer candy bars if the candy bars are a normal good, but more if they are an inferior good.
d. fewer candy bars if the candy bars are an inferior good, but more if they are a normal good.
e. fewer candy bars if her income elasticity for the candy bars is between 0 and 1.

13. The income effect of a change in the price of a good tends to be more important:

a. the larger the proportion of income that the consumer spends on the good is and the smaller the income elasticity is.
b. the smaller the proportion of income that the consumer spends on the good is and the smaller the income elasticity is.
c. the larger the proportion of income that the consumer spends on the good is and the smaller the price elasticity is.
d. the smaller the proportion of income that the consumer spends on the good is and the larger the income elasticity is.

e. the larger the proportion of income that the consumer spends on the good is and the larger the income elasticity is.

14. Kim spends all her income on beer and pizza. Both beer and pizza are normal goods. If the price of beer rises, the substitution effect of this price change on the demand for pizza:

    a. encourages consumption of pizza, but the income effect of the price change discourages consumption of pizza.
    b. encourages consumption of pizza, and this is reinforced by the income effect of the price change.
    c. depends upon whether pizza is a necessity or a luxury good.
    d. discourages consumption of pizza, and this is reinforced by the income effect of the price change.
    e. discourages consumption of pizza, but the income effect of the price change encourages consumption of pizza.

15. The distinction between total and marginal utility is that total utility:

    a. measures the willingness to pay for one more unit and marginal utility measures total willingness to pay.
    b. diminishes as consumption increases but marginal utility does not.
    c. measures total willingness to pay and marginal utility measures the willingness to pay for one more unit.
    d. refers to all consumers but marginal utility refers to a particular consumer.
    e. is expressed in dollars but marginal utility is not.

16. Diminishing marginal utility means that:

    a. the utility of one more unit declines as more units are consumed.
    b. utility declines the longer you own something.
    c. the budget constraint is not a straight line.
    d. total utility declines as more units are consumed.
    e. adding more workers to a fixed quantity of land reduces total production.

17. If Fred is willing to pay $100 for one espresso maker and $140 for two, then the marginal utility of the second espresso maker is:

    a. $20.
    b. $40.
    c. $50.
    d. $70.
    e. $140.

18. Henry is a big fan of a certain type of candy bar. He is still a rational consumer and adjusts his consumption as the price changes. He chooses his quantity by equating:

    a. total utility and total expenditure.
    b. marginal utility and price.
    c. total utility and price.
    d. marginal utility and total expenditure.
    e. total utility and income.

19. Henry is a big fan of a certain type of candy bar. The difference between what he is willing to pay for the quantity he buys and the amount he has to pay is called his:

    a. marginal utility.
    b. price elasticity of demand.
    c. consumer surplus.
    d. income elasticity of demand.
    e. total utility.

20. All of the following, except one, are true statements about the budget constraint. Which is the odd one out?

    a. Points outside the constraint indicate unattainable combinations of goods.
    b. The slope of the constraint is determined by the relative price of the good that is measured on the horizontal axis.
    c. If all prices rise by 10 percent, the constraint shifts out parallel to itself.
    d. The slope of the constraint measures the consumer's trade-off.
    e. A change in price changes the slope of the constraint.

Completion

1. The opportunity set for the consumer is defined by the _____, which says that expenditures cannot exceed disposable income.

2. The slope of the budget line equals the _____ of one good in terms of the other.

3. The benefits of consumption are called _____.

4. The willingness to pay for an extra unit of some good is its _____.

5. When income increases, the budget constraint shifts outwards _____ to itself.

6. The _____ of demand measures how consumption of a good changes in response to a change in income.

7. When the price of the good on the horizontal axis _____, the budget constraint becomes steeper.

8. When the price of the good on the vertical axis decreases, the budget constraint becomes _____.

9. When the price of a good falls, the substitution effect of the price change results in the consumer buying _____ units of the good.

10. The difference between what the consumer is willing to pay for a good and what she has to pay is called _____.

Answers to Self-Test

True or False

1. t	4. f	7. f	10. t	13. f
2. t	5. t	8. f	11. t	14. t
3. f	6. t	9. f	12. t	15. t

Multiple Choice

1. a	6. d	11. b	16. a
2. b	7. c	12. d	17. b
3. e	8. a	13. e	18. b
4. d	9. c	14. a	19. c
5. b	10. e	15. c	20. c

Completion

1. budget constraint
2. relative price
3. utility
4. marginal utility
5. parallel
6. income elasticity
7. increases
8. steeper
9. more
10. consumer surplus

Doing Economics: Tools and Practice Problems

The most important model in this chapter is the opportunity set for the consumer: the budget constraint. This section will first review how to construct the budget constraint and then explain how the budget constraint changes when price and income change. A somewhat more advanced topic follows, as we explore how to illustrate the substitution and income effects of price changes. Next, there are some applications: in-kind transfers and tax-subsidy schemes. Finally, we consider marginal utility.

THE BUDGET CONSTRAINT

Because we have limited income, we can only afford certain combinations of goods. The budget constraint divides those combinations we can afford from those we cannot. Tool Kit 6.1 shows you how to plot the budget constraint.

Tool Kit 6.1: Plotting the Budget Constraint

Constructing the budget constraint is one of the essential techniques needed in Part Two. Follow these steps to see how it is done.

Step one: Draw a set of coordinate axes. Label the horizontal axis as the quantity of one good consumed and the vertical axis as the quantity of a second good consumed.

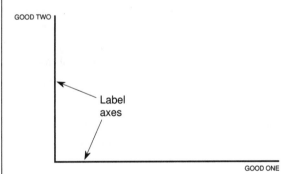

Step two: Calculate the quantity of the good measured on the horizontal axis that can be purchased if all the consumer's money is spent on it. Plot this quantity along the horizontal axis.

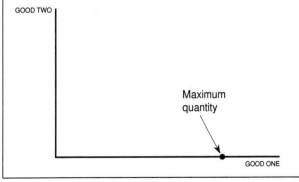

Step three: Calculate the quantity of the good measured on the vertical axis that can be purchased if all the consumer's money is spent on it. Plot this quantity along the vertical axis.

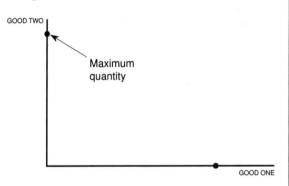

Step four: Draw a line segment connecting the two points. This line segment is the budget constraint.

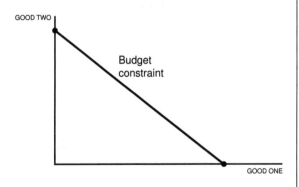

Step five: Verify that the slope of the budget constraint is (minus) the price of the good measured on the horizontal axis divided by the price of the good measured on the vertical axis.

1. (Worked problem: budget constraint) Dick has a budget of $500 to paint and paper the rooms in his new condominium. The price of enough paint for 1 room is $25; the price of wallpaper is $50 per room. Draw Dick's budget constraint.

Step-by-step solution

Step one: Draw a set of coordinate axes, and label the horizontal one "Rooms painted" and the vertical one "Rooms papered." (There is no rule as to which good goes on which axis. It is fine either way.)

Step two: Calculate how many rooms can be painted with the entire $500. This number is $500/$25 = 20 rooms. Plot this quantity along the horizontal axis.

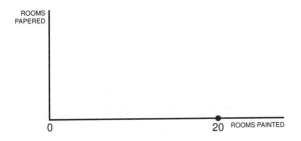

Step three: Calculate how many rooms can be papered with the entire $500. This number is $500/$50 = 10 rooms. Plot this quantity along the vertical axis.

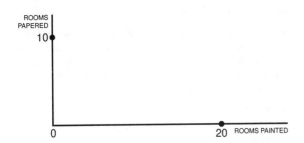

Step four: Draw a line segment connecting these two points. This line segment is the budget constraint.

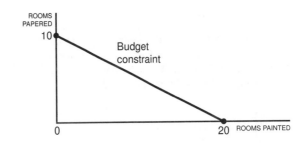

Step five: Verify the slope. The slope of the budget constraint is 10/20 = 1/2. The price ratio is $25/$50 = 1/2.

2. (Practice problem: budget constraint) The head of the music department would like to have some of the practice pianos tuned in the charming but decaying music building. She could use some of the $1,000 in the supplies and services budget, but that money must also pay for repairing broken lockers. The piano tuner charges $50 per piano, and the carpenter charges $40 per locker. Plot her budget constraint and verify that the slope is the relative price.

3. (Practice problem: budget constraint). Draw the following budget constraints.

   a. Budget for hiring groundskeepers = $100,000; price of a full-time employee = $20,000; price of a part-time employee = $8,000.

   b. Budget for food = $250; price of microwave snacks = $2.00. (Plot expenditures on all other food on the vertical axis.)

   c Budget for landscaping = $2,000; price of lilac bushes = $50; price of cherry trees = $80.

   d Budget for library acquisitions = $50,000; price of books = $40; price of journal subscriptions = $100.

CHANGES IN THE BUDGET CONSTRAINT

When either income or price changes, the budget constraint moves. The shift is a parallel one when income changes, because the ratio of the prices is unchanged; this means there is no change in the slope of the constraint. If price changes, this changes the relative price, and hence the slope of the constraint. The next five problems require you to plot budget constraints before and after a change in income or price. Refer to Tool Kit 6.1 if you need to be reminded of how to plot constraints. Then plot the old and new constraints, compare the two, and verify that the shift is a parallel one when income changes, and a change in the slope when price changes.

4. (Worked problem: budget constraint with income and price changes) Bill, a somewhat lazy student, has decided to take a course on the nineteenth-century American novel. Many books are assigned, and all are available in the abridged "Fred's Notes" versions at $8 each. The unabridged versions are $3 each. Bill has $72 to spend.

   a. Plot his budget constraint.

   b. Show how it changes when Bill finds that he has another $24 (for a total of $96).

Step-by-step solution

Step one (a): Plot Bill's budget constraint using the procedure outlined above. He can afford $72/$8 = 9 abridged and $72/$3 = 24 unabridged books. Note that the absolute value of the slope is 9/24 = $3/$8, the ratio of the prices.

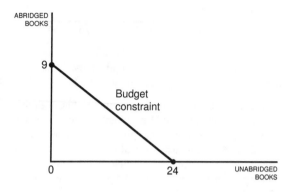

Step two (b): Plot Bill's budget constraint with $96 to spend. He can now afford $96/$8 = 12 abridged and $96/$3 = 32 unabridged books.

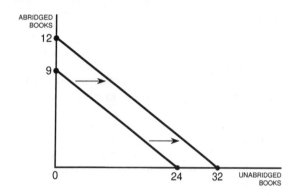

Step three: Verify that the shift in the budget constraint is parallel. The slope is 12/32 = $3/$8, which is the ratio of the prices. Because the prices have not changed, the slope has not changed. The income increase causes a parallel shift.

5. (Practice problem: budget constraint with income and price changes) Helen is nervous about graduate school. She is considering hiring a tutor for her economics course at $10 per hour. Another possibility is to attend sessions on how to improve the score of her GMAT test. These cost $30 each. She has $90.

   a. Plot her budget constraint.
   b. Oops! Unexpectedly stuck with the tab at the restaurant, Helen now has only $60 to spend. Plot her new budget constraint.

6. (Worked problem: budget constraint with income and price changes) Dissatisfied with his social life, Horatio has budgeted $400 for self-improvement. He is considering elocution lessons at $25 per hour and ballroom dancing classes at $10 each.

   a. Plot Horatio's budget constraint.
   b. Good news! A new elocution studio offers lessons at the introductory price of $20. Plot the new budget constraint.

Step-by-step solution

Step one (a): Plot the budget constraint at the $25 price. Horatio can afford $400/$25 = 16 elocution lessons or $400/$10 = 40 classes. Note that the slope is 40/16 = $25/$10, which is the ratio of the prices.

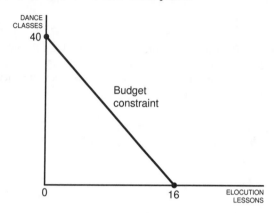

Step two (b): Plot the budget constraint at the $20 price. Horatio can now afford $400/$20 = 20 elocution lessons, which is 4 more, but he still can only buy 40 dance lessons.

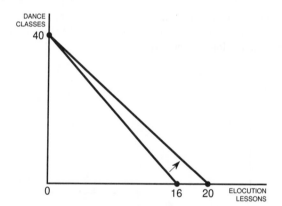

Step three: Verify that the slope of the budget constraint changes. The slope is now 40/20 = $20/$10, which is the ratio of the new prices and is flatter. The price decrease rotated the budget constraint. The vertical intercept, the point at 0 elocution lessons and 40 dance classes, does not change, because when no elocution lessons are purchased, the price change makes no difference.

7. (Practice problem: budget constraint with income and price changes) With some of her extra cash ($100 each month), Sho-Yen buys meals and blankets and donates them to the nearby shelter for the homeless. The meals cost $2 each, and the blankets $5 each.

   a. Plot Sho-Yen's budget constraint.
   b. The supplier of meals cuts the price to $1. Plot the new budget constraint.

8. (Practice problem: budget constraint with income and price changes) For each of these problems, draw the budget constraints before and after the change. Plot expenditures on all other goods on the vertical axis.

   a. Income = $400; price of potatoes = $1 per sack; price of potatoes rises to $2 per sack.

b. Income = \$5,000; price of therapy sessions = \$100 per hour; income rises to \$6,000.

c. Income = \$450; price of housecleaning = \$45; income falls to \$225.

d. Income = \$100; price of pizzas = \$5; price increases to \$10.

Substitution and Income Effects

A consumer's response to a price change—how the quantity demanded changes with the price—is broken down into a substitution effect and an income effect. The substitution effect is the response to the change in relative prices. The income effect is the response to the change in purchasing power when price changes. The substitution effect is always in the opposite direction to the price change. If, for example, the price falls, the good is cheaper relative to other goods, and the substitution effect leads to increased consumption. The income effect usually reinforces the substitution effect. A price fall, for example, increases purchasing power, and in most cases, this will result in increased consumption. Tool Kit 6.2 shows you how to distinguish the substitution and income effects and demonstrates how it is possible for the income effect to oppose the substitution effect.

Tool Kit 6.2: Distinguishing between Substitution and Income Effects

Follow these steps to see how a consumer's response to a price change can be broken down into a substitution effect and an income effect.

Step one: Draw the budget line with the original price.

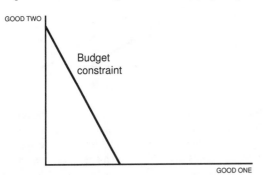

Step two: Arbitrarily select the chosen quantities along the budget line. Label this point *A*.

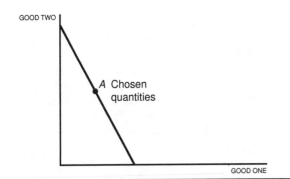

Step three: Draw the budget line with the new price.

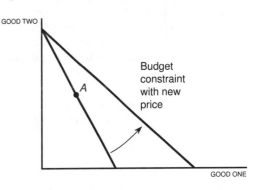

Step four: Draw a dashed line through point *A* and parallel to the *new* budget line.

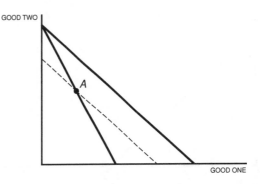

Step five: Darken the portion of the dashed line that lies above the original budget line. The points along this darkened segment represent the quantities not previously attainable. The change to the new quantity the consumer chooses is the substitution effect of the price change. Note that the substitution effect is necessarily in the opposite direction to the price change: the consumer will only choose from the points along the darkened segment, and all indicate an increase in consumption relative to *A*.

Arbitrarily select a point for the new consumption resulting from the substitution effect. Label this point *B*. The income effect is the change from *B* to the quantity the consumer chooses on the new budget line drawn in step three. If good one is normal, the income effect will result in higher consumption relative to *B*, for example, point *C*. If good one is inferior, the income effect will result in lower consumption relative to B, for example, point *D*.

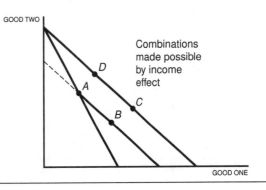

9. (Worked problem: substitution and income effects) Always diligent in keeping up with out-of-town friends and acquaintances, Colleen budgets $30 per month for postage and phone calls. A long-distance call costs her $2 on average, and the price of a stamped envelope is $.30. She makes 6 calls and mails 60 letters each month.

a. Plot her budget constraint, and label the point that she has chosen.
b. The price of a stamped envelope falls to $.20. Illustrate the substitution and income effects of the price change.

Step-by-step solution

Step one (a): Draw the original budget constraint. The maximum quantity of calls is $30/$2 = 15, and the maximum quantity of letters is $30/$.30 = 100.

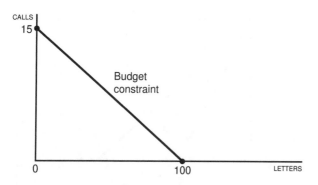

Step two: Plot and label the chosen point (6 calls, 60 letters). Note that this is on the budget constraint because (6 × $2) + (60 × $.30) = $30. Label this point *A*.

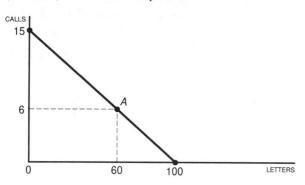

Step three (b): Draw the new budget constraint. The maximum quantities are 15 calls and 30/$.20 = 150 letters.

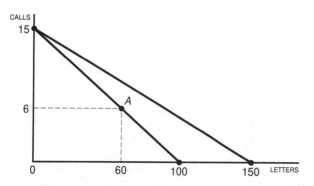

Step four: Draw a dashed line segment through *A* parallel to the new budget constraint.

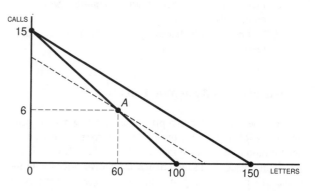

Step five: Darken the portion of the dashed line segment that lies above the original budget constraint. Notice that the substitution effect would lead Colleen to choose a point like *B* along this segment, where the quantity of letters is greater. We say that the substitution effect of a price decrease is always to increase the quantity demanded. The income effect moves this darkened segment out to the new budget constraint. Colleen would write more letters if letters were a normal good, but she would write fewer if letters were inferior. The income effect can go either way in principle, although most goods are normal.

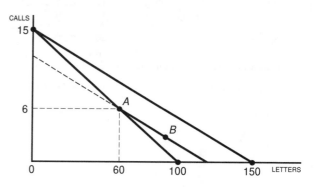

10. (Practice problem: substitution and income effects) Yves loves to wear whites for tennis. He sends his outfits to the cleaners at a price of $3.60 each. Playing tennis also requires new balls, which cost $2.25 per can. Yves' tennis budget is $36 per week, which allows him his current consumption levels of 8 cans of balls and 5 clean outfits.

a. Plot his budget constraint, and show his current consumption choice.
b. The price of tennis balls has risen to $4.50. Illustrate the substitution and income effects of this price increase.

11. (Practice problem: substitution and income effects) For each of the following, illustrate the substitution and income effects of the price change. Plot expenditures on all other goods on the vertical axis, and pick any point on the original budget line as the quantities consumed before the price change.

a. Income = $100; price of bricks = $.10 each; price changes to $.20.

b. Income = $1,000; price of haircuts = $20; price changes to $25.

c. Income = $500; price of pies = $5; price changes to $4.

d. Income = $10; price of baseball cards = $.50; price changes to $.25

APPLICATIONS OF SUBSTITUTION AND INCOME EFFECTS

12. (Worked problem: applications) Many government programs deliver benefits in kind to people. For example, the U.S. government issues food stamps, which can only be used to buy food. Economists often argue that cash transfers are better. The typical food stamp recipient has $200 per week in income in addition to $80 per week in food stamps.

    a. Draw the budget constraint.

    b. One proposal is to substitute $80 in cash for the stamps. Draw the budget constraint that results from this proposal.

    c. Which would the recipient prefer? Why?

Step-by-step solution

Step one (a): Draw the budget constraint with the food stamps. Label the axes "Food" and "Other goods." The slope is 1 because $1 not spent on other goods means $1 spent on food. Note that no more than $200 may be spent on other goods.

Step two (b): Draw the budget constraint with the cash grants replacing the food stamps.

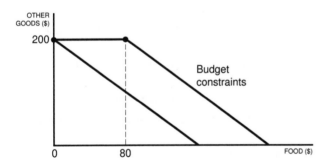

Step three (c): Compare. The difference is that the cash grant allows the recipient to choose the points between *A* and *B*. Many recipients would not choose these low levels of food consumption anyway; so there would be no difference. Some might, however, and these people would prefer the cash.

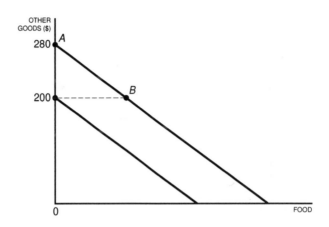

13. (Practice problem: applications) The city of Arbor, recently planted 2 trees (worth $50 each) in every yard. The typical Arbor resident has $400 in disposable income this summer.

    a. Plot the budget constraint with the in-kind transfer of 2 trees.

    b. Plot the budget constraint with the $100 refunded through the tax system.

    c. Which opportunity set is preferred?

14. (Worked problem: applications) When lower consumption of some good or service is needed, economists often recommend putting a tax on the good or service. One objection is that the taxes lead to higher prices, which make people worse off. If the tax revenue is refunded, however, people can be approximately as well off, yet still face higher prices for the good or service. In essence, it is possible to put the substitution effect to work and reduce consumption of the good or service without reducing the well-being of consumers very much. The city of Pleasantville is running out of room at the dump. The typical resident has an income of $100 and puts out 5 bags of garbage each week. The garbage collectors will not pick up the garbage unless it is in official bags, which cost $1 each.

    a. Plot the budget constraint for the typical resident, and show the current consumption choice.

    b. In an effort to encourage recycling and discourage disposal, the city council votes to increase the price of official bags to $2 and to refund the extra revenue collected to residents. Each resident receives 5 × $1 = $5. Plot the new budget constraint.

Step-by-step solution

Step one (a): Plot the budget constraint when the price is $1 and there is no tax refund. Label the resident's chosen point *A*.

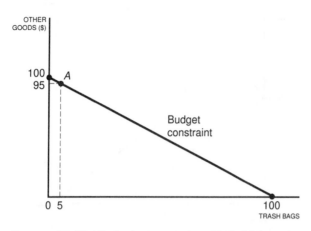

Step two (b): Plot the budget constraint with the higher price and the tax refund.

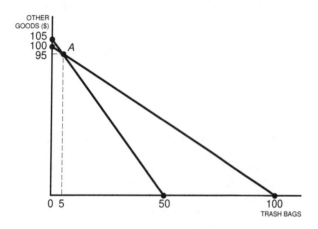

Step three (c): We see that the net effect of the scheme is only the substitution effect of the increase in the price of bags to $2. The resident is no worse off (because he can still consume as he did before the user fee), but he will be motivated to use fewer bags. (One flaw in the programme is that as people substitute away from trash bags, they will pay less in user fees than is needed to finance the tax relief.)

15. (Practice problem: applications) Environmental activists propose a tax that will increase gas prices at the pump from $1 to $2 per litre. The government, not wishing to appear lacking in environmental consciousness, imposes the tax but chooses to modify income taxes so that any consumer can still buy the same amount of gas that he or she was buying before the price increase.

    a. Plot the budget constraint with no added gas tax.
    b. Plot the budget constraint with the gas tax and the refund.
    c. The chief environmentalist, Kirk Greensleeves, writes a letter to the newspaper complaining that "the plan will have no effect. The government takes money away with one hand and gives it back with the other." Is he right? Why or why not?

MARGINAL UTILITY

The first step in the consumption decision is to determine what is attainable, given income and prices. This defines the budget constraint. The second step is to choose the best bundle of goods from among those that lie on the constraint. Here, we are asking the question: which of those bundles that the consumer can afford does the consumer most prefer? Economists say that the bundle selected gives maximum utility.

As the text explains, at the point on the budget constraint chosen by the consumer, marginal utility (measured as willingness to pay for one more unit) equals the good's price. The difference between the consumer's willingness to pay and the price (what the consumer would be happy to pay for all the units bought less the amount actually spent) is called the consumer surplus.

As the price changes, the consumer readjusts the amount of the good purchased to restore equality between price and marginal utility. Tool Kit 6.3 shows you how to use marginal utitlity to determine demand for a commodity as its price changes and how to calculate the consumer surplus.

Tool Kit 6.3: Marginal Utility

Follow these steps to see how equating marginal utility and price determines the consumer's quantity demanded, and how to calculate consumer surplus.

Step one: Identify the product price and the total utility (total willingness to pay) at each quantity of the good.

Step two: Compute marginal utility at each quantity. This tells you the willingness to pay for one more unit of the good. It is calculated as follows:

marginal utility = change in total utility
                 = utility – utility from consuming
                   one unit less.

Step three: Choose the quantity for which marginal utility equals price.

Step four: Compute expenditure at this quantity. It is calculated as follows:

expenditure = price × quantity.

Step five: Compute consumer surplus. It is calculated as follows:

consumer surplus = total utility – expenditure.

---

16 (Worked problem: marginal utility) Table 6.1 gives Junsen's willingness to pay (his total utility) for various quantities (hours per week) of on-line access to the Internet. The price is $12 per hour.

Table 6.1

Number of on-line hours	Utility (willingness to pay)
0	0
1	$ 20
2	$ 38
3	$ 54
4	$ 68
5	$ 80
6	$ 90
7	$ 98
8	$104

a. Compute marginal utility for each additional hour.
b. How many hours of on-line access does Junsen buy?
c. Compute Junsen's consumer surplus for this good.

Step one (a): Identify price and utility for each quantity. The price is $12 and utility is given in Table 6.1.

Step two: Compute marginal utility. The first unit raises utility from $0 to $20. The difference (marginal utility) is $20. The second unit raises utility from $20 to $38. The marginal utility is $18 ($38 − $20). Continuing, we obtain the information in Table 6.2. Notice that marginal utility diminishes as quantity increases.

Table 6.2

Number of on-line hours	Utility	Marginal utility
0	0	
1	$ 20	$20
2	$ 38	$18
3	$ 54	$16
4	$ 68	$14
5	$ 80	$12
6	$ 90	$10
7	$ 98	$ 8
8	$104	$ 6

Step three (b): Choose the quantity for which marginal utility equals price. Marginal utility equals $12 when Junsen buys 5 hours of on-line access. So, when the price is $12, Junsen demands 5 hours of access.

Step four (c): Calculate expenditure. Expenditure is $12 × 5 = $60.

Step five: Calculate consumer surplus. Junsen's total utility when he buys 5 hours of access is $80. Consumer surplus is $80 − $60 = $20.

17. (Practice problem: marginal utility) Marlene is considering going to a concert series. There are 7 concerts. Table 6.3 gives Marlene's willingness to pay for concert tickets. The tickets cost $20 each.

Table 6.3

Number of concert tickets	Willingness to pay
0	$ 0
1	$ 35
2	$ 65
3	$ 90
4	$110
5	$125
6	$135
7	$140

a. Compute the marginal utility for each concert.
b. How many concerts does Marlene go to?
c. Compute Marlene's consumer surplus.

18. (Practice problem: marginal utility) Charlie loves to play tennis. He has his own court and his time is his own, so he pays attention only to the price of balls. Being a perfectionist, he uses a new can of balls for every game. Table 6.4 gives Charlie's willingness to pay for cans of tennis balls per week. Each can costs $2.

Table 6.4

Number of cans of tennis balls	Willingness to pay
0	$ 0.00
1	$10.00
2	$16.00
3	$20.00
4	$22.00
5	$23.00
6	$23.50
7	$23.75

a. Compute the marginal utility for each game of tennis (that is, each can of balls).
b. How many games does Charlie play each week?
c. Compute Charlie's consumer surplus.

Answers to Problems

2.

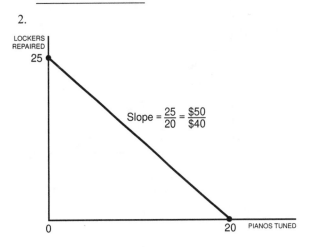

3.

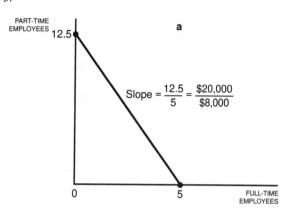

a

$$\text{Slope} = \frac{12.5}{5} = \frac{\$20,000}{\$8,000}$$

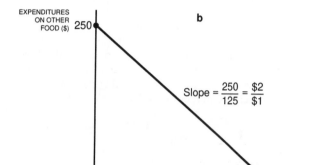

b

$$\text{Slope} = \frac{250}{125} = \frac{\$2}{\$1}$$

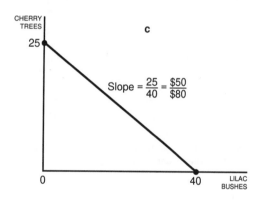

c

$$\text{Slope} = \frac{25}{40} = \frac{\$50}{\$80}$$

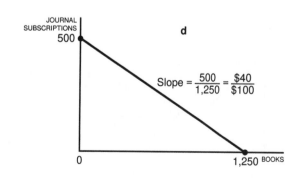

d

$$\text{Slope} = \frac{500}{1,250} = \frac{\$40}{\$100}$$

5.

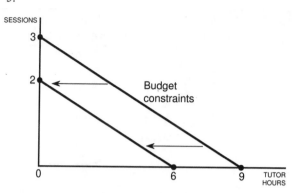

Budget constraints

7.

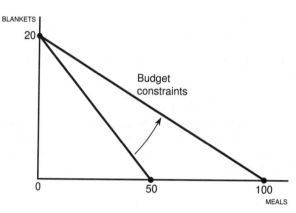

Budget constraints

8.

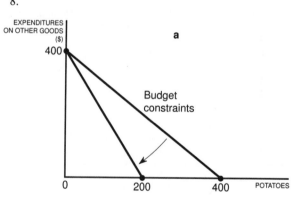

a

Budget constraints

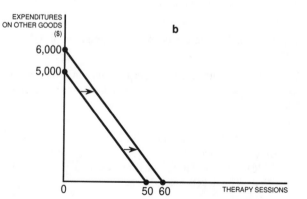

b

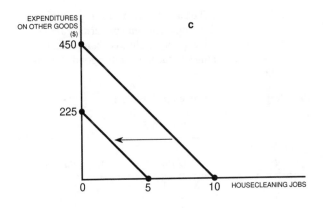

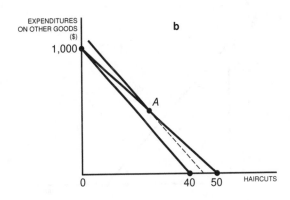

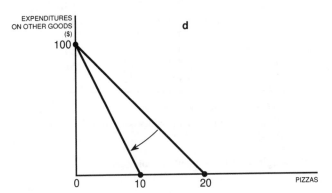

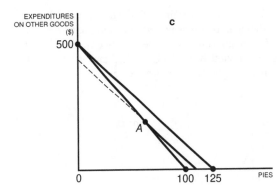

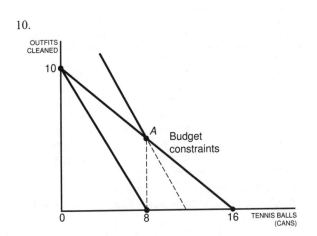

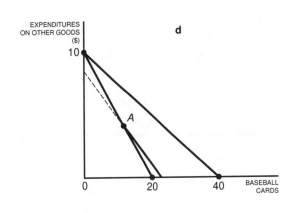

10.

11.

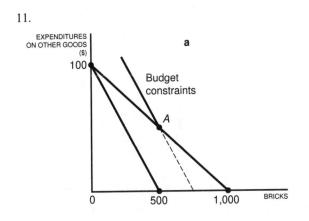

13.

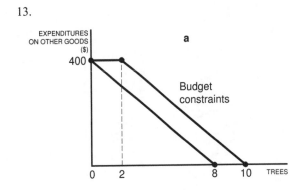

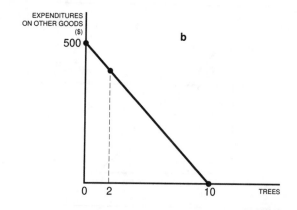

c. The budget constraint with the tax refund, which is shown in part b, is preferred by anyone who would like to consume along the section of the constraint not previously available, that is, anyone who would not voluntarily buy at least 2 trees.

15.

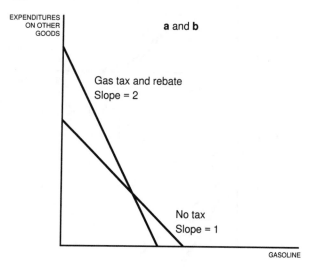

c. He is wrong. The gas tax and rebate programme results in a budget constraint with preferred alternatives that involve lower gasoline consumption. It motivates individuals to substitute other goods for gasoline.

17. Marginal utility is given in Table 6.5.

Table 6.5

Number of concert tickets	Utility	Marginal utility
0	0	
1	$ 35	$35
2	$ 65	$30
3	$ 90	$25
4	$110	$20
5	$125	$15
6	$135	$10
7	$140	$ 5

a. Marlene goes to 4 concerts.
b. Marlene's consumer surplus is $110 − ($20 × 4) = $30.

18. Marginal utility is given in Table 6.6.

Table 6.6

Number of cans of tennis balls	Utility	Marginal utility
0	$ 0.00	
1	$10.00	$10.00
2	$16.00	$ 6.00
3	$20.00	$ 4.00
4	$22.00	$ 2.00
5	$23.00	$ 1.00
6	$23.50	$ 0.50
7	$23.75	$ 0.25

a. Charlie plays 4 games of tennis.
b. Charlie's consumer surplus is $22 − ($2 × 4) = $14.

Chapter 7

LABOUR SUPPLY

Chapter Review

This chapter continues the discussion of household decision making. Here, the focus is on the labour supply decision; the choice is between leisure and the income needed for consumption. As with the consumption decision in Chapter 6, the individual chooses the best alternative in an opportunity set: how much labour time to offer, what type of job to seek, and how much training to undertake.

ESSENTIAL CONCEPTS

1. The decision to supply labour is primarily a time-allocation problem. Individuals have only so much time available, and they must divide their time between working and other activities. To keep life simple, any time not devoted to working and earning money, whether it is spent in recreation, sleep, chores, or errands, is called leisure. The income earned while working is available for consumption; therefore, the *trade-off* is between **leisure** and **consumption,** between consuming time and consuming goods.

2. The chapter focuses on the budget constraint between leisure and consumption, shown here in Figure 7.1. The slope is the wage rate, and changes in the wage rate rotate the budget constraint and cause income and substitution effects. When an individual's wage increases, leisure becomes more expensive; thus, the **substitution effect** encourages less leisure and more work. On the other hand, the **income effect** leads the individual to want to consume more leisure, and this results in less work. Because the income and substitution effects work

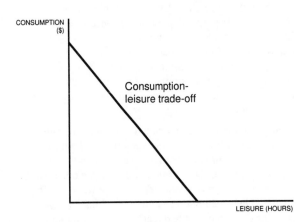

Figure 7.1

in opposite directions, the supply curve for labour may be upward-sloping or downward-sloping, depending upon the relative sizes of the income and substitution effects.

3. There are more dimensions to labour supply than hours worked. Individuals choose whether or not to participate in the work force. They must also decide what sort of job to pursue, how much education and training to acquire, and when to retire. Finally, in the long run, the labour supply for the economy depends upon how many children families decide to have, a decision that, perhaps surprisingly, is quite subject to the influence of economic forces. Each of these decisions can be understood as the choice of the best alternative within an appropriately specified budget constraint.

4. Government policy also affects labour supply. Taxation reduces the consumption that a given amount of labour will yield. Both the substitution and income effects of the welfare system encourage recipients to work less or not at all. Each of these policies can be analyzed in terms of how it alters the consumption-leisure budget constraint.

5. According to **human capital** theory, individuals invest in education and training to acquire human capital, or skills that increase their productivity and wages. The resulting **productivity differentials** in wages provide one explanation of why wages differ among workers. Differentials can also arise for other reasons. For example, **compensating differentials** arise in response to differences in the characteristics of jobs.

BEHIND THE ESSENTIAL CONCEPTS

1. The basic diagram of the chapter is the budget constraint for leisure and consumption. It is important to understand that this diagram is very much like the consumer's budget constraint in Chapter 6. Each shows which combinations are affordable. The slopes are the relative prices; in this case, the relative price of leisure is the wage rate. If the individual wants to consume another hour of leisure, the opportunity cost is the money that could be earned in that hour. Changes in nonwage income, such as investment returns, bring about a parallel shift in the budget constraint, but changes in the wage rate rotate it. Again, this is very similar to the other budget constraint.

2. Changes in the wage rate rotate the budget constraint and cause substitution and income effects. The income effect leads to more leisure (less work) when the wage rate increases. The substitution effect, on the other hand, causes less leisure (more work) when the wage rate increases. The substitution and income effects of wage changes work in opposite directions. For consumption, however, they work in the same direction. Thus, while the demand curves for goods and services is downward-

sloping, the supply curves for savings and labour may be upward-sloping or bend backwards.

3. Table 7.1 may help you keep straight the substitution and income effects.

Table 7.1

If the wage rate rises:
    the *substitution* effect leads to more work because leisure is more expensive.
    the *income* effect leads to less work because the worker is better off and demands more leisure.
If the wage rate falls:
    the *substitution* effect leads to less work because leisure is less expensive.
    the *income* effect leads to more work because the worker is worse off and demands less leisure.

4. Be sure not to confuse the budget constraint with the labour supply curve. The budget constraint shows the combinations of leisure and consumption the individual can afford given the wage rate and any nonwage income. The labour supply curve shows the quantity of labour supplied at each wage rate. As usual, it is important to pay attention to what is measured along each axis.

5. Compensating differentials are the higher wages that must be paid to workers in risky jobs or jobs with unpleasant working conditions. Individuals seek desirable characteristics in their jobs. Competition for jobs with desirable characteristics drives these jobs' wages down. In equilibrium, the relatively higher wages will compensate for the undesirable characteristics.

SELF-TEST

True or False

1. The percentage change in labour supply resulting from a 1 percent change in the wage is the elasticity of the supply of labour.

2. The income effect of a decrease in wages is to increase the quantity of labour supplied.

3. The substitution effect of a decrease in wages is to increase the quantity of labour supplied.

4. When the income effect of a wage increase is bigger than the substitution effect, the worker works more hours than before the wage increase.

5. An increase in nonwage income usually results in a reduction in hours worked.

6. The female elasticity of labour supply is smaller than the male elasticity of labour supply.

7. Labour force participation of women has more than doubled since the 1950s.

8. A cut in marginal income taxes will always increase hours worked.

9. Investment in education produces human capital.

10. The only costs of going to school are the direct costs, like tuition, room, and board.

11. According to human capital theory, education increases the productivity of students and enables them to earn more in the labour market.

12. Jobs that are generally less attractive must pay compensating differentials, in the form of higher wages.

13. The proportion of workers in public-sector unions has declined since World War II.

14. The proportion of workers in private-sector unions has declined since World War II.

15. Unions favour minimum-wage laws and free trade.

Multiple Choice

1. The labour supply decision is depicted as a trade-off between:
   a. eating and sleeping.
   b. sleeping and working.
   c. consumption today and consumption tommorrow.
   d. consumption and leisure.
   e. leisure and sleeping.

2. When the wage:
   a. increases, the price of leisure falls.
   b. increases, there is no effect on the price of leisure.
   c. increases, the price of leisure increases.
   d. falls, the effect on the price of leisure depends on the income elasticity of leisure.
   e. falls, the price of leisure increases.

3. Dave has a week's worth of hours (168) to allocate between hours of leisure and dollars of consumption (paid for by giving up hours of leisure to work). He can earn $10 per hour and has nonwage income (from investments) of $168 per week. If his consumption-leisure budget constraint is plotted with leisure on the horizontal axis, the absolute value of its slope equals:
   a. 16.8
   b. 10.
   c. 11.
   d. 1.10.
   e. 0.10.

4. Dave has a week's worth of hours (168) to allocate between hours of leisure and dollars of consumption (paid for by giving up hours of leisure to work). If his consumption-leisure budget constraint is plotted with leisure on the horizontal axis, an increase in his non-wage income means his constraint:
   a. becomes steeper.
   b. becomes flatter.
   c. shifts out parallel to itself.
   d. shifts in parallel to itself.
   e. is unaffected.

5. Dave has a week's worth of hours (168) to allocate between hours of leisure and dollars of consumption (paid for by giving up hours of leisure to work). If his consumption-leisure budget constraint is plotted with leisure on the horizontal axis, an increase in his hourly wage means his constraint:
   a. becomes steeper.
   b. becomes flatter.
   c. shifts out parallel to itself.
   d. shifts in parallel to itself.
   e. is unaffected.

6. Dave has a week's worth of hours (168) to allocate between hours of leisure and dollars of consumption (paid for by giving up hours of leisure to work). When Dave's hourly wage rate increases, the substitution effect of this change is:
   a. Dave's response to the rise in the relative price of leisure, and the income effect is his response to the reduction in his purchasing power.
   b. Dave's response to the fall in the relative price of leisure, and the income effect is his response to the reduction in his purchasing power.
   c. determined by Dave's price elasticity of demand for leisure.
   d. Dave's response to the fall in the relative price of leisure, and the income effect is his response to the increase in his purchasing power.
   e. Dave's response to the rise in the relative price of leisure, and the income effect is his response to the increase in his purchasing power.

7. Dave has a week's worth of hours (168) to allocate between hours of leisure and dollars of consumption (paid for by giving up hours of leisure to work). When his hourly wage rate increases, the substitution effect of the wage change encourages him to allocate:
   a. more hours to leisure.
   b. fewer hours to leisure.
   c. more hours to leisure only if leisure is a normal good.
   d. fewer hours to leisure only if leisure is an inferior good.
   e. more hours to leisure only if his income elasticity for leisure is between 0 and 1.

8. Dave has a week's worth of hours (168) to allocate between hours of leisure and dollars of consumption (paid for by giving up hours of leisure to work). When his hourly wage rate increases, the substitution effect of the wage change encourages him to allocate:
   a. more hours to work.
   b. fewer hours to work.
   c. fewer hours to work only if leisure is an inferior good.
   d. fewer hours to work only if leisure is a normal good.
   e. more hours to work only if his income elasticity for leisure is between 0 and 1.

9. Dave has a week's worth of hours (168) to allocate between hours of leisure and dollars of consumption (paid for by giving up hours of leisure to work). When his hourly wage rate increases, the income effect of the wage change encourages him to allocate:

a. more hours to leisure.
b. fewer hours to leisure.
c. more hours to leisure if leisure is a normal good.
d. more hours to leisure if leisure is an inferior good.
e. fewer hours to leisure if his income elasticity for leisure is between 0 and 1.

10. Dave has a week's worth of hours (168) to allocate between hours of leisure and dollars of consumption (paid for by giving up hours of leisure to work). When his hourly wage rate increases, the income effect of the wage change encourages him to allocate:

a. more hours to work.
b. fewer hours to work.
c. fewer hours to work if leisure is an inferior good.
d. fewer hours to work if leisure is a normal good.
e. more hours to work if his income elasticity for leisure is between 0 and 1.

11. Dave has a week's worth of hours (168) to allocate between hours of leisure and dollars of consumption (paid for by giving up hours of leisure to work). When leisure is a normal good, an increase in Dave's wage:

a. always increases his hours worked.
b. always reduces his hours worked.
c. reduces his hours worked if the substitution effect of the wage change dominates the income effect.
d. increases his hours worked if the income effect of the wage change dominates the substitution effect.
e. reduces his hours worked if the income effect of the wage change dominates the substitution effect.

12. Dave has a week's worth of hours (168) to allocate between hours of leisure and dollars of consumption (paid for by giving up hours of leisure to work). When leisure is a normal good, an increase in Dave's non-wage income results in:

a. a decrease in hours worked through the income effect.
b. a decrease in hours worked through the income effect.
c. an increase in hours worked through the substitution effect.
d. an increase in hours worked through the income effect.
e. none of the above

13. Dave has a week's worth of hours (168) to allocate between hours of leisure and dollars of consumption (paid for by giving up hours of leisure to work). When leisure is a normal good:

a. Dave's labour supply curve is upward-sloping if the substitution effect dominates the income effect.
b. Dave's labour supply curve is upward-sloping if the income effect dominates the substitution effect.
c. Dave's labour supply curve is upward-sloping if the substitution effect is in the same direction as the income effect.
d. Dave's labour supply curve is negatively sloped if the substitution effect dominates the income effect.
e. Dave's labour supply curve is perfectly elastic if the substitution effect exactly cancels the income effect.

14. The most likely effect of a decrease in marginal income tax rates is:

a. a big increase in the quantity of labour supplied because the substitution effect dominates the income effect.
b. a big decrease in the quantity of labour supplied because the income effect dominates the substitution effect.
c. little change in the quantity of labour supplied because the income effect offsets the substitution effect.
d. a big increase in the quantity of labour supplied because the income effect reinforces the substitution effect.
e. a big decrease in the quantity of labour supplied because the income effect reinforces the substitution effect.

15. In Canada, the elasticity of female labour supply is:

a. much smaller than the elasticity of male labour supply.
b. much larger than the elasticity of male labour supply.
c. equal to the elasticity of male labour supply.
d. difficult to measure because few women work.
e. very small.

16. In Canada, the effective tax rate for the secondary earner in a household:

a. is irrelevant, because almost invariably only one spouse works.
b. is the same as for the primary earner.
c. is lower than for the primary earner.
d. is higher than for the primary earner.
e. provides a strong incentive for the secondary earner to find employment.

17. Which of the following is not an example of investment in human capital?

a. university education
b. on-the-job learning
c. technical training
d. community college education
e. plant and equipment

18. All of the following, except one, are included in the opportunity costs of postsecondary education. Which is the odd one out?

a. books
b. tuition
c. room and board
d. forgone earnings
e. educational software

19. Unions:

 a. raise the wages of union workers and lower the wages of nonunion workers.
 b. raise the wages of both union and nonunion workers.
 c. have no effect on the wages of union or nonunion workers.
 d. lower the wages of both union and nonunion workers.
 e. lower the wages of union workers and raise the wages of nonunion workers.

20. All of the following, except one, are possible reasons for the decline in private-sector union membership in Canada. Which is the odd one out?

 a. Improvements in working conditions have meant that workers see less need for unions.
 b. Employers have volunarily raised wages beyond the unions' wage demands and rendered unions redundant.
 c. Reduced trade barriers have increased competition and left less scope for union power.
 d. Unions tend to be strongest in sectors, like manufacturing, that have declined in importance.
 e. Unions tend to be weakest in sectors, like services, that have increased in importance.

Completion

1. The decision concerning how much labour to supply is a choice between _____ and _____.

2. The slope of the budget line is equal to (minus) the _____.

3. When the nonwage income of an individual decreases, the individual's labour supply _____.

4. The _____ effect of a wage decrease leads individuals to decrease their labour supply.

5. If an individual's labour supply is backward-bending, then the _____ effect is stronger.

6. The labour supply of women is usually _____ elastic than the labour supply of men.

7. An investment in education produces _____.

8. The increase in the wage needed to attract workers to unpleasant jobs is called a _____.

9. The proportion of workers in private-sector unions has _____ since the 1960s.

10. Unions tend to _____ wages for nonunion workers.

Answers to Self-Test

True or False

1. t	4. f	7. t	10. f	13. f
2. t	5. t	8. f	11. t	14. t
3. f	6. f	9. t	12. t	15. f

Multiple Choice

1. d	6. e	11. e	16. d
2. c	7. b	12. b	17. e
3. b	8. a	13. a	18. c
4. c	9. c	14. c	19. a
5. a	10. d	15. b	20. b

Completion

1. leisure, consumption
2. wage
3. increases
4. substitution
5. income
6. more
7. human capital
8. compensating differential
9. fallen
10. lower

Doing Economics: Tools and Practice Problems

The important model in this chapter is the opportunity set for the labour supply decision: the consumption-leisure budget constraint, or trade-off. In this section, we first review how to construct the budget constraint. We then see how the budget constraint changes when the wage rate or nonwage income changes. As in the previous chapter, substitution and income effects can be illustrated using the budget constraint. Finally, there are some applications. The effects of many government programs and also of many private sector incentive schemes, such as overtime pay and attendance bonuses, become much clearer when you understand how they alter the consumption-leisure budget constraint. Several problems explore how to use the budget constraint to analyze these issues. You'll notice that some are quite similar in form to some problems in Chapter 6. This fact underscores how valuable it is to see the similarities between the consumer's budget constraint of Chapter 6 and the consumption-leisure budget constraint of this chapter.

THE CONSUMPTION-LEISURE BUDGET CONSTRAINT

We work to earn money for consumption, but to work, we must give up time we could devote to leisure pursuits. The decision of how much to work is therefore a trade-off between consumption and leisure. If we receive nonwage income (e.g., interest on investments), this provides consumption opportunities without the need to sacrifice any leisure hours. The trade-off and the effect on the trade-off of non-wage income are captured in the consumption-leisure budget constraint. Tool Kit 7.1 shows you how to construct this budget constraint.

Tool Kit 7.1: Plotting the Consumption-Leisure Budget Constraint

The budget constraint shows what combinations of consumption and leisure can be afforded given the wage rate and the amount of nonwage income. To plot the budget constraint, follow these steps.

Step one: Draw a set of coordinate axes. Label the horizontal axis as the quantity of leisure consumed and the vertical axis as the consumption level.

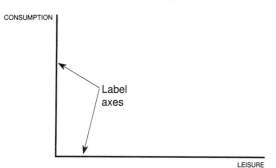

Step two: If an individual chooses to do no work, leisure equals the total time available, and consumption is equal to the nonwage income. Plot this point.

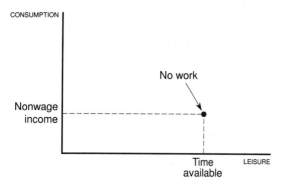

Step three: Calculate the maximum earnings if the individual consumes no leisure. Add this amount to the nonwage income, and plot this quantity along the vertical axis.

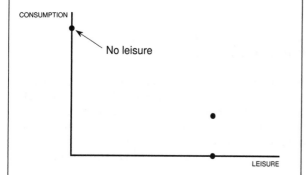

Step four: Draw a line segment connecting the two points. This line segment is the consumption-leisure budget constraint.

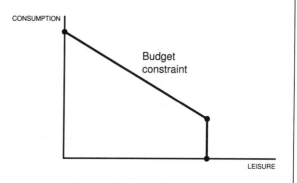

Step five: Verify that the slope of the budget constraint is (minus) the wage rate.

---

1. (Worked problem: consumption-leisure budget constraint) In his spare time, Mike, a student at Magic Johnson University, referees intramural basketball games. Each game pays $7, and if he could stand the abuse, Mike could referee as many as 60 each month. On average, each game takes 1 hour. This is not Mike's only source of income; each month his parents send him $200 for expenses.

   a. Construct Mike's budget constraint.
   b. Suppose that Mike chooses to referee 20 games. Label his chosen alternative, and indicate his total income, income from refereeing, hours worked, and leisure.

Step-by-step solution

Step one (a): Draw the two axes, and label the vertical one "Consumption" and the horizontal one "Leisure."

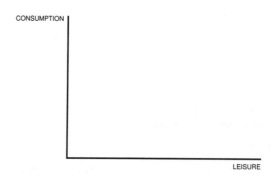

Step two: Plot the no-work consumption point. If Mike referees no games, he consumes all 60 hours as leisure. This leaves him $200 (from his parents) for consumption, his nonwage income. Plot this point.

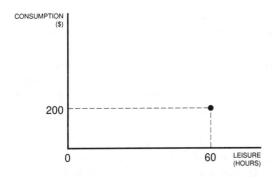

Step three: Calculate total income if Mike works all the time available. If he referees the maximum number of games, 60, he earns $420 from refereeing and retains the $200 from his parents. This leaves him with $620 for consumption but no time for leisure. Plot this point.

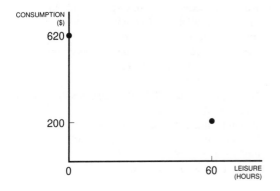

Step four: Draw a line segment between the two plotted points. This is the budget constraint.

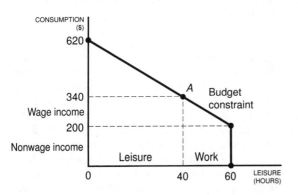

Step five: The slope of the budget constraint is (620 − 200)/60 = 7, which is the wage.

Step six (b): If Mike referees 20 games, he is left with 40 hours of leisure, and earns $140 in wage income for a total of $340. Plot the point, and label appropriately.

2. (Practice problem: consumption-leisure budget constraint) University professors can earn extra cash by reviewing papers for journals. Editors pay around $50 per paper for an academic opinion about whether it should be accepted for publication. Reviewing a paper takes 1 hour. Professor Cavendish has 15 hours available each month for outside work such as reviewing. She draws $3,000 monthly from Vineland University and that is her only other source of income.

    a. Plot Professor Cavendish's budget constraint.
    b. Suppose that the professor reviews 6 papers in March. Plot and label her chosen alternative.

3. (Practice problem: consumption-leisure budget constraint) For each of the following, draw a budget constraint. Also, choose a point along the budget constraint, and show the corresponding amount of leisure, work, nonwage income, and wage income.

	Wage	Total time	Nonwage income
a.	$25/hour	80 hours	$ 1,000
b.	$200/day	30 days	$ 0
c.	$1,000/week	50 weeks	$15,000
d.	$5/hour	100 hours	$ 0

CHANGES IN THE BUDGET CONSTRAINT

When either nonwage income or the wage rate changes, the budget constraint moves. The basic technique here is to draw the budget constraint using the original nonwage income and wage rate, following the procedure shown in Tool Kit 7.1. Then draw a new budget constraint using the new nonwage income and wage rate. Compare the two budget constraints, and verify that the budget constraint shifts parallel to itself when nonwage income changes and that the slope of the budget constraint changes when the wage rate changes.

4. (Worked problem: consumption-leisure budget constraint) Art supplements his pension by repairing automatic teller machines. Each service call takes an hour, and he receives $50 per call. His pension and other nonwage income is $200 per week. Art has 30 hours available and can work as much as he likes.

    a. Plot Art's budget constraint.
    b. His pension fund has done well with its investments and increases Art's nonwage income to $300. Plot his new budget constraint.
    c. How will Art change his work effort?

Step-by-step solution

Step one (a): Plot his budget constraint in the usual way. If he consumes all 30 hours as leisure, Art can consume $200. If he works all 30 hours, he can consume $200 + ($50 × 30) = $1,700. Note that the slope is (1,700 − 200)/30 = 50, which is the wage.

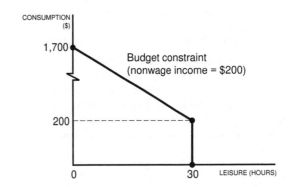

Step two (b): Plot his budget constraint with nonwage income equal to $300. His no-work consumption is now $300 + (30 × $50) = $1,800, if he works all the available time. Note that the nonwage income increase brings about a parallel shift.

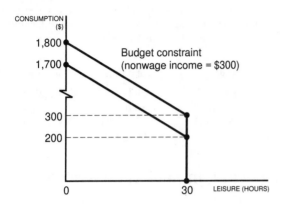

Step three (c): The change in the budget constraint causes an income effect. The income effect leads to a reduction in work effort when income rises. Art will work less.

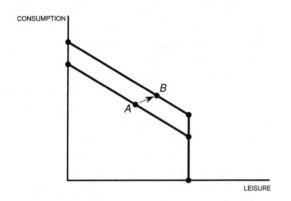

5. (Practice problem: consumption-leisure budget constraint) Liza's job as a broker requires making unsolicited, or "cold," calls to potential clients in an attempt to persuade them to put their portfolios in her hands. On average, cold calls earn Liza $10 each. She can make 4 per hour, and she can work as many as 80 hours per week. Her base salary (nonwage income) is $100 per week.

   a. Plot her budget constraint.
   b. Suppose that the firm offers her an increase in the base salary to $150 per week. Plot her new budget constraint.
   c. Will Liza make more or fewer cold calls? Why?

6. (Practice problem: consumption-leisure budget constraint) Sara is offered a position as tour guide for a local museum. She can conduct 2 tours per hour and earn $10 each. She has no nonwage income, but she must pay 25 percent of her salary in taxes. The museum will allow her to work as many as 20 hours each week.

   a. Plot her budget constraint.
   b. Taxes are reduced to 20 percent. Plot her budget constraint.

7. (Practice problem: consumption-leisure budget constraint) Theodore tutors some of his fellow students in economics for $10 per hour. He also receives $2,000 per semester from his scholarship. He can work as many as 100 hours per semester.

   a. Plot his budget constraint.
   b. Students realize that there is a plethora of semi-intelligent grad students who will take less pay. Theodore now only receives $8 per hour. Plot his new budget constraint.

8. (Practice problem: consumption-leisure budget constraint) For each of the following, plot the budget constraint before and after the change.

   a. Nonwage income = $100; wage = $20 hour; total time available = 40 hours; nonwage income changes to $0.
   b. Nonwage income = $0; wage = $500/week; total time available = 52 weeks; wage changes to $300/week.
   c. Nonwage income = $10,000; wage = $40/hour; total time available = 50 hours; available time increases to 60 hours.
   d. Nonwage income = $500; wage = $200/week; total time available = 52 weeks; wage changes to $400/week.

SUBSTITUTION AND INCOME EFFECTS OF WAGE CHANGES

If you can earn $10 per hour, taking an hour of leisure means giving up the $10 you could have earned. You have paid $10 for the hour of leisure. Thus the price of an hour of leisure is the hourly wage rate. A wage change is therefore just a particular example of a price change: it represents a change in the price of leisure. The response to the change in the wage rate can be analyzed using the same techniques you learned in Chapter 6. This means that there are two effects, a substitution effect and an income effect. Tool Kit 7.2 shows you how to distinguish these two effects. It also shows you why the two effects work in opposite directions, which is a major difference from the analysis you learned in Chapter 6.

9. (Worked problem: wage changes) John currently works 45 hours per week tuning pianos at a wage of $20 per hour. This is his only income. He is offered a raise to $30 per hour. He has 80 hours available for work each week.
   a. Draw the budget constraint at $20 per hour. Label his chosen alternative along this budget constraint.
   b. Draw the budget constraint at $30 per hour.
   c. Show the substitution effect of the wage increase.

Tool Kit 7.2: Distinguishing Between Substitution and Income Effects of Wage Changes

When the wage rate changes, this causes a substitution effect and an income effect, both of which can be illustrated using the consumption-leisure budget constraint. Follow these steps to see how it is done.

Step one: Draw the budget constraint with the original wage.

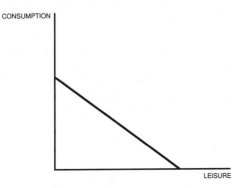

Step two: Find the chosen point along this budget constraint. Label this point *A*.

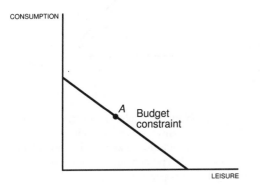

Step three: Draw the budget constraint with the new wage.

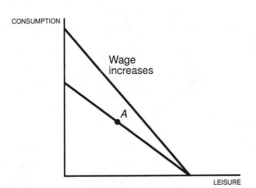

Step four: Draw a dashed line segment through point *A* and parallel to the *new* budget constraint.

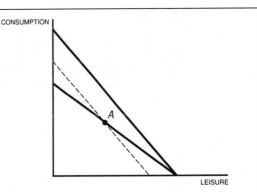

Step five: Darken the portion of the dashed line segment that lies above the original budget constraint. The points along this darkened segment represent the new alternatives made possible by the substitution effect of the wage change.

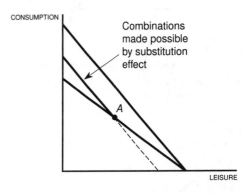

Step six: Select a point for the new consumption-leisure combination after the substitution effect has occurred. Label this point *B*. The income effect is the change from *B* to the point the consumer chooses on the new budget constraint drawn in step three. Select a point for the new combination after the income effect has occurred. Label this point *C*. Normally, *C* will be to the right of *B*. In other words, the income effect opposes the substitution effect.

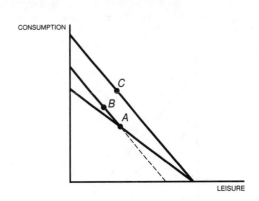

Step-by-step solution

Step one (a): Draw the budget constraint at the original wage. We label the horizontal axis "Leisure" and the vertical one "Consumption." If John does not work, he has 80 hours of leisure and no consumption. If he works all 80 hours (leisure = 0), he consumes $1,600. Draw John's budget constraint connecting the two points.

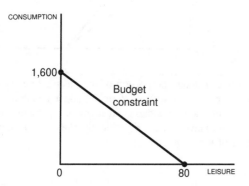

Step two: Find the chosen point along this budget line. John chooses 80 − 45 = 35 hours of leisure, which give him 45 × $20 = $900. Label this point *A*, and note that it does lie along the budget constraint.

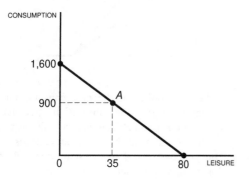

Step three (b): Draw the budget constraint when the wage is $30. The no-work alternative still offers consumption equal to $0, but now if John works the 80 hours available, he consumes $30 × 80 = $2,400. Plot and connect the two end points.

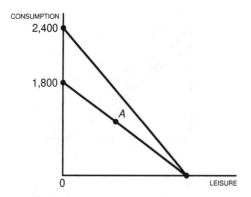

Step four (c): Draw a dashed line parallel to the $30 budget constraint through point *A*.

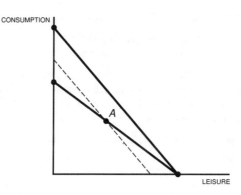

Step five: Darken the portion that lies above the budget constraint drawn in step one. These are the alternatives made possible by the substitution effect of the wage increase. All these points involve more work than at point *A*, the alternative chosen when the wage is $20.

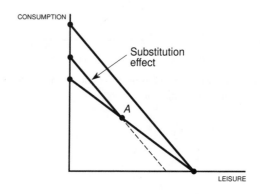

10. (Practice problem: wage changes) Arna loves her job as a design consultant. She can earn $60 per hour and has been able to work as much as she likes up to 50 hours per week. She has no nonwage income. She is currently working 15 hours per week.

a. Plot her budget constraint. Find her chosen alternative, and label the point *A*.
b. A new provincial income tax of 10 percent is passed. Arna now takes home only $54 per hour. Plot her new budget constraint.
c. Show the substitution effect of the wage decrease.

11. (Practice problem: wage changes) For each of the following, draw the budget constraint with the wage in the first column and a new budget constraint with the wage in the second column. Pick an alternative along the first budget constraint, and show the substitution effect. There is no nonwage income.

	Old wage	New wage	Total time
a.	$25/hour	$50/hour	80 hours
b.	$200/day	$100/day	30 days
c.	$1,000/week	$1,500/week	50 weeks
d.	$5/hour	$4/hour	100 hours

APPLICATIONS OF THE CONSUMPTION-LEISURE BUDGET CONSTRAINT

The consumption-leisure budget constraint has many applications. Welfare programmes, overtime pay, and even divorce arrangements can be analyzed, and income and substitution effects identified. For each application, the technique is the same. Determine what has changed and draw budget constraints with and without the change incorporated. Then compare the two constraints in terms of the substitution and income effects.

12. (Worked problem: applications) In Smithsville, the welfare system pays $100 per week. Anyone in Smithsville can earn the minimum wage of $4.00 per hour at the local pickle plant, but welfare recipients cannot receive more than $100 per week. This means that any earnings are subtracted from welfare benefits. There are 80 hours available for work.

   a. Draw the budget constraint for a Smithsville welfare recipient.
   b. A new proposal would substitute a job subsidy for the welfare system. Under the job subsidy proposal, the town pays nothing to those who do not work and $.50 for every dollar earned, up to a total payment of $100. Draw the new budget constraint.

Step-by-step solution

Step one (a): Draw a set of axes labelled "Leisure" and "Consumption." If the recipient does no work, he consumes $100. Plot this point, and label it *A*.

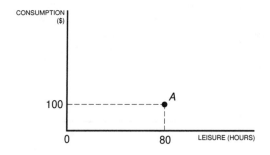

Step two: If the recipient earns $100, he loses all of his benefits and still consumes $100. At $4 per hour, $100 is earned in $100/$4 = 25 hours, which leaves 80 − 25 = 55 hours of leisure. Plot the point (100,55). Label this point *B*.

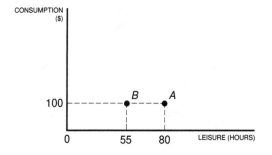

Step three: If the recipient works all 80 hours, he consumes $4 × 80 = $320. Plot this point, and label it *C*. Draw line segments connecting points *A* and *B* and points *B* and *C*. This is the budget constraint under the welfare system.

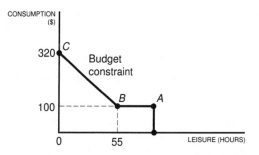

Step four (b): Under the job subsidy program, if the person works no hours, he consumes nothing. Plot the point (0,80). Label it *D*.

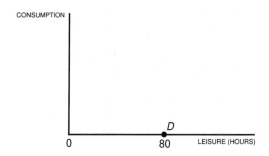

Step five: If the person earns $200, he receives the maximum subsidy, which is $100. The total consumption is then $300. To earn $200 (and consume $300) takes $200/$4 = 50 hours of work; this leaves 80 − 50 = 30 hours of leisure. Plot the point (300, 30), and label it *E*.

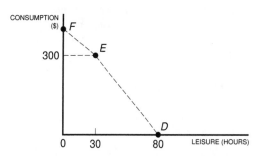

Step six: If the person works all 80 hours, he consumes $100 + (80 × $4) = $420. Plot the point (420, 80), and label it *F*.

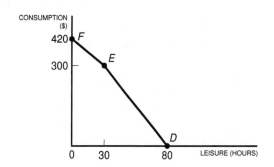

Step seven: Draw line segments connecting *DEF*. This is the budget constraint with the job subsidy.

13. (Practice problem: applications) The management at Acme Manufacturing is disturbed that although the typical factory worker is required to work 250 days each year, most only work 230. It proposes a $100 bonus for any employee who works more than 240 days each year. The wage of the typical factory worker is $120 per day.

    a. Draw the budget constraint without the attendance bonus.
    b. Draw the budget constraint with the attendance bonus. How is attendance likely to change for the typical factory worker?
    c. Suppose that the company simply gives each worker $100. How is the opportunity set different from the one with the attendance bonus?
    d. Under which scheme will the typical worker work more? Why?

14. (Practice problem: applications) The Quantity Bakery Company has paid its workers $6 per hour to make donuts, cakes, and pies. There are always sweets to make, and the workers can work as many hours as they choose, up to 80 hours per week. The typical worker chooses to work 40 hours per week. Recently, the company union won a new contract that keeps the wage at the same level, but allows for overtime pay of "time and a half" for any hours worked in excess of 40 per week.

    a. Draw the budget constraint under the old contract with no provision for overtime pay.
    b. Draw the budget constraint with the overtime pay.
    c. What is likely to happen to the number of hours that Quantity Bakery workers work under the new contract? Explain.

15. (Practice problem: applications) Assume that earnings below $20,000 are taxed at 15 percent. Any earnings above $20,000 incur a 28 percent tax rate. Lucinda Gamez, a private investigator, earns $800 per week, and she has 50 weeks per year available for work.

    a. Draw her budget constraint if she pays no taxes.
    b. Draw her budget constraint under the schedule described above. How do progressive income taxes shape the budget constraint?

16. (Practice problem: applications) Harry Gold makes $5,000 by working 20 days each month as a plumber. His wage is $250 per day, and he can work as many as 30 days each month (except February, of course). The income tax rate for Harry is 20 percent. Also, he pays $1,000 monthly in property taxes on a very nice condo down by the river. His nonwage income is $4,000 per month. (Hint: Review the solutions to problems 14 and 15 in Chapter 6.)

    a. What is Harry's wage per day after taxes?
    b. Draw his budget constraint.
    c. The new government proposes eliminating the income tax and increasing property taxes. Harry figures that his property tax bill will rise to $2,000.

Draw his budget constraint under the government's proposed tax changes.

    d. Will Harry work more or less under the new tax plan? Why?
    e. Is Harry better off under the new tax plan? Why or why not?

17. (Practice problem: applications) After 10 miserable years, Al and Norma Bennet are getting a divorce. They have agreed that Norma will retain custody of their two children. Al makes $50 per hour from his job as a marriage counsellor, and this is his only income. Although he could work as much as 40 hours, Al is only working 20 hours currently. The court has ruled that Al must pay $250 per week in child support regardless of his earnings. (Hint: Review the solutions to problems 14 and 15 in Chapter 6.)

    a. Draw Al's (postdivorce) consumption-leisure budget constraint.
    b. Many U.S. states (for example, Wisconsin and Michigan) have established fixed guidelines for child support payments. Suppose there is a guideline that requires noncustodial parents to pay 12.5 percent of their income per child. Draw Al's budget constraint for this child care payment.
    c. Under which plan will Al work more? Why?

Answers to Problems

2.

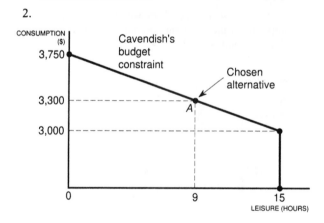

3.

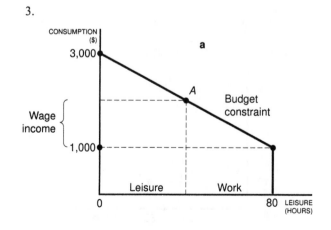

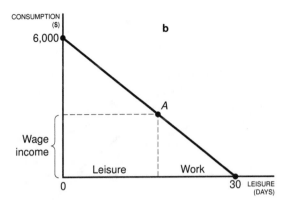

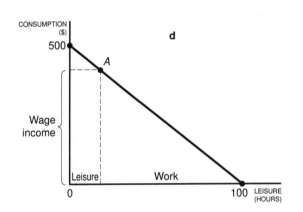

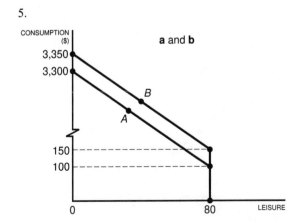

5.

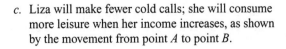

c. Liza will make fewer cold calls; she will consume more leisure when her income increases, as shown by the movement from point *A* to point *B*.

6.

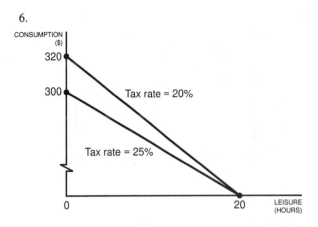

7.

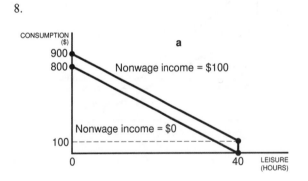

8.

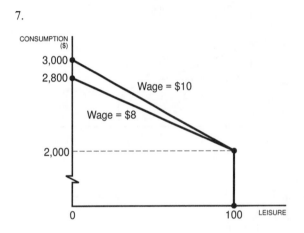

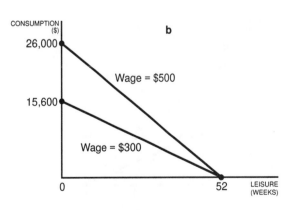

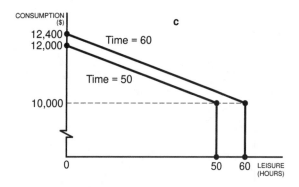

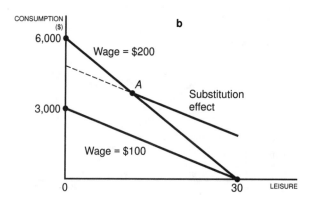

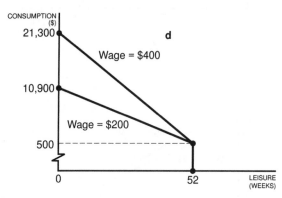

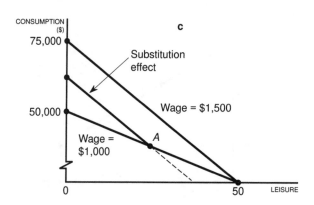

10.

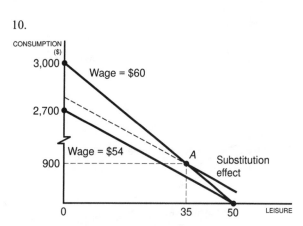

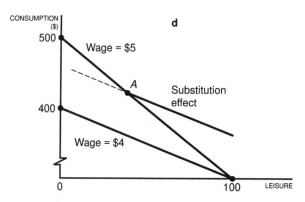

13.

11.

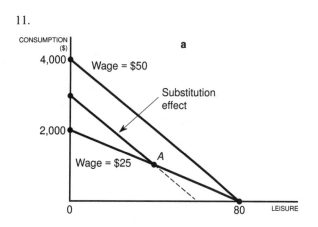

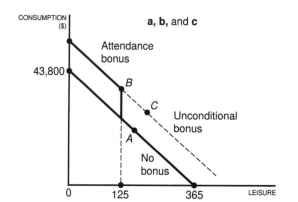

d. An unconditional bonus of $100 simply shifts the budget constraint up in a parallel way, and so causes an income effect. The typical worker consumes more leisure at point C. The attendance bonus does not offer the points along the dashed budget constraint. Point B or another point involving even more work will be chosen. Clearly, there is a greater incentive to work with the attendance bonus.

14.

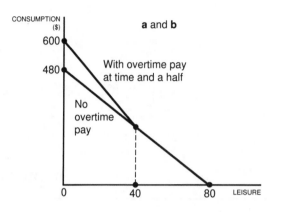

c. All the new alternatives made possible by the overtime provision involve working more than 40 hours. There is only a substitution effect, and work time will increase.

15.

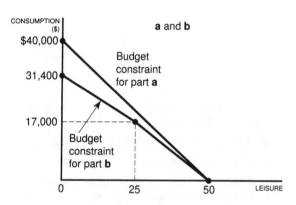

16. *a.* $200/day.

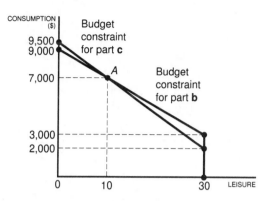

d. He will work more because the tax change offers him new alternatives with more work. In effect it leaves him with the substitution effect of a wage increase; the income effect is cancelled by the property tax increase.

e. He is better off because he can continue to choose point A, but he also has some new alternatives.

17.

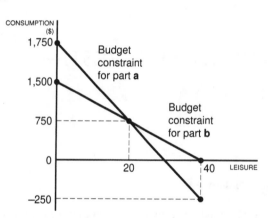

c. Al will work more under the lump-sum child care requirement. The other system leaves him with the substitution effect of a wage decrease.

SAVING AND INVESTING

Chapter Review

Chapter 8 introduces a future-oriented aspect to our study of economics. When trades involve the future, as they do when individuals borrow money, both the borrowers and lenders must be concerned with the time value of money. As a reflection of this, the price in the market for loanable funds is the interest rate. In deciding how much to borrow or save, individuals face yet another budget constraint: a trade-off between current and future consumption. They also face the question of what to do with their savings. Financial markets offer a wide array of investment opportunities, all with different characteristics. Chapter 8 addresses all these issues and concludes with some rules for intelligent investing.

ESSENTIAL CONCEPTS

1. The value of a dollar today is greater than the value of a dollar to be received in the future. In other words, money has a time value. Any decision that involves present and future dollars must account for the time value of money. Economists calculate the present discounted value; they convert future dollars to their present equivalent. The formula is as follows:

   present value = future dollars/$(1 + \text{interest rate})^n$.

   where n represents the number of years in the future.

2. The market for loanable funds brings together all those who want to borrow and those who want to save. The price in this market is the **interest rate.** Figure 8.1 shows the demand curve for loanable funds sloping

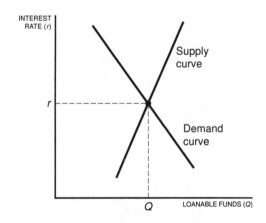

Figure 8.1

downwards; this indicates that at lower interest rates, more borrowers would like to borrow more funds. The supply curve slopes upwards because at higher interest rates, individuals will save more. The interest rate adjusts to clear the market, and the equilibrium quantity of savings equals the equilibrium quantity of borrowing.

3. The **savings decision** is basically a decision about *when* to consume; households choose whether to spend all their income now or save it for future consumption. The **two-period budget constraint** employs the techniques we learned in Chapter 6 to show what combinations of consumption in the present and consumption in the future are affordable, given present and future incomes and the interest rate. As in Chapter 6, the slope of the budget constraint indicates the *trade-off,* and it equals the relative price. Since current consumption is measured on the horizontal axis, the slope is the **relative price of current consumption,** which is **1 plus the interest rate**.

4. When the interest rate changes, the budget constraint rotates; it becomes steeper if the interest rate increases and flatter if it decreases. In exactly the same manner as in Chapter 6's analysis of the consumption decision, the change in the budget constraint causes income and substitution effects. Higher interest rates make savers better off, and because current consumption is a normal good, the **income effect** makes them want to consume more today, and thus reduces savings. On the other hand, higher interest rates lower the relative price of future consumption. The resulting **substitution effect** increases savings. In the decision to save, the substitution and income effects work in opposite directions, as they did in the analysis of labour supply in Chapter 7.

5. There are several motives for saving. People set aside **precautionary savings** to guard against the chance of accident or illness. The **bequest motive** leads people to save for their heirs. Finally, people save to meet a particular goal, such as buying a house or starting a business. We call this motive **target savings.**

6. Aggregate savings are lower in Canada than in some other countries. There are a number of possible reasons: an aging population, government dissaving (budget deficits), pay-as-you-go pensions, high levels of consumer durables, and improvements in capital markets that make consumer borrowing easier.

7. Financial investments are purchases of financial assets in the expectation of receiving returns. Examples include bank accounts, real estate, bonds, and shares of stock. Investors receive returns in the form of interest, dividends, rent, and capital gains.

8. There are four important properties of financial investments: expected return, risk, tax treatment, and liquidity.

   a. Since returns are uncertain, the investor must balance the high returns with the low. The **expected return** is calculated by multiplying the possible returns by the probability each will occur.

   b. Assets with a greater chance of very low and very high returns are **risky.** Most individuals are **risk averse;** they prefer safer assets. An important risk characteristic of an investment is how its returns vary with the market as a whole. Assets that pay high returns when the economy is weak are in greater demand because they allow the investor to reduce the riskiness of the overall portfolio.

   c. The returns from some assets, such as housing and municipal bonds, are taxed less than the returns from other assets. The **tax advantages** make these assets more appealing to investors.

   d. The ease with which an investment can be converted to cash is called **liquidity.** Bank accounts are very liquid; housing is illiquid. Most investors prefer liquidity.

9. The chapter closes with some investment advice. Although unlikely to appear on a test, this advice is immensely valuable.

   a. Carefully evaluate the characteristics of each asset you own as it relates to your personal situation.

   b. Diversify. Give your portfolio a broad base.

   c. Consider all your risks, not just those in your financial investment portfolio.

   d. Think again before you imagine that you can beat the market.

BEHIND THE ESSENTIAL CONCEPTS

1. The distinction between real and nominal interest rates is very important. When you deposit money in your bank account, the bank pays you the nominal interest rate. Say it is 5 percent. Your money grows at 5 percent each year, but your purchasing power may not, because each year prices may also be changing. Suppose that the inflation rate (the rate of increase in the general price level) is 4 percent. This means that each year goods become 4 percent more expensive, and you can buy only 5 percent – 4 percent = 1 percent more goods. Thus, 1 percent is the real interest rate, and also the rate of increase in your purchasing power.

2. The basic diagram in this chapter is the two-period budget constraint shown in Figure 8.2. It is important to see how similar this diagram is to the consumer's budget

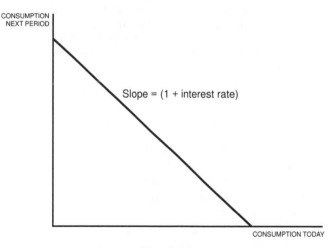

Figure 8.2

constraint of Chapter 6. There, the trade-off was between consuming different goods. Here, the trade-off involves consuming in different time periods. In each case, the slope is the relative price. When the relative price changes, there are substitution and income effects. Price changes rotate the buget constraint, but income changes bring about a parallel shift. This basic approach was also used for the labour supply decision in Chapter 7.

3. Think about the slope of the two-period budget constraint. To consume more in the future, an individual can save today. One dollar saved today results in $(1 + r)$ dollars of consumption in the future, where r is the interest rate. That is, the individual can buy $(1 + r)$ dollars of future consumption at an opportunity cost of only 1 dollar today. Conversely, to buy 1 more dollar of current consumption, the individual must give up $(1 + r)$ dollars of future consumption. The relative price of future consumption is, then, 1 plus the interest rate.

4. One plus the interest rate is also the slope of the budget constraint; therefore, only changes in the interest rate can change the slope. If the interest rate rises, the budget constraint becomes steeper. If the interest rate falls, the budget constraint becomes flatter. Income changes, either now or in the future, only shift the budget constraint in a parallel way.

5. Table 8.1 may help you keep the substitution and income effects straight.

Table 8.1

If the interest rate rises:
  the *substitution* effect leads to more savings because current consumption is relatively more expensive.
  the *income* effect leads to reduced savings because the saver is better off and desires to consume more today.

If the interest rate falls:
  the *substitution* effect leads to reduced savings because current consumption is relatively less expensive.
  the *income* effect leads to more savings because the saver is worse off and desires to consume less today.

6. The **efficient market theory** says that market prices reflect the characteristics of assets, incorporate all currently available information, and change unpredictably. An important implication of this theory is that without inside information, investors cannot earn more than average returns.

7. What do investors want from their financial assets? In addition to high expected returns, individuals value investments with low risk, favourable tax treatment, and liquidity. The demand for investments with these characteristics is higher; therefore, their price is higher. The fact that market prices are higher for assets with desirable characteristics—in other words, that asset prices reflect these characteristics—is one of the central ideas of efficient market theory.

8. Many people are mystified by the notion that in an efficient market, asset prices change randomly. Once you understand the logic, however, you can see why this must be true. Since market prices reflect available information, you can only beat the market if you have information others do not. Anyone who had known in April 1990 that Iraq would invade Kuwait could have bought oil stocks before their prices rose. Once the invasion happened, however, it was too late. Prices had already risen. Since the invasion was a surprise, the sudden changes in the prices of oil stocks were also surprises. This is what is meant by random movements in prices: the changes are unpredictable, though they are not without rational cause.

SELF-TEST

True or False

1. The present discounted value of a future dollar is what one would pay today for that future dollar.

2. The interest rate is the price in the market for loanable funds.

3. The real interest rate is the nominal interest rate plus the rate of inflation.

4. An increase in the interest rate increases the relative price of future consumption.

5. The income effect of an increase in the interest rate results in increased saving.

6. When the interest rate changes, saving may rise or fall because the income and substitution effects of the change work in opposite directions.

7. Increased taxes on interest income will discourage saving.

8. Pay-as-you-go pension programmes tend to decrease aggregate savings.

9. One reason for the fall in the aggregate savings rate in Canada is that borrowing has become easier.

10. Housing is a tax-favoured investment.

11. Bondholders bear no risk from inflation.

12. If the interest rate increases, bond prices fall.

13. Illiquid assets pay lower rates of return on average.

14. A fund that gathers money from many investors and purchases a range of assets is called a mutual fund.

15. If stock prices vary randomly, the stock market cannot be efficient.

Multiple Choice

1. If you deposit $1,100 in the bank today and the interest rate on your deposit is 10 percent, how much money will be in your account at the end of one year?

   a. $2,310
   b. $1,210
   c. $1,110
   d. $990
   e. $110

2. If you are to receive $1,100 from a client one year from today and the interest rate is 10 percent, what is the present discounted value of that future receipt?

   a. $1,200
   b. $1,000
   c. $1,000
   d. $900
   e. $100

3. When the interest rate _____, the present discounted value of the future returns from an investment project _____.

   a. increases; rises
   b. decreases; remains unchanged
   c. decreases; falls
   d. increases; remains unchanged
   e. increases; falls

4. Suppose that the interest rate offered on certificates of deposit is 8 percent. The inflation rate is expected to be 5 percent. What is the real rate of interest?

   a. 13 percent
   b. 8 percent
   c. 5 percent
   d. 3 percent
   e. minus 3 percent

5. Let r be the rate of interest. The relative price of $1 consumed today is:

   a. $1/(1 + r)$.
   b. $1/(1 - r)$.
   c. $1 + r$.
   d. $1 - r$.
   e. r.

6. If the interest rate falls, the two-period budget constraint (with current consumption on the horizontal axis):

   a. shifts inwards parallel to itself.
   b. becomes flatter.
   c. is unaffected.
   d. becomes steeper.
   e. shifts outwards parallel to itself.

7. Sonja lives for two periods. In the first, she receives income from work, some of which she saves for her retirement in the second period. If the interest rate falls in the two-period model of current and future consumption:

   a. the relative price of current consumption falls, and the substitution effect results in lower current consumption.
   b. the relative price of consumption rises, and the substitution effect results in lower current consumption.
   c. the relative price of consumption rises, and the substitution effect results in higher future consumption.
   d. the relative price of current consumption rises, and the substitution effect results in higher current consumption.
   e. the relative price of current consumption falls, and the substitution effect results in higher current consumption.

8. Sonja lives for two periods. In the first, she receives income from work, some of which she saves for her retirement in the second period. If the interest rate falls in the two-period model of current and future consumption:

   a. both the income and substitution effects mean Sonja saves more.
   b. the income effect means Sonja saves less but the substitution effect means she saves more.
   c. there is no income effect, only a substitution effect.
   d. the income effect means Sonja saves more but the substitution effect means she saves less.
   e. both the income and substitution effects mean Sonja saves less.

9. If the government were to announce a reduction in benefits to be paid in the future to recipients of the Canada Pension Plan, this would be likely to:

   a. reduce national savings.
   b. increase national savings through the income effect but reduce national savings through the substitution effect.
   c. have no effect on national savings.
   d. reduce national savings through the income effect but increase national savings through the substitution effect.
   e. increase national savings.

10. All of the following, except one, are possible explanations of Canada's low savings rate. Which is the odd one out?

    a. public-sector dissaving
    b. increased demand for consumer durables
    c. low interest rates
    d. high public pension benefits
    e. improved captial markets

11. When the interest rate falls:

    a. long-term bond prices rise but short-term bond prices fall.
    b. bond prices rise.
    c. bond prices are unaffected.
    d. bond prices fall.
    e. long-term bond prices fall but short-term bond prices rise.

12. Junk bonds are assets with:

    a. high rates of return and a low risk of default.
    b. low rates of return and a low risk of default.
    c. high rates of return and no risk of default.
    d. low rates of return and a high risk of default.
    e. high rates of return and a high risk of default.

13. The amount of a firm's earnings not paid out to stockholders is called:

    a. corporate profits.
    b. a capital gain.
    c. retained earnings.
    d. the dividend.
    e. corporate income.

14. If an investor sells a share of stock for more than he paid for it, this represents:

a. a liquidity premium.
b. a capital gain.
c. retained earnings.
d. a risk premium.
e. a dividend.

15. An asset purchased today for $100 can be sold in a year's time for an uncertain price. If there is a 25 percent chance the price will be $104, a 50 percent chance the price will be $108, and a 25 percent chance the price will be $110, the expected return to holding the asset for one year is:

a. 8 percent.
b. 7.5 percent.
c. 7 percent.
d. 6.5 percent.
e. 6 percent.

16. An asset that sells at a premium has:

a. a lower-than-average rate of return.
b. undesirable attributes.
c. an average rate of return.
d. the status of a junk bond.
e. a higher-than-average rate of return.

17. Housing is:

a. an investment that is easily liquidated.
b. tax-favoured because mortgage interest is tax deductible.
c. tax-favoured because any capital gain on a principal residence is untaxed.
d. tax-favoured because there are no property taxes.
e. none of the above

18. Which of the following assets is the most illiquid?

a. long-term bonds
b. certificates of deposit
c. shares of stock
d. housing
e. mutual funds

19. The _____ argues that asset prices accurately reflect the assets' characteristics.

a. efficient market theory
b. principle of diminishing returns
c. random walk theory
d. principle of comparative advantage
e. arbitrage theory

20. The advice to diversify your portfolio means:

a. stay away from risky assets.
b. choose assets that beat the market.
c. own a wide variety of assets with different risks.
d. follow a random walk strategy.
e. buy low and sell high.

Completion

1. The _____ of a future dollar is the value of that future dollar today.

2. The interest rate is the price in the market for _____.

3. The nominal interest rate minus the real interest rate is the _____.

4. The substitution effect of an increase in the interest rate is _____ savings.

5. The income effect of an increase in the interest rate is _____ savings.

6. If r is the rate of interest, the relative price of consumption today versus consumption in the future is _____.

7. The Canadian public pension system, in which benefits to retirees are financed by current taxes paid by younger workers, is called a _____ scheme.

8. A _____ asset is one that is easily turned into cash.

9. The demand for an asset depends on its average return, its _____, its liquidity, and its treatment by the tax system.

10. The theory that market prices accurately reflect assets' attributes is called the _____ theory.

Answers to Self-Test

True or False

1. t	4. f	7. f	10. t	13. f
2. t	5. f	8. t	11. f	14. t
3. f	6. t	9. t	12. t	15. f

Multiple Choice

1. b	6. b	11. b	16. a
2. c	7. e	12. e	17. c
3. e	8. d	13. c	18. d
4. d	9. e	14. b	19. a
5. c	10. c	15. b	20. c

Completion

1 present discounted value
2 loanable funds
3 rate of inflation
4 increased
5 decreased
6 $1 + r$
7 pay-as-you-go
8 liquid
9 risk
10 efficient market

Doing Economics: Tools and Practice Problems

We begin with several examples of how to convert streams of future payments to present discounted values. Then we turn to a detailed analysis of the two-period budget constraint. We see how it changes with changes in income or the interest rate, identify the substitution and income effects of a change in the interest rate, and examine several applications of the two-period model. Finally, we introduce the concept of expected returns; learn how the investor perceives tradeoffs of risk and expected return, and liquidity and expected return; and investigate the relationship between bond prices and interest rates.

PRESENT DISCOUNTED VALUE

A dollar to be received in the future is not worth as much as a dollar received today. There is a time value of money. To compare present and future payments, it is necessary to compute the present discounted value. Tool Kit 8.1 shows you how to do this.

Tool Kit 8.1: Calculating the Present Discounted Value

Follow these steps to compute the present discounted value of a stream of future payments.

Step one: Make a table with four columns, and label them as shown.

Year	Amount	Discount factor	Present discounted value

Step two: For every payment or receipt, enter the year and the amount. Let Y_1 be the amount in the first year, Y_2 the amount in the second year, and so on.

Year	Amount	Discount factor	Present discounted value
1	Y_1		
2	Y_2		

Step three: Calculate the discount factor for each year. The formula is $1/(1 + r)^n$, where r is the interest rate and n is the number of years until the payment or receipt. Enter these discount factors in the table.

Year	Amount	Discount factor	Present discounted value
1	Y_1	$1/(1 + r)$	
2	Y_2	$1/(1 + r)^2$	

Step four: Multiply the number in the amount column by the corresponding discount factor. Enter the product in the present discounted value column.

Year	Amount	Discount factor	Present discounted value
1	Y_1	$1/(1 + r)$	$Y_1 \times 1/(1 + r)$
2	Y_2	$1/(1 + r)^2$	$Y_2 \times 1/(1 + r)^2$

Step five: Add the numbers in the right-hand column. The sum is the present discounted value.

Year	Amount	Discount factor	Present discounted value
1	Y_1	$1/(1 + r)$	$Y_1 \times 1/(1 + r)$
2	Y_2	$1/(1 + r)^2$	$Y_2 \times 1/(1 + r)^2$

Present discounted value
$$= Y_1 \times 1/(1 + r) + Y_2 \times 1/(1 + r)^2.$$

---

1. (Worked problem: present discounted value) Ethel has two years before retirement from a career of teaching unruly high school delinquents. Her salary is $40,000, paid at the end of each year. The school board has offered her $70,000 now to retire early. The relevant interest rate is 7 percent. In monetary terms alone, is working worth more than retiring?

Step-by-step solution

First, calculate the present discounted value of continuing to work.

Step one: Make a table with four columns, and label them as shown.

Year	Amount	Discount factor	Present discounted value

Step two: For every payment or receipt, enter the year and the amount. Ethel receives $40,000 each year for two years.

Year	Amount	Discount factor	Present discounted value
1	$40,000		
2	$40,000		

Step three: Calculate the discount factor for each year. For the first year, the discount factor is $1/(1 + .07) = 0.93$, and for the second year it is $1/(1 + .07)^2 = 0.86$. Enter these discount factors in the table.

Year	Amount	Discount factor	Present discounted value
1	$40,000	0.93	
2	$40,000	0.86	

Step four: Multiply the number in the amount column by the corresponding discount factor. Enter the product in the present discounted value column.

Year	Amount	Discount factor	Present discounted value
1	$40,000	0.93	$37,380
2	$40,000	0.86	$34,400

Step five: Add the numbers in the right-hand column. The sum is the present discounted value.

Year	Amount	Discount factor	Present discounted value
1	$40,000	0.93	$37,380
2	$40,000	0.86	$34,400

Present discounted value = $71,780.

Next, compare the lump-sum payment with the present discounted value of continuing to work. Ethel can postpone retirement and increase the present discounted value of her earnings by only $1,780. The reason that the gain is so little is that earnings come in the future and must be discounted, while the retirement bonus is paid now.

2. (Practice problem: present discounted value) The Transportation Department is considering the bids of two paving companies for repaving South Street. The Do-It-Rite firm will do the job for $200,000, and they will guarantee that their new process will make the road free of potholes for 3 years. The Let-It-Go company only charges $100,000, but estimated pothole repair costs are $40,000 each year. The interest rate is 8 percent.

   a. Calculate the present discounted value of the entire cost with the Let-It-Go firm.

   b. Which is the less expensive bid?

3. (Practice problem: present discounted value) Calculate the present discounted value of each of the following.

  a. Interest rate equals 10 percent.

Year	Amount	Discount factor	Present discounted value
1	$10,000		
2	$15,000		

  b. Interest rate equals 5 percent.

Year	Amount	Discount factor	Present discounted value
1	$ 0		
2	$20,000		

  c. Interest rate equals 15 percent.

Year	Amount	Discount factor	Present discounted value
1	$5,000		
2	$5,000		
3	$5,000		

  d. Interest rate equals 5 percent.

Year	Amount	Discount factor	Present discounted value
1	$ 5,000		
2	$ 0		
3	$25,000		

THE TWO-PERIOD BUDGET CONSTRAINT

The most important model in this chapter is the two-period budget constraint. The constraint shows the combinations of present and future consumption that are available to the individual, once we know her income and the interest rate she faces. Tool Kit 8.2 shows you how to construct the two-period budget constraint.

Tool Kit 8.2: Plotting the Two-Period Budget Constraint

Follow the steps to construct the two-period budget constraint.

Step one: Draw a set of coordinate axes. Label the horizontal axis "Consumption in period one" and the vertical axis "Consumption in period two."

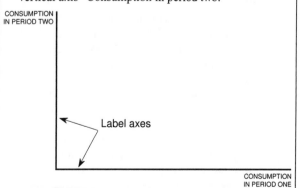

Step two: Calculate the maximum possible consumption in period one. (This quantity is the present discounted value of income.) Plot this quantity along the horizontal axis.

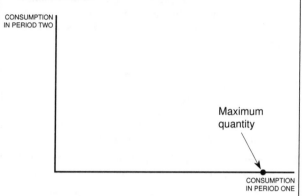

Step three: Calculate the maximum possible consumption in period two. (This quantity is the future value of income.) Plot this quantity along the vertical axis.

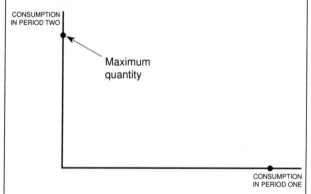

Step four: Draw a line segment connecting the two points. This line segment is the two-period budget constraint.

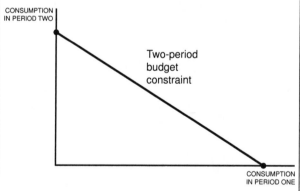

Step five: Verify that the slope of the budget constraint is (minus) $1 + r$, where r is the interest rate.

---

4. (Worked problem: two-budget constraint) Nancy won the lottery! It is only $5,000, but that looks pretty good to someone making $18,000 per year. Her interest rate is 6 percent, and the capital market is perfect. Plot her budget constraint for consumption this year and next year.

Step-by-step solution

Step one: Draw coordinate axes, labelling the horizontal axis "Consumption now" and the vertical axis "Consumption next year."

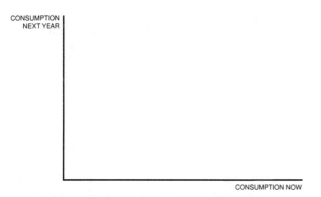

Step two: The maximum consumption today is the present discounted value of all income. Make the following table, and compute and plot the amount along the horizontal axis.

Year	Income	Discount factor	Present discounted value
Now	$23,000	1	$23,000
Next year	$18,000	1/(1.06)	$16,980

Present discounted value = $39,980.

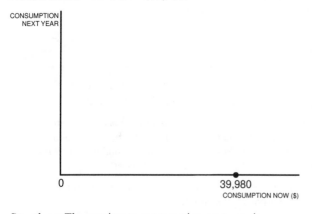

Step three: The maximum consumption next year is

$$\$23,000 \, (1 + .06) + \$18,000 = \$42,380.$$

Plot this point.

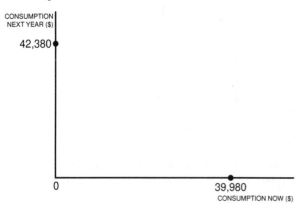

Step four: Draw a line segment connecting the two points.

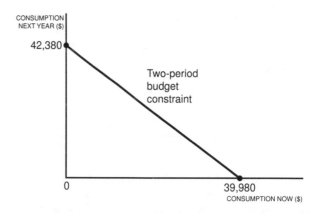

Step five: Verify that the slope equals 1 plus the interest rate. It is 42,380/39,980 = 1.06 = 1 + r.

5. (Practice problem: two-period budget constraint) Current income is $40,000. Retirement income is $15,000. The interest rate for the period between now and retirement is 150 percent. Plot the two-period budget constraint.

6. (Practice problem: two-period budget constraint) Plot the two-period budget constraints for the following:

	Interest rate	Present income	Future income
a.	100%	$100,000	$ 25,000
b.	50%	$ 40,000	$ 10,000
c.	250%	$ 20,000	$ 0
d.	80%	0	$150,000

CHANGES IN THE TWO-PERIOD BUDGET CONSTRAINT

When the interest rate, current income, or future income changes, the two-period budget constraint moves. The basic technique here is to draw the two-period budget constraint using the original incomes and interest rate, and then draw a new two-period budget constraint using the new incomes and interest rate. Compare the two budget constraints and verify that the budget constraint shifts parallel to itself when there is a change in current or future income and that the budget constraint changes its slope when the interest rate changes.

7. (Worked problem: two-period budget constraint) Michael is earning $25,000 as an executive assistant and expects to earn the same next year. His interest rate is 5 percent.

   a. Plot his two-period budget constraint.
   b. He receives word that his aunt is sick and has one year to live. She plans to leave him $50,000. Plot his two-period budget constraint.

Step-by-step solution

Step one (a): Follow the procedure to plot the two-period budget constraint. The slop is 1 + r = 1.05, and it passes through the point $25,000 now and $25,000 next year.

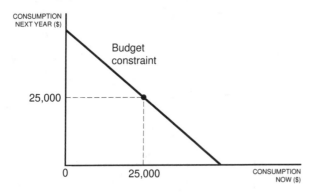

Step two (b): Plot the new budget constraint. Because the interest rate is the same, the slope does not change. The new budget constraint passes through the point $25,000 now and $75,000 next year.

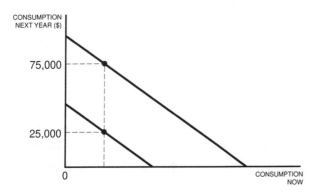

8. (Practice problem: two-period budget constraint) Boris currently takes home $45,000 as a skilled lathe operator. His union contract guarantees him the same salary next year. The credit union at the plant pays 8 percent interest.

   a. Plot his two-period budget constraint.
   b. Boris' employer is experiencing low profits this year. She proposes that Boris accept $35,000 this year and $55,000 next year. Plot his two-period budget constraint. Does his employer's offer shift Boris' budget constraint? How?

9. (Practice problem: two-period budget constraint) Monica plans to retire in 20 years. She now takes home $40,000 and expects $20,000 in retirement income. The interest rate for the 20 years is 180 percent.

   a. Plot her budget constraint.
   b. A new broker promises her a 20-year return of 250 percent. She believes him. Plot her new budget constraint.

10. (Practice problem: two-period budget constraint) The Coddingtons now take home $375,000 per year, but they have no retirement income planned. Their portfolio will earn them 100 percent over the 12 years left until retirement.

    a Plot their budget constraint.
    b. Tax increases reduce their after-tax return to 60 percent. Plot their new budget constraint.

11. (Practice problem: two-period budget constraint) Plot the budget constraints before and after the change.

	Current income	Future income	Interest rate	Change
a.	$100,000	$ 0	40%	Interest rate = 60%.
b.	$100,000	$ 0	40%	Future income = $100,000.
c.	$ 0	$50,000	10%	Current income = $25,000.
d.	$ 60,000	$80,000	50%	Interest rate = 20%.

SUBSTITUTION AND INCOME EFFECTS

If the interest rate (r) is 10 percent, giving up $1 for a year yields you $1.10 in one year's time. The price of consuming (that is, spending) $1 today is therefore $1.10, or equivalently $1 + r$. A change in r is therefore just a particular example of price change: it represents a change in the price of consumption today. The response to the change in the interest rate can be analyzed using the same techniques you learned in Chapter 6 and applied to labour supply in Chapter 7. This means there are two effects, a substitution effect and an income effect. Tool Kit 8.3 shows you how to identify these two effects. It also shows you why the two effects work in opposite directions; this is a major difference from the analysis you learned in Chapter 6 but reflects the application to labour supply in Chapter 7.

Tool Kit 8.3: Substitution and Income Effects of Changes in Interest Rates

When the interest rate changes, this causes a substitution effect and an income effect, both of which can be illustrated using the two-period budget constraint. Follow these steps to see how it is done.

Step one: Draw the two-period budget constraint with the original interest rate.

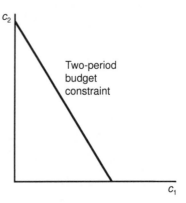

Step two: Find the chosen current and future consumption level along this budget constraint. Label this point *A*.

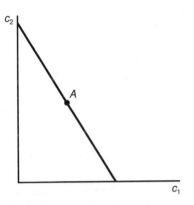

Step three: Draw the two-period budget constraint with the new interest rate.

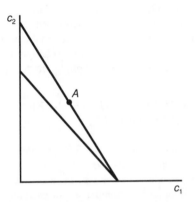

Step four: Draw a dashed line segment through point A and parallel to the *new* budget constraint.

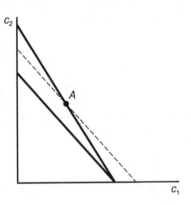

Step five: Darken the portion of the dashed line that lies above the orignianl budget constraint. The points

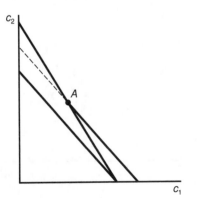

along this darkened segment represent the quantities made possible by the substitution effect of the interest rate change. The income effect is the response to moving from this new budget constraint to the lower, parallel budget constraint drawn in step three.

Step six: Select a point for the new combination of c_1 and c_2 after the substitution effect has occured. Label this point B. The income effect is the change from B to the point the consumer chooses on the new budget constraint drawn in step three. Select a point for the new combination after the income effect has occurred. Label this point C. Normally, C will be to the left of B. In other words, the income effect opposes the substitution effect.

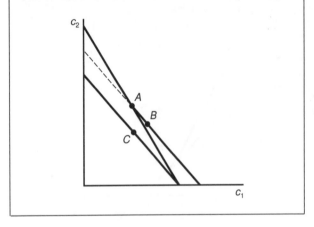

12. (Worked problem: substitution and income effects) Show the substitution and income effects of the change in the rate of return for Monica's portfolio in problem 9. She is currently saving $5,000 per year.

Step-by-step solution

Step one: Draw the two-period budget constraint with the interest rate equal to 180 percent. It must pass through the point ($40,000, $20,000).

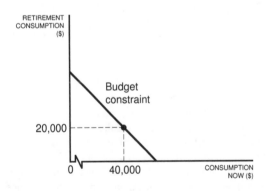

Step two: Label Monica's current consumption ($40,000 − $5,000 = $35,000) point A.

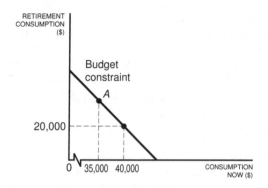

Step three: Draw the two-period budget constraint with the intereste rate equal to 250 percent. It also must pass through the point ($40,000, $20,000).

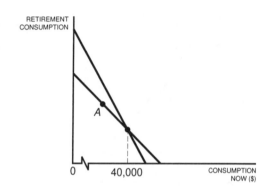

Step four: Draw a dotted line with a slope of 1 + 2.50 = 3.50 through *A*.

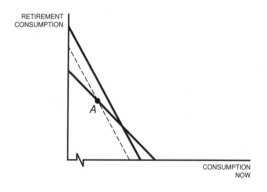

Step five: Darken the portion of the dashed line that lies above the original budget constraint drawn in step one. These are the alternatives made possible by the substitution effect of the interest rate change. All these involve more savings; thus, the substitution effect of an increase in the interest rate is an increase in savings. The income effect is the response to the shift from the darkened line segment to the parallel budget constraint drawn in step two and reduces savings.

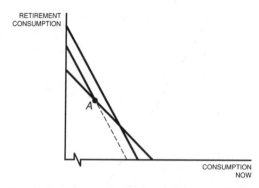

13. (Practice problem: substitution and income effects) Show the substituion and income effects for the change in the Coddingtons' after-tax interest rate in problem 10. Currently they have no savings.

14. (Practice problem: substitution and income effects) Show the substitution and income effects for parts a through d in problem 11. Assume that current consumption before the interest rate changes is $50,000 in a and b, $25,000 in c, and $60,000 in d.

APPLICATIONS OF THE TWO-PERIOD BUDGET CONSTRAINT

The two-period budget constraint has many applications. Imperfect capital markets, tax-free savings plans, and pay-as-you-go pension schemes can be analyzed, and income and substitution effects identified. For each application, the technique is the same. Determine what has changed and draw budget constraints with and without the change incorporated. Then compare the two constraints in terms of the substitution and income effects.

15. (Worked problem: applications) If the capital market were perfect, then the interest rates for borrowing and lending would be the same. The rates for borrowing, however, are higher. Haywood and Myrna take home $40,000 each year. They can earn 4 percent on any savings, but they must borrow at 14 percent. Plot their two-period budget constraint.

Step-by-step solution

This is an application of the opportunity set with multiple constraints introduced in Chapter 2.

Step one: Plot the budget constraint with the 4 percent interest rate. The slope is 1.04, and it passes through the point $40,000 now and $40,000 next year.

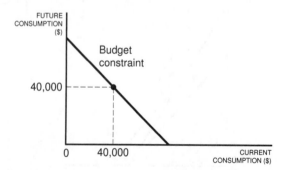

Step two: Plot the budget constraint with the 14 percent interest rate. The slope is 1.14, and it passes through the point $40,000 now and $40,000 next year.

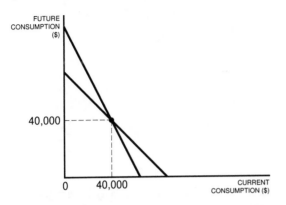

Step three: Darken the portion of each budget constraint that lies under the other constraint.

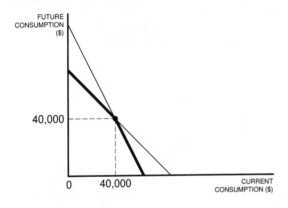

16. (Practice problem: applications) Bob takes home $20,000 this year, but he anticipates taking home $30,000 next year. He can earn 8 percent on savings, but he has a poor credit rating and must pay 19 percent to borrow. Plot his two-period budget constraint.

17. (Worked problem: applications) The Davidsons take home $100,000 per year after taxes and save $3,500. Their son, David, will enter university in three years' time if he can improve his grades sufficiently. The Davidsons are offered the opportunity to participate in a new government plan that will make it easier to pay for David's education: a special university savings account in which up to $3,000 can be deposited without attracting taxes so long as any money withdrawn is used to pay for university tuition.

   a. Draw the Davidsons' two-period budget constraint if the real rate of return over the three-year period is 25 percent before taxes.

   b. The Davidsons face a 40 percent marginal tax rate. Draw their budget constraint if their interest were taxed at this rate.

   c. Draw the Davidsons' budget constraint after the introduction of the university savings plan.

   d. Use the concepts of income and substitution effects to explain how their savings will be affected by the plan.

Step-by-step solution

Step one (a): Plot the two-period budget constraint. The slope is $1 + 0.25 = 1.25$, and the budget constraint must pass through the point where current and future income are each $100,000.

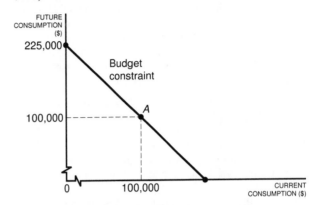

Step two (b): Plot the two-period budget constraint with the tax on interest. Taxes take 40 percent of the interest, so their after-tax interest rate for the three years is 15 percent. The slope is now 1.15. Interest taxes make the budget constraint flatter.

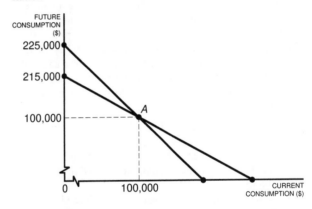

Step three (c): The university savings plan allows the Davidsons to save along the tax-free budget constraint, where the slope is 1.25 until their savings reach $3,000. At that point (*B*), there is a kink, and the slope of the budget constraint returns to the flatter after-tax slope of 1.15.

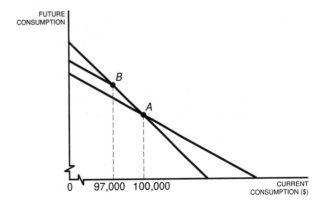

Step four (d): Since the Davidsons save more than $3,000, the program will have only an income effect. The program will not change their after-tax marginal rate of return, because only the first $3,000 of savings is tax exempt.

18. (Practice problem: applications) The Johnsons do not know where they will find the money to send their four bright children to university in 5 years. They make $26,000 per year and have been unable to save a nickel. Their marginal tax rate is 20 percent, and they could earn 40 percent interest on savings over the 5-year period.

   a Plot the Johnsons' two-period budget constraint ignoring the tax on interest.
   b. Plot their two-period budget constraint including the tax on interest.
   c. Plot their two-period budget constraint under the university savings plan spelled out in problem 17.
   d. Use the concepts of substitution and income effects to explain how their savings will be affected by the university savings plan.

19. (Worked problem: applications) Unfunded pension benefits reduce the incentives for individuals to save for retirement. Melissa is already fantasizing about retirement, even though it is 40 years away. She estimates that a dollar deposited today will return $3.50 in interest when she retires. She currently takes home $25,000 after paying $3,250 annually in taxes and expects to draw $14,625 in pension benefits. Although she is thinking about retirement, Melissa has no savings.

   a. Calculate the present discounted value of Melissa's pension benefits.
   b Draw her two-period budget constraint, and label her levels of consumption now and in the future.
   c. Suppose that the future pension benefits and current taxes are eliminated. Draw her two-period budget constraint.
   d. How much does Melissa save?

Step-by-step solution

Step one (a): The present discounted value of her benefit payment is $14,625/(1 + r) = $3,250, which is exactly her taxes.

Step two (b): Draw Melissa's two-period budget constraint. Label the axes "Current consumption" and "Consumption 40 years in the future." The slope is $1 + r$, and the interest rate for the 40-year period is 350 percent. Also, the budget constraint must pass through her current choice: $25,000 now and $14,625 in 40 years.

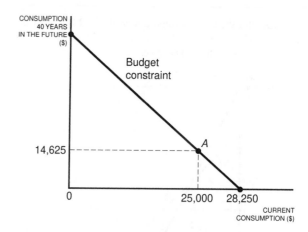

Step three (c): Eliminating pension benefits reduces her future income to $0, but because she no longer pays taxes, her current income rises to $28,250. Because the present discounted value of her two-period income does not change, the budget constraint does not change. (In general, this would shift out the budget constraint for low-income people and shift it in for high-income people.)

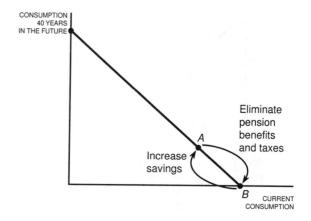

Step four (d): Because Melissa has the same budget constraint, she chooses the same point. This means that she must save $3,250 (which returns $14,625 in 40 years), which is exactly the amount she now pays in taxes. Eliminating pensions and taxes would (for Melissa) lead to the same consumption, but greater savings.

20. (Practice problem: applications) Melissa's uncle is only 10 years from retirement. He can expect to receive $1 in interest for every $1 saved for retirement. He takes home $50,000 annually, saves $10,000, and expects benefits of $20,000 when he retires.

   a. Plot his two-period budget constraint.
   b. Suppose there is a 50 percent increase in benefits. Taxes also rise, so that the budget constraint of Melissa's uncle does not change. How will his savings change? How will his consumption now and during retirement change?

EXPECTED RETURNS

In the two-period budget constraint, there is a single rate of interest, which is known with certainty. But for many financial investments, the investor, at the time he makes the investment, is uncertain about what the returns will be. Good investors think carefully about all the possibilities and calculate the expected return. Tool Kit 8.4 shows you how to do this.

Tool Kit 8.4: Calculating Expected Returns

Follow these steps to calculate an asset's expected return when different returns are possible, each with its own probability.

Step one: Make a three-column table showing all the possible returns in the left-hand column and the corresponding probabilities in the middle column.

Returns	Probability	Product
r_1	P_1	
r_2	P_2	

Step two: Multiply each possible return by its probability, and enter the product in the right-hand column.

Returns	Probability	Product
r_1	P_1	$r_1 \times P_1$
r_2	P_2	$r_2 \times P_2$

Step three: Add the numbers in the right-hand column. The sum is the expected return.

Returns	Probability	Product
r_1	P_1	$r_1 \times P_1$
r_2	P_2	$r_2 \times P_2$

Average returns $= (r_1 \times P_1) + (r_2 \times P_2)$.

---

21. (Worked problem: expected returns) Envious of his brother's life-style, Dr. Mendez is considering investing in one of his brother's real estate ventures. His brother promises a return of 100 percent in one year, but Dr. Mendez thinks the probability that this will happen is only 1/4. More likely (probability = 1/2) is a return of 8 percent. Finally, there is another 1/4 probability that the project will go under and the doctor will lose all his money (return = −100 percent). Calculate the expected return.

Step-by-step solution

Step one: Make a table, and enter the possible returns and the corresponding probabilities.

Returns	Probability	Product
100%	1/4	
8%	1/2	
−100%	1/4	

Step two: Multiply each return by its probability, and enter the result.

Returns	Probability	Product
100%	1/4	25%
8%	1/2	4%
−100%	1/4	−25%

Step three: Add the numbers in the right-hand column.

Returns	Probability	Product
100%	1/4	25%
8%	1/2	4%
−100%	1/4	−25%

Expected returns = 4%.

Thus, in spite of the considerable risk, the investment pays an average of only 4 percent. The good doctor should stick to medicine and put his money in a safe investment.

22. (Practice problem: expected returns) Climax, flush with a consultant's prediction of its future as a high-technology centre, is issuing bonds for a new city government building. The bonds pay 20 percent. Most financial analysts think the probability of default is 1/10. In case of default, the bondholders lose their investments (returns = −100 percent). Calculate the expected return on the Climax bond.

23. (Practice problem: expected returns) Calculate the expected return on each of the following.

a.

Returns	Probability	Product
50%	1/4	
12%	5/8	
−100%	1/8	

b.

Returns	Probability	Product
10%	1/4	
20%	3/4	

c.

Returns	Probability	Product
200%	1/3	
40%	1/3	
−100%	1/3	

d.

Returns	Probability	Product
50%	1/3	
12%	2/3	

24. (Worked problem: expected returns) There are four characteristics of financial investments: expected returns, risk, task treatment, and liquidity. Seeking the best combination of these characteristics, an investor faces trade-offs. The table below gives the returns on six bond issues if there is no default, and also the probabilities of default for each. If there is a default, the investor loses all invested money (return = −100 percent). Also, note that if the probability of default is .1, then the probability of not experiencing a default must be .9.

   a. Compute the expected return for each bond.
   b. Measure risk as the probability of default. Construct the opportunity set, and interpret its outer edge as the risk-return trade-off.

c. Are there any bonds a rational investor would never buy? Why or why not?

Company	Returns (if no default)	Probability of default
Do Music Co.	5%	0
Re Music Co.	19%	.1
Mi Music Co.	30%	.2
Fa Music Co.	12%	.05
Sol Music Co.	8%	.02
Fred's Music Co.	15%	.07

Step-by-step solution

Step one (a): Calculate the expected returns for each bond. Follow the procedure for calculating expected returns.

Do Music Co.	$(5\% \times 1) - (100\% \times 0) = 5\%$.
Re Music Co.	$(19\% \times .9) - (100\% \times .1) = 7.1\%$.
Mi Music Co.	$(30\% \times .8) - (100\% \times .2) = 4\%$.
Fa Music Co.	$(12\% \times .95) - (100 \times .05) = 6.4\%$.
Sol Music Co.	$(8\% \times .98) - (100\% \times .02) = 5.84\%$.
Fred's Music Co.	$(15\% \times .93) - (100\% \times .07) = 6.95\%$.

Step two (b): Plot the expected returns on the vertical axis and risk (measured as the probability of default) on the horizontal. This is the risk-return trade-off.

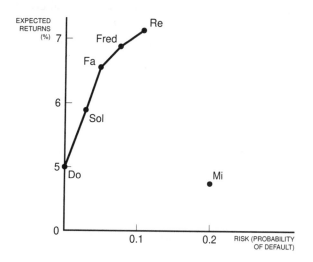

Step three (c): Since Mi Music Company's bonds do not lie on the outer edge, no one will buy them. All of the other issues offer higher average returns and lower risk, as shown in the figure.

25. (Practice problem: expected returns) The four hospitals in Greenville are racing to install the latest medical technologies. Each is trying to raise money in the bond market, and their returns and default risks are given below. If there is a default, the return is –100 percent.

   a Calculate the expected returns for each.
   b Plot the risk-return trade-off.

Hospital	Returns (if no default)	Probability of default
Northside	6%	0
Southside	18%	.09
Eastside	22%	.1
Westside	12%	.05

26. (Practice problem: expected returns) The Kannapans have set aside some money in case of emergency. They are considering where to invest it, but they are concerned about how quickly they will have access to the money when it is needed. The four possible assets, their returns, and the times needed to withdraw the principal (or sell the asset) are given below. Construct the liquidity-return trade-off.

Asset	Returns	Waiting period
Bank account	5%	None
Bond	7%	2 days
Diamonds	4%	1 week
Rental housing	9%	1 month

27. (Worked problem: expected returns) When interest rates rise, bond prices fall. This fact of financial markets follows from the concept of present discounted value. The market price for a bond is the present discounted value of the promised repayments. Bonds issued by Hitek, Inc., promise to pay $100 at the end of the year for 2 years. In addition, the face value equal to $1,000 is repaid at the end of 3 years. The market interest rate is 8 percent.

   a. Calculate the present discounted value of the bond.
   b. The interest rate rises to 10 percent. Recalculate the bond value.

Step-by-step solution

Step one (a): Make a table, and enter the years and the payments.

Year	Amount	Discount factor	Present discounted value
1	$ 100		
2	$ 100		
3	$1,000		

Step two: Calculate and enter the discount factors for each year. For the first year, the discount factor is $1/(1 + .08) = 0.92$. For the second year, it is $1/(1 + .08)^2 = 0.85$, and for the third, it is $1/(1 + .08)^3 = 0.78$.

Step three: Multiply the amounts by the corresponding discount factor. Enter the product in the right-hand column.

Step four: Add the numbers in the right-hand column.

Year	Amount	Discount factor	Present discounted value
1	$ 100	0.92	$ 92
2	$ 100	0.85	$ 85
3	$1,000	0.78	$780

Present discounted value = $957.

Step five (b): Repeat the procedure for a 10 percent interest rate. The table looks like this.

Year	Amount	Discount factor	Present discounted value
1	$ 100	0.90	$ 90
2	$ 100	0.81	$ 81
3	$1,000	0.73	$730

Present discounted value = $901.

The rise in the interest rate from 8 percent to 10 percent causes the bond price to fall by $56 ($957 – $901). It should be clear why ripples in interest rates cause waves in the bond market.

28. (Practice problem: expected returns) Deuce Hardwear, a franchiser of motorcycle clothing, has issued a bond that promises to pay $800 at the end of each of the next two years and $12,000 at the end of the third year. The interest rate is 7 percent.

   a. Calculate the present discounted value of the bond.
   b. The interest rate falls to 6 percent. How much does the price of the bond change?

29. (Practice problem: expected returns) For each of the following, calculate the change in the price of the bond.

   a. The interest rate falls from 10 percent to 8 percent.

Year	Amount	Discount factor	Present discounted value
1	$ 88		
2	$ 88		
3	$1,000		

   Present discounted value = $

   b. The interest rate rises from 10 percent to 13 percent.

Year	Amount	Discount factor	Present discounted value
1	$ 800		
2	$ 700		
3	$13,000		

   Present discounted value = $

Answers to Problems

2. *a.*

Firm	Cost
Do-It-Rite	$200,000

Let-It-Go $100,000 + $\dfrac{\$40,000}{1.08}$ +

$\dfrac{\$40,000}{(1.08)^2} + \dfrac{\$40,000}{(1.08)^3} =$

$203,083.

   b. The Do-It-Rite bid.

3. *a.* $21,488
   b. $18,141
   c. $12,447
   d. $26,358

5.

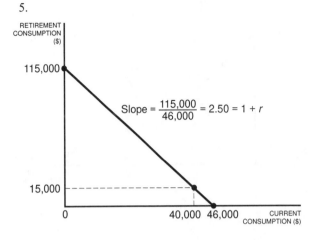

6.

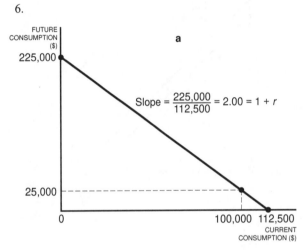

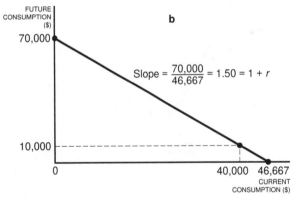

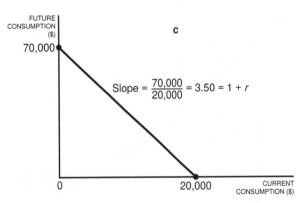

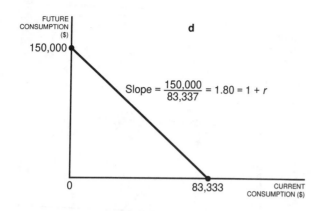

d

FUTURE CONSUMPTION ($)

150,000

Slope = $\frac{150,000}{83,337}$ = 1.80 = 1 + r

0   83,333   CURRENT CONSUMPTION ($)

8.

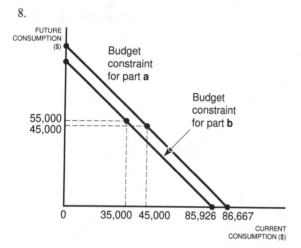

FUTURE CONSUMPTION ($)

Budget constraint for part **a**

Budget constraint for part **b**

55,000
45,000

0   35,000   45,000   85,926   86,667   CURRENT CONSUMPTION ($)

9.

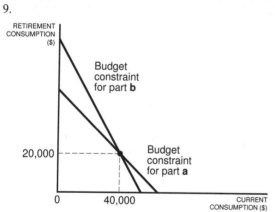

RETIREMENT CONSUMPTION ($)

Budget constraint for part **b**

Budget constraint for part **a**

20,000

0   40,000   CURRENT CONSUMPTION ($)

10.

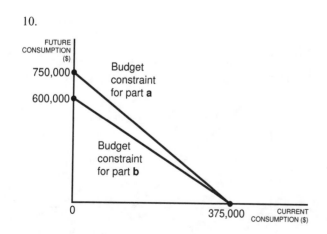

FUTURE CONSUMPTION ($)

750,000
600,000

Budget constraint for part **a**

Budget constraint for part **b**

0   375,000   CURRENT CONSUMPTION ($)

11.

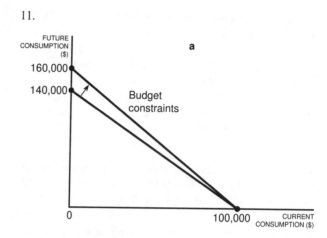

FUTURE CONSUMPTION ($)

a

160,000
140,000

Budget constraints

0   100,000   CURRENT CONSUMPTION ($)

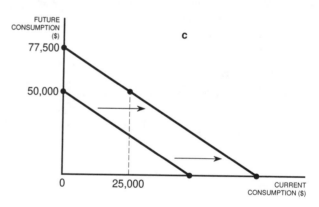

FUTURE CONSUMPTION ($)

b

240,000

140,000
100,000

0   100,000   CURRENT CONSUMPTION ($)

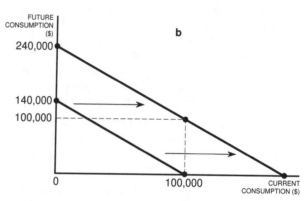

FUTURE CONSUMPTION ($)

c

77,500

50,000

0   25,000   CURRENT CONSUMPTION ($)

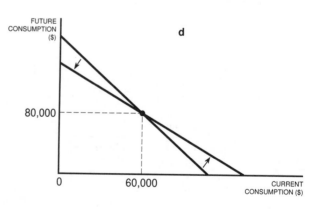

FUTURE CONSUMPTION ($)

d

80,000

0   60,000   CURRENT CONSUMPTION ($)

13.

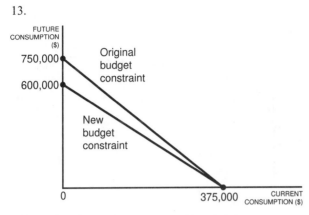

14.

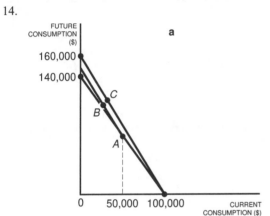

A to B is the substitution effect.
B to C is the income effect.

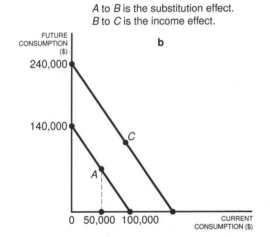

A to C is the income effect.
There is no substitution effect.

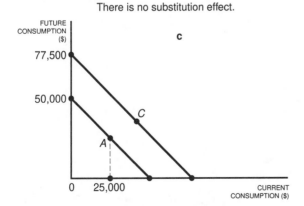

A to C is the income effect.
There is no substitution effect.

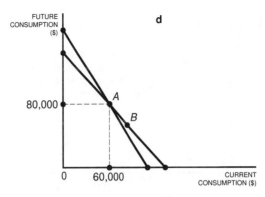

A to B is the substitution effect.
There is no income effect.

16.

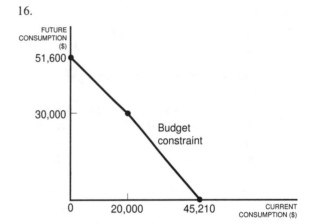

18.

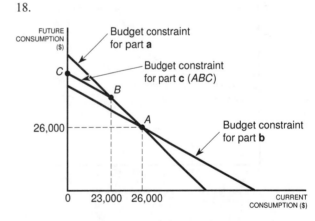

d. If the Johnsons save less than $3,000, the program
has both substitution and income effects. If they save
more than $3,000, there is only an income effect.

20.

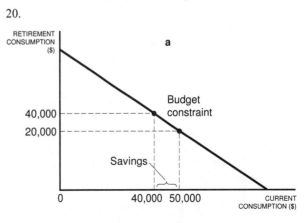

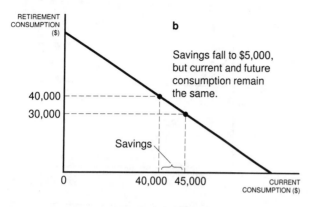

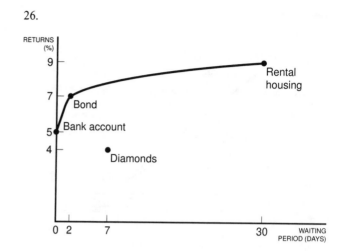

26.

22. Expected return = $(9 \times 20) - (.1 \times 100) = 8\%$.

23. *a.* 7.5%
    b. 17.5%
    c. 46.7%
    d. 24.7%

25. *a.* The expected returns for each bond are given in the table.

Hospital	Returns (if no default)	Probability of default	Expected returns
Northside	6%	0	6%
Southside	18%	0.09	7.38%
Eastside	22%	0.1	9.8%
Westside	12%	0.05	6.4%

28. *a.* Present discounted value = $800/(1.07) + $800/(1.07)^2 + $12,000/(1.07)^3 = $11,243.
    b. Present discounted value = $11,542.

29. *a.* Price of the bond rises from $904 to $950.
    b. Price of the bond falls from $11,073 to $10,263.

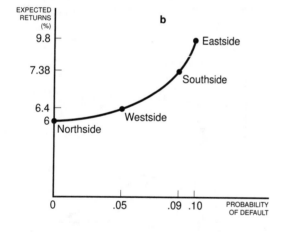

Chapter 9

THE FIRM'S COSTS

Chapter Review

We have now completed the analysis of the households' side of the competitive model. Business enterprises—firms—occupy the other side. This chapter begins the discussion of the role of firms in a market-based economy. We learn about the production function, which summarizes the relationship between the inputs that the firm demands (especially in the labour market) and the outputs that it supplies in the product market. Payments for inputs make up most of the firm's costs, and this chapter treats these costs in depth. How the costs are balanced against revenue is the subject of Chapter 10.

ESSENTIAL CONCEPTS

1. In the basic competitive model, the firm's objective is to maximize its market value. Because the value of the firm depends on its profit-making potential, another way to put this is to say the firm's objective is to maximize its (long-term) profits. **Profits** equal revenue minus costs, and revenue is simply price times quantity.

2. The **production function** shows the relationship between inputs and outputs. The increase in output resulting from a small increase in the use of an input is called the **marginal product**. The **principle of diminishing returns** states that as more of one input is used, holding other inputs fixed, the marginal product declines. While diminishing returns represent the usual case, some production functions exhibit **increasing returns,** where the marginal product increases as more of an input is used. If doubling the input doubles the output, then there are **constant returns.** When the quantity of an input does not depend on the level of output, the input is called a **fixed input;** when the quantity varies with output, it is called a **variable input.**

3. There are costs associated with each type of input: either **fixed costs,** which do not change when output changes, or **variable costs,** which do. The important concept to grasp is how the various measures of costs change as output changes. The **average cost** curve is typically U-shaped; the **marginal cost** curve lies below it when average cost falls, equals average cost at minimum average cost, and lies above it when average cost increases.

4. The **principle of substitution** says that as the price of an

input increases, firms substitute other inputs. The firm always chooses the least-cost production technique. In the long run, all inputs are variable; the firm has more choices. The **long-run average cost curve** is the lower boundary of all possible short-run average cost curves.

5. In the long run, there are **constant returns to scale** if output increases in proportion with an increase in all inputs. If output increases by less, there are **decreasing returns to scale**. **Increasing returns to scale** imply that output increases by a greater proportion than do inputs. **Economies of scope** refer to the cost savings from producing several goods together rather than separately.

BEHIND THE ESSENTIAL CONCEPTS

1. Of the many diagrams in this chapter, there are four that you should particularly take care to master. Each is explained below. Notice how the economic idea (such as diminishing returns or increasing returns to scale) determines the shape of the curves.

   a. The first diagram to master is the production function (Figure 9.1, which is similar to Figure 9.3 in the text). The production function indicates how output (measured on the vertical axis) changes as the quantity of the variable input (measured on the horizontal axis) changes. There are two important facts to know. The first is that the shape indicates whether the production function has diminishing, constant, or increasing returns. Over the range of outputs for which the function in Figure 9.1 is drawn, there are diminishing returns. Also, the slope of the line from the origin to the curve is equal to the average product. The slope of the line drawn in Figure 9.1 therefore measures average product at L_1. Average product is actually at its highest at L_1; that is, the slope of this line is steeper than any other you can draw through the origin to any other point on the production function. If this is not obvious to you, you should try drawing additional lines through the origin to other points on the function to demonstrate it to yourself.

   b. The total cost curves are shown in Figure 9.2 (which summarizes Figure 9.4 A, B, and C of the text). Output is measured along the horizontal axis, and cost along the vertical one. Again, there are two important features to observe. First, total cost is the sum of fixed and variable costs. By definition, fixed costs do not change (otherwise they would not be fixed!). It follows that the variable cost curve and the total cost curve will be parallel to one another, since the difference between them is the total of the fixed costs. The second feature is that the total cost curve inherits its shape from the production function. This will be explored in the analysis part of this chapter.

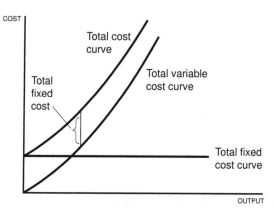

Figure 9.2

   c. Third, there is the average cost–marginal cost diagram, shown in Figure 9.3 (which duplicates Figure 9.5 in the text). The important concept here is the relationship between the marginal and average cost curves. The average cost curve is typically U-shaped. When marginal cost is below average cost, average cost is downward-sloping. Marginal cost equals average cost at the minimum of average cost, and marginal cost is above average cost when average cost is upward-sloping. Average cost falls as fixed costs are spread over more units. Average cost rises because diminishing returns drive the marginal cost curve above the average cost curve.

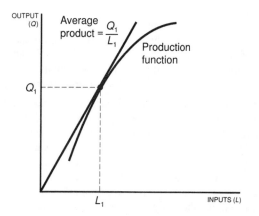

Figure 9.1

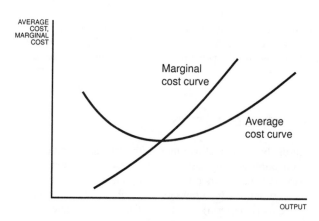

Figure 9.3

d.. Finally, there is the long-run average cost curve. For every production process, there are fixed inputs and an associated average cost curve. The long-run average cost curve is the lower boundary, as shown in Figure 9.4 (which duplicates Figure 9.12 in the text). The curve is drawn flat, which represents constant returns to scale.

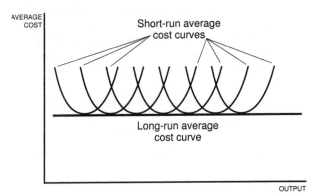

Figure 9.4

2. In reviewing these four diagrams, keep in mind three pointers.

   a. Remember to note what is measured along each axis. It's easy to make the mistake of memorizing the shapes of the curves while forgetting how to label the axes.

   b. Note the relationships among the curves, especially the marginal cost and average cost relationship.

   c. The shapes of the curves illustrate the economic properties. It's important to be able to recognize economic properties like diminishing returns and economies of scale in the diagrams of production functions and cost curves.

3. Diminishing returns refer to production processes in which some, but not all, inputs are variable. Diminishing returns imply that the marginal product decreases as more inputs are used. Economists add the words "to scale" when describing a production process in which all inputs are variable. Thus, decreasing returns to scale mean that as all inputs are increased by a certain proportion, output increases by less than that proportion.

SELF-TEST

True or False

1. In the basic competitive model, firms are assumed to maximize the value of the firm.

2. Firms in competitive markets are price takers.

3. The marginal product is the last unit of output produced.

4. If all inputs are increased by 10 percent and output rises by less than 10 percent, this represents an example of the principle of diminishing returns.

5. If there are constant returns to scale, average and marginal cost are constant.

6. Costs associated with inputs that change as output changes are called variable costs.

7. Total costs are the sum of average and marginal costs.

8. If labour is the only variable input, then average cost equals the wage divided by the marginal product.

9. Average fixed cost does not vary with output.

10. If marginal cost is rising, average cost must be rising too.

11. The average cost curve intersects the marginal cost curve at the minimum of the marginal cost curve.

12. If the price of an input rises, the firm will substitute other inputs to some extent, but its cost curves will still shift up.

13. Short-run average cost curves are typically U-shaped.

14. If there are economies of scale, the long-run average cost curve slopes downwards.

15. When there are economies of scope, producing a set of goods together is less expensive than producing each of them separately.

Multiple Choice

1. In the basic competitive model, a firm that charges more than the going price:

   a. will lose some of its customers.
   b. faces a downward-sloping demand curve.
   c. will lose all of its customers.
   d. faces a perfectly inelastic demand curve.
   e. will lose none of its customers.

2. Total profit equals:

   a. revenue minus fixed cost.
   b. price minus marginal cost.
   c. revenue minus variable cost.
   d. price minus average cost.
   e. revenue minus total cost.

3. The marginal product of an input is the :

   a. cost of the units of the input that must be hired to produce one more unit of output.
   b. number of units of output produced when one more unit of the input is hired.
   c. cost of hiring one more unit of the input.
   d. total output divided by the total number of units of the input.
   e. number of units of the input that must be hired to produce one more unit of output.

4. If a firm's production function exhibits diminishing returns to labour, this means that when labour is increased with all other inputs held constant:

   a. marginal cost falls.
   b. the average product of labour falls.
   c. total output falls.
   d. the marginal product of labour falls.
   e. average cost falls.

5. If a firm's production function exhibits initially increasing returns and then diminishing returns to labour, this means that when labour is increased with all other inputs held constant, the marginal and average products of labour both initially:

   a. increase and then decrease, with marginal product being the first to begin falling.
   b. decrease and then increase, with marginal product being the first to begin rising.
   c. increase and then decrease, with both beginning to fall simultaneously.
   d. decrease and then increase, with average product being the first to begin rising.
   e. increase and then decrease, with average product being the first to begin falling.

6. Fixed inputs are inputs that:

   a. are bolted down.
   b. can be purchased at a fixed price.
   c. can be purchased only in certain quantities.
   d. do not vary with the level of output.
   e. must not be moved.

7. Fixed costs:
   I. are the costs associated with fixed inputs.
   II. do not change with the level of output.
   Which of the following is true?

   a. I is correct; II is incorrect.
   b. I is incorrect; II is correct.
   c. Both I and II are correct.
   d. Neither I nor II is correct.
   e. Either I or II is correct, but not both simultaneously.

8. Marginal cost is the:

   a. wage divided by the marginal product.
   b. wage multiplied by the marginal product.
   c. average product divided by the marginal product.
   d. wage multiplied by the average product.
   e. wage divided by the average product.

9. If a firm's production function exhibits diminishing returns to labour, this means that when labour is increased with all other inputs held constant, marginal product:

   a. rises and marginal cost falls.
   b. and marginal cost both fall.
   c. rises but marginal cost is unaffected.
   d. and marginal cost both rise.
   e. falls and marginal cost rises.

10. When marginal cost exceeds average cost, average cost is:

    a. at its minimum.
    b. rising.
    c. equal to zero.
    d. falling.
    e. at its maximum.

11. When marginal cost is below average cost, average cost is:

    a. at its minimum.
    b. rising.
    c. equal to zero.

    d. falling.
    e. at its maximum.

12. What is the defining difference between the long run and the short run?

    a. The big run is six months longer than the short run.
    b. In the short run, there are constant returns; in the long run, there are diminishing returns.
    c. In the short run, some inputs are fixed; in the long run, all inputs can be varied.
    d. In the short run, average cost is falling; in the long run, it is constant.
    e. The long run is 32 kilometres longer than the short run.

13. In the short run, the typical average cost curve is:

    a. upward-sloping.
    b. horizontal.
    c. vertical.
    d. U-shaped.
    e. downward-sloping.

14. Which of the following statements is true?

    a. All fixed costs are overhead costs; not all overhead costs are fixed costs.
    b. All overhead costs are fixed costs; not all fixed costs are overhead costs.
    c. Overhead costs are never fixed costs; fixed costs are never overhead costs.
    d. The term "overhead costs" is just another name for fixed costs.
    e. None of the above statements is true.

15. The long-run total cost curve is:

    a. the upper boundary of the short-run total cost curves.
    b. horizontal.
    c. the sum of the short-run total cost curves.
    d. U-shaped.
    e. the lower boundary of the short-run total cost curves.

16. The long-run average cost curve is:

    a. upward-sloping.
    b. the upper boundary of the short-run average cost curves.
    c. horizontal.
    d. the lower boundary of the short-run average cost curves.
    e. downward-sloping.

17. If the firm's production function exhibits constant returns to scale:

    a. it is less expensive to produce a variety of goods together than to produce them separately.
    b. when all inputs are increased, output rises less than proportionately.
    c. when all inputs are increased, output rises in proportion.
    d. when all inputs are increased, output rises more than proportionately.
    e. the marginal product of the variable input rises as more of the input is used.

18. If the firm's production function exhibits increasing returns to scale, the long-run average cost curve is:

 a. upward-sloping.
 b. horizontal.
 c. vertical.
 d. U-shaped.
 e. downward-sloping.

19. If the firm's production function exhibits decreasing returns to scale, the long-run marginal cost curve is:

 a. upward-sloping and lies above the long-run average cost curve.
 b. upward-sloping and lies below the long-run average cost curve.
 c. horizontal and coincides with the long-run average cost curve.
 d. downward-sloping and lies below the long-run average cost curve.
 e. downward-sloping and lies above the long-run average cost curve.

20. If a firm can take advantage of economies of scope:

 a. it is more expensive to produce a variety of goods together than to produce them separately.
 b. marginal cost falls as more output is produced.
 c. average cost falls as more output is produced.
 d. overhead costs fall as more output is produced.
 e. it is less expensive to produce a variety of goods together than to produce them separately.

Completion

1. The relationship between the inputs used in production and the level of output is called the _____.

2. The increase in output that results from using one more unit of an input is the _____.

3. The principle of _____ says that as more and more of one input is added, while other inputs remain unchanged, the marginal product of the added input diminishes.

4. Costs that do not depend upon output are called _____ costs.

5. The _____ is the extra cost of producing one more unit of output.

6. The marginal cost curve intersects the average cost curve at the _____ of the average cost curve.

7. If marginal cost is above average cost, then producing an additional unit will _____ average cost.

8. An increase in the price of one input will lead a firm to substitute other inputs. This is a statement of the _____ of _____.

9. If the average cost is lower when the firm produces a larger quantity, then there are economies of _____.

10. If it is less expensive to produce a variety of goods together than to produce each good separately, then there are economies of _____.

Answers to Self-Test

True or False

1. t	4. f	7. f	10. f	13. t
2. t	5. t	8. f	11. f	14. t
3. f	6. t	9. f	12. t	15. t

Multiple Choice

1. c	6. d	11. d	16. d
2. e	7. c	12. c	17. c
3. b	8. a	13. d	18. e
4. d	9. e	14. b	19. a
5. a	10. b	15. e	20. e

Completion

1. production function
2. marginal product
3. diminishing returns
4. fixed
5. marginal cost
6. minimum
7. increase
8. principle of substitution
9. scale
10. scope

Doing Economics: Tools and Practice Problems

There is quite a bit of technical detail in this chapter, including production functions and a host of cost curves. First, we explore the production function, calculating the marginal and average product and plotting the curves. It is important to understand how the shape of the production function exhibits diminishing, constant, or increasing returns. Next, we turn our attention to the cost curves; we calculate the various cost concepts and plot the curves. Again, it is important to understand the relationships between the curves and the economic meaning of the shapes of the curves.

AVERAGE AND MARGINAL PRODUCT

The production function summarizes the relationship between inputs and output. It shows the level of output that results from the efficient use of each possible quantity of the inputs. Average and marginal products are two concepts closely related to the production function. The average product of an input is simply output per unit of the input. An input's marginal product is the extra output produced when one additional unit of the input is used in the production process. Table 9.1 describes the relationships among the production function, the average product, and the marginal product. Once we know the production function, we can obtain the average product and marginal product for an input. Tool Kit 9.1 shows you how to do this.

**Table 9.1
Production Function**

The marginal product is the slope of the production
  function:
  marginal product = change in output/change in number
    of units of input.
The average product is the slope of a line from the origin
  to the production function:
  average product = output/input.
If returns are diminishing:
  the marginal product is decreasing.
  the slope of the production function is becoming flatter.
If returns are constant:
  the marginal product is constant.
  the slope of the production function is constant.
If returns are increasing:
  the marginal product is increasing.
  the slope of the production function is becoming steeper.

Tool Kit 9.1: Calculating Average
and Marginal Products

Follow these steps to learn how you determine an
input's average and marginal products when you
know the production function.

Step one: Identify and graph the production function.

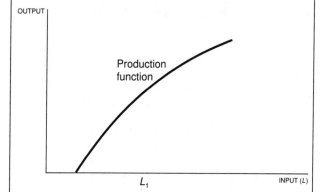

Step two: Calculate the average product, which is output per unit of the input:

average product = output/number of units of input.

The average product is the slope of a line from the
origin to the production function.

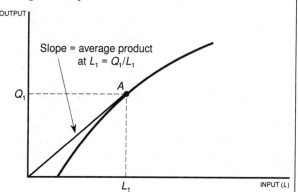

Step three: Calculate the marginal product, which is
the extra output resulting from the use of one more
unit of the input:

marginal product = change in output/change in input.

The marginal product equals the slope of the production function.

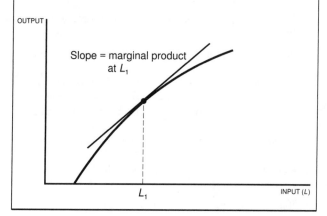

1. (Worked problem: average and marginal products) Table
   9.2 gives the production function for keyboards at Tek-
   Tek computer products.

Table 9.2

Number of workers	Output	Average product	Marginal product
1	80		
2	150		
3	210		
4	260		
5	300		

a. Compute the average and marginal product, and fill
   in the table.
b. Plot the production function. For each point, verify
   that the slope of the line from the origin to the production function equals the average product.
c. Between each two adjacent points on the production
   function, verify that the slope equals the marginal
   product.
d. Does the production function exhibit diminishing,
   constant, or increasing returns?

Step-by-step solution

Step one (a): Identify the production function. This is given
in Table 9.2.

Step two: Calculate and graph the average product. The average product is output divided by the number of workers. If
output is 80, the average product is 80/1 = 80. Enter this
number. If output is 150, the average product is 150/2 = 75.
Complete the average product column. The result is given in
Table 9.3.

Step three: Calculate the marginal product. The marginal product is the extra output resulting from using one more input. The marginal product of the first worker is 80. Enter this number. When the second worker is used, output rises to 150. The marginal product of this worker is 150 – 80 = 70. Enter this number. Complete the marginal product column. Table 9.3 gives the result.

Table 9.3

Number of workers	Output	Average product	Marginal product
1	80	80	80
2	150	75	70
3	210	70	60
4	260	65	50
5	300	60	40

Step four (b): Plot the production function.

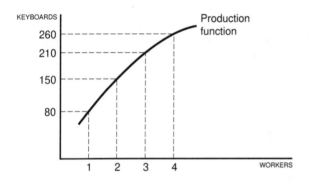

Step five: Choose a point on the production function, and verify that the slope of a line from the origin to that point is equal to the average product. Choose the point labelled *A,* where output is 210 and the number of workers is 3. Draw a line from the origin to point *A.* The slope is rise/run = 210/3 = 70, which is the average product.

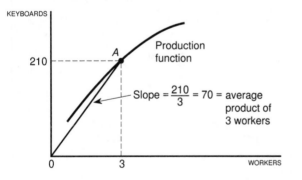

Step six (c): Verify that the slope of the production function is the marginal product. Consider the effect of adding an additional worker when moving from point *A,* where the firm is employing 3 workers and producing 210 keyboards. This takes the firm to point *B,* where the firm is employing 4

workers and producing 260 keyboards. The slope of the production function is therefore (260 – 210)/(4 – 3) = 50, which is indeed the marginal product of the fourth worker (see Table 9.3).

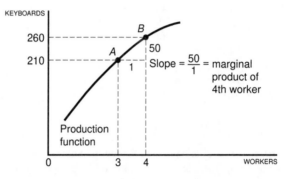

Step seven (d): When a fifth worker is added to the production process, this yields a marginal product of (300 – 260)/(5 – 4) = 40. Marginal product is falling; this means there are diminishing returns to labour.

2. (Practice problem: average and marginal products) Table 9.4 gives the production function for the insect spray Nobeetle at Bugout Pesticide Company.

Table 9.4

Number of workers	Output	Average product	Marginal product
1	1,200		
2	2,200		
3	3,000		
4	3,600		
5	4,000		

a. Compute the average and marginal products, and fill in the table.
b. Plot the production function. For each point, verify that the slope of the line from the origin to the production function equals the average product.
c. Between each two adjacent points on the production function, verify that the slope equals the marginal product.
d. Does the production function exhibit diminishing, constant, or increasing returns?

3. (Practice problem: average and marginal products) For the following production functions, answer parts a through d in problem 2.

a. Bedford Waterbeds

Number of workers	Output	Average product	Marginal product
1	24		
2	42		
3	57		
4	68		
5	75		

b. Worry-Free Insurance

Number of sellers	Policies	Average product	Marginal product
10	200		
20	500		
30	700		
40	800		
50	850		

COST CURVES

A firm's costs are its payments for inputs. Some of the inputs are fixed (their levels are independent of output) and the costs of these inputs are called fixed costs; some inputs are variable (their levels vary with output) and their costs are called variable costs. Average and marginal costs are two concepts closely related to total cost. Average cost is simply total cost per unit of output. Marginal cost is the extra cost of producing one more unit of output. Table 9.2 described the relationships among total cost, average cost, and marginal cost. Once we know total cost, we can obtain the average cost and marginal cost for any level of output. Tool Kit 9.2 shows you how to do this, and Table 9.5 summarizes the key information about cost curves.

Table 9.5
Cost Curves

Variable cost is parallel to the total cost curve, and below it by the amount of fixed cost:
   variable cost = total cost − fixed cost.
Marginal cost is the slope of the total cost curve:
   marginal cost = change in total cost/change in output.
Average cost is the slope of the line from the origin to the total cost curve:
   average cost = total cost/output.
If returns are diminishing:
   the marginal cost is increasing.
   the slope of the total cost curve is becoming steeper.
If returns are constant:
   the marginal cost is constant.
   the slope of the total cost curve is constant.
If returns are increasing:
   the marginal cost is decreasing.
   the slope of the total cost curve is becoming flatter.
If marginal cost is below average cost:
   the average cost curve is decreasing.
If marginal cost equals average cost:
   the average cost curve is at its minimum.
If marginal cost is above average cost:
   the average cost curve is increasing.

Tool Kit 9.2: Cost Curves

Following these steps will help you to identify the components of total cost—variable cost and fixed cost—and to understand the relationship between total cost and average and marginal costs.

Step one: Identify and graph the total cost curve.

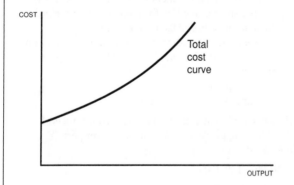

Step two: Calculate and graph the variable cost curve:

   variable cost = total cost − fixed cost.

The variable cost curve is parallel to the total cost curve, and lies below it by the amount of fixed costs.

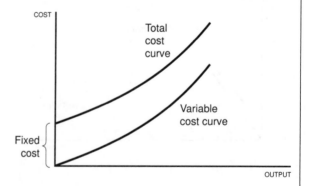

Step three: Calculate and graph the average cost curve: average cost = total cost/output.

Average cost equals the slope of a line from the origin to the total cost curve.

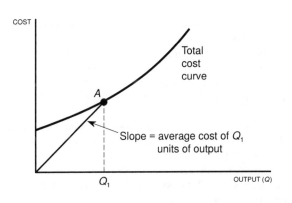

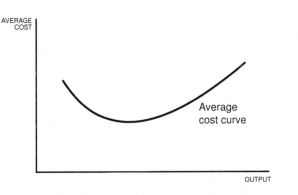

Step four: Calculate and graph the marginal cost curve: marginal cost = change in cost/change in output.

Marginal cost is the slope of the total cost curve.

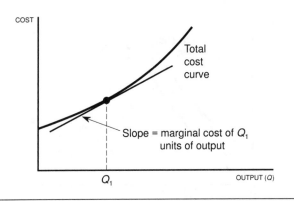

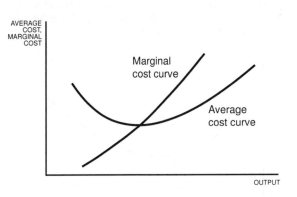

4. (Worked problem: cost curves) The total fixed costs at Stay-Brite Cleaning Company are $100,000. Table 9.6 gives their total costs for different levels of output measured in truckloads of Stay-Brite Cleaning Solution.

Table 9.6

Output	Total cost	Variable cost	Average cost	Marginal cost
1,000	$180,000			
2,000	$280,000			
3,000	$420,000			
4,000	$600,000			
5,000	$800,000			

a. Compute variable, average, and marginal cost, and enter in the table.
b. Plot the total cost and variable cost curves on one diagram, and verify the relationships given in Table 9.5.
c. Plot the average cost and marginal cost curves, and verify the marginal-average relationship.
d. Do the cost curves exhibit increasing, constant, or diminishing returns?

Step-by-step solution

Step one (a): Identify and graph the total cost curve.

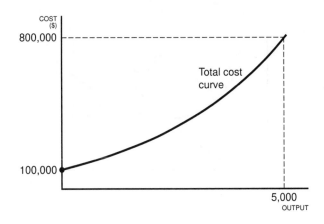

Step two: Calculate and graph the variable cost curve. Variable cost is just the difference between total cost and total fixed cost. The variable cost of 1,000 units is $180,000 − $100,000 = $80,000. Enter this number. Complete the variable cost column.

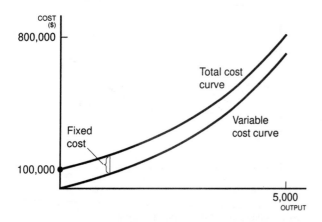

Step three: Calculate and graph the average cost curve. Average cost is total cost divided by output. The average cost of 1,000 units is $180,000/1,000 = $180. Enter this number. Complete the average cost column.

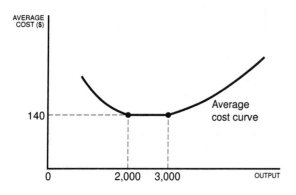

Step four: Calculate and graph the marginal cost curve. Marginal cost is the extra cost of producing one more unit. The marginal cost per unit for the first 1,000 units is $80,000/1,000 = $80. Enter this number, and continue to fill in the column. The complete information appears in Table 9.7.

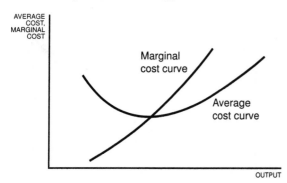

Table 9.7

Output	Total cost	Variable cost	Average cost	Marginal cost
1,000	$180,000	$ 80,000	$180	$ 80
2,000	$280,000	$180,000	$140	$100
3,000	$420,000	$320,000	$140	$140
4,000	$600,000	$500,000	$150	$180
5,000	$800,000	$700,000	$160	$200

Step five (b): Choose a point on the total cost curve, and verify the relationships.

Variable cost is parallel to total cost. For example, between *A* and *B*, the slope of the total cost curve is ($600,000 − $420,000)/(4,000 − 3,000) = 180. The slope of the variable cost curve for the same levels of output is ($500,000 − $320,000)/(4,000 − 3,000) = 180.

The variable cost curve lies below the total cost curve by the amount of the fixed cost. The difference all along the curves is $100,000, which is the fixed cost.

The slope of the total cost curve equals the marginal cost. Between *A* and *B*, the slope is 180, which is the marginal cost at 4,000 workers.

The slope of a line from the origin to the total cost curve equals average cost. At point *A*, the slope of the line is $420,000/3,000 = 140, which is the average cost.

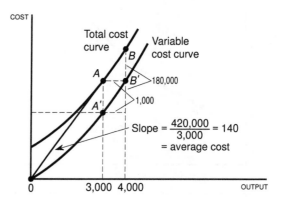

Step six (c): Plot the average and marginal cost curves, and verify the average-marginal relationship. As you can see, marginal cost is below average cost at *A*, where average cost is falling; they are equal at *B*, which is the minimum of average cost; and marginal cost is above average cost at *C*, where average cost is rising.

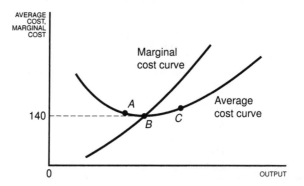

Step seven: The cost curves exhibit diminishing returns. Marginal cost is increasing, and total cost is becoming steeper.

5. (Practice problem: cost curves). The fixed costs at Pestle Mortar Company are $50,000. Table 9.8 gives their costs for different levels of output.

Table 9.8

Output	Total cost	Variable cost	Average cost	Marginal cost
1,000	$ 250,000			
2,000	$ 500,000			
3,000	$ 800,000			
4,000	$1,200,000			
5,000	$1,800,000			

a. Compute variable, average, and marginal costs, and enter in the table.

b. Plot the total cost and variable cost curves on one diagram, and verify the relationships given in Table 9.5.

c. Plot the average cost and marginal cost curves, and verify the marginal-average relationship.

d. Do the cost curves exhibit increasing, constant, or diminishing returns?

6. (Practice problem: cost curves) For the following cost data, answer parts a through d in question 5.

a. Fixed costs are $1,000.

Output	Total cost	Variable cost	Average cost	Marginal cost
10	$1,500			
20	$2,200			
30	$3,000			
40	$4,000			
50	$6,000			

b. Fixed costs are $0.

Output	Total cost	Variable cost	Average cost	Marginal cost
100	$1,000			
200	$1,800			
300	$2,400			
400	$2,800			
500	$3,200			
600	$3,600			

c. Fixed costs are $80,000.

Output	Total cost	Variable cost	Average cost	Marginal cost
1	$140,000			
2	$180,000			
3	$220,000			
4	$260,000			
5	$300,000			
6	$340,000			

Answers to Problems

2. a. The marginal and average products are given in Table 9.9.

Table 9.9

Number of workers	Output	Average product	Marginal product
1	1,200	1,200	1,200
2	2,200	1,100	1,000
3	3,000	1,000	800
4	3,600	900	600
5	4,000	800	400

b. The production function is drawn in the figure. The average product for 3 workers, which is 1,000, is shown as the slope of the line from the origin to point B. The average product for 4 workers is similarly the slope of a line from the origin to point C.

c. The marginal product of the fourth worker, which is 600, is the slope between points B and C.

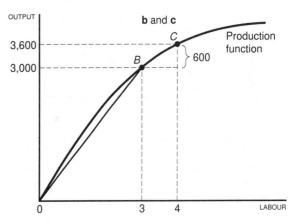

d. The production function exhibits diminishing returns.

3. a. Bedford Waterbeds—diminishing returns

Number of workers	Output	Average product	Marginal product
1	24	24	24
2	42	21	18
3	57	19	15
4	68	17	11
5	75	15	7

b. Worry-Free Insurance—diminishing returns

Number of sellers	Policies	Average product	Marginal product
10	200	20.0	20
20	500	25.0	30
30	700	23.3	20
40	800	20.0	10
50	850	17.0	5

5 a. The completed table is given in Table 9.10.

Table 9.10

Output	Total cost	Variable cost	Average cost	Marginal cost
1,000	$ 250,000	$ 200,000	$250	$200
2,000	$ 500,000	$ 450,000	$250	$250
3,000	$ 800,000	$ 750,000	$267	$300
4,000	$1,200,000	$1,150,000	$300	$400
5,000	$1,800,000	$1,750,000	$360	$600

b. The diagram shows the total cost and variable cost curves. The variable cost curve is parallel and lies below the total cost curve by $50,000, which is the amount of fixed cost.

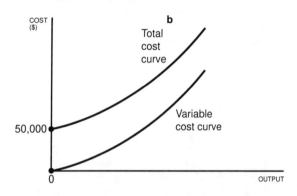

c. The diagram shows the average and marginal cost curves. Average and marginal costs are equal at $250, which is the minimum of the average cost curve. Average cost rises after this point, and marginal cost lies above average cost.

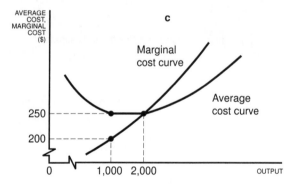

d. The cost curves exhibit diminishing returns.

6. The completed cost tables appear below.

a. These cost curves show diminishing returns.

Output	Total cost	Variable cost	Average cost	Marginal cost
10	$1,500	$ 500	$150	$ 50
20	$2,200	$1,200	$110	$ 70
30	$3,000	$2,000	$100	$ 80
40	$4,000	$3,000	$100	$100
50	$6,000	$5,000	$120	$200

b. These cost curves show increasing returns.

Output	Total cost	Variable cost	Average cost	Marginal cost
100	$1,000	$1,000	$10.00	$10
200	$1,800	$1,800	$ 9.00	$ 8
300	$2,400	$2,400	$ 8.00	$ 6
400	$2,800	$2,800	$ 7.00	$ 4
500	$3,200	$3,200	$ 6.50	$ 4
600	$3,600	$3,600	$ 6.00	$ 4

c. These cost curves show increasing returns until output equals 2, and constant returns thereafter.

Output	Total cost	Variable cost	Average cost	Marginal cost
1	$140,000	$ 60,000	$140,000	$60,000
2	$180,000	$100,000	$ 90,000	$40,000
3	$220,000	$140,000	$ 73,333	$40,000
4	$260,000	$180,000	$ 65,000	$40,000
5	$300,000	$220,000	$ 60,000	$40,000
6	$340,000	$260,000	$ 56,667	$40,000

Chapter 10

PRODUCTION IN A COMPETITIVE INDUSTRY

Chapter Review

This chapter moves the discussion from firms' costs to decisions firms must make regarding production. In the process, it shows the role of the firm in the competitive model. The firm is a supplier in product markets and a demander in input markets, especially in the labour market. The chapter also explains why and when new firms will enter an industry and why and when existing firms will shut down. Each of these issues requires carefully distinguishing opportunity costs from sunk costs, and profits from rents. This close examination of the firm's production decision completes the discussion of all the individual parts of the basic competitive model that began in Chapter 6. What remains is to put them together and evaluate how the model works. This is done in Chapter 11.

ESSENTIAL CONCEPTS

1. Firms choose output to **maximize profit.** Profit is the difference between total revenue and total costs. The output decision can be illustrated in two ways. One way, shown in Figure 10.1A, is to draw the total revenue and total cost curves and find the output where the total revenue curve is above the total cost curve by the greatest amount. At this point, the curves are parallel and their slopes are equal. The second way, shown in panel B, uses the marginal revenue curve. The slope of the total revenue curve is marginal revenue, which for the competitive firm equals the price of its product. The slope of the total cost curve is marginal cost. Therefore, at this point, marginal revenue (price) equals marginal cost, and profit maximization can be shown by the intersection of these two curves.

2. Entry of new firms occurs whenever the price exceeds minimum average cost, or equivalently, when revenue exceeds total cost (including all opportunity costs). Entering firms can earn higher profits in this industry than elsewhere in the economy. As more firms enter, price falls. In the long run, price falls to the point where it equals minimum average cost for the least efficient firm. For this firm, all costs, including opportunity costs, are just being covered.

3. In deciding whether to exit from a market, a firm must consider which costs it can recover. Costs that the firm must pay whether or not it leaves the market are called **sunk costs.** The firm should stay in the market whenever it can earn revenues greater than all the costs not sunk. If all the fixed costs are nonrecoverable sunk costs, then

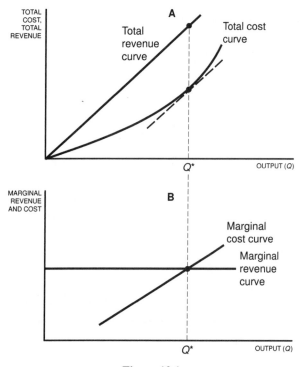

Figure 10.1

the firm will exit when price falls below the minimum of the average variable cost curve.

4. The **supply curve of the firm** is the marginal cost curve above the minimum price needed to keep the firm from exiting. The **market supply curve** is the sum of the quantities supplied by all firms in the market, and it takes into account both the adjustments made by existing firms and the new entrants attracted to the market as the price rises. This curve is more elastic in the long run than in the short run, because existing firms have time to adjust to the lowest-cost production techniques and new firms have time to enter the market and produce.

5. The firm's demand for inputs follows from its decision about how much to produce. More formally, the demand for an input is the **value of its marginal product,** which equals its marginal product (how much extra output the marginal input produces) times the product price (how much revenue the firm receives in selling each unit of the output). Again, the market demand is just the sum of the quantities demanded by all firms in the market. Because labour is by far the most important input in production, it is used as the main example of an input in the text. Nevertheless, the demand for any input is the value of its marginal product.

BEHIND THE ESSENTIAL CONCEPTS

1. Production costs include all opportunity costs of production borne by the firm. Not only are such explicit costs as wages, energy, raw materials, and interest included,

but also **opportunity costs** are taken into account, such as the value of the entrepreneur's time or the alternative earnings on the equity invested by the owners of the firm. These are considered opportunity costs because if the firm did not produce, the entrepreneur would devote time to some other activity, and the owners would take their investment capital elsewhere.

When a firm is making zero **economic** profits, its revenues are sufficient to cover all costs, including normal returns on the invested financial capital. An economist would say that the firm is making just enough to compensate the owners for the opportunity cost of putting their money into the firm. An accountant would view the situation differently, saying that a firm earning normal returns was actually making positive accounting profits.

2. Another difference between the way economists and accountants view profits concerns rent. **Rent** is the return to anything that is supplied inelastically. For example, suppose a firm's superior location enables it to earn 50 percent more than its competitors. An accountant would say that this firm's profits are 50 percent higher. An economist would call this extra return a rent, because the firm's earnings are higher than the minimum necessary to induce it to stay in its location. Although land is a good example, the concept of rent applies to any payment to a factor of production above the minimum necessary to bring the factor on to the market.

3. Sunk costs and fixed costs are related to, but distinct from, each other. **Sunk costs** cannot be recovered no matter what the firm does. The firm can shut down production, sell off all its assets, and even go out of business, but it cannot recover its sunk costs. **Fixed costs** do not change as output changes, but they may be recoverable if the firm exits the industry. For example, the firm may own a plant, and the alternative earnings (the opportunity cost) of its plant do not depend on whether the firm produces a little or a great deal of output. If the firm can sell the factory when it exits the industry, then the costs of the plant are fixed but not sunk.

4. There is only one way to maximize profits. If the firm produces goods for the least cost and sets price equal to marginal cost, then it must set the input price equal to the value of the marginal product of that input. Thus, the profit-maximizing demand for labour is just the other side of the coin of the profit-maximizing supply of output. This fact is illustrated in Figure 10.2, where in panel A the firm sets the product price equal to marginal cost and produces Q^* units of output. (Note that this is the usual diagram turned on its side.) The production function, drawn in panel B, shows that this level of output requires L^* hours of labour. Finally, panel C shows that when the firm sets the wage equal to the value of the marginal product of labour, it chooses exactly L^* hours of labour.

5. The competitive firm has four basic decisions to make: when to enter, when to exit, how much to produce, and how many inputs to hire. Table 10.1 summarizes the decision rules.

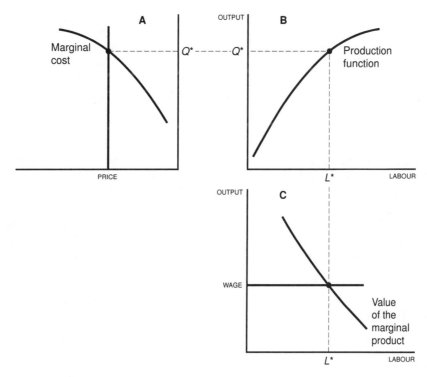

Figure 10.2

Table 10.1

Entry	Enter when price > minimum average cost.
Exit	Exit when revenues < recoverable costs.
Supply	Produce the quantity of output for which price equals marginal cost.
Demand	Hire the input up to the point where the input price equals the value of the marginal product.

6. The theory of contestable markets argues that entry is not required to drive price down to minimum average cost, so long as sunk costs are low. The threat of entry is sufficient to keep the firm from pushing up its price. If sunk costs are high, however, the threat of competition diminishes. Firms considering entry reason that the existing firm(s) could drive price below average cost but still find it worthwhile to continue to produce, and thereby make life very uncomfortable for the new entrant. So long as the firm does not enter, it does not incur the sunk costs. In this case, the prospect of bearing these costs serves as a deterrent to entry.

SELF-TEST

True or False

1. The firm's profit-maximizing level of output occurs when price equals marginal cost.

2. The firm's profit-maximizing level of any input occurs when the input price equals the value of the marginal product.

3. The value of the marginal product equals the wage divided by the marginal product.

4. In the competitive model, marginal revenue is less than price because increasing output leads to a fall in price.

5. All sunk costs are fixed, but not all fixed costs are sunk.

6. Accounting profits are always less than economic profits.

7. In the long run in a competitive industry, economic profits are zero for any potential entrant.

8. Firms exit the industry when price falls below the minimum of average cost.

9. A firm will enter an industry if the price is above the minimum of the average variable cost curve.

10. Economic rent is any payment to an input in excess of that needed to keep the input in its current use.

11. Land is the only input that can earn economic rent.

12. The long-run supply is more elastic than the short-run supply for the industry but not for the individual firm.

13. The long-run supply curve is the sum of the supply curves of individual firms, including those that enter at high prices.

14. Even if a firm's supply curve is upward-sloping in the short run, it may be perfectly elastic in the long run.

15. Correctly measured, total cost should include all opportunity costs of operating.

Multiple Choice

1. The extra cost of producing an additional unit of output is called:

   a. marginal cost.
   b. fixed cost.
   c. overhead cost.
   d. sunk cost.
   e. average cost.

2. All of the following are true statements about the firm, except that one applies only to the competitive firm. Which is the odd one out?

   a. Marginal revenue is the revenue from the sale of one more unit of output.
   b. Average revenue equals price.
   c. Marginal revenue equals price.
   d. Profit is revenue minus cost.
   e. Profit is maximized where marginal revenue equals marginal cost.

3. A profit-maximizing firm determines output by equating:

   a. marginal revenue and price.
   b. average cost and average revenue.
   c. average cost and marginal revenue.
   d. marginal cost and marginal revenue.
   e. average revenue and price.

4. The competitive firm supplies the profit-maximizing level of output when:

   a. marginal revenue equals price.
   b. marginal cost equals price.
   c. economic profits are zero.
   d. accounting profits are zero.
   e. marginal revenue equals zero.

5. If a competitive firm finds that, at its current level of output, marginal revenue is less than marginal cost, it:

   a. can increase total profit by increasing output until marginal cost has fallen enough that it equals marginal revenue.
   b. can increase total profit by increasing output until marginal revenue has risen enough that it equals marginal cost.
   c. is maximizing profit.
   d. can increase total profit by decreasing output until marginal revenue has risen enough that it equals marginal cost.
   e. can increase total profit by decreasing output until marginal cost has fallen enough that it equals marginal revenue.

6. A competitive, profit-maximizing firm will enter a market if:

   a. price exceeds minimum average cost.
   b. revenue exceeds variable costs.
   c. price exceeds minimum average variable cost.
   d. revenue exceeds fixed costs.
   e. price exceeds minimum marginal cost.

7. Sunk costs are:

   a. the same thing as fixed costs.
   b. opportunity costs.
   c. variable costs.
   d. nonrecoverable costs.
   e. all costs other than variable costs.

8. When all fixed costs are sunk costs, a competitive, profit-maximizing firm will leave the market if:

   a. price falls below minimum average cost.
   b. revenue falls below total cost.
   c. price falls below minimum average variable cost.
   d. revenue falls below total fixed cost.
   e. price falls below minimum marginal cost.

9. When all fixed costs are sunk costs, a competitive, profit-maximizing firm will leave the market if:

   a. it cannot at least cover its fixed costs.
   b. price falls below minimum average cost.
   c. it cannot cover all its costs.
   d. price falls below minimum marginal cost.
   e. it cannot at least cover its variable costs.

10. If a competitive, profit-maximizing firm is already in the market and all its fixed costs are sunk costs, its supply curve is its:

    a. marginal cost curve above minimum average variable cost.
    b. average cost curve above minimum average variable cost.
    c. marginal cost curve above minimum average cost.
    d. average cost curve above minimum average cost.
    e. average cost curve above minimum marginal cost.

11. If a competitive, profit-maximizing firm is not already in the market, so that it has not yet committed to any sunk costs, its supply curve is its:

    a. average cost curve above minimum average cost.
    b. marginal cost curve above minimum average variable cost.
    c. average cost curve above minimum marginal cost.
    d. average cost curve above minimum average variable cost.
    e. marginal cost curve above minimum average cost.

12. In the long run, a shift in the demand curve in a competitive market will have:

    a. a smaller effect on both quantity and price than in the short run.
    b. a smaller effect on quantity and a larger effect on price than in the short run.
    c. exactly the same effect on quantity and price as in the short run.
    d. a larger effect on quantity and a smaller effect on price than in the short run.
    e. a larger effect on both quantity and price than in the short run.

13. All of the following, except one, are true of long-run equilibrium in a competitive industry. Which is the odd one out?

    a. The marginal firm is making zero profit.
    b. The marginal firm's price is equal to average cost.

c. All firms determine output by equating price and marginal cost.
d. The inframarginal firms are making positive profits.
e. Industry demand is perfectly elastic.

14. If some fixed costs are sunk and some are recoverable, a competitive, profit-maximizing firm will leave the market if it cannot at least cover its:

a. sunk costs.
b. total costs.
c. recoverable costs.
d. variable costs.
e. fixed costs.

15. The theory of contestable markets only holds if:

a. sunk costs are low.
b. sunk costs and fixed costs are low.
c. fixed costs are low.
d. sunk costs and fixed costs are high.
e. sunk costs are high.

16. When a firm is making zero economic profit, its accounting profit:

a. is negative.
b. is undefined.
c. is positive.
d. is zero.
e. may be positive or negative, but it cannot be zero.

17. The opportunity cost of the time of a firm's owner is:

a. taken into account when calculating economic profits but not when calculating accounting profits.
b. not taken into account when calculating either accounting or economic profits.
c. never taken into account when calculating any measure of profit.
d. taken into account when calculating both accounting and economic profits.
e. taken into account when calculating accounting profits but not when calculating economic profits.

18. The rent on a natural resource is:

a. its value in its next-best alternative use.
b. its value minus its extraction cost.
c. the present value of future profits that it will yield.
d. its value minus what it will sell for.
e. the value imputed to it before it is extracted.

19. The value of a firm's output that results from hiring one more worker is the worker's:

a. average produce multiplied by marginal cost.
b. marginal product multiplied by the product price.
c. average product multiplied by the product price.
d. marginal product multiplied by the worker's wage.
e. average produce multiplied by the worker's wage.

20. A competitive, profit-maximizing firm determines the quantity of labour it wishes to hire by equating labour's nominal wage to the:

a. worker's average product multiplied by the product price.
b. worker's average product.
c. marginal cost of output.
d. worker's marginal product.

e. worker's marginal product multiplied by the product price.

Completion

1. The extra revenue that a firm receives for selling another unit of output is the _____.
2. In the competitive model, the marginal revenue equals the _____.
3. The extra cost that the firm bears for producing another unit of output is the _____.
4. The level of output that maximizes a competitive firm's profit is found by setting _____ equal to _____.
5. The supply curve of the competitive firm is the same as the _____ curve when price is high enough to keep the firm in the market.
6. Costs that are not recoverable are called _____ costs.
7. Economic profits equal revenues received in excess of the _____ cost of operating the firm.
8. The demand for an input is the _____ of the _____.
9. New firms enter the industry whenever price is greater than the minimum of the _____ curve.
10. The value of the marginal product is found by multiplying the _____ by the _____.

Answers to Self-Test

True or False

1. t	4. f	7. t	10. t	13. t
2. t	5. t	8. f	11. f	14. t
3. f	6. f	9. f	12. f	15. t

Multiple Choice

1. a	6. a	11. e	16. c
2. c	7. d	12. d	17. a
3. d	8. c	13. e	18. b
4 b	9. e	14. c	19. b
5. e	10. a	15. a	20. e

Completion

1. marginal revenue
2. price
3. marginal cost
4. price, marginal cost
5. marginal cost
6. sunk
7. total
8. value, marginal product
9. average cost
10. marginal product, product price

Doing Economics: Tools and Practice Problems

When the firm sets its profit-maximizing output, it also decides how much of each input it will use. When there is only one variable input, the decision is even simpler: the production function dictates a unique level of the input for any given output level. The problems in this chapter look at how the firm makes input and output decisions. The output decision is sometimes to produce nothing if the firm is better off doing this than continuing to produce. This issue is also examined. Finally, two problems draw all the threads together.

SUPPLY OF OUTPUT

A firm maximizes profit by equating marginal revenue and marginal cost. A competitive firm is a price taker, so marginal revenue equals price. The profit-maximizing condition reduces then to equating price and marginal cost. When these are equal, the firm has located its profit-maximizing level of output. Took Kit 10.1 shows you how this level of output is found.

Tool Kit 10.1: Finding the Quantity of Output to Supply

Follow these steps to see how a competitive firm's profit-maximizing level of output is determined.

Step one: Calculate the marginal cost for each unit of output.

Step two: Identify the market price.

Step three: Find the greatest level of output for which price equals marginal cost. This is the quantity supplied.

---

1. (Worked problem: supply of output) Barbara's Carpet Cleaners has fixed costs of $100 per month and a total cost curve as given in Table 10.2. Output is the number of carpets cleaned.

Table 10.2

Output	Total cost
10	$ 200
20	$ 320
30	$ 460
40	$ 620
50	$ 800
60	$1,000

a. The current price for cleaning a carpet is $18. How many carpets must be cleaned to maximize profits? What will the profit be?
b. Suppose that the price falls to $14. Calculate the profit-maximizing output and the total profits.

Step-by-step solution

Step one (a): Marginal cost is the extra cost of cleaning another carpet. When output is increased from 0 to 10, total

costs increase by $200 − $100 = $100; therefore, the marginal cost is $100/10 = $10. Derive the marginal cost curve shown in Table 10.3.

Table 10.3

Output	Total cost	Marginal cost
10	$ 200	10
20	$ 320	12
30	$ 460	14
40	$ 620	16
50	$ 800	18
60	$1,000	20

Step two: Identify the market price. It is $18.

Step three: Find the greatest level of output for which price equals marginal cost. The $18 price equals marginal cost when output is 50.

Step four: Calculate profits. Profits equal revenues minus costs. Revenues equal $900 (50 × $18); profits equal $900 − $800 = $100. So the firm makes profits equal to $100.

Step five (b): If the price falls to $14, then price equals marginal cost at 30 units. Profits = (30 × $14) − $460 = −$40, and the firm loses $40.

2. (Practice problem: supply of output) The fixed cost for Martin Block, Inc., is $10,000. The company's cost curve is given in Table 10.4.

Table 10.4

Output	Total cost	Marginal cost
10,000	$21,000	
20,000	$32,100	
30,000	$43,300	
40,000	$54,600	
50,000	$66,000	
60,000	$77,500	

a. The current price for blocks is $1.12. Find the profit-maximizing quantity of blocks to produce. What will the profit be?
b. Suppose that the price rises to $1.15. Calculate the profit-maximizing output and the total profits.

3. (Practice problem: supply of output) For each of the following, find the profit-maximizing output level, and calculate total profits.

a. Fixed costs = $40,000; price = $600.

Output	Total cost	Marginal cost
100	$ 80,000	
200	$120,000	
300	$170,000	
400	$230,000	
500	$300,000	
600	$380,000	
700	$470,000	

b. Fixed costs = $900; price = $3.

Output	Total cost	Marginal cost
1,000	$ 1,900	
2,000	$ 2,900	
3,000	$ 4,600	
4,000	$ 6,600	
5,000	$ 9,400	
6,000	$12,400	
7,000	$16,000	
8,000	$20,000	

c. Fixed costs = $0; price = $80.

Output	Total cost	Marginal cost
1	$ 40	
2	$ 90	
3	$150	
4	$210	
5	$280	
6	$360	
7	$450	
8	$550	

INPUT DEMAND

A firm maximizes profit by equating the value of an input's marginal product and the input price, which is just the same as equating the marginal cost of another unit of the input with the marginal revenue the firm receives by employing that unit. The value of an input's marginal product is the price of output multiplied by the input's marginal product. When the input price equals the value of marginal product, the firm has located its profit-maximizing level of the input. Tool Kit 10.2 shows you how this input level is found.

Tool Kit 10.2: Finding the Quantity of an Input to Demand

Follow these steps to see how a competitive firm's profit-maximizing level of output is determined.

Step one: Calculate the marginal product for each level of the input.

Step two: Identify the product price.

Step three: Compute the value of the marginal product by multiplying the marginal product by the product price for each level of the input:

value of the marginal product
= marginal product × product price.

Step four: Identify the input price. (In the case of labour, this is the wage.)

Step five: Find the level of the input for which the value of the marginal product equals the input price. This is the quantity demanded.

---

4. (Worked problem: input demand) The new company The Hair Cuttery is ready to start hiring. The price of haircuts is $8, and the production function is given in Table 10.5.

Table 10.5

Stylists	Haircuts per day	Marginal product	Value of the marginal product
1	9		
2	17		
3	24		
4	30		
5	35		
6	39		

a. The wage paid to hair stylists is $40 per day. Find the profit-maximizing number of hair stylists to hire.
b. Suppose that the wage rises to $64 per day. Find the number of hair stylists that maximizes profits.

Step-by-step solution

Step one (a): The marginal product is the extra output that results from hiring one more input. When the first hair stylist is hired, output rises from 0 to 9. The marginal product is 9. Enter this number. When the second hair stylist is hired, output rises from 9 to 17. The marginal product is 17 − 9 = 8; enter this number and continue. The marginal product column is given in Table 10.6.

Table 10.6

Stylists	Haircuts per day	Marginal product	Value of the marginal product
1	9	9	
2	17	8	
3	24	7	
4	30	6	
5	35	5	
6	39	4	

Step two: The product price is $8.

Step three: The value of the marginal product equals the product price multiplied by the marginal product. The value of the marginal product of the first worker is 9 × $8 = $72. Continue to enter the results in the appropriate column. The completed information is given in Table 10.7.

Table 10.7

Stylists	Haircuts per day	Marginal product	Value of the marginal product
1	9	9	$72
2	17	8	$64
3	24	7	$56
4	30	6	$48
5	35	5	$40
6	39	4	$32

Step four: The wage is $40 per day.

Step five: Profits are maximized when the wage is set equal to the value of the marginal product. The wage is $40, which equals the value of the marginal product when 5 hair stylists are hired.

Step six (b): When the wage is $64, it equals the value of the marginal product if 2 stylists are hired.

5. (Practice problem: input demand) Moe's Lawn Service mows lawns for $20 each. Moe's production function is given in Table 10.8. Output is measured as the number of lawns mowed.

Table 10.8

Workers	Output per day	Marginal product	Value of the marginal product
1	5.0		
2	9.0		
3	13.0		
4	16.5		
5	19.5		
6	22.0		
7	24.0		

Moe pays his lawn mowers $40 per day.

a. Find the profit-maximizing number of mowers to hire.

b. Suppose that the wage rises to $70 per day. Find the profit-maximizing number of mowers to hire.

6. (Practice problem: input demand) For each of the following, complete the table and find the profit-maximizing number of inputs.

a. Product price = $10; wage = $100 per day.

Workers	Output per day	Marginal product	Value of the marginal product
10	200		
20	360		
30	500		
40	620		
50	720		
60	800		

b. Product price = $10,000; wage = $10,000 per month.

Workers	Output per day	Marginal product	Value of the marginal product
10	20		
20	40		
30	55		
40	65		
50	70		
60	70		

c. Product price = $5; input price = $40.

Workers	Output per day	Marginal product	Value of the marginal product
1,000	10,000		
2,000	18,000		
3,000	25,500		
4,000	31,500		
5,000	36,000		
6,000	40,000		

ENTRY AND EXIT PRICES

A firm will enter a market when it can make positive economic profit, which occurs when price exceeds minimum average cost. A firm will exit a market when it is making losses larger than those it would sustain by producing nothing. This means that it will exit if it cannot at least cover its recoverable costs. If all fixed costs are nonrecoverable, its only recoverable costs are its variable costs, and the firm will exit from the market when price falls below minimum average variable cost. If all fixed costs are recoverable, the firm will exit when price falls below minimum average cost. If some fixed costs are recoverable, the exit price will lie somewhere between these two points. Tool Kit 10.3 shows you how to determine the firm's exit price.

Tool Kit 10.3: Determining Entry and Exit Prices

The firm's entry price is the price at which the firm will enter the market. The firm's exit price is the price below which it will exit the market and prefer to product nothing. Follow these steps to see how the entry and exit prices are determined.

Step one: Calculate the average cost for each level of output.

Step two: Find the minimum average cost; this is the entry price. When the price is greater than or equal to the minimum average cost, then the firm should enter the market.

Step three: Identify all costs that are recoverable.

Step four: Calculate the average of the costs that are recoverable.

Step five: Find the minimum average recoverable cost; this is the exit price. When the price falls below this level, the firm should exit the market.

---

7. (Worked problem: entry and exit prices) Let's return to Barbara's Carpet Cleaners in problem 1. The total cost curve is given in Table 10.9.

Table 10.9

Output	Total cost
10	$ 200
20	$ 320
30	$ 460
40	$ 620
50	$ 800
60	$1,000

a. Find the entry price, which is the minimum price that will induce the firm to enter the market.

b. Assume that all the fixed costs are sunk. Find the exit price, which is the price below which the firm will exit the market.

c. Now assume that $50 of the fixed cost is recoverable. Find the exit price.

Step-by-step solution

Step one (a): Calculate the average cost for each level of output, and enter in the table. The average cost at 10 carpets is $200/10 = $20. Continue to fill in the column as in Table 10.10.

Table 10.10

Output	Total cost	Average cost
10	$ 200	$20.00
20	$ 320	$16.00
30	$ 460	$15.33
40	$ 620	$15.50
50	$ 800	$16.00
60	$1,000	$16.66

Step two: The minimum of the average cost curve is $15.33, and this is the entry price. This is the answer to part a.

Step three (b): Identify the costs that are not sunk. If all fixed costs are sunk, then only the variable costs can be recovered. In this case, the exit price is the minimum of the average variable cost curve. First, compute variable cost by subtracting fixed costs from total cost. The variable cost for 10 units of output is $200 – $100 = $100. Continue to fill in this column as in Table 10.11.

Table 10.11

Output	Total cost	Variable cost
10	$ 200	$100
20	$ 320	$220
30	$ 460	$360
40	$ 620	$520
50	$ 800	$700
60	$1,000	$900

Step four: Compute average variable cost. For 10 carpets, the average variable cost is $100/10 = $10. Enter the results as given in Table 10.12.

Table 10.12

Output	Total cost	Variable cost	Average variable cost
10	$ 200	$100	$10
20	$ 320	$220	$11
30	$ 460	$360	$12
40	$ 620	$520	$13
50	$ 800	$700	$14
60	$1,000	$900	$15

Step five: The minimum of the average variable cost curve is $10; therefore, the firm should exit when the price falls below $10. This is the answer to part b.

Step six (c): Only $50 is sunk; thus, the firm exits when revenues fall below variable costs plus $50. To find the recoverable costs, simply add $50 to the variable cost. Next, find the average of these numbers, and the minimum of these averages is the exit price. The results appear in Table 10.13.

Table 10.13

Output	Variable cost	Recoverable cost	Average recoverable cost
10	$100	$150	$15.00
20	$220	$270	$13.50
30	$360	$410	$13.66
40	$520	$570	$14.25
50	$700	$750	$15.00
60	$900	$950	$15.83

The minimum of the average recoverable cost column is $13.50, which is the exit price. When the price is $13.50, the firm loses $50, which means that revenues cover all but the nonrecoverable costs.

8. (Practice problem: entry and exit prices) Now let's return to Martin Block in problem 2. The total cost curve is reprinted in Table 10.14. Fixed costs equal $10,000.

Table 10.14

Output	Total cost
10,000	$21,000
20,000	$32,100
30,000	$43,300
40,000	$54,600
50,000	$66,000
60,000	$77,500

a. Find the entry price, which is the minimum price that will induce the firm to enter the market.

b. Assume that all of the fixed costs are sunk. Find the exit price.

9. (Practice problem: entry and exit prices) Find the entry price and the exit price for the firms in problem 3. Assume that all the fixed costs are sunk.

10. (Worked problem: applications) The competitive firm is a price taker in product and input markets. It has a production function and a level of fixed costs. Given this information, we can derive all the firm's cost curves, its supply curve, its demand curve, and the price at which it will enter or exit the industry. Remo's Repos recovers the automobiles of delinquent borrowers. Local banks pay him $50 per car recovered. Remo hires agents at $100 per night to repossess the cars. He runs a low-budget operation with fixed costs of only $500. The production function is given in Table 10.15, where output is measured as the number of cars repossessed.

a. Complete the table below, and calculate the profit-maximizing number of agents to hire.

Table 10.15

Agents	Output	Marginal product	Value of the marginal product
1	8		
2	15		
3	21		
4	26		
5	30		
6	33		
7	35		
8	36		
9	37		

b. Complete the cost table below, and calculate the profit-maximizing number of automobiles to repossess.

Output	Total cost	Variable cost	Average cost	Average variable cost	Marginal cost

c. Verify that the number of agents hired repossesses the quantity of output produced.
d. Find the entry price.
e. Assume that all the fixed costs are sunk, and find the exit price.

Step-by-step solution

Step one (a): Follow the solution to problem 4, and complete the table given above. The results are given in Table 10.16.

Table 10.16

Agents	Output	Marginal product	Value of the marginal product
1	8	8	$400
2	15	7	$350
3	21	6	$300
4	26	5	$250
5	30	4	$200
6	33	3	$150
7	35	2	$100
8	36	1	$ 50
9	37	1	$ 50

Step two: Set the input price ($100) equal to the value of the marginal product, which is $100 when 7 agents are hired.

Step three (b): Compute the cost for each output level in the production function. For 8 cars repossessed, 1 agent is hired at $100 and fixed costs are $500; therefore, total costs equal $100 + $500 = $600. Enter this number. For 15 cars, 2 agents at $100 each added to the $500 gives a total cost of $700. Continue and complete the total cost column. The result is given in Table 10.17.

Table 10.17

Output	Total cost
8	$ 600
15	$ 700
21	$ 800
26	$ 900
30	$1,000
33	$1,100
35	$1,200
36	$1,300
37	$1,400

Step four: Follow the solution to problems 1 and 7, and complete the table. Be careful with marginal cost. For example, the marginal cost at 8 cars is ($600 − $500)/8 = $12.50. The marginal cost at 15 cars is ($700 − $600)/(15 − 8) = $14.29. The complete information is given in Table 10.18.

Table 10.18

Output	Total cost	Variable cost	Average cost	Average variable cost	Marginal cost
8	$ 600	$100	$75.00	$12.50	$ 12.50
15	$ 700	$200	$46.66	$13.33	$ 14.29
21	$ 800	$300	$38.09	$14.28	$ 16.66
26	$ 900	$400	$34.61	$15.38	$ 20.00
30	$1,000	$500	$33.33	$16.66	$ 25.00
33	$1,100	$600	$33.33	$18.18	$ 33.33
35	$1,200	$700	$34.28	$20.00	$ 50.00
36	$1,300	$800	$36.11	$22.22	$100.00
37	$1,400	$900	$37.83	$24.32	$100.00

Step five: Set price equal to marginal cost. The price is $50, which equals marginal cost when 35 cars are repossessed.

Step six (c): Check the production function to make sure that when 7 agents are hired, 35 cars are repossessed.

Step seven (d): The entry price is the minimum of the average cost curve, which is $33.33. Note that marginal cost equals average cost at the minimum of the average cost curve.

Step eight (e): The exit price for the case in which all fixed costs are sunk is the minimum of the average variable cost, which is $12.50. Again, note that at the minimum of average variable cost, it is equal to marginal cost.

11. (Practice problem: applications) Perry's Perfect Pet Place hires workers to give baths to dogs. Perry pays

each woker $20 per day and charges the dogs $10 per bath. His fixed costs are $50. The production function is given in Table 10.19.

a. Complete the table below, and calculate the profit-maximizing number of workers to hire.

Table 10.19

Bathers	Baths	Marginal product	Value of the marginal product
1	6		
2	11		
3	15		
4	18		
5	20		
6	21		

b. Complete the cost table below, and calculate the profit-maximizing number of baths.

Output	Total cost	Variable cost	Average cost	Average variable cost	Marginal cost

c. Verify that the number of workers hired does give the profit-maximizing number of baths.
d. Find the entry price.
e. Assume that all the fixed costs are sunk, and find the exit price.

Answers to Problems

2. a. The marginal cost is given in Table 10.20.

Table 10.20

Output	Total cost	Marginal cost
10,000	$21,000	—
20,000	$32,100	$1.11
30,000	$43,300	$1.12
40,000	$54,600	$1.13
50,000	$66,000	$1.14
60,000	$77,500	$1.15

When the price is $1.12, output is 30,000, and profits equal ($1.12 × 30,000) – $43,300 = –9,700.

b. When the price is $1.15, output is 60,000, and profits equal ($1.15 × 60,000) – $77,500 = –$8,500.

3. a. The marginal cost is given in Table 10.21.

Table 10.21

Output	Total cost	Marginal cost
100	$ 80,000	$400
200	$120,000	$400
300	$170,000	$500
400	$230,000	$600
500	$300,000	$700
600	$380,000	$800
700	$470,000	$900

Output = 400; profits = ($600 × 400) – $230,000 = $10,000.

b. The marginal cost is given in Table 10.22.

Table 10.22

Output	Total cost	Marginal cost
1,000	$ 1,900	$1.00
2,000	$ 2,900	$1.00
3,000	$ 4,600	$1.70
4,000	$ 6,600	$2.00
5,000	$ 9,400	$2.80
6,000	$12,400	$3.00
7,000	$16,000	$3.60
8,000	$20,000	$4.00

Output = 6,000; profits = ($3.00 × 6,000) – $12,400 = $5,600.

c. The marginal cost is given in Table 10.23.

Table 10.23

Output	Total cost	Marginal cost
1	$ 40	$ 40
2	$ 90	$ 50
3	$150	$ 60
4	$210	$ 60
5	$280	$ 70
6	$360	$ 80
7	$450	$ 90
8	$550	$100

Output = 6; profits = (6 × $80) – $360 = $120.

5. The value of the marginal product is given in Table 10.24.

Table 10.24

Workers	Output per day	Marginal product	Value of the marginal product
1	5.0	5.0	$100
2	9.0	4.0	$ 80
3	13.0	4.0	$ 80
4	16.5	3.5	$ 70
5	19.5	3.0	$ 60
6	22.0	2.5	$ 50
7	24.0	2.0	$ 40

a. When the wage is $40, it equals the value of marginal product if 7 are hired.
b. When the wage is $70, it equals the value of marginal product if 4 are hired.

6. a. The value of the marginal product is given in Table 10.25. The quantity demanded is 50 workers.

Table 10.25

Workers	Output per day	Marginal product	Value of the marginal product
10	200	20	$200
20	360	16	$160
30	500	14	$140
40	620	12	$120
50	720	10	$100
60	800	8	$ 80

b. The value of the marginal product is given in Table 10.26. The quantity demanded is 40 workers.

Table 10.26

Workers	Output per day	Marginal product	Value of the marginal product
10	20	2.0	$20,000
20	40	2.0	$20,000
30	55	1.5	$15,000
40	65	1.0	$10,000
50	70	0.5	$ 5,000
60	70	0	$ 0

c. The value of the marginal product is given in Table 10.27. The quantity demanded is 2,000 workers.

Table 10.27

Workers	Output per day	Marginal product	Value of the marginal product
1,000	10,000	10.0	$50.00
2,000	18,000	8.0	$40.00
3,000	25,500	7.5	$37.50
4,000	31,500	6.0	$30.00
5,000	36,000	4.5	$22.50
6,000	40,000	4.0	$20.00

8. The cost measures are given in Table 10.28.

Table 10.28

Output	Total cost	Average cost	Variable cost	Average variable cost
10,000	$21,000	$2.10	$11,000	$1.10
20,000	$32,100	$1.61	$22,100	$1.11
30,000	$43,300	$1.43	$33,300	$1.11
40,000	$54,600	$1.37	$44,600	$1.12
50,000	$66,000	$1.32	$56,000	$1.12
60,000	$77,500	$1.29	$67,500	$1.13

a. Entry price = $1.29.
b. Exit price = $1.10.

9. a. The cost measures appear in Table 10.29.

Table 10.29

Output	Total cost	Average cost	Variable cost	Average variable cost
100	$ 80,000	$800	$ 40,000	$400
200	$120,000	$600	$ 80,000	$400
300	$170,000	$567	$130,000	$433
400	$230,000	$575	$190,000	$475
500	$300,000	$600	$260,000	$520
600	$380,000	$633	$340,000	$567
700	$470,000	$671	$430,000	$614

Entry price = $567; exit price = $400.
b. The cost measures appear in Table 10.30.

Table 10.30

Output	Total cost	Average cost	Variable cost	Average variable cost
1,000	$ 1,900	$1.90	$ 1,000	$1.00
2,000	$ 2,900	$1.45	$ 2,000	$1.00
3,000	$ 4,600	$1.53	$ 3,700	$1.23
4,000	$ 6,600	$1.65	$ 5,700	$1.43
5,000	$ 9,400	$1.88	$ 8,500	$1.70
6,000	$12,400	$2.07	$11,500	$1.92
7,000	$16,000	$2.29	$15,100	$2.16
8,000	$20,000	$2.50	$19,100	$2.39

Entry price = $1.45; exit price = $1.00.
c. The cost measures appear in Table 10.31.

Table 10.31

Output	Total cost	Average cost	Variable cost	Average variable cost
1	$ 40	$40.00	$ 40	$40.00
2	$ 90	$45.00	$ 90	$45.00
3	$150	$50.00	$150	$50.00
4	$210	$52.50	$210	$52.50
5	$280	$56.00	$280	$56.00
6	$360	$60.00	$360	$60.00
7	$450	$64.29	$450	$64.29
8	$550	$68.75	$550	$68.75

Entry price = $40; exit price = $40.

11. a. The complete information is given in Table 10.32.

Table 10.32

Workers	Baths	Marginal product	Value of the marginal product
1	6	6	$60
2	11	5	$50
3	15	4	$40
4	18	3	$30
5	20	2	$20
6	21	1	$10

Perry should hire 5 workers.

b. The completed cost information appears in Table 10.33.

Table 10.33

Output	Total cost	Variable cost	Average cost	Average variable cost	Marginal cost
6	$ 70	$ 20	$11.67	$3.33	$ 3.33
11	$ 90	$ 40	$ 8.18	$3.64	$ 4.00
15	$110	$ 60	$ 7.33	$4.00	$ 5.00
18	$130	$ 80	$ 7.22	$4.44	$ 6.33
20	$150	$100	$ 7.50	$5.00	$10.00
21	$170	$120	$ 8.10	$5.71	$20.00

Perry should sell 20 baths.

c. 5 workers give 20 baths.

d. Entry price = $7.22.

e. Exit price = $3.33.

COMPETITIVE EQUILIBRIUM

Chapter Review

The elements of the basic competitive model have been presented over the last five chapters of the text. In Chapter 11, these elements—from individuals and their decisions regarding consumption, savings, investment, and work to firms and their choices regarding production and costs—are brought together in the general equilibrium model. The focus of the model is the interdependencies of the product, labour, and capital markets. Another major topic is a normative one: how well does the competitive economy perform? The notion of Pareto efficiency provides a tool with which economists can evaluate how well the market economy answers the basic economic questions. This chapter completes the presentation of the competitive model and closes Part Two. In Part Three, attention shifts to imperfect markets.

ESSENTIAL CONCEPTS

1. **Partial equilibrium** analysis looks at one market in isolation. This kind of analysis can be inappropriate if changes in the market under consideration cause disturbances in the rest of the economy, which then feed back in an important way to the original market. General equilibrium analysis takes into account the relationships among different markets and keeps track of the interactions.

2. The three-market competitive model is a relatively simple **general equilibrium** model, yet it is very good for analyzing the interactions among markets. The three markets are the labour, capital, and product markets. They are interdependent: as the price changes in one market, demand and supply curves shift in the others.

3. General equilibrium in the competitive model occurs when the three prices—the wage, the interest rate, and the product price—are such that demand is equal to supply in the market for labour, the market for capital, and the output market. All markets clear.

4. Another view of the general equilibrium of the economy is given by the **circular flow model**. The simple version given in Figure 11.1 shows that households supply labour and financial capital to firms and demand products. Firms demand labour and capital and supply products. The flows of funds balance. For example, the revenues that firms receive for the sale of their goods equal the payments to labour as wages and to capital as dividends and interest. The circular flow model can be expanded to keep track of flows between one country and

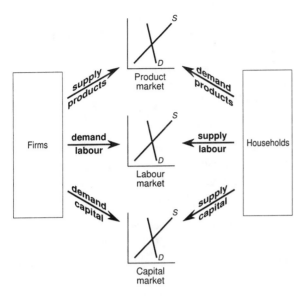

Figure 11.1

the rest of the world and between the private sector and the government.

5. The concept of efficiency used by economists is called **Pareto efficiency**. An allocation of resources is Pareto efficient if there is no way to reallocate resources to make anyone better off without hurting someone else. The equilibrium of the competitive economy is Pareto efficient. There is **exchange efficiency** because the goods and services produced by the economy are distributed efficiently among individuals, **production efficiency** because the economy is on its production possibilities curve, and **product-mix efficiency** because the mix of goods matches consumers' tastes.

6. Although the equilibrium of the competitive economy allocates resources efficiently, there are no forces to ensure that it distributes them equally. How much of the economy's output any individual receives depends upon how the market values the individual's labour and how much capital the individual is endowed with. This process is not necessarily equal or fair. Some economists argue that the needs of efficiency allow only a limited role for government. Others maintain that there are many market imperfections and therefore fewer limits on government intervention. All economists agree, however, that government action can create distortions just as easily as it can solve them.

BEHIND THE ESSENTIAL CONCEPTS

1. The interdependencies of markets demonstrate another facet of the principle of substitution. When the price of one good rises, the demand for its substitutes rises, while the demand for its complement falls. When the price of one input rises, firms substitute other inputs. A change in the capital market affects the wealth of consumers and the costs of firms. The economy is a spider's web, and a

movement in any one part reverberates throughout the whole.

2. Even though there are connections between all markets, in many cases the effects beyond a single market may be small. When this is true, it is sufficient to concentrate on the one market, that is, to employ partial equilibrium analysis, and ignore any general equilibrium repercussions. The art of economic analysis is to bring to light the important general equilibrium considerations and leave aside the portion of the economy that remains relatively unaffected.

3. If a firm produces several goods and there exists a way to rearrange its production and increase the output of one good without reducing the output of any other, an economist would say that this firm is inefficient. The firm is wasting inputs, because it is not getting the maximum output from the inputs. The output of the economy is the satisfaction (the utility) of its members. Therefore, if the economy is doing things one way, and there exists another way to do things that increases the utility of one individual (makes that individual better off) without reducing the utility of anyone else, then, just like the firm above, the economy is inefficient. Pareto efficiency is a natural definition of efficiency for the economy, the important output of which is ultimately not goods and services but human satisfaction.

SELF-TEST

True or False

1. A general equilibrium analysis takes into account all the important interactions between markets.

2. A partial equilibrium analysis focuses on one market only.

3. General equilibrium and partial equilibrium analyses always differ quite dramatically.

4. For the most part, in the capital market, firms are demanders and households are suppliers.

5. In the product market, firms are demanders and households are suppliers.

6. In the labour market, firms are demanders and households are suppliers.

7. The economy is in equilibrium when at least one of its markets clears.

8. In the circular flow model, the flows to households must equal the flows from households.

9. In the circular flow model, exports plus funds lent abroad must equal imports plus money borrowed from abroad.

10. The allocation of resources is Pareto efficient in competitive equilibrium.

11. The allocation of resources is equal in competitive equilibrium.

12. Pareto efficiency means that everyone can be made better off by some reallocation of resources.

13. Exchange efficiency means there is no scope for further trade among individuals.

14. All points along the production possibilities curve are Pareto efficient.

15. Pareto efficiency requires exchange efficiency, production efficiency, and product-mix efficiency.

Multiple Choice

1. When an analysis focuses on the interactions between markets, it is called _____ analysis.

    a. equilibrium
    b. partial equilibrium
    c. interactive
    d. general equilibrium
    e. disequilibrium

2. When an analysis looks only at the changes in one market, it is called _____ analysis.

    a. equilibrium
    b. partial equilibrium
    c. noninteractive
    d. general equilibrium
    e. disequilibrium

3. A general equilibrium analysis of an increase in the corporate income tax argues that the increase will be borne:

    a. by the owners of the corporations, the consumers who buy the corporations' products, and the workers in the corporations.
    b. solely by the workers in the corporations.
    c. by the owners of the corporations and the consumers who buy the corporations' products, but not by the workers in the corporations.
    d. solely by the owners of the corporations.
    e. by the owners of the corporations and the workers in the corporations, but not by the consumers who buy the corporations' products.

4. A general equilibrium analysis of an increase in the corporate income tax argues that the increase will result in a:

    a. higher product price, a higher wage, and a higher interest rate.
    b. lower product price, a lower wage, and a lower interest rate.
    c. higher product price, a lower wage, and a higher interest rate.
    d. lower product price, a higher wage, and a higher interest rate.
    e. higher product price, a lower wage, and a lower interest rate.

5. Partial equilibrium analysis is useful when the change being analyzed has effects in other markets that are:

    a. not widely dispersed.
    b. widely dispersed and small in any one market.
    c. widely dispersed and large in any one market.
    d. not widely dispersed and large in any one market.
    e. large and reverberate throughout the entire economy.

6. Which of the following probably does not require a general equilibrium analysis for its effects to be studied appropriately?

    a. an increase in the corporate income tax
    b. a ban on foreign investment
    c. a tariff on all imports
    d. elimination of trade restrictions
    e. a tax on cigarettes

7. In a three-sector, general equilibrium model, the supply of labour depends upon:

    a. only the wage.
    b. only the product price.
    c. only the rate of interest.
    d. the wage and the product price.
    e. the wage, the product price, and the rate of interest.

8. In a three-sector, general equilibrium model, the supply curve in the product market will shift to the left in response to:

    a. an increase in the wage or a reduction in the interest rate.
    b. an increase in either the wage or the interest rate.
    c. equal proportionate reductions in the wage and the interest rate.
    d. a reduction in either the wage or the interest rate.
    e. an increase in the interest rate or a reduction in the wage.

9. In general equilibrium in a three-sector model:

    a. only the product market clears.
    b. the product market and the labour market both clear, but the capital market does not.
    c. the capital market and the labour market both clear, but the product market does not.
    d. the product market and the capital market both clear, but the labour market does not.
    e. the product market, the labour market, and the capital market all clear.

10. In the simplest model of the circular flow of funds:

    a. firms pay households for goods and services and receive wages, rent, and profit from the households.
    b. households pay firms for goods and services and pay wages, rent, and profit to the firms.
    c. firms pay households for goods and services and pay wages, rent, and profit to the households.
    d. households pay firms for goods and services and receive wages, rent, and profit from the firms.
    e. the only flow of funds is from households and firms to the government.

11. In the expanded model of the circular flow of funds, including government and the foreign sector:

    a. households demand goods and services.
    b. firms supply goods and services.
    c. households supply labour and financial capital.
    d. firms demand labour and financial capital.
    e. all of the above

12. In the expanded model of the circular flow of funds, including government and the foreign sector, the balancing condition for the foreign sector is:

a. imports plus savings invested abroad equal exports plus borrowing from abroad.

b. imports equal exports.

c. exports plus savings invested abroad equal imports plus borrowing from abroad.

d. savings invested abroad equal borrowing from abroad.

e. imports plus exports equal savings invested abroad plus borrowing from abroad.

13. The balancing condition for government in the circular flow model means that a cut in income tax must be accompanied by any one of the following, except one. Which is the odd one out?

a. an increase in government borrowing from households

b. an increase in some other tax

c. a reduction in government borrowing from abroad

d. a reduction in government spending

e. a reduction in government spending and an increase in some other tax

14. Exchange efficiency means:

a. a redistribution of resources can make everyone better off.

b. there are no unexploited gains from trade between individuals.

c. the mix of goods in the economy matches consumer preferences.

d. more of one good cannot be produced without producing less of another.

e. a redistribution of resources will make everyone worse off.

15. Production efficiency means:

a. a redistribution of resources can make everyone better off.

b. there are no unexploited gains from trade between individuals.

c. the mix of goods in the economy matches consumer preferences.

d. more of one good cannot be produced without producing less of another.

e. a redistribution of resources will make everyone worse off.

16. Product-mix efficiency means:

a. a redistribution of resources can make everyone better off.

b. there are no unexploited gains from trade between individuals.

c. the mix of goods in the economy matches consumer preferences.

d. more of one good cannot be produced without producing less of another.

e. a redistribution of resources will make everyone worse off.

17. An economy is Pareto efficient if it satisfies:

a. only exchange efficiency.

b. any two of exchange efficiency, product-mix efficiency, and production efficiency.

c. only product-mix efficiency.

d. exchange efficiency, product-mix efficiency, and production efficiency.

e. only production efficiency.

18. Competitive markets guarantee:

a. only exchange efficiency.

b. exchange efficiency, product-mix efficiency, and production efficiency.

c. only product-mix efficiency.

d. any two of exchange efficiency, product-mix efficiency, and production efficiency.

e. only production efficiency.

19. Those economists who believe that markets left to themselves are the path to economic efficiency are called:

a. imperfect-market economists.

b. Pareto efficient economists.

c. efficient-market economists.

d. interventionist economists.

e. free-market economists.

20. Those economists who believe that the basic competitive model is not a good description of the economy and that markets left to themselves do not product economically efficient outcomes are called:

a. imperfect-market economists.

b. Pareto efficient economists.

c. efficient-market economists.

d. interventionist economists.

e. free-market economists.

Completion

1. Focusing on a single market while ignoring any spillover effects on other markets is called _____ analysis.

2. _____ analysis takes into account all the interactions and interdependencies between various parts of the economy.

3. In the simple circular flow model of the economy, households _____ labour and savings (financial capital) to firms and _____ goods and services.

4. In the simple circular flow model of the economy, firms _____ labour and financial capital from households and _____ goods and services.

5. When there is no way to make anyone better off without hurting someone else, the allocation of resources is _____.

6. An economy in _____ is Pareto efficient.

7. _____ requires that the economy's output of goods and services be distributed efficiently among its consumers.

8. When the economy is productively efficient, it is operating on its _____ curve.

9. The competitive economy results in distribution of income that are _____.

10. Environmental pollution and unemployment are examples of _____.

Answers to Self-Test

True or False

1.	t	4.	t	7.	f	10.	t	13.	t
2.	t	5.	f	8.	t	11.	f	14.	f
3.	f	6.	t	9.	f	12.	f	15.	t

Multiple Choice

1.	´d	6.	c	11.	e	16.	c
2.	b	7.	e	12.	a	17.	d
3.	a	8.	b	13.	c	18.	b
4.	c	9.	e	14.	b	19.	e
5.	b	10.	d	15.	d	20.	a

Completion

1. partial equilibrium
2. General equilibrium
3. supply, demand
4. demand, supply
5. Pareto efficient
6. competitive equilibrium
7. Exchange efficiency
8. production possibilities
9. unequal
10. market failure

Doing Economics: Tools and Practice Problems

There are three major markets: the labour, capital, and product markets. They are interrelated in that the demand and supply in any market depend upon all the prices, not just the price in that market. Because of this interdependence, there are important second-round effects in the three-market model. A change in the wage rate, for example, will shift the supply of output. The skill in general equilibrium analysis lies in choosing which interdependencies are important and which can be safely ignored. Tool Kit 11.1 shows you how to approach this task. Then, in the problem set, you apply what you have learned, by using the three-market model to analyze the effects of major changes in the economy. A few problems also focus on the connections between two markets.

Tool Kit 11.1: Using General Equilibrium Analysis

When applying general equilibrium analysis, follow these steps.

Step one: Identify the relevant markets.

Step two: Start with an equilibrium in each market, as in the figure.

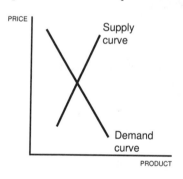 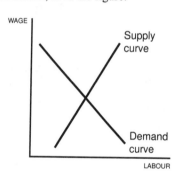 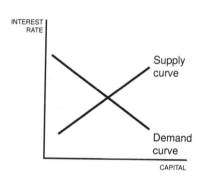

Step three: Identify a change, and determine which curves shift as a direct result of the change. In the second row of the figure, the demand for labour shifts outwards.

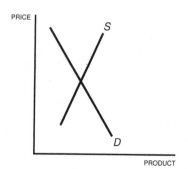 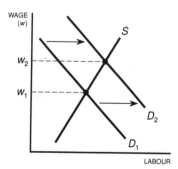 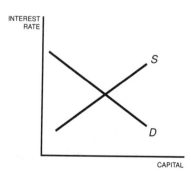

Step four: Shift the curves, and find the new equilibrium. In the general equilibrium model, this is only a temporary equilibrium because there are second-round effects to be accounted for. Observe which prices have changed. In the diagram, wages increase.

Step five: Determine which curves shift as a result of the price changes observed in step four.

Step six: Shift the curves, as shown here by lower supply in the product market and higher demand in the capital market, and find the new equilibrium.

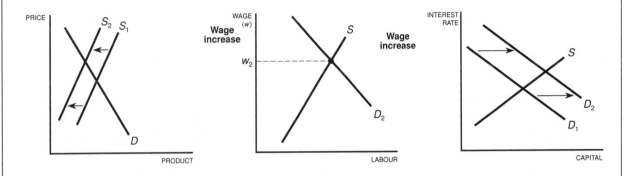

Step seven: Stop. Usually a second round is enough. Compare the new equilibrium with that in step two.

1. (Worked problem: general equilibrium analysis) Most European countries have a value-added tax, a national sales tax that is similar in some respects to the Goods and Services Tax.

    a. Use the three-market model to evaluate the effects of a value-added tax.

    b. Who pays the value-added tax?

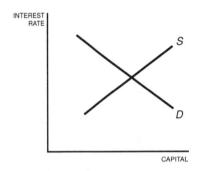

Step-by-step solution

Step one (a): Identify the relevant markets. We will use the labour, capital, and product markets.

Step two: Start with an equilibrium in each market.

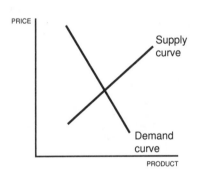

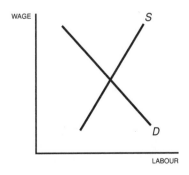

Step three: The value-added tax shifts the product market supply curve up by the amount of the tax. (This step is exactly like the analysis of the effects of taxes in Chapter 5.)

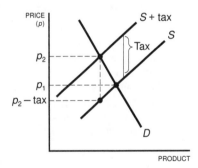

Step four: Find the new (temporary) equilibrium. Note that some of the tax is paid by consumers in the form of higher product prices. On the other hand, firms also receive less after the tax. This completes the first round.

Step five: Determine which curves shift as a result of the price changes observed in step four. The lower net of tax product price observed in step four implies that the value of the marginal product of inputs is lower. This means that the demand curve for labour and the demand curve for capital must shift to the left.

Step six: Shift the curves, and find the new equilibrium.

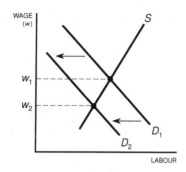

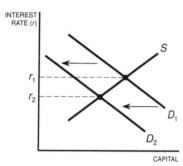

Step seven: Compare the new equilibrium with that in step two. We see that the wage and the interest rate are lower.

Step eight (b): The value-added tax is paid for in three ways. First, it is shifted forwards to consumers in the form of higher product prices. Second, it is shifted backward to workers through lower wages. Third, it is shifted backward to savers in terms of lower interest rates. A vital lesson of the general equilibrium approach is that all taxes are ultimately paid by individuals. A partial equilibrium treatment in the product market alone would imply that firms pay some of the tax. The full general equilibrium analysis reveals that the producers' share of the tax is passed backward to workers and savers.

2. (Practice problem: general equilibrium analysis) A substantial part of in the growth of developed countries is accounted for by technological advance, by improvements in how goods and services are produced, and by the introduction of new and better products. The hope for continued economic progress rests on technological advance in production. Use the three-market model to analyze the effects of a major technological advance.

   a. Start with an equilibrium in the three markets.
   b. Better technology increases the marginal products of labour and capital. Which curves are shifted? (Hint: Remember the formula for the value of the marginal product and the relationship between marginal product and marginal cost.)
   c. In the second round, how does the equilibrium change?

3. (Practice problem: general equilibrium analysis) Suppose that households decrease their consumption and increase their savings. Trace through the effects using the three-market model.

4. (Worked problem: general equilibrium analysis) Often when a change occurs in one market, there is another market closely linked to the first. In these cases, both markets must be included in the analysis. Investors seeking the highest possible returns can choose to buy stock in corporations or to invest their money in other noncorporate businesses. If the returns were higher in the corporate sector of the economy, then no one would invest in the noncorporate sector. If the returns were higher in the noncorporate sector, all money would flow out of the corporate sector. In equilibrium, then, the rate of return must be equal in the two sectors.

   a. Illustrate an equilibrium in the markets for corporate and noncorporate investment.
   b. In Canada, corporations must pay taxes on their income. The corporate income tax is in addition to the taxes paid by investors on their dividend income. Show how a tax on corporate income affects the market for corporate investment.
   c. Show how the noncorporate investment market will adjust to restore both markets to equilibrium.
   d. Who pays the corporate income tax?

Step-by-step solution

Step one (a): Start with an equilibrium. In this case, not only must supply and demand be equal in each market, but also each market must pay the same returns.

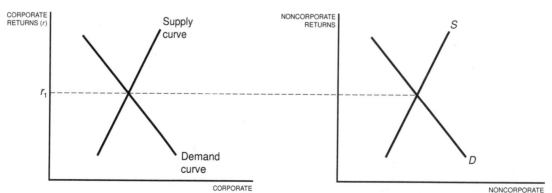

Step one

Step two (b): Determine which curve shifts. The corporate tax is paid by the demanders (corporations); therefore, the demand curve in the market for corporate investment shifts down.

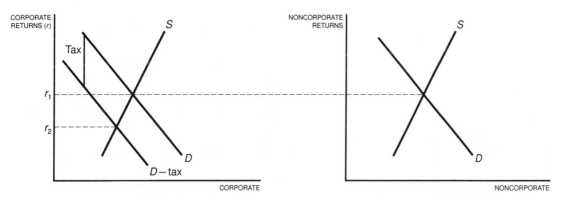

Step two

Step three: The (temporary) equilibrium in the market for corporate investment has a lower rate of return than in the market for noncorporate investment.

Step four (c): Determine the effects in the noncorporate investment market. Because they can earn higher after-tax returns in the noncorporate sector, corporate investors will move their money. The supply of corporate investment will shift left, and the supply of noncorporate investment will shift right, until the returns are equal.

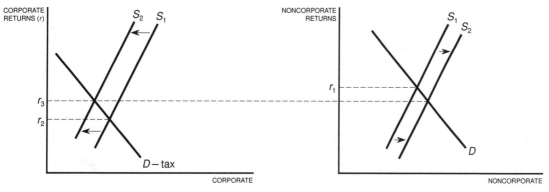

Step four

Step five (d): Find the new equilibrium and compare. In the new equilibrium, the returns are equal in each sector, but overall the returns are lower. We conclude that the corporate tax is paid by both noncorporate and corporate investors.

5. (Practice problem: general equilibrium analysis) Differences in wages that reflect differences in the characteristics of jobs are called compensating differentials. Truck drivers who haul freight over long distances are paid more than those who drive local routes. Suppose that the difference is $50 per week in equilibrium.

   a. Start with an equilibrium in the markets for local truck drivers and long-haul drivers. Be sure that the difference in wages is $50 per week.

   b. A new policy, agreed upon by both union and management, specifies that each driver must earn the same amount. Explain how the markets will adjust.

6. (Practice problem: general equilibrium analysis) Many people are concerned about the possible exhaustion of the limited supplies of natural resources, such as oil. To understand the economics of this issue, consider a two-period problem. Known reserves of oil equal 100,000 barrels. The oil can be sold now or be saved and sold in the future period. The discount rate is 50 percent over the time between the periods. The demand is the same now and in the future, and it is given in Table 11.1.

Table 11.1

Price	Quantity	Present discounted value of the future price
$50	20,000	
$45	30,000	
$40	40,000	
$35	55,000	
$30	70,000	
$25	80,000	
$20	90,000	
$10	100,000	

a. Calculate the present discounted value of each of the prices for the future demand. This is the current value of waiting to sell at the future price.

b. If the current price is greater than the present discounted value of the future price, all the oil will be sold today. If the reverse is true, the oil will be sold in the future. In equilibrium, current price must equal the present discounted value of the future price, and the total quantity sold in both periods must equal

100,000 barrels. Find the equilibrium price today, the price in the future, and the quantity sold in each period.

Answers to Problems

2. a. The initial equilibrium price is p_1, the wage is w_1, and the interest rate is r_1 .

b. The technological advance shifts the demands for labour and capital to the right because both factors are made more productive, and it shifts the supply of output to the right because costs are lower. The product price falls to p_2, the wage rises to w_2, and the interest rate rises to r_2.

c. In the second round, the supply curve for output shifts left (mitigating the effects of the original shift) because wages and interest rates are higher. The demand curves for labour and capital shift back to the left (offsetting somewhat the effects of the original shift) because the product price is lower. (Recall that the demand for a factor of production is the value of the marginal product, which is price multiplied by

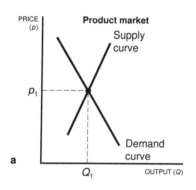

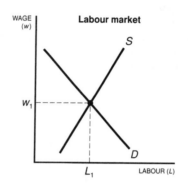

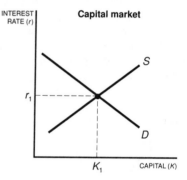

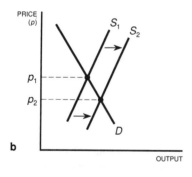

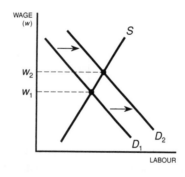

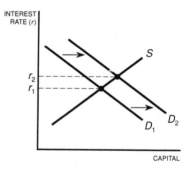

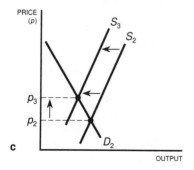

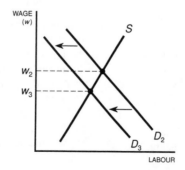

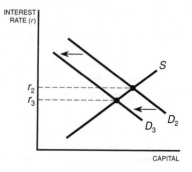

marginal product.) The ultimate price is p_3, which is higher than p_1 but lower than p_2, because of the general equilibrium repercussions. Similarly, w_3 is greater than w_1 and r_3 is greater than r_1, but the changes are less great than a partial equilibrium analysis would imply.

3. a. The initial equilibrium price is p_1, the wage is w_1, and the interest rate is r_1.
    b. As people consume less, the demand for output falls. As they save more, the supply shifts to the right in the capital market. Product prices and interest rates fall as a result.
    c. In the second round, the fall in interest rates shifts the supply of output to the right and further reduces product prices. The fall in product prices, observed in part b, reduces the demand for capital and leads to a further decrease in the interest rate. In the labour market, demand shifts up because of lower interest rates, but shifts down because of lower product prices. The ultimate impact on the wage is not certain.

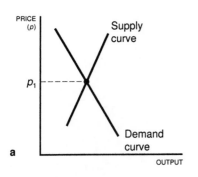

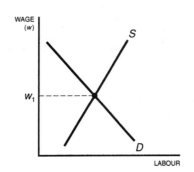

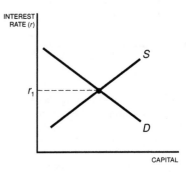

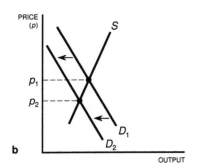

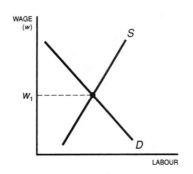

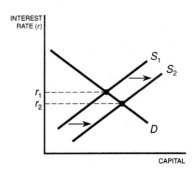

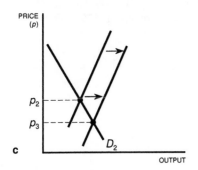

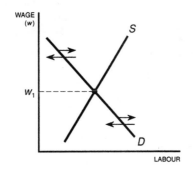

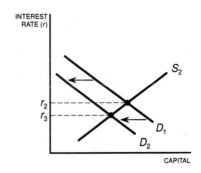

5. *a.* In the initial equilibrium, both markets clear, and the weekly wage is $50 higher in the long-haul market.

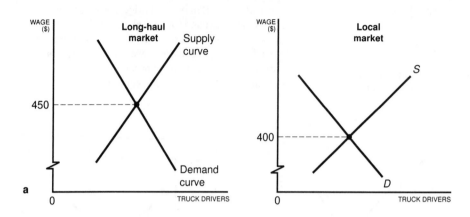

b. When the same wage is paid in the two markets, there is a shortage of long-haul drivers, and a surplus of drivers in the local market.

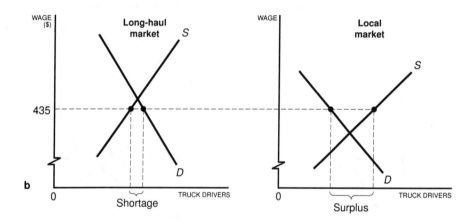

6. *a.* The present discounted value of the future price is given in Table 11.2.

Table 11.2

Price	Quantity	*Present discounted value of the future price*
$50	20,000	$50/(1 + $.50) = $33.33
$45	30,000	$30.00
$40	40,000	$26.67
$35	55,000	$23.33
$30	70,000	$20.00
$25	80,000	$16.67
$20	90,000	$13.33
$10	100,000	$ 6.67

b. The current price is $30, and 70,000 barrels are sold. The future price is $45, and 30,000 barrels are sold. The total is 70,000 + 30,000 = 100,000. The present discounted value of the future price is $30, which is the current price.

Part Three

Imperfect Markets

Chapter 12

MONOPOLIES AND IMPERFECT COMPETITION

Chapter Review

This chapter begins the study of imperfect competition. The real world differs from the basic competitive model of Part Two in many important ways, and these differences shape the discussion in Part Three of the text.

The first difference involves setting prices. While the competitive firm must accept the market price as a given fact, most firms in the real world have some control over their prices. How prices are set in monopolies, where there is only one seller, is the first topic taken up in Chapter 12. The chapter then turns to a discussion of barriers to entry, which keep new firms from competing in an established industry, and competition among many firms producing similar but not identical products.

ESSENTIAL CONCEPTS

1. There are four important types of **market structure: perfect competition, monopoly, monopolistic competition**, and **oligopoly.** The differences among these market structures are summarized in Table 12.1.

Table 12.1

Market structure	Firm's demand curve	Entry	Examples
Perfect competition	Horizontal	Free entry	Wheat, corn
Monopoly	Downward-sloping	Barriers to entry	Major league baseball, holders of patents
Monopolistic competition	Downward-sloping	Free entry	Restaurants, designer clothing
Oligopoly	Downward-sloping	Barriers to entry	Steel, automobiles

2. Monopolistic competition and oligopoly are collectively referred to as imperfect competition. Together with monopoly, they share an important characteristic that sets them apart from perfect competition: the demand curve they face is downward sloping. All three market structures also share something with perfect competition:

they maximize profit by equating marginal cost and marginal revenue. But because their demand curves are downward-sloping, marginal revenue is less than price.

3. Marginal revenue is less than price because these firms can only increase sales by lowering price. The relationship between marginal revenue and price is captured by the following formula:

$$\text{marginal revenue} = \text{price}\left(1 - \frac{1}{\text{elasticity of demand}}\right).$$

When demand is perfectly elastic (the case of perfect competition), marginal revenue equals price. But if demand is downward-sloping, the term in parentheses is less than 1, and marginal revenue is therefore less than price. This means that, at the profit maximum, price is higher than marginal cost. (In perfect competition, marginal revenue equals price, so the profit-maximizing condition is equality between price and marginal cost.)

4. Factors that prevent entry into markets are called **barriers to entry.** Government policies such as licence requirements and patents create barriers to entry. The cost structure of the industry, specifically the fraction of market demand accounted for by the output at the minimum of the firm's average cost curve, can also be a barrier. If one firm can produce the entire market demand for less than it could if it shared the market, the structure is called a **natural monopoly.** A monopoly can be sustained if a firm has control over an essential resource or if the firm has information advantages. Finally, strategies of existing firms can create barriers if they can credibly convince potential competitors that entry would be met with fierce competition.

5. Monopolistic competition describes the market structure made up of many firms, each of which ignores the reactions of the others. The demand curves facing the firms slope down (thus, price is above marginal cost), but new firms enter when there are profit opportunities (thus, in equilibrium, price equals average cost). New entrants produce close substitutes for the products of existing firms. Each entry shifts the demand curves facing existing firms to the left, and so reduces firms' profits.

BEHIND THE ESSENTIAL CONCEPTS

1. One important idea in the theory of imperfect competition is the relationship between marginal revenue and price. Marginal revenue is the extra revenue that the firm takes in when it sells another unit. In perfect competition, this amount is the price. But in imperfect competition, the price falls as more output is sold. Thus, there are two effects on revenue, shown in Figure 12.1. The firm is initially selling 10 units for $10 each. If it chooses to produce and sell 11 units, the price falls to $9.50. The first effect on revenue is that the firm sells more units at $9.50. This is shown as the area with pluses. If the demand curve facing the firm were horizontal, as under perfect competition, this would be the end of the story: the extra revenue would be price times the extra quantity

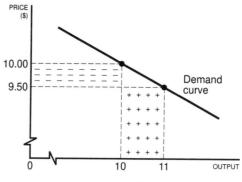

Figure 12.1

sold. However, the downward-sloping demand curve means the price must drop in order to sell one extra unit. This is the second effect: the firm loses revenue on all its existing sales (because the price is lower for all units). This effect is shown as the area with minuses, and it is this that makes marginal revenue less than price.

2. All imperfectly competitive firms face a downward-sloping demand curve. Thus, their profit-maximizing price is greater than marginal cost. In monopoly, there are barriers to entry, which allow monopolies to earn pure profits without attracting new competition. Monopoly prices are greater than average costs. In monopolistic competition, however, new entry drives economic profits to zero. When profits are zero, price equals average cost. To sum up:

   a. downward-sloping demand implies that price is greater than marginal cost.
   b. barriers to entry imply that price is greater than average cost.

3. Monopoly and monopolistic competition are similar in that each firm faces a downward-sloping demand curve and sets marginal revenue equal to marginal cost, which is less than price. The similarities stop here, however, because in a monopoly no new firm may enter even though a firm may earn pure profits. In monopolistically competitive industries, new firms enter, produce close substitutes, and capture customers. This entry shifts demand to the left until price equals average cost. The basic difference in the equilibria is that monopolies earn pure profits.

4. Monopolies are inefficient because price (which equals the marginal benefit of the good to consumers) is greater than marginal cost. Producing another unit would benefit customers more than it would cost. In monopolistic competition, things are not so simple. If all firms produce more goods, there are gains to both consumers and firms because, though price is greater than marginal cost, average cost falls. (Remember that the monopolistically competitive firm produces along the downward-sloping part of average cost.) On the other hand, the overall industry demand is only so large, and if the firms become bigger, there will be room for fewer firms. Fewer firms mean fewer types of goods, so there is a trade-off between costs and variety.

SELF-TEST

True or False

1. The demand curve facing the firm is downward-sloping in perfect competition.

2. The demand curve facing the firm is downward-sloping in monopolistic competition.

3. When the demand curve facing the firm is downward-sloping, marginal revenue is less than price.

4. In imperfect competition, marginal revenue is less than price because price must fall for sales to increase.

5. An industry with a single seller is a monopoly.

6. The demand curve facing a monopolist is the same as the industry demand curve.

7. Price is greater than marginal cost in monopoly.

8. Price is greater than marginal cost in monopolistic competition.

9. Compared to perfect competition, monopolies produce more but charge higher prices.

10. If there is a barrier to entry, firms may continue to earn pure profits.

11. Product differentiation is caused by barriers to entry.

12. In a natural monopoly, one firm can produce at a lower average cost than it could if it shared the market with other firms.

13. In equilibrium in monopolistic competition, price is greater than average cost.

14. A firm that practises limit pricing charges less than the monopoly price and produces more than the monopoly output.

15. The more elastic the monopolist's demand, the more price exceeds marginal cost.

Multiple Choice

1. All of the following, except one, are true of the competitive model. Which is the odd one out?

    a. Marginal revenue equals market price.
    b. The firm cannot raise the market price without losing all its customers.
    c. The firm can sell as much as it wants at the market price.
    d. The firm is a price taker.
    e. The firm faces a downward-sloping demand curve.

2. Which of the following groups of market structures includes only price makers?

    a. oligopoly, monopolistic competition, monopoly
    b. perfect competition, imperfect competition, monopoly
    c. monopolistic competition, perfect competition, oligopoly
    d. monopoly, monopolistic competition, perfect competition
    e. perfect competition, oligopoly, monopoly

3. When one firm supplies the entire market, the market structure is called:

    a. perfect competition.
    b. oligopoly.
    c. monopolistic competition.
    d. monopoly.
    e. imperfect competition.

4. When the market is dominated by several firms, each of which has to pay attention to what its rivals are doing, the market structure is called:

    a. perfect competition.
    b. oligopoly.
    c. monopolistic competition.
    d. monopoly.
    e. imperfect competition.

5. The market structure in which there are many firms in the industry, each selling slightly differentiated products, is called:

    a. perfect competition.
    b. oligopoly.
    c. monopolistic competition.
    d. monopoly.
    e. imperfect competition.

6. The market structures that lie between the extremes of one firm supplying the market and many firms acting as price takers are collectively referred to as:

    a. perfect competition.
    b. oligopoly.
    c. monopolistic competition.
    d. monopoly.
    e. imperfect competition.

7. In imperfect competition, the demand curve facing the firm is:

    a. the market demand curve.
    b. horizontal.
    c. perfectly elastic.
    d. vertical.
    e. downward-sloping.

8. Efficiency requires that marginal cost equal price. For which of the following market structures does marginal cost equal price?

    a. perfect competition
    b. monopoly
    c. monopolistic competition
    d. oligopoly
    e. imperfect competition

9. When the demand curve facing the firm is downward-sloping, marginal revenue is less than price because:

    a. the firm can sell more units without lowering its price.
    b. the firm can only sell more units by lowering its price on all units.
    c. a very large number of firms are producing essentially the same product.
    d. if the firm raises its price, it loses all its customers.
    e. the firm is behaving as a price taker.

10. In which of the following market structures does the firm face the market demand curve?

 a. perfect competition
 b. oligopoly
 c. monopolistic competition
 d. monopoly
 e. imperfect competition

11. If p denotes price and e denotes the (absolute value of the) elasticity of demand, marginal revenue can be written as:

 a. $p(1 + 1/e)$.
 b. $p/(1 + 1/e)$.
 c. $p(1 - 1/e)$.
 d. $p/(1 - 1/e)$.
 e. $p(1 - e)$.

12. Efficiency requires that marginal cost equal price. In the case of a monopoly, price exceeds marginal cost. The difference between price and marginal cost is:

 a. at its greatest when the demand curve facing the firm is perfectly elastic.
 b. greater the more inelastic the demand curve facing the firm is.
 c. smaller the more inelastic the demand curve facing the firm is.
 d. greater the more elastic the demand curve facing the firm is.
 e. at its greatest when the demand curve facing the firm is horizontal.

13. If an industry in which the entire market is supplied by one firm were converted to a competitive industry:

 a. output would fall and price would rise.
 b. output and price would both fall.
 c. nothing would happen to either output or price.
 d. output and price would both rise.
 e. output would rise and price would fall.

14. A monopoly makes a profit by restricting output and raising price. This profit is sometimes called:

 a. a monopoly rent.
 b. accounting profit.
 c. a normal rate of return.
 d. short-run profit.
 e. opportunity cost.

15. When a monopoly practises price discrimination, it:

 a. charges a higher price in the market with the higher elasticity of demand.
 b. charges a higher price in the market with the higher marginal cost.
 c. sets the same price in both markets but sells a different quantity in each market.
 d. charges a higher price in the market with the lower marginal cost.
 e. charges a higher price in the market with the lower elasticity of demand.

16. A firm's market power is greater when the:

 a. difference between marginal cost and price is smaller.
 b. demand curve the firm faces is more elastic.

 c. market for the firm's product is larger.
 d. demand curve the firm faces is more inelastic.
 e. difference between marginal revenue and price is smaller.

17. The four-firm concentration ratio measures the:

 a. proportion of the economy's output produced by the four biggest firms in the economy.
 b. elasticity of demand for the four biggest firms in the industry.
 c. proportion of industry output produced by the four biggest firms in the industry.
 d. proportion of industries that contain four firms or less.
 e. proportion of the world's output produced by the four biggest firms in the world.

18. All of the following, except one, are sources of market power and imperfect competition. Which is the odd one out?

 a. product differentiation
 b. competition from foreign firms
 c. barriers to entry
 d. single ownership of an essential input
 e. patents

19. A firm has a natural monopoly when:

 a. it is the only firm supplying the market for a natural resource.
 b. the firm faces a downward-sloping demand curve.
 c. marginal revenue is less than price.
 d. the monopoly is maintained without a barrier to entry.
 e. one firm can supply the entire market at lower average cost than any larger number of firms.

20. The major characteristic that distinguishes firms in monopolistic competition from monopoly firms is that, in long-run equilibrium, firms in monopolistic competition:

 a. make zero economic profits.
 b. equate marginal revenue and marginal cost.
 c. face a downward-sloping demand curve.
 d. charge a price that exceeds marginal cost.
 e. do not produce at minimum average cost.

Completion

1. The way in which an industry is organized is called its _____.

2. A few firms dominate an industry in _____.

3. An industry with a single seller is called _____.

4. In monopolistic competition, there are enough firms that each firm _____ the reactions of rivals.

5. In industries where the characteristics of products are different, there is said to be _____.

6. In imperfect competition, marginal revenue is _____ than price.

7. Any factor that prevents new firms from coming into an industry is called a _____.

8. If the market demand curve intersects the average cost curve for the firm at a point where it is decreasing, the industry is a _____.

9. In monopolistic competition, there is a trade-off between lower prices and more _____.

10. In equilibrium in monopolistic competition, price equals _____.

Answers to Self-Test

True or False

1. f	4. t	7. t	10. t	13. f
2. t	5. t	8. t	11. f	14. t
3. t	6. t	9. f	12. t	15. f

Multiple Choice

1. e	6. e	11. c	16. d
2. a	7. e	12. b	17. c
3. d	8. a	13. e	18. b
4. b	9. b	14. a	19. e
5. c	10. d	15. e	20. a

Completion

1. market structure
2. oligopoly
3. monopoly
4. ignores
5. product differentiation
6. less
7. barrier to entry
8. natural monopoly
9. variety
10. average cost

Doing Economics: Tools and Practice Problems

In this section, we start with two basic topics and several applications. First, we calculate marginal revenue and find the profit-maximizing price and quantity for the monopolist. The second topic is price discrimination, the practice in which firms in imperfectly competitive markets charge different prices to different consumers in order to raise profits. Finally, several problems provide extensions to the standard application of profit-maximizing behaviour when demand is downward-sloping.

MARGINAL REVENUE

Monopoly and imperfect competition are distinguished from perfect competition in one important respect: the demand curve facing monopolistic and imperfectly competitive firms is downward-sloping. This means marginal revenue is less than price. Tool Kit 12.1 shows you how to calculate marginal revenue when demand is downward-sloping. Once marginal revenue has been determined, the profit-maximizing output is found by equating marginal revenue and marginal cost. The price associated with this output is obtained from the demand curve.

> **Tool Kit 12.1:** Calculating Marginal Revenue
>
> Follow these steps to calculate marginal revenue when demand is downward-sloping.
>
> *Step one*: Make a table with four column headings: "Price," "Quantity," "Revenue," and "Marginal revenue." Enter the demand curve in the first two columns.
>
> Price   Quantity   Revenue   Marginal revenue
>
> *Step two*: Calculate revenues for each point on the demand curve, and enter the result in the table. Revenue is price multiplied by quantity:
>
> $$revenue = price \times quantity.$$
>
> *Step three*: Calculate marginal revenue for each interval along the demand curve, and enter the result in the table. Marginal revenue is the change in total revenue divided by the change in quantity:
>
> marginal revenue
> = change in revenue/change in quantity.
>
> After calculating marginal revenue, choose the price and quantity for which marginal revenue equals marginal cost.

---

1. (Worked problem: marginal revenue) As the only cement producer within 200 kilometres, Sam's Cement faces a downward-sloping demand curve, which is given in Table 12.2.

Table 12.2

Price	Quantity (tonnes)
$4.00	400
$3.50	800
$3.00	1,400
$2.50	2,800
$2.00	4,000

Sam's marginal cost is $2 per ton, and he has fixed costs of $1,000.

a. Calculate revenue and marginal revenue, and add these two columns to the table.
b. Find the profit-maximizing price and quantity.
c. Compute Sam's costs and profits at this price.
d. Suppose that Sam's fixed costs fall to $500. What is his profit-maximizing price and quantity, and how much does he earn in profits?
e. Illustrate your answer with a diagram.

Step-by-step solution

Step one (a): Make a table.

Price   Quantity   Revenue   Marginal revenue

Step two: Calculate revenue for each point on the demand

curve. When the price is $4, revenue is $4 × 400 = $1,600. Continuing, we derive Table 12.3.

Table 12.3

Price	Quantity	Revenue	Marginal revenue
$4.00	400	$1,600	
$3.50	800	$2,800	
$3.00	1,400	$4,200	
$2.50	2,800	$7,000	
$2.00	4,000	$8,000	

Step three: Calculate marginal revenue for each interval along the demand curve. For the first 400 units, revenue rises from $0 to $1,600. Thus, marginal revenue is $1,600/400 = $4. As output is increased to 800, total revenue grows from $1,600 to $2,800. Marginal revenue is ($2,800 − $1,600)/(800 − 400) = $3. Complete the marginal revenue column as shown in Table 12.4.

Table 12.4

Price	Quantity	Revenue	Marginal revenue
$4.00	400	$1,600	$4.00
$3.50	800	$2,800	$3.00
$3.00	1,400	$4,200	$2.33
$2.50	2,800	$7,000	$2.00
$2.00	4,000	$8,000	$0.83

Step four (b): To find the monopoly output and price, set marginal revenue equal to marginal cost. This occurs when the price is $2.50 and output is 2,800.

Step five (c): To find total costs, add fixed costs, which are $1,000, plus total variable costs. Each unit costs $2, and 2,800 units are produced. Total costs equal $1,000 + ($2 × 2,800) = $6,600. Profits equal revenue minus costs. Revenue is $7,000, so profits equal $7,000 − $6,600 = $400.

Step six (d): If fixed costs fall, marginal cost does not change. The profit-maximizing price is still $2.50, but total profits now equal $7,000 − ($500 + $5,600) = $900. Unless the firm decides to shut down, fixed costs do not affect the output and pricing decisions.

Step seven (e): The solution is illustrated in the diagram.

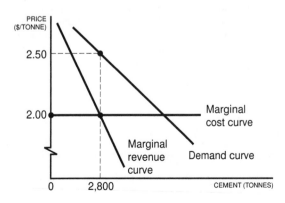

2. (Practice problem: marginal revenue) The Mudville Nine is the only professional baseball team within several hundred kilometres. The marginal cost of admitting another fan is $1. Fixed costs, which include player salaries, are $100,000. The demand curve is given in Table 12.5. The quantity column gives the season's attendance.

Table 12.5

Price	Quantity	Revenue	Marginal revenue
$8	100,000		
$7	150,000		
$6	200,000		
$5	250,000		
$4	300,000		
$3	350,000		
$2	400,000		

a. Compute marginal revenue, and complete the column.
b. Find the profit-maximizing price and quantity.
c. Compute Mudville's costs and profits at this price.
d. Suppose that the players win the right to negotiate with any team, and the increase in salaries raises fixed costs to $150,000. What is Mudville's profit-maximizing price and quantity, and how much profit does the team earn?
e. Illustrate your answer with a diagram.

3. (Practice problem: marginal revenue) For each of the following firms, find the profit-maximizing price and quantity and total profits earned.

a. Fixed costs = $0; marginal cost = $8.

Price	Quantity	Revenue	Marginal revenue
$10	1		
$ 9	2		
$ 8	3		
$ 7	4		
$ 6	5		
$ 5	6		
$ 4	7		

b. Fixed costs = $50,000; marginal cost = $.10.

Price	Quantity	Revenue	Marginal revenue
$.50	500,000		
$.45	600,000		
$.40	700,000		
$.35	800,000		
$.30	900,000		

c. Compute marginal cost from the table.

Price	Quantity	Revenue	Marginal revenue	Total costs	Marginal costs
$20	400			$ 5,000	
$18	800			$ 7,000	
$16	1,200			$ 9,400	
$14	1,600			$12,600	
$12	2,000			$16,200	
$10	2,400			$21,000	

d. Compute marginal cost from the table.

Price	Quantity	Revenue	Marginal revenue	Total costs	Marginal costs
$1.00	1,000			$ 200	
$0.90	2,000			$ 300	
$0.80	3,500			$ 450	
$0.70	5,500			$ 650	
$0.60	8,000			$ 900	
$0.50	11,000			$1,230	
$0.40	15,000			$1,730	
$0.30	20,000			$2,355	

PRICE DISCRIMINATION

When it is possible (and legal) to do so, a monopoly or imperfectly competitive firm can increase its profit by charging different prices to different consumers for reasons unconnected to cost. This practice is called price discrimination. The idea is to segment the market and exploit differences in elasticities of demand across markets. Examples abound. For example, next time you are on a plane flying somewhere, find out how much the person next to you paid for his or her ticket. Chances are, you did not pay the same price as your fellow traveller. The airlines' practice of charging different prices to passengers on the same plane flying to the same destination is a common form of price discrimination. Another common example is dumping, which occurs when a firm faces less competition in its home market than in its overseas market.

4. (Worked problem: price discrimination) Although the sale of the product is illegal, a drug enterprise operates according to sound business practices. It sells addictive designer drugs to two types of customers: nonaddicted experimenters and addicts (former experimenters). The demands for each type of customer are given in Table 12.6. The drug has no fixed costs and has marginal cost equal to $10 per dose.

Table 12.6

	Nonaddicts				Addicts		
Price	Quantity	Revenue	Marginal revenue	Price	Quantity	Revenue	Marginal revenue
$50	100			$50	500		
$40	300			$40	700		
$30	500			$30	1,050		
$20	1,000			$20	1,650		

a. Calculate marginal revenue for each demand curve.
b. Find the profit-maximizing price and quantity for each type of consumer.
c. Calculate total profits.

Step-by-step solution

Step one (a): Follow the procedure outlined above to calculate marginal revenue. The result should look like Table 12.7.

Table 12.7

	Nonaddicts				Addicts		
Price	Quantity	Revenue	Marginal revenue	Price	Quantity	Revenue	Marginal revenue
$50	100	$ 5,000	$50	$50	500	$25,000	$50.00
$40	300	$12,000	$35	$40	700	$28,000	$15.00
$30	500	$15,000	$15	$30	1,050	$31,500	$10.00
$20	1,000	$20,000	$10	$20	1,650	$33,000	$ 2.50

Step two (b): Find the profit-maximizing price in each market. Marginal cost, which is $10, equals marginal revenue for nonaddicts at a price of $20 and a quantity of 1,000. For addicts, marginal revenue equals marginal cost at a price of $30 and a quantity of 1,050.

Step three (c): Calculate total profits. Revenues are $20,000 from the nonaddicts and $31,500 from the addicts. Costs are $10 × (1,000 + 1,050) = $20,500; so profits equal $51,500 – $20,500 = $31,000.

5. (Practice problem: price discrimination) Opus Company sells carpet fibres in the foreign and domestic markets. Its marginal cost is $1 per spool, and it has fixed costs of $5,000. The domestic and foreign demands are given in Table 12.8.

Table 12.8

	Home market				Foreign market		
Price	Quantity	Revenue	Marginal revenue	Price	Quantity	Revenue	Marginal revenue
$10	2,000			$10	2,000		
$ 9	2,500			$ 9	3,000		
$ 8	3,000			$ 8	4,000		
$ 7	3,500			$ 7	5,000		
$ 6	4,000			$ 6	6,000		
$ 5	4,500			$ 5	7,000		
$ 4	5,000			$ 4	8,000		

a. Calculate marginal revenue for each demand curve.
b. Find the profit-maximizing price and quantity for each type of consumer.
c. Calculate total profits.

6. (Practice problem: price discrimination) Mark's Markets is one of the few chains that has not closed its inner-city stores. Mark's has expanded to the suburbs, but it faces more competition there. An example of a product it sells in both markets is hamburger, which has a marginal cost equal to $1. The space required to sell hamburger costs Mark's Markets about $100, and the demand curves in the suburbs and inner city are given in Table 12.9.

Table 12.9

	Suburbs				Inner city		
Price	Quantity	Revenue	Marginal revenue	Price	Quantity	Revenue	Marginal revenue
$4.00	200			$4.00	100		
$3.50	400			$3.50	120		
$3.00	600			$3.00	140		
$2.50	800			$2.50	160		
$2.00	1,000			$2.00	180		
$1.50	1,200			$1.50	200		

a. Calculate marginal revenue for each demand curve.
b. Find the profit-maximizing price and quantity for each type of consumer.
c. Calculate total profits.

APPLICATIONS

The following problems provide extensions to the standard application of profit-maximizing behaviour in cases in which the demand curve is downward-sloping. Artists, entertainers, and authors are often paid a percentage of revenues. You will see why this means they prefer their work to be sold at a lower price than the profit-maximizing price set by producers and publishers. Other problems explore the effects of taxes and price ceilings in monopoly markets and show why monopolists always produce where demand is price elastic.

7. (Worked problem: applications) After the surprising success of her first novel, Imelda has negotiated a deal in which she receives 20 percent of the revenues from the sale of her second novel. The demand curve is given in Table 12.10. The publisher has fixed costs of $20,000, and the marginal cost of printing and distributing each book printed is $20.

Table 12.10

Price	Quantity	Revenue	Marginal revenue	Imelda's revenue
$40	10,000			
$35	20,000			
$30	30,000			
$25	40,000			
$20	50,000			

a. Calculate marginal revenue, and enter in the table.
b. Find the profit-maximizing price and quantity.
c. Compute Imelda's revenue for each price, and enter in the table.
d. What price maximizes Imelda's revenue?
e. Draw a diagram illustrating your answer.

Step-by-step solution

Step one (a): Calculate marginal revenue. Follow the usual procedure. The answer is in Table 12.11.

Table 12.11

Price	Quantity	Revenue	Marginal revenue	Imelda's revenue
$40	10,000	$ 400,000	$40	
$35	20,000	$ 700,000	$30	
$30	30,000	$ 900,000	$20	
$25	40,000	$1,000,000	$10	
$20	50,000	$1,000,000	$ 0	

Step two (b): Find the profit-maximizing price and quantity. Marginal cost equals marginal revenue for the publisher at a price of $30, where the quantity sold is 30,000.

Step three (c): Calculate Imelda's revenue. She receives 20 percent of the total. At a price of $40, she receives .20 × $400,000 = $80,000. Continue to calculate, and enter the results. They are given in Table 12.12.

Table 12.12

Price	Quantity	Revenue	Marginal revenue	Imelda's revenue
$40	10,000	$ 400,000	$40	$ 80,000
$35	20,000	$ 700,000	$30	$140,000
$30	30,000	$ 900,000	$20	$180,000
$25	40,000	$1,000,000	$10	$200,000
$20	50,000	$1,000,000	$ 0	$200,000

Step four (d): Imelda prefers a price of $25 or $20, which earns her $200,000, more than the $180,000 that she earns at the publisher's preferred price.

Step five (e): Draw a diagram. Note that the publisher sets marginal revenue equal to marginal cost. Imelda is only concerned with revenues, so she prefers the point where marginal revenue equals zero.

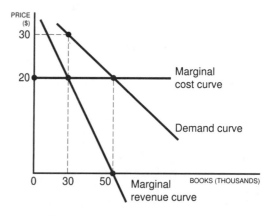

8. (Practice problem: applications) Magdalena, a budding female recording artist, has just completed her first album. She will receive 25 percent of the revenues. The record company reports that its demand curve is as given in Table 12.13, and its marginal costs are $6 per CD.

Table 12.13

Price	Quantity	Revenue	Marginal revenue	Magdalena's revenue
$20	20,000			
$18	25,000			
$16	30,000			
$14	35,000			
$12	40,000			
$10	48,000			

a. Calculate marginal revenue, and enter in the table.
b. Find the profit-maximizing price and quantity.
c. Compute Magdalena's revenue for each price, and enter in the table.
d. What price maximizes Magdalena's revenue?
e. Draw a diagram illustrating your answer.

9. (Practice problem: applications) Like most cities, Southam City is a one-newspaper town. The *Southam Truth* distributes its daily paper for a marginal cost of $.10. The demand curve is given in Table 12.14.

Table 12.14

Price	Quantity	Revenue	Marginal revenue
$1.00	30,000		
$0.95	40,000		
$0.90	50,000		
$0.85	60,000		
$0.80	70,000		
$0.75	80,000		
$0.70	90,000		
$0.65	100,000		
$0.60	110,000		
$0.55	120,000		

a. Calculate marginal revenue, and enter in the table.
b. Find the profit-maximizing price and quantity.
c. Suppose that a tax of $.10 per paper is instituted. The tax will be paid by the newspaper company. Find the new profit-maximizing price and quantity.
d. How much of the tax is paid by consumers?
e. Draw a diagram illustrating your answer.

10. (Practice problem: applications) In competitive markets, price ceilings lower price and reduce the quantity sold. This is not necessarily true in monopoly markets. The demand for cable subscriptions in Motelville is given in Table 12.15. The marginal cost, including payments to the cable programming providers, is $15.

Table 12.15

Price	Quantity	Revenue	Marginal revenue
$45	60,000		
$40	80,000		
$35	100,000		
$30	120,000		
$25	140,000		

a. Calculate marginal revenue, and enter in the table.
b. Find the profit-maximizing price and quantity of subscriptions.
c. Now suppose that the town sets a price ceiling equal to $25. How much will the company charge, and how many subscriptions will be sold?
d. Draw a diagram illustrating your answer.

11. (Practice problem: applications) Because a monopoly is a single seller of a good, it has no competition. Since price elasticity is generally lower when consumers have little opportunity to find substitutes, you might think that the demand for the monopolist's product is always inelastic. Nevertheless, the monopolist always produces on the elastic portion of its demand curve. To see this, compute elasticity along the demand curve given in question 3a. Show that at the chosen price and quantity, the price elasticity of demand is greater than 1.

Answers to Problems

2. *a.* Marginal revenue appears in Table 12.16.

Table 12.16

Price	Quantity	Revenue	Marginal revenue
$8	100,000	$ 800,000	—
$7	150,000	$1,050,000	$5
$6	200,000	$1,200,000	$3
$5	250,000	$1,250,000	$1
$4	300,000	$1,200,000	–$1
$3	350,000	$1,050,000	–$3
$2	400,000	$ 800,000	–$5

b. Profits are maximized when the price is $5 and the number of fans is 250,000.
c. Costs = $100,000 + (250,000 × $1) = $350,000; profits = $1,250,000 – $350,000 = $900,000.
d. The price and quantity remain as in part a, but profits fall to $1,250,000 – $400,000 = $850,000.
e. The solution is illustrated in the diagram.

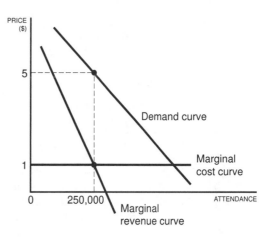

3. *a.* Marginal revenue appears in Table 12.17.

Table 12.17

Price	Quantity	Revenue	Marginal revenue
$10	1	$10	—
$ 9	2	$18	$8
$ 8	3	$24	$6
$ 7	4	$28	$4
$ 6	5	$30	$2
$ 5	6	$30	$0
$ 4	7	$28	–$2

Price = $9; quantity = 2;
profits = $18 – ($8 × 2) = $2.

b. Marginal revenue appears in Table 12.18.

Table 12.18

Price	Quantity	Revenue	Marginal revenue
$.50	500,000	$250,000	—
$.45	600,000	$270,000	$0.20
$.40	700,000	$280,000	$0.10
$.35	800,000	$280,000	$0
$.30	900,000	$270,000	–$0.10

Price = $.40; quantity = 700,000;
profits = $280,000 – [$50,000 + (700,000 × $.10)] = $160,000.

c. The complete table appears in Table 12.19.

Table 12.19

Price	Quantity	Revenue	Marginal revenue	Total costs	Marginal cost
$20	400	$ 8,000	—	$ 5,000	—
$18	800	$14,400	$16	$ 7,000	$ 5
$16	1,200	$19,200	$12	$ 9,400	$ 6
$14	1,600	$22,400	$ 8	$12,600	$ 8
$12	2,000	$24,000	$ 4	$16,200	$ 9
$10	2,400	$24,000	$ 0	$21,000	$12

Price = $14; quantity = 1,600;
profits = $22,400 – $12,600 = $9,800.

d. The completed table appears in Table 12.20.

Table 12.20

Price	Quantity	Revenue	Marginal revenue	Total costs	Marginal cost
$1.00	1,000	$1,000	—	$ 200	—
$0.90	2,000	$1,800	$.80	$ 300	$.10
$0.80	3,500	$2,800	$.67	$ 450	$.10
$0.70	5,500	$3,850	$.52	$ 650	$.10
$0.60	8,000	$4,800	$.38	$ 900	$.10
$0.50	11,000	$5,500	$.23	$1,230	$.11
$0.40	15,000	$6,000	$.12	$1,730	$.12
$0.30	20,000	$6,000	$.00	$2,355	$.14

Price = $.40; quantity = 15,000;
profits = $4,270.

5. *a.* The marginal revenue figures appear in Table 12.21.

Table 12.21

	Home market				Foreign market		
Price	Quantity	Revenue	Marginal revenue	Price	Quantity	Revenue	Marginal revenue
$10	2,000	$20,000	—	$10	2,000	$20,000	—
$ 9	2,500	$22,500	$5	$ 9	3,000	$27,000	$7
$ 8	3,000	$24,000	$3	$ 8	4,000	$32,000	$5
$ 7	3,500	$24,500	$1	$ 7	5,000	$35,000	$3
$ 6	4,000	$24,000	–$1	$ 6	6,000	$36,000	$1
$ 5	4,500	$22,500	–$3	$ 5	7,000	$35,000	–$1
$ 4	5,000	$20,000	–$5	$ 4	8,000	$32,000	–$3

b. Home market price = $7; quantity = 3,500.
Foreign market price = $6; quantity = 6,000.

c. Profits = $24,500 + $36,000 – [(3,500 + 6,000) × $1] – $5,000 = $46,000.

6. *a.* The completed table appears in Table 12.22.

Table 12.22

	Suburbs				Inner city		
Price	Quantity	Revenue	Marginal revenue	Price	Quantity	Revenue	Marginal revenue
$4.00	200	$ 800	—	$4.00	100	$400	—
$3.50	400	$1,400	$3	$3.50	120	$420	$1
$3.00	600	$1,800	$2	$3.00	140	$420	$0
$2.50	800	$2,000	$1	$2.50	160	$400	–$1
$2.00	1,000	$2,000	$0	$2.00	180	$360	–$2
$1.50	1,200	$1,800	–$1	$1.50	200	$300	–$3

b. Suburbs price = $2.50; quantity = 800.
Inner city price = $3.50; quantity = 120.

c. Profits = $2,000 + $420 – [(800 + 120) × $1] = $1,500.

8. *a, c.* The marginal revenue and Magdalena's revenue are given in Table 12.23.

Table 12.23

Price	Quantity	Revenue	Marginal revenue	Magdalena's revenue
$20	20,000	$400,000	—	$100,000
$18	25,000	$450,000	$10	$112,500
$16	30,000	$480,000	$ 6	$120,000
$14	35,000	$490,000	$ 2	$122,500
$12	40,000	$480,000	–$ 2	$120,000
$10	48,000	$480,000	$ 0	$120,000

b, d. The profix-maximizing price is $16 and the quantity is 30,000, but Magdalena's revenues are maximized at a price of $14, where 35,000 CDs are sold.

e. The solution is illustrated in the diagram.

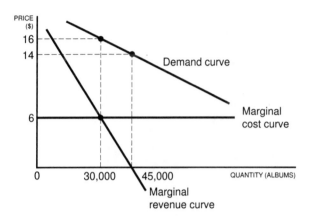

9. *a.* Marginal revenue is given in Table 12.24.

Table 12.24

Price	Quantity	Revenue	Marginal revenue
$1.00	30,000	$30,000	—
$0.95	40,000	$38,000	$.80
$0.90	50,000	$45,000	$.70
$0.85	60,000	$51,000	$.60
$0.80	70,000	$56,000	$.50
$0.75	80,000	$60,000	$.40
$0.70	90,000	$63,000	$.30
$0.65	100,000	$65,000	$.20
$0.60	110,000	$66,000	$.10
$0.55	120,000	$66,000	$.00

b. Price = $.60; quantity = 110,000.
c. The tax increases marginal cost to $.20. The price becomes $.65 and the quantity, 100,000.
d. Consumers pay $.05 of the tax.
e. The solution is illustrated in the diagram.

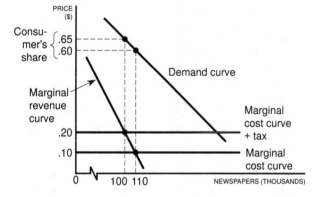

10. *a.* Marginal revenue is given in Table 12.25.

Table 12.25

Price	Quantity	Revenue	Marginal revenue
$45	60,000	$2,700,000	—
$40	80,000	$3,200,000	$25
$35	100,000	$3,500,000	$15
$30	120,000	$3,600,000	$ 5
$25	140,000	$3,500,000	−$ 5

b. Price = $35; quantity = 100,000.
c. Price = $25; quantity = 140,000.
d. The solution is illustrated in the diagram.

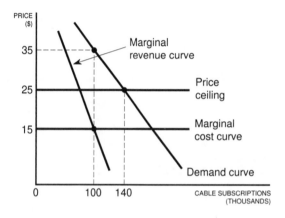

11. The elasticity for each point on the demand curve is given in Table 12.26.

Table 12.26

Price	Quantity	Revenue	Marginal revenue	Elasticity
$10	1	$10	—	—
$ 9	2	$18	$8	19/3
$ 8	3	$24	$6	17/5
$ 7	4	$28	$4	15/7
$ 6	5	$30	$2	13/9
$ 5	6	$30	$0	11/11
$ 4	7	$28	−$2	9/11

Along the elastic portion of the demand curve, which is where price exceeds $5, marginal revenue is positive. Marginal revenue equals marginal cost at a price of $9, which is on the elastic portion.

OLIGOPOLIES

Chapter Review

Chapter 12 dealt with two market structures, monopoly and monopolistic competition, in which firms face downward-sloping demand curves. The third market structure for which this is the case, oligopoly, is the subject of Chapter 13.

Oligopolies are industries that are dominated by a few firms. In a limiting case, duopoly, there are only two firms in the industry. Each firm watches its competitors closely, because each firm's best price, output level, or strategy depends upon what its rivals choose. The North American automobile industry is a perfect example of an oligopolistic market. Even today, with foreign firms competing in the Canadian market, it is still easy to see how the "big three" (General Motors, Ford, and Chrysler) respond to one another with competing rebate programmes, lower prices, or cheap financing. The chapter introduces the Prisoner's Dilemma models to examine the possibilities and motives for collusion. Chapter 14 builds upon the insights of this chapter and Chapter 12 to explore government policy towards competition.

ESSENTIAL CONCEPTS

1. In an **oligopoly**, a few firms dominate the industry. If any one firm changes its price, produces more, or adopts a new strategy, then the other firms in the oligopoly will notice the change and react to it. This strategic interaction is the essential feature of oligopolies, and it makes the study of oligopolies both difficult and fascinating.

2. Because total profits are lower when firms compete, oligopolists have an incentive to form a cartel and to collude, fix prices, and share the market. This behaviour is not only illegal in Canada but it is also difficult to sustain. First, individual firms are tempted to cheat and take advantage of the higher prices charged by others by undercutting their prices. Further, as demand and costs change over time, oligopolies have trouble renegotiating their tacit agreements. Finally, the pure profits earned by successful colluders attract entry and new competition.

3. The conflict between collusion and competition is at the heart of oligopoly. The combined profits of firms are highest if they collude. Collectively, their incentives are to fix prices and share the market. But each individual firm is tempted by its own self-interest. If its rivals keep their price high, a firm can undercut this price and capture the market. The **Prisoner's Dilemma** summarizes this conflict and shows how collusion might work. If the game is played only once and self-interest quickly takes over, all firms cheat and the equilibrium is competition. If the game is played repeatedly for an indefinite period of time, firms may be able to threaten cheaters with

competitive price wars and motivate one another to collude.

4. Firms use **restrictive practices** to restrict rival firms' abilities to compete effectively. These include imposing **market restrictions** (or **exclusive territories**), which give exclusive rights to a wholesaler or retailer in a particular area; requiring **exclusive dealing** at retail outlets, so that the outlet is prevented from stocking competing products; and insisting on **tied selling** arrangements, which force a customer who buys one product to buy an additional product too. These practices can reduce competition by increasing the costs of capturing the customers of rival firms. Firms also restrict competition through such practices as matching their rivals' low-price offers.

5. Existing firms always face the problem of entry, and the threat can sometimes be so strong that it keeps prices close to production costs. When potential competition induces competitive prices, markets are called **contestable.** Costs of entry and exit must be relatively small, however, and the persistence of certain oligopolies through time suggests that significant barriers to entry exist in these industries, and hence that these particular markets are not contestable.

6. There are three important models of competition in oligopolies.

   a. If firms are committed to producing a given amount of output, as is the case in industries where fixed costs are high and changing capacity is very expensive, there is quantity or **Cournot competition.** One such example is the steel industry. Setting up a factory to commence or expand production is very expensive, so the firm gets locked in at certain capacities. It tries to select capacities corresponding to a price where profits will be maximized. The equilibrium is given by the intersection of **reaction** functions, which indicate the quantity that one firm will produce for each possible quantity choice of its rival.

   b. If the costs of increasing capacity are low, then price or **Bertrand competition** reigns. An example of this is a particular route flown by an airline—for example, between Toronto and Montreal. Varying capacity is easy, and the airline selects a price corresponding to a quantity where profits will be maximized. The equilibrium is again given by the intersection of reaction functions. The reaction functions in this model show the price that one firm will charge for each possible price of its rival.

   c. The **kinked demand curve** model shows that if firms expect rivals to match a price cut but not price increases, then they are unlikely to change price or quantity.

BEHIND THE ESSENTIAL CONCEPTS

1. The world of perfect competition is simple and precise. The firm cannot affect the market of any competitor; it simply chooses its quantity to maximize profits. The world of oligopoly is rich and varied. Firms try to limit competition and promote collusion. They have a wealth of strategies to choose from: price and quantity, of course, but also such practices as matching offers of rivals and threatening price wars with new entrants or existing firms who cheat on tacit agreements to limit price competition. Oligopoly is an area in which economics has made much progress in the last 10 or 15 years.

2. As a group, firms in an oligopoly want to cooperate, charge high prices, and share monopoly profits, but they always run up against the problem of self-interest. Each individual firm would like to cheat while the others abide by the cooperative strategy. It is this noncooperative behaviour by individual firms that promotes economic efficiency, because it keeps the oligopolists from cooperating to gouge customers with high prices. It is ironic that if firms were more cooperative, the economy would not work so well.

3. The most important technique for studying oligopolies is the reaction function. The equilibrium in the industry is at the intersection of reaction functions, but the reasoning is not the same as in the supply and demand model. Because there are few firms, the profit-maximizing price, quantity, or other strategy depends upon what the other firms do. How is the individual firm to decide without actually knowing the choices of rivals? The reaction function shows what the choice would be for every possible choice by the rival. Putting the reaction functions of both firms together gives the equilibrium. At the intersection, each firm is choosing what is best for it in response to the actual choice of the rival. Since neither can improve matters unilaterally, there are no forces for change, and the market is in equilibrium.

SELF-TEST

True or False

1. In an oligopoly, there are so few firms that any one firm need not worry about how its rivals will react to anything it does.

2. A cartel is a group of firms engaging in price competition.

3. The incentive for a cartel member to cheat arises because its marginal revenue is greater than the marginal revenue for the cartel as a whole.

4. Anti-combines laws allow cartels to sign collusive agreements.

5. Price leadership facilitates collusion.

6. Offers to match prices charged by competing firms result in more price competition.

7. In contestable markets the threat of entry keeps price from rising.

8. In the Prisoner's Dilemma, both parties are made worse off by pursuing their self-interest.

9. Resale price maintenance is an example of a vertical restraint.

10. In Cournot competition, each oligopolist assumes its rivals will change their outputs in response to its output decision.

11. In Cournot competition, industry output is less than it would be under competitive conditions but greater than it would be under monopoly conditions.

12. In Bertrand competition, firms believe they face a more elastic demand than firms in the Cournot model do.

13. If the firms' goods are perfect substitutes, the price in Bertrand competition is the monopoly price.

14. In the kinked demand curve model, the curve is more elastic below the current price than above it.

15. A prediction of the kinked demand curve model is that small changes in marginal cost have large effects on output and price.

Multiple Choice

1. Firms in oligopolies differ from firms in monopolistic competition in that firms in oligopolies:

   a. face downward-sloping demand curves.
   b. face demand curves for which price exceeds marginal revenue.
   c. must worry about how rivals will react to their decisions.
   d. maximize profit when price exceeds marginal cost.
   e. do not set price and output at levels that are efficient.

2. When firms in an industry act jointly to maximize profits in the industry, this is called:

   a. monopolistic competition.
   b. a cartel.
   c. perfect competition.
   d. a monopsony.
   e. oligopolistic competition.

3. One difficulty that colluding firms often face is that a firm may cheat on the collusive understanding by:

   a. undercutting the cartel price and restricting output.
   b. charging more than the cartel price and expanding output.
   c. maintaining the cartel price and expanding output.
   d. undercutting the cartel price and expanding output.
   e. charging more than the cartel price and restricting output.

4. The incentive for colluding firms to cheat on the collusive understanding arises because:

   a. the marginal revenue perceived by the firm is greater than it is for the cartel as a whole.
   b. the marginal revenue perceived by the firm is less than it is for the cartel as a whole.
   c. collusion is not mutually beneficial.
   d. the marginal cost perceived by the firm is greater than it is for the cartel as a whole.
   e. the marginal cost perceived by the firm is less than it is for the cartel as a whole.

5. Price leadership is an example of:

   a. a facilitating practice.
   b. a restrictive practice.
   c. exclusive territories.
   d. exclusive dealing.
   e. tied selling.

6. In the practice known as price leadership, the leader:

   a. sets the industry's highest price.
   b. sets the industry's price and the other firms follow.
   c. deters entry by threatening to lower price.
   d. is always the largest firm in the industry.
   e. stands ready to match the industry's lowest price.

7. The public offer by a firm to "meet the competition" by matching any price charged by any competing firm is an example of:

   a. a restrictive practice.
   b. exclusive territories.
   c. tied selling.
   d. exclusive dealing.
   e. a facilitating practice.

8. When a firm makes a public offer to "meet the competition" by matching any price charged by any competing firm, this typically represents an attempt to:

   a. undermine a collusive agreement.
   b. reduce price competition.
   c. maintain price competition.
   d. increase price competition.
   e. facilitate coordinated price reductions.

9. Markets in which it is believed that potential entry is sufficient to keep prices competitive are called:

   a. oligopolistically competitive markets.
   b. competitive markets.
   c. contestable markets.
   d. efficienct markets.
   e. monopolistically competitive markets.

10. The Prisoner's Dilemma illustrates that the pursuit of self-interest by the prisoners:

    a. will make one prisoner worse off and one no better off.
    b. always makes both prisoners better off.
    c. will make one prisoner better off and one no worse off.
    d. can make both prisoners worse off.
    e. will leave both prisoners no worse off and no better off.

11. All of the following, except one, are examples of restrictive practices. Which is the odd one out?

    a. matching the competition's prices
    b. exclusive territories
    c. exclusive dealing
    d. tied selling
    e. market restrictions

12. Tied selling is:

    a. a requirement that a retailer charge list price for a firm's product.
    b. an agreement granting the sole right to sell a good within a region.
    c. a requirement that any customer who buys one product must buy another.
    d. a practice in which firms set their prices by following a leader.
    e. a requirement that a retailer sell no competing firm's product.

13. Market restrictions are:

    a. requirements that a retailer charge list price for a firm's product.

    b. agreements granting the sole right to sell a good within a region.

    c. requirements that any customer who buys one product must buy another.

    d. practices in which firms set their prices by following a leader.

    e. requirements that a retailer sell no competing firm's products.

14. Exclusive dealing is:

    a. a requirement that a retailer charge list price for a firm's product.

    b. an agreement granting the sole right to sell a good within a region.

    c. a requirement that any customer who buys one product must buy another.

    d. a practice in which firms set their prices by following a leader.

    e. a requirement that a retailer sell no competing firm's products.

15. Resale price maintenance is:

    a. a requirement that a retailer charge list price for a firm's product.

    b. an agreement granting the sole right to sell a good within a region.

    c. a requirement that any customer who buys one product must buy another.

    d. a practice in which firms set their prices by following a leader.

    e. a requirement that a retailer sell no competing firm's products.

16. All of the following, except one, are possible effects of restrictive practices. Which is the odd one out?

    a. reduced economic efficiency
    b. restricted competition
    c. lower prices for consumers
    d. higher costs for rivals
    e. duplication of distribution systems

17. In Cournot competition, oligopolistic firms:

    a. match rivals' price cuts but not their price increases.

    b. compete by choosing price, assuming rivals' prices are fixed.

    c. finish up setting the price that would occur under perfect competition.

    d. compete by choosing quantity, assuming rivals' output is fixed.

    e. collude to fix prices and earn monopoly profits.

18. In Bertrand competition, oligopolistic firms:

    a. match rivals' price cuts but not their price increases.

    b. compete by choosing price, assuming rivals' prices are fixed.

    c. finish up setting the price that would occur under perfect competition.

    d. compete by choosing quantity, assuming rivals' output is fixed.

    e. collude to fix prices and earn monopoly profits.

19. When a firm stands ready to match rivals' price cuts but not rivals' price increases, the demand curve facing the firm:

    a. is more price-elastic above the current price than below it.

    b. has a kink at the price that would be set under competition.

    c. is less price-elastic above the current price than below it.

    d. has a kink at the price that will yield zero profit.

    e. is more price-elastic below the current price than above it.

20. Marginal revenue for the firm with a kinked demand curve:

    a. equals price for outputs below the level at which the kink in the demand curve occurs.

    b. rises sharply at the output at which the kink in the demand curve occurs.

    c. is horizontal, except for a spike at the output at which the kink in the demand curve occurs.

    d. drops sharply at the output at which the kink in the demand curve occurs.

    e. equals price for outputs above the level at which the kink in the demand curve occurs.

Completion

1. In an oligopoly, there are so few firms that each must consider how its rival will _____ to any change in strategy.

2. A group of companies operating jointly as if they were a monopoly is called a _____.

3. Collusive behavior is prohibited by _____ laws.

4. The _____ is a game that illustrates the problem cartels have in enforcing collusive behavior.

5. Markets in which the threat of competition impels firms to charge the competitive price are called _____.

6. A firm that insists that any other firm selling its products refrain from selling those of its rivals is engaging in _____.

7. Meeting competitors' prices is known as a _____.

8. Tied selling is a form of _____.

9. If a firm believes that its rivals will match its price cuts but not its price increases, then it will perceive its demand curve to be _____ at the current price.

10. Firms that compete by setting price believe that they face _____ elastic demand curves than firms that compete by setting quantity.

Answers to Self-Test

True or False

1. f	4. f	7. t	10. f	13. f
2. f	5. t	8. t	11. t	14. f
3. t	6. f	9. t	12. t	15. f

Multiple Choice

1. c	6. b	11. a	16. c
2. b	7. e	12. c	17. d
3. d	8. b	13. b	18. b
4. a	9. c	14. e	19. a
5. a	10. d	15. a	20. d

Completion

1. react
2. cartel
3. anti-combines
4. Prisoner's Dilemma
5. contestable
6. exclusive dealing
7. facilitating practice
8. vertical restraint
9. kinked
10. more

Doing Economics: Tools and Practice Problems

This section looks at several issues pertaining to oligopoly. First, we consider collusion and the incentive it creates for any individual firm to increase output. Then, we turn to quantity competition. Next, some examples of the Prisoner's Dilemma game are presented. Finally, we demonstrate how restrictive practices may help support a collusive agreement.

COLLUSION AND CHEATING

Collusion among price-taking firms enables them to share monopoly profits if they are able to prevent entry. By establishing a cartel, an agreement to set the monopoly price, they can divide the monopoly output among them. But the success of a cartel sows the seeds of its own destruction. To charge the monopoly price, each firm must produce less than it wants to at that price. The temptation to cheat is usually too great. Firms produce more than their assigned amounts, and collectively they undercut the cartel's price. Tool Kit 13.1 shows you how firms can establish a cartel and illustrates the potential for cheating on the agreement.

Tool Kit 13.1: Collusion and Cheating

Follow these steps to see how a group of price-taking firms can establish a cartel.

Step one: Identify and add up the supply curves of the individual firms. The result is the cartel's marginal cost curve.

Step two: Identify the market demand curve, and find its marginal revenue.

Step three: Find the profit-maximizing price and quantity for the cartel by setting marginal revenue equal to marginal cost.

Step four: Determine each firm's output by evenly dividing the cartel's output among its members.

Step five: Given the profit-maximizing price, determine how much each firm would like to produce. Remember that each firm will behave as if this price is its marginal revenue and will want to equate this to its marginal cost (which is also the individual firm's supply curve).

Step six: If all firms cheat, collusion breaks down completely and the market becomes competitive. Determine the competitive output and price by equating market supply and market demand.

---

1. (Worked problem: collusion and cheating) The Quebec Maple Syrup Board is a cartel of 1,000 maple syrup producers. The demand for maple syrup and the supply curve of a typical producer are given in Table 13.1. The quantity represents litres.

Table 13.1

Market demand		Firm's supply	
Price	Quantity	Price	Quantity
$10	10,000	$10	60
$ 9	15,000	$ 9	55
$ 8	20,000	$ 8	50
$ 7	25,000	$ 7	45
$ 6	30,000	$ 6	40
$ 5	35,000	$ 5	35
		$ 4	30
		$ 3	25
		$ 2	20

a. Find the profit-maximizing price for the cartel as a whole. How many litres will be sold at this price? How many must each firm produce to sustain this price?

b. If the cartel charges the price computed in part a, how many units would the individual firm like to produce?

c. Now suppose that all firms cheat and the market becomes competitive. Find the equilibrium price and quantity.

Step-by-step solution

Step one (a): Add up the individual supplies. Since there are 1,000 firms, the market supply is simply the quantity supplied by the firm multiplied by 1,000. The market supply is given in Table 13.2.

Table 13.2

Firm's supply		Market supply	
Price	Quantity	Price	Quantity
$10	60	$10	60,000
$ 9	55	$ 9	55,000
$ 8	50	$ 8	50,000
$ 7	45	$ 7	45,000
$ 6	40	$ 6	40,000
$ 5	35	$ 5	35,000
$ 4	30	$ 4	30,000
$ 3	25	$ 3	25,000
$ 2	20	$ 2	20,000

Step two: Derive marginal revenue. First find total revenue, and enter it in the appropriate column. Marginal revenue is the change in total revenue divided by the change in quantity. The answer is given in Table 13.3.

Table 13.3

Market demand		Total revenue	Marginal revenue
Price	Quantity		
$10	10,000	$100,000	
$ 9	15,000	$135,000	$7
$ 8	20,000	$160,000	$5
$ 7	25,000	$175,000	$3
$ 6	30,000	$180,000	$1
$ 5	35,000	$175,000	–$1

Step three: Find the profit-maximizing price for the cartel. The market supply curve is the cartel's marginal cost. Marginal cost equals marginal revenue when the quantity is 25,000. The corresponding price is $7. Each firm produces 25 litres.

Step four (b): Find how much the firm would like to supply at the cartel price. At a price of $7, the firm would like to produce 45 litres (this number is read off the firm's supply curve), which is 20 more than it is assigned.

Step five (c): If all firms cheat, then the market will become a competitive market and will clear at a price of $5, where each firm produces 35 litres.

2. (Practice problem: collusion and cheating) The 500 mail-order computer equipment suppliers are (discreetly) forming a cartel. The market demand curve and the supply curve of a typical equipment supplier are given in Table 13.4. The quantity represents the number of computers.

Table 13.4

Market demand		Total revenue	Marginal revenue
Price	Quantity		
$1,000	300,000		
$ 900	400,000		
$ 800	500,000		
$ 700	600,000		
$ 600	700,000		
$ 500	800,000		
$ 400	900,000		
$ 300	1,000,000		

Firm's supply		Market supply	
Price	Quantity	Price	Quantity
$1,000	4,000		
$ 900	3,500		
$ 800	3,000		
$ 700	2,400		
$ 600	2,000		
$ 500	1,600		
$ 400	1,000		
$ 300	500		
$ 200	100		

a. Derive the marginal revenue for the computer equipment supplier market.

b. Add up the 500 individual firm supplies to derive the market supply.

c. Find the profit-maximizing price for the cartel as a whole. How many computers will be sold at this price? How many must each firm sell to sustain this price?

d. If the cartel charges the price computed in part c, how many units would the individual firm like to sell?

e. Now suppose that all firms cheat, and the market becomes competitive. Find the equilibrium price and quantity.

QUANTITY COMPETITION

In industries like steel and aluminum, the fixed costs of plant and equipment are a major proportion of total costs, and variable costs are relatively unimportant. Once capital goods are in place, adding new machines would be expensive, and not using machinery to its capacity would save the firm little money. In such circumstances, a firm might reasonably presume that it can take its rival's output as fixed in the short term. Tool Kit 13.2 shows you how a duopoly (a two-firm industry) might initially divide up the market, only for one firm to find it profitable to increase output if it believes the other firm will not change its output. In such cases, the industry price is whatever clears the market, given the combined output of the firms.

Tool Kit 13.2: Collusion and Quantity Competition between Duopolists

Follow these steps to determine the details of a collusive agreement between duopolists that have high fixed costs and low variable costs. The procedure also includes the calculation of the first round of quantity competition that might result because of the incentive provided by the collusive agreement for one firm to increase production.

Step one: Identify the market demand, marginal revenue, marginal cost, and profit-maximizing price and output if the firms collude.

Step two: Identify the market demand, marginal cost, and output of the opponent firm.

Step three: Subtract the output of the opponent firm from the market demand. The difference is called the **residual demand curve**:

residual demand =
   market demand – opponent's output.

Step four: Find the marginal revenue for the residual demand curve.

Step five: Choose the output for which marginal revenue equals marginal cost.

Step six: Find industry output and the price that clears the market, given this output.

3. (Worked problem: quantity competition) The New Chairs for Old Company shares the furniture-refinishing market in Southpoint with the Like New Company. Each uses enormous vats of chemicals, which are expensive to set up but cheap to operate. One vat will permit the refinishing of 10 pieces of furniture per day. The marginal cost for each firm is constant and equal to $4. Table 13.5 gives the market demand.

Table 13.5

Price	Quantity
$7.50	0
$7.00	10
$6.50	20
$6.00	30
$5.50	40
$5.00	50
$4.50	60
$4.00	70

a. Suppose that the two firms try to operate as a cartel and share the market equally. Find the profit-maximizing quantity for each.
b. Now look at the problem from the point of view of the owner of New Chairs for Old. The owner conjectures that the rival firm will commit to the quantity solved for in part a. Find the profit-maximizing quantity.
c. Determine total output on the assumption that the rival firm does not adjust its output. Find the price that will clear the market.

Step-by-step solution

Step one (a): We follow the usual procedure for the monopolist: find the marginal revenue and set marginal revenue equal to marginal cost. Table 13.6 gives the marginal revenue.

Table 13.6

Price	Quantity	Total revenue	Marginal revenue
$7.50	0	$ 0	—
$7.00	10	$ 70	$7
$6.50	20	$130	$6
$6.00	30	$180	$5
$5.50	40	$220	$4
$5.00	50	$250	$3
$4.50	60	$270	$2
$4.00	70	$280	$1

Marginal revenue equals marginal cost when the total quantity is 40. Each firm then buys two vats and refinishes 20 pieces of furniture.

Step two (b): Identify the market demand, marginal cost, and output of the opponent firm. The market demand is given in Table 13.5, the marginal cost is $4, and Like New is expected to produce 20.

Step three: Subtract the output of the opponent firm from the market demand, as shown in Table 13.7.

Table 13.7

Price	Quantity
$7.00	0
$6.50	20 − 20 = 0
$6.00	30 − 20 = 10
$5.50	40 − 20 = 20
$5.00	50 − 20 = 30
$4.50	60 − 20 = 40
$4.00	70 − 20 = 50

Step four: Find the marginal revenue for the residual demand curve, as given in Table 13.8.

Table 13.8

Price	Quantity	Total revenue	Marginal revenue
$7.00	0	0	—
$6.50	0	0	—
$6.00	10	$ 60	$6
$5.50	20	$110	$5
$5.00	30	$150	$4
$4.50	40	$180	$3
$4.00	50	$200	$2

Step five: Choose the output for which marginal revenue equals marginal cost. When output is 30, marginal revenue and marginal cost both equal $4.

Step six (c): New Chairs for Old now has an output of 30, and Like New is still at an output of 20. Total output is 50, and Table 13.5 reveals that the price that will clear the market is $5, compared with $5.50 when the firms were colluding by setting total output at 40.

4. (Practice problem: quantity competition) The Davis Lead Company competes with its rival Anderson Lead. Because the plant and equipment are so expensive and because marginal production costs are so low (only $5 per tonne) until capacity is reached, the two firms compete by choosing quantity. The market demand is given in Table 13.9.

Table 13.9

Price	Quantity (tonnes)
$22.50	0
$20.00	100
$17.50	200
$15.00	300
$12.50	400
$10.00	500
$ 7.50	600

a. Suppose that the two firms try to operate as a cartel and share the market equally. Find the profit-maximizing quantity for each.

b. Now look at the problem from the point of view of the owner of Davis. The owner conjectures that the rival firm will commit to the quantity solved for in part a. Find the profit-maximizing quantity.

c. Determine total output under the assumption that the rival firm does not adjust its output. Find the price that will clear the market.

PRISONER'S DILEMMA

The Prisoner's Dilemma demonstrates that both parties are made worse off by pursuing their self-interest. In terms of a collusive agreement, what is good for the cartel conflicts with what is good for the individual firm in the cartel. Once again, there are pressures operating from within to break down collusion. Tool Kit 13.3 shows you how to represent this conflict in terms of the Prisoner's Dilemma.

Tool Kit 13.3: The Prisoner's Dilemma

Follow these steps to present cooperative (that is, collusive) and competitive outcomes as a Prisoner's Dilemma.

Step one: Draw a box with four cells, and label it as shown.

	FIRM A cooperate	compete
FIRM B cooperate		
compete		

Step two: Identify the payoffs for each party if both cooperate, and enter in the appropriate cell.

	FIRM A cooperate	compete
FIRM B cooperate	A's profits = B's profits =	
compete		

Step three: Identify the payoffs for each party if both compete, and enter in the appropriate cell.

	FIRM A cooperate	compete
FIRM B cooperate		
compete		A's profits = B's profits =

Step four: Identify the payoffs for each party if one competes while the other cooperates, and enter in the corresponding cells.

	FIRM A cooperate	compete
FIRM B cooperate		A's profits = B's profits =
compete	A's profits = B's profits =	

Step five: In the classic Prisoner's Dilemma, competing is always the best strategy, whatever the opponent chooses. Show that competition is the equilibrium.

---

5. (Worked problem: Prisoner's Dilemma) Chiaravelli and Fiegenshau are the only two dentists in Plainville. They have been colluding, sharing the market and earning monopoly profits of $100,000 each for several years. Fiegenshau is considering reducing his price. Fiegenshau estimates that if Chiaravelli keeps the price at current levels, Fiegenshau would earn $150,000, although Chiaravelli's earnings would fall to $25,000. There is also the possibility that Chiaravelli would compete against Fiegenshau. The resulting price war would reduce the earnings of each to $40,000.

a. Represent this market as a Prisoner's Dilemma game.

b. Explain why competition between the dentists is the equilibrium outcome.

Step-by-step solution

Step one (a): Draw a box with four cells, and label it as shown.

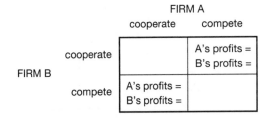

	CHIARAVELLI cooperate	compete
FIEGENSHAU cooperate		
compete		

Step two: Identify the payoffs for each party if both cooperate, and enter in the appropriate cell. If both cooperate, they each earn $100,000.

	CHIARAVELLI cooperate	compete
FIEGENSHAU cooperate	C = $100,000 F = $100,000	
compete		

Step three: Identify the payoffs for each party if both compete, and enter in the appropriate cell. If both compete, they each earn $40,000.

	CHIARAVELLI	
	cooperate	compete
FIEGENSHAU cooperate	C = $100,000 F = $100,000	
compete		C = $40,000 F = $40,000

Step four: Identify the payoffs for each party if one competes while the other cooperates, and enter in the corresponding cell. In this case, the dentist who competes earns $150,000, and the other is left with $25,000.

	CHIARAVELLI	
	cooperate	compete
FIEGENSHAU cooperate	C = $100,000 F = $100,000	C = $150,000 F = $25,000
compete	C = $25,000 F = $150,000	C = $40,000 F = $40,000

Step five (b): Show that competition is the equilibrium. For each party, competition is always the best alternative. If Chiaravelli cooperates, then Fiegenshau can earn more by competing ($150,000 > $100,000). If Chiaravelli competes, Fiegenshau still earns more by competing ($40,000 > $25,000). The same is true for Chiaravelli, and both choose to compete.

6. (Practice problem: Prisoner's Dilemma) Upper Peninsula Airlines and Northern Airways share the market from Toronto to the winter resorts in the South. If they cooperate, they can extract enough monopoly profits to earn $400,000 each, but unbridled competition would reduce profits to $50,000 each. If one is foolish enough to cooperate in its pricing policy while the other undercuts it, the cooperating firm would earn $0, and the competing firm would earn $800,000.

    a. Represent this market as a Prisoner's Dilemma game.
    b. Explain why competition is the equilibrium outcome.

7. (Practice problem: Prisoner's Dilemma) Hill College and Allan College are the best private schools in the city. Each also prides itself on its lacrosse team. If neither offers scholarships for promising players, then obviously the cost of scholarships will be zero. For $20,000 in scholarships, either could attract the best players (if the other did not offer scholarships), win the provincial championship, and attract at least $50,000 in new donations. In this case, however, donations at the losing school would fall by $30,000. On the other hand, if both offered scholarships, there would be no advantage, no extra donations, and each would have spent the $20,000 for nothing.

    a. Represent this market as a Prisoner's Dilemma game.
    b. Explain why competition is the equilibrium outcome.

FACILITATING AND RESTRICTIVE PRACTICES

Coordination and enforcement are two major problems faced by firms in a collusive agreement. Facilitating and restrictive practices help to make collusion easier. The final two problems adapt previous questions to provide examples of how this might occur.

8. (Worked problem: facilitating and restrictive practices) This problem builds upon problem 3. Having accumulated several years of experience with the unpleasant results of competition, the owners of Southpoint's two furniture-refinishing firms decide to try a new method of collusion. Henceforth, the New Chairs for Old Company will specialize in refinishing chairs, and the Like New Company will take care of the table share of the market. It so happens in Southpoint that exactly half of the business involves tables and half involves chairs. Their marginal costs remain at $4.

    a. Compute the profit-maximizing quantity of chairs and tables and the corresponding prices for both companies.
    b. Compare your answer with the collusive solution in part a of problem 3.

Step-by-step solution

Step one (a): Divide the market into chair and table markets. The result is given in Table 13.10.

Table 13.10

Price	Quantity of chairs	Quantity of tables
$7.50	0	0
$7.00	5	5
$6.50	10	10
$6.00	15	15
$5.50	20	20
$5.00	25	25
$4.50	30	30
$4.00	35	35

Step two: Compute the marginal revenue for each firm. These are shown in Table 13.11. Note that since the demands are exactly the same, so are the marginal revenues. Only one is shown.

Table 13.11

Price	Quantity of chairs	Quantity of tables	Total revenue	Marginal revenue
$7.50	0	0	$ 0	—
$7.00	5	5	$ 35	$7
$6.50	10	10	$ 65	$6
$6.00	15	15	$ 90	$5
$5.50	20	20	$110	$4
$5.00	25	25	$125	$3
$4.50	30	30	$135	$2
$4.00	35	35	$140	$1

Step three (b): Marginal revenue equals marginal cost at a quantity of 20 for each. The market price will be $5.50, which is exactly the outcome that was solved for in part a of problem 3. Dividing the market promotes collusion.

9. (Practice problem: facilitating and restrictive practices) This problem builds upon problem 4. The Davis and Anderson companies have come up with a scheme to promote collusion. From now on, Davis will advertise and take orders from customers in the West and leave the eastern half of the market to Anderson. They divide the territories so that exactly half the customers will go to each firm. The marginal cost remains at $5 per tonne, and the market demand is as given in Table 13.9.

   a. Compute the profit-maximizing quantity and price for each firm.
   b. Compare your answer with the collusive solution in part a of problem 4.

Answers to Problems

2. *a,b.* The marginal revenue and the market supply appear in Table 13.12.

Table 13.12

Market demand		Total revenue	Marginal revenue
Price	Quantity		
$1,000	300,000	$300,000,000	—
$ 900	400,000	$360,000,000	$600
$ 800	500,000	$400,000,000	$400
$ 700	600,000	$420,000,000	$200
$ 600	700,000	$420,000,000	$ 0
$ 500	800,000	$400,000,000	–$200
$ 400	900,000	$360,000,000	–$400
$ 300	1,000,000	$300,000,000	–$600

Firm's supply		Market supply	
Price	Quantity	Price	Quantity
$1,000	4,000	$1,000	2,000,000
$ 900	3,500	$ 900	1,750,000
$ 800	3,000	$ 800	1,500,000
$ 700	2,400	$ 700	1,200,000
$ 600	2,000	$ 600	1,000,000
$ 500	1,600	$ 500	800,000
$ 400	1,000	$ 400	500,000
$ 300	500	$ 300	250,000
$ 200	100	$ 200	50,000

   c. Cartel price = $800; market quantity = 500,000; each firm's quantity = 1,000.
   d. 3,000.
   e. Price = $500; quantity = 800,000.

4. *a.* Marginal revenue for the market demand is given in Table 13.13.

Table 13.13

Price	Quantity (tonnes)	Total revenue	Marginal revenue
$22.50	0	$ 0	
$20.00	100	$2,000	$20
$17.50	200	$3,500	$15
$15.00	300	$4,500	$10
$12.50	400	$5,000	$ 5
$10.00	500	$5,000	$ 0
$ 7.50	600	$4,500	–$ 5

Price = $12.50; market quantity = 400; each firm sells 200 tonnes.

   b. The residual demand is found by subtracting 200 from the market demand. This and marginal revenue appear in Table 13.14.

Table 13.14

Price	Quantity (tonnes)	Total revenue	Marginal revenue
$22.50	0	$ 0	
$20.00	0	$ 0	
$17.50	0	$ 0	
$15.00	100	$1,500	$15
$12.50	200	$2,500	$10
$10.00	300	$3,000	$ 5
$ 7.50	400	$3,000	$ 0

Davis will produce 300. The market quantity will be 200 + 300 = 500, and the price will be $10 per tonne.

6. *a.*

	Upper Peninsula	
	cooperate	compete
Northern cooperate	UP = $400,000 N = $400,000	UP = $800,000 N = $0
compete	UP = $0 N = $800,000	UP = $50,000 N = $50,000

   b. If Northern cooperates, UP prefers to compete ($800,000 > $400,000). If Northern competes, UP still prefers to compete ($50,000 > $0). If UP cooperates, Northern prefers to compete ($800,000 > $400,000). If UP competes, Northern still prefers to compete ($50,000 > $0) Since both always prefer competition, the equilibrium is that both compete and profits are $50,000 each.

7. *a.*

		Allan	
		cooperate	compete
Northern	cooperate	A = $0 H = $0	A = +$30,000 H = –$30,000
	compete	A = –$30,000 H = +$30,000	A = –$20,000 H = –$20,000

b. If Hill cooperates and does not offer scholarships, Allan prefers to compete and offer them because the return by doing so when Hill cooperates, which is $30,000, exceeds the return of $0 if Allan cooperates too. If Hill competes and offers scholarships, Allan is better off offering them (–$20,000) than not offering them (–30,000). If Allan cooperates and does not offer scholarships, Hill prefers to offer them ($30,000 > $0). If Allan competes and offers scholarships, Hill still prefers to offer them (–$20,000 > –$30,000). Since each prefers to compete and offer scholarships, regardless of the ac-tions of the other, the equilibrium is that both compete.

9. The demand for each firm's share of the market and the corresponding marginal revenue appear in Table 13.15.

Table 13.15

Price	Quantity (tonnes)	Revenues	Marginal revenue
$22.50	0	$ 0	—
$20.00	50	$1,000	$20
$17.50	100	$1,750	$15
$15.00	150	$2,250	$10
$12.50	200	$2,500	$ 5
$10.00	250	$2,500	$ 0
$ 7.50	300	$2,250	–$ 5

a. Each firm charges $12.50 and sells 200.

b. The price and quantity are the same as under monopoly.

Chapter 14

GOVERNMENT POLICIES TOWARDS COMPETITION

Chapter Review

Monopolies and oligopolies, studied in Chapters 12 and 13, produce too little output and charge prices that exceed marginal cost. Wherever possible, there will be a benefit from eliminating these inefficiencies. This chapter examines the role government can play in this regard. A primary focus is government policy to promote competition. The chapter also examines government responses to natural monopolies. Natural monopolies occur when a single firm can produce the good more cheaply than multiple firms. In Chapter 15, the focus shifts to how firms compete to introduce new products and discover better ways of producing.

ESSENTIAL CONCEPTS

1. Competitive industries allocate resources efficiently. Monopolies and other imperfectly competitive industries, however, often operate inefficiently. Economists study four types of inefficiency.

   a. Monopolies restrict output below what it would be if the industry were competitive. The lower output results in higher prices and a transfer of wealth from consumers to the monopoly. There is an additional loss in consumer surplus, because output is below the level at which all gains from trade are realized. This loss is called the deadweight loss of monopoly.

   b. Although monopoly profits are higher when their costs are lower, monopolies are not forced to produce at the lowest cost. There is some room for **managerial slack**, which allows monopolies to be inefficient.

   c. Although there are examples of monopolies that engage in effective **research and development**, the incentives for technological progress are reduced under monopoly.

   d. Because monopolies earn rents (profits above the level necessary to compensate investors), resources are expended to acquire and retain these existing rents. This type of activity is called **rent seeking** and is socially wasteful.

2. In some industries, where there are high fixed and low marginal costs, the lowest cost of production occurs when there is only one firm. Such an industry is called a **natural monopoly**. Figure 14.1 shows the typical cost curves for a natural monopoly. The average cost is downward-sloping, and as a result, marginal cost lies below average cost. Governments sometimes nationalize and operate natural monopolies, but more often governments regulate them. A regulatory agency sets prices designed

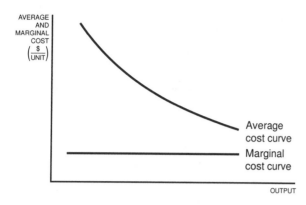

Figure 14.1

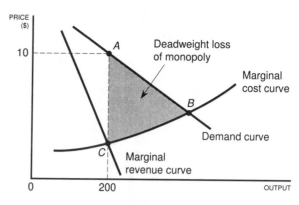

Figure 14.2

to limit the firm to a normal rate of return on capital. This policy in turn motivates firms to overinvest in capital. Also, because the pricing decisions in both the nationalized and regulated cases are made politically, products may be sold below cost in some markets and above cost in others. This practice is called **cross subsidization.** A further problem is that regulators are often captured by the firms they set out to regulate, so that the regulators tend to lose sight of the public interest and side too often with the firms.

3. A final way of dealing with natural monopolies is to increase competition. Examples in Canada include the deregulation of long-distance telephone service and the trucking and airline industries. Competition provides firms with incentives to innovate and reduce costs, and it eliminates cross subsidization. On the other hand, with more firms in the industry, each firm produces less, that is, chooses a point higher up the average cost curve.

4. The various ways in which the government attempts to promote competition were referred to historically as anti-combines legislation. More recently, the Competition Act of 1986 replaced the Combines Investigation Act. It set up a Competition Tribunal to investigate the effect of large corporate mergers on competition according to seven factors. Additionally, it defined "abuse of a dominant position" as constituting various types of "anticompetitive acts," rather than declaring monopoly itself an offence. The Competition Act also prohibited certain restrictive practices where it can be proved that they do economic harm.

BEHIND THE ESSENTIAL CONCEPTS

1. The problem of deadweight loss lies at the heart of economic arguments about making exchange efficient. As an example, look at Figure 14.2, which shows a monopoly output equal to 200. The firm sets the price at $10 and maximizes its profits. Notice, however, that at this point the marginal benefit to consumers of one more unit (measured, as usual, by the price they are willing to pay) is greater than the marginal cost. This means that producing and selling this unit and additional units would create value; there would be gains from trade. The total possible additional gains equal the area of the triangle *ABC*. But these gains are not realized; they are called the deadweight loss of monopoly.

2. Firms desiring greater profits seek them in two ways. First, they offer better products or devise better ways of producing and doing business. These activities do make profits, and they create value and enhance efficiency as well. Second, firms try to convince government to protect them against competition or devise strategies to deter entry. Practices of this type do not create anything; they only redistribute money and reduce economic efficiency. Such behaviour is called rent seeking.

3. In competitive industries, firms are forced to produce at the lowest possible cost. If they do not, new firms will enter the market, undercut the price, and drive existing firms out. In a monopoly, however, whether it is private, nationalized, or regulated, the firm can get away with some slack. It can pay its workers a little more than the going wage, it can postpone adopting the most efficient production techniques, or it can overlook the low-cost suppliers. You can probably see how this could happen in an unregulated monopoly, where there are extra profits, or in a nationalized industry, where the government makes up any losses, but it is also possible in a regulated monopoly because regulators do not always know the lowest cost. The firm has an incentive and the ability to make the regulators believe that it is more costly to do business than it really is. Regulators can prevent fraud, but it is very difficult to find and eliminate waste.

4. In order to determine whether a merger will inhibit competition, the number of firms in an industry and their size relative to the market needs to be determined. The geographical size of the market should be considered, as some industries are local, while many have become international. For example, the gold market is a world market. The cement industry, on the other hand, is local. The product is very expensive to transport, and only nearby firms could merge. The similarity of the products also needs to be considered. Is plastic wrap in the same industry as aluminum foil? If so, does a single producer of plastic wrap have a monopoly, or is it simply another firm in the food-wrapping industry?

SELF-TEST

True or False

1. A monopoly produces less output than would be produced if the industry were competitive.

2. Monopolies must produce at the lowest cost.

3. Rent seeking refers to the use of resources to obtain or retain monopoly profits.

4. Monopolies have stronger incentives to undertake research and development than do competitive firms.

5. In a natural monopoly, the cost of production is higher because of the lack of competition.

6. Cross subsidization refers to the practice of selling below cost in one market and above cost in another.

7. Regulated natural monopolies are usually forced to charge a price equal to marginal cost.

8. A natural monopoly that is forced to set price equal to marginal cost will make a loss.

9. In a horizontal agreement, a firm colludes with a distributor or supplier.

10. The vertical agreement known as resale price maintenance is illegal per se, not just if competition is restricted.

11. The Competition Act of 1986 defined anticompetitive acts that constituted abuses of a dominant position.

12. Anticompetitive behaviour can sometimes be successfully defended by claiming that the behaviour also enhances economic efficiency.

13. Collusive aggreements are examples of vertical agreements.

14. The liberalization of trade between Canada and other countries reduces domestic firms' market power, and hence their tendency to indulge in anticompetitive behaviour.

15. A natural monopoly can only be prevented from taking advantage of its market power by nationalization.

Multiple Choice

1. All of the following, except one, are problems associated with monopolies. Which is the odd one out?

    a. reduced incentives for research and development
    b. restricted output
    c. managerial slack
    d. rent seeking
    e. low prices

2. Monopolists maximize profit by setting output where _____ marginal cost; this means that _____ marginal cost.

    a. marginal revenue exceeds; price equals
    b. price equals; marginal revenue equals
    c. marginal revenue equals; price exceeds
    d. price exceeds; marginal revenue equals
    e. marginal revenue equals; price equals

3. Compared with the competitive outcome, a monopoly produces _____ of output, which it sells at a _____.

    a. fewer units of output; lower price
    b. fewer units of output; higher price
    c. the same quantity of output; higher price
    d. more units of output; higher price
    e. more units of output; lower price

4. Consider a monopoly for which, for simplicity, we assume marginal cost is constant and equal to average cost. Let A denote consumer surplus if the industry were competitive, B denote actual consumer surplus under monopoly, and C denote the monopoly's profit. The deadweight loss of monopoly is:

    a. $A - B$.
    b. $B + C$.
    c. $A + B + C$.
    d. $A - B + C$.
    e. $A - B - C$.

5. The term managerial slack, when used in connection with monopolies, refers to the:

    a. lack of efficiency because of the absence of competition.
    b. use of resources to obtain or maintain a monopoly position.
    c. weakness of those charged with administering anti-combines policies.
    d. reduced incentives for research and development.
    e. loss in consumer surplus as a result of restricted output.

6. The term rent seeking, when used in connection with monopolies, refers to the:

    a. lack of efficiency because of the absence of competition.
    b. use of resources to obtain or maintain a monopoly position.
    c. weakness of those charged with administering anti-combines policies.
    d. reduced incentives for research and development.
    e. loss in consumer surplus as a result of restricted output.

7. All of the following, except one, are examples of rent-seeking behaviour. Which is the odd one out?

    a. research aimed at reducing the cost of production
    b. lobbying government to introduce protectionist policies
    c. political contributions
    d. activities designed to deter entry
    e. lobbying government to grant a monopoly

8. If one firm can supply the entire market at lower average cost than if there were a greater number of firms, this is termed:

    a. collusion.
    b. rent-seeking behaviour.
    c. monopolistic competition.
    d. a natural monopoly.
    e. a cartel.

9. In a natural monopoly:

   a. average cost is upward-sloping, and marginal cost is above average cost.
   b. average cost is upward-sloping, and marginal cost is below average cost.
   c. average cost is horizontal, and marginal cost equals average cost.
   d. average cost is downward-sloping, and marginal cost is above average cost.
   e. average cost is downward-sloping, and marginal cost is below average cost.

10. If a natural monopoly is required to set price equal to:

   a. average cost, it will make a loss.
   b. marginal cost, it will make a loss.
   c. average variable cost, it will make a profit.
   d. marginal cost, it will make a profit.
   e. average cost, it will make a profit.

11. Cross subsidization occurs when a firm:

   a. sells at below marginal cost in some markets and above marginal cost in other markets.
   b. sells at below marginal cost in all markets.
   c. subsidizes another firm's operations.
   d. sells at above marginal cost in all markets.
   e. charges different profit-maximizing prices in markets with different elasticities of demand.

12. When a natural monopoly is regulated, it is usually required to set price equal to:

   a. marginal revenue.
   b. marginal product.
   c. average cost.
   d. average revenue.
   e. marginal cost.

13. Many economists argue that regulation of natural monopolies provides too:

   a. weak an incentive to invest in capital and too strong an incentive to innovate.
   b. weak an incentive to invest in capital and innovate.
   c. strong an incentive to be efficient.
   d. strong an incentive to invest in capital and innovate.
   e. strong an incentive to invest in capital, and too weak an incentive to innovate.

14. When regulators lose sight of the public interest and serve the interests of the industry they are supposed to be regulating, this is termed:

   a. a restrictive practice.
   b. rent seeking.
   c. regulatory capture.
   d. a natural monopoly.
   e. exclusive dealing.

15. Anti-combines policy is designed to:

   a. convert industries to public ownership.
   b. regulate natural monopolies.
   c. provide incentives for rent-seeking behaviour.
   d. promote competition.
   e. encourage restrictive practices.

16. The Competition Act of 1986 sets out seven factors that the Competition Tribunal may use in determining the effect of a merger on competition. All of the following, except one, are among these seven factors. Which is the odd one out?

   a. the gap between price and marginal cost
   b. the availability of close substitutes
   c. the existence of barriers to entry
   d. the extent of foreign competition
   e. the extent of innovation

17. The Competition Act of 1986 prohibits abuse of a dominant position and defines anticompetitive acts that constitute abuse. The Act quotes all of the following, except one, as examples of anticompetitive acts. Which is the odd one out?

   a. selling one of the firm's brands at a discount
   b. setting price equal to marginal cost
   c. withholding resources from a competitor
   d. selling below cost
   e. adopting product specifications designed to eliminate competition

18. According to the four-firm concentration ratio, which of the following Canadian industries is most heavily dominated by the largest four firms in the industry?

   a. food
   b. finance
   c. transportation
   d. tobacco products
   e. communications

19. The Competition Act of 1986 makes all of the following, except one, criminal offences. Which is the odd one out?

   a. collusion
   b. price discrimination
   c. predatory pricing
   d. resale price maintenance
   e. exclusive dealing

20. Restrictive practices can be classified as either horizontal or vertical agreements. Which of the following is a horizontal agreement?

   a. exclusive dealing
   b. tied selling
   c. bid rigging
   d. resale price maintenance
   e. market restrictions

Completion

1. Monopolies restrict output and cause a loss in consumer surplus, part of which is a transfer to the monopolist; the remainder is called the _____.

2. The fact that, shielded from competition, monopolists may not produce for the lowest costs is called _____.

3. Political contributions and lobbying expenses for the purpose of winning regulations to restrict competition are examples of _____.

4. Regulated or nationalized firms may sell below cost in some markets and above cost in others, a practice known as _____.

5. In a _____, the average cost of production of any level of industry output is lowest if there is only one firm in the industry.

6. Before 1986, government efforts to promote competition by restricting anticompetitive tactics or opposing mergers were called _____ legislation.

7. When a firm buys a competitor that was producing a competing product, it is called a _____.

8. The purchase by one firm of a supplier or distributor is called a _____.

9. Prior to the Competition Act, most convictions under anti-combines legislation were for _____.

10. The Competition Act established the _____ to enforce certain aspects of competition policy.

Answers to Self-Test

True or False

1. t	4. f	7. f	10. t	13. f
2. f	5. f	8. t	11. t	14. t
3. f	6. t	9. f	12. t	15. f

Multiple Choice

1. e	6. b	11. a	16. a
2. c	7. a	12. c	17. b
3. b	8. d	13. e	18. d
4. e	9. e	14. c	19. e
5. a	10. b	15. d	20. c

Completion

1. deadweight loss
2. managerial slack
3. rent seeking
4. cross subsidization
5. natural monopoly
6. anti-combines
7. horizontal merger
8. vertical merger
9. restrictive practices
10. Competition Tribunal

Doing Economics: Tools and Practice Problems

One of the important costs that monopolies impose on the economy is the deadweight loss, which reflects the losses resulting from the fact that monopolies restrict output. Here, we study how to compute the deadweight loss and then move on to consider the regulation of natural monopolies.

DEADWEIGHT LOSS

A monopoly sets output below the level where price equals marginal cost. By doing so, the monopoly reduces the number of mutually beneficial trades. Because these trades do not occur, there is a loss in consumer surplus, and this loss is called the deadweight burden. Consumer surplus falls still

further because of the higher price that the monopoly charges, but this loss in consumer surplus is only a transfer from consumers to the monopolist and is not part of the deadweight loss. Tool Kit 14.1 shows you how to calculate the deadweight loss caused by monopoly.

Tool Kit 14.1: Finding the Deadweight Loss of Monopoly

Follow these steps to calculate the deadweight loss caused by monopoly.

Step one: Identify the demand and marginal cost curves.

Step two: Calculate marginal revenue.

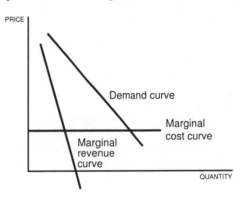

Step three: Find the monopoly output (Q_m) and price (p_m) by choosing the quantity for which marginal revenue equals marginal cost (MC).

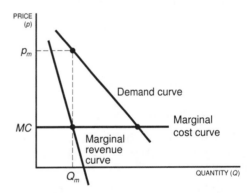

Step four: Find the "competitive" quantity (Q_c) by choosing the quantity for which demand equals marginal cost.

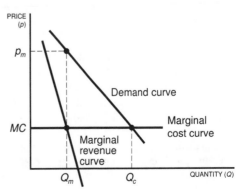

Step five: Compute the deadweight loss as the area between the demand and marginal cost curves:

deadweight loss = ½ $(Q_c - Q_m) \times (p_m - MC)$.

(This formula exactly measures the area only when demand is a straight line and marginal cost is constant.)

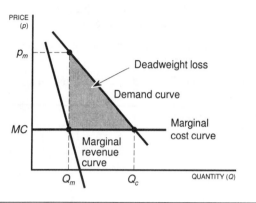

1. (Worked problem: deadweight loss) The West India Tea Company has been granted the sole franchise to sell green tea in Greenville. Its marginal cost is $5 per box. Demand is given in Table 14.1. Solve for its output and price and the deadweight loss.

Table 14.1

Price	Quantity
$10	10,000
$ 9	15,000
$ 8	20,000
$ 7	25,000
$ 6	30,000
$ 5	35,000

Step-by-step solution

Step one: Identify the demand and marginal cost curves. The demand curve is given in Table 14.1; marginal cost is constant and equal to $5.

Step two: Calculate marginal revenue. The marginal revenue for the West India Tea Company is given in Table 14.2.

Table 14.2

Price	Quantity	Total revenue	Marginal revenue
$10	10,000	$100,000	—
$ 9	15,000	$135,000	$7
$ 8	20,000	$160,000	$5
$ 7	25,000	$175,000	$3
$ 6	30,000	$180,000	$1
$ 5	35,000	$175,000	–$1

Step three: Find the monopoly output by choosing the quantity for which marginal revenue equals marginal cost. Mar-

ginal revenue equals marginal cost when price is $8 and 20,000 boxes are sold.

Step four: Find the competitive quantity by choosing the quantity for which demand equals marginal cost. The competitive price is $5, and the quantity is 35,000.

Step five: Compute the deadweight loss as the area between the demand and marginal cost curves.

Deadweight loss = ½ $(Q_c - Q_m) \times (p_m - MC)$
$$= ½ (35,000 - 20,000) \times (\$8 - \$5)$$
$$= \$22,500.$$

2. (Practice problem: deadweight loss) Although its marginal cost is only $4 for each ride, the Calloway Cab Company has bribed the city council in Venal City to grant it monopoly status at the local airport. The demand for rides is given in Table 14.3.

Table 14.3

Price	Quantity
$7.50	0
$7.00	10
$6.50	20
$6.00	30
$5.50	40
$5.00	50
$4.50	60
$4.00	70

Solve for the company's output and price and the deadweight loss.

3. (Practice problem: deadweight loss) As all baseball fans know, there is only one team in Mudville. The marginal cost of admitting another fan in the park is $1, and the demand for tickets is given in Table 14.4.

Table 14.4

Price	Quantity
$3.00	1,500
$2.50	3,000
$2.00	4,500
$1.50	6,000
$1.00	7,500

Solve for the team's output and price and the deadweight loss.

NATURAL MONOPOLY

Natural monopolies are industries with high fixed and low marginal costs. Costs in these industries are lowest when there is only one firm. Many natural monopolies, such as public utilities, cable television companies, and phone companies, are regulated by a public commission that prevents the entry of competitors and sets prices just high enough to allow the firms to earn a normal rate of return. This practice mandates that price equal average cost. Tool Kit 14.2 shows you how to find the regulated price for a natural monopoly.

Tool Kit 14.2: Finding the Price for a Regulated Natural Monopoly

Follow these steps to determine the price a regulated natural monopoly will be required to charge.

Step one: Identify the demand curve, marginal cost, and fixed costs.

Step two: Compute the average cost by dividing total cost by quantity:

average cost = total cost/quantity.

Step three: Find the price for which average cost crosses the demand curve. This is the price for a regulated natural monopoly.

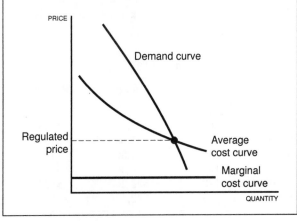

---

4. (Worked problem: natural monopoly) Cutthroat Co-Axial Cable Company is the only provider of cable television services in Kings. Most of its costs are access fees and maintenance expenses, and these fixed costs, which do not vary with the number of customers, total $760,000 monthly. The marginal cost of another subscriber is only $1 per month. The company's demand curve is given in Table 14.5.

Table 14.5

Price (per month)	Number of subscribers
$50	10,000
$40	20,000
$30	30,000
$20	40,000
$10	50,000
$ 1	100,000

The Kings Telecommunications Commission regulates the price of cable service and wants to set the price so that Cutthroat makes a normal rate of return. What price should it mandate?

Step-by-step solution

Step one: Identify the demand curve, marginal cost, and fixed costs. Demand is given in Table 14.5; marginal cost is $1, and fixed costs are $760,000.

Step two: Compute average cost. When price is $50, there are 10,000 subscribers, and total costs are $760,000 + (10,000 × $1) = $770,000. Average cost is $770,000/10,000 = $77. Continuing this procedure, we derive Table 14.6.

Table 14.6

Price	Number of subscribers	Total cost	Average cost
$50	10,000	$770,000	$77.00
$40	20,000	$780,000	$39.00
$30	30,000	$790,000	$26.33
$20	40,000	$800,000	$20.00
$10	50,000	$810,000	$16.20
$ 1	100,000	$860,000	$ 8.60

Step three: Find the price for which average cost crosses the demand curve. This price is $20, and it is the price that the Commission will choose.

5. (Practice problem: natural monopoly) The new big-cat exhibit at the Potter Park Zoo is bringing in the public. Demand is given in Table 14.7. The zoo costs the park service only $1 per visitor, but its fixed costs equal $12,000. The government has declared that no public funds will be used to support zoos, so Potter Park must charge a price just high enough to cover its costs. What price will solve this problem?

Table 14.7

Price	Number of visitors
$8	1,000
$7	2,000
$6	3,000
$5	4,000
$4	5,000
$3	6,000
$2	7,000
$1	8,000

6. (Practice problem: natural monopoly) Country Line Commuter Service runs from rural areas into the city. It has fixed costs of $20,400 and a marginal cost of $10 per commuter. Demand is given in Table 14.8. The Metro Transportation Commission sets the monthly price for a pass on Country Line, and it wants to allow the firm to earn a normal rate of return. Find the price that allows the service to cover its costs.

Table 14.8

Price (per month)	Number of commuters
$200	100
$180	120
$160	140
$140	160
$120	180
$100	200

Answers to Problems

2. The marginal revenue is given in Table 14.9.

Table 14.9

Price	Quantity	Total revenue	Marginal revenue
$7.50	0	$ 0	—
$7.00	10	$ 70	$7
$6.50	20	$130	$6
$6.00	30	$180	$5
$5.50	40	$220	$4
$5.00	50	$250	$3
$4.50	60	$270	$2
$4.00	70	$280	$1

The monopoly output and price are 40 and $5.50, respectively. The competitive output and price would be 70 and $4, respectively. The deadweight loss is

$$\tfrac{1}{2}\,(70 - 40) \times (\$5.50 - \$4.00) = \$22.50.$$

3. The marginal revenue is given in Table 14.10.

Table 14.10

Price	Quantity	Total revenue	Marginal revenue
$3.00	1,500	$4,500	$3
$2.50	3,000	$7,500	$2
$2.00	4,500	$9,000	$1
$1.50	6,000	$9,000	$0
$1.00	7,500	$7,500	–$1

The monopoly price and output are $2 and 4,500, respectively. The competitive price and output would be $1 and 7,500, respectively. The deadweight loss is

$$\tfrac{1}{2} \times (7,500 - 4,500) \times (\$2 - \$1) = \$1,500.$$

5. Average cost is given in Table 14.11.

Table 14.11

Price	Number of visitors	Total cost	Average cost
$8	1,000	$13,000	$13.00
$7	2,000	$14,000	$ 7.00
$6	3,000	$15,000	$ 5.00
$5	4,000	$16,000	$ 4.00
$4	5,000	$17,000	$ 3.40
$3	6,000	$18,000	$ 3.00
$2	7,000	$19,000	$ 2.70
$1	8,000	$20,000	$ 2.50

The price that allows Potter Park to cover its costs is $3.

6. Average cost is given in Table 14.12.

Table 14.12

Price	Number of commuters	Total cost	Average cost
$200	100	$21,400	$214
$180	120	$21,600	$180
$160	140	$21,800	$156
$140	160	$22,000	$138
$120	180	$22,200	$123
$100	200	$22,400	$112

Average cost equals price when price is $180. The Commission should choose this price.

Chapter 15

TECHNOLOGICAL CHANGE

Chapter Review

Think back once again to the history of the automobile in Chapter 1. At the beginning of this century, the automobile had not been invented, much less produced in any quantity or in the form we know it today. The enormous technological change in the automobile industry during this century is astounding.

This chapter looks at the process of technological change: the discovery of new products and of new ways of producing. Although many firms may be involved, many aspects of the material covered in Chapters 12 to 14 are relevant to the analysis, since industries in which technological change are important are almost necessarily imperfectly competitive. Indeed, the benefits that technological change yields mean that imperfect competition has its virtues, as well as the disadvantages that were stressed in the earlier chapters. Government policy to promote technological change recognizes this by, for example, granting patents, which are essentially government-enforced monopolies. The chapter explores the trade-offs involved in formulating patent policy, and also explains why the government provides direct subsidies to basic research.

ESSENTIAL CONCEPTS

1. In the basic competitive model, there is one lowest-cost way of producing, and all firms adopt this technology. The entry of new firms into the market soon drives away any profits, and all firms settle down to produce at the minimum of the average cost curve. The world of **technological change**, however, is vastly different. Firms compete aggressively to develop new products or production processes so that they can earn monopoly profits, at least for a while.

2. A **patent** is a property right to an idea, and it gives the owner monopoly status and the opportunity to earn monopoly profits for the duration of the patent. Firms compete in **patent races**, a winner-take-all system in which the first firm with a discovery is awarded that patent, and its competitors get nothing. Because not all ideas are patentable and because to obtain a patent the firm must disclose details of the idea, firms sometimes forgo applying for one and keep the idea a **trade secret.** In this case, the firm earns monopoly profits until its competitors discover the idea or a better one.

3. Patent policy involves two types of trade-offs:

   a. The first issue is the **length** of the patent. Longer patents offer greater rewards for winning the race, and at the same time they promote research and development (R & D). On the other hand, for the duration of the patent, the firm sells at the monopoly price, which is above marginal cost, and so causes short-run inefficiency, that is, a deadweight loss.

   b. The second issue is the **breadth** of the patent. Should patents be given for the narrowly defined idea or something more general? More broadly defined patents increase the rewards for R & D but access to the idea is restricted, and this restriction inhibits any subsequent innovative activity that might build on the patented idea.

4. Several features of research and development encourage large-sized firms.

   a. First, R & D is a fixed cost, in the sense that once discovered, an idea can be used many times without additional cost. Fixed costs increase the efficient scale of the firm.

   b. Second, the **learning curve** shows that costs fall with experience. The more the firm learns, the more it produces, and thus learning by doing encourages firms to increase their size.

   c. Third, firms have difficulty borrowing to finance R & D. Larger firms with more retained earnings can finance more of their own research.

5. **Basic research** on the nature of fundamental ideas generates such widespread external benefits that it has the two characteristics of what economists refer to as **public goods:** basic research produces knowledge, and it is difficult (not to mention undesirable) to exclude others from learning and taking advantage of new knowledge. Also, the marginal cost of giving another user access to new knowledge is zero. Because basic research has these characteristics, the government has an important role to play in providing funding for such work.

6. Because R & D creates these external benefits, most economists advocate government policies to encourage it. Tax credits for R & D spending are one form of subsidy used in Canada. Also, the **infant industry argument** for protection argues that new industries require protection against foreign competition until they move down the learning curve and acquire sufficient expertise to compete effectively. Finally, anti-combines laws can be relaxed to allow for joint ventures.

BEHIND THE ESSENTIAL CONCEPTS

1. Most of microeconomics sings the praises of perfect competition, especially to the extent that it allocates resources efficiently given the existing production technology. But a perfectly competitive economy does not always find the best way to generate more-advanced technologies of production, better products, and new ways of doing things. In order to encourage R & D, the government set up the patent system to motivate innovation among firms by rewarding the winner with a period of freedom from competition.

2. Technological advance is a vital engine of economic growth. Because it is so important, government promotes it with a wide range of complementary policies. Longer-lived and more broadly defined patents increase the rewards for R & D, while tax subsidies reduce the cost. Government also provides direct funding for basic research.

3. Economists consider the infant industry argument for protection to be valid but dangerous. Sometimes the protected industry gains expertise through experience and becomes a world-class competitor; other times the industry becomes inefficient and requires constant government support to survive. Some infant industries never grow up, and the difficulty lies therefore in determining which industries will thrive and which will not.

4. This chapter is your first introduction to the concept of externalities and public goods. Part Four of the textbook deals more fully with these issues. For now, the important thing to note is that inefficiencies can arise when costs or benefits arising from some decision are not borne by, or do not accrue to, the decision maker. In the context of technological change, there are often external benefits from investment in R & D that are not captured by the firm making the investment. These benefits include the fruits of subsequent R & D following an initial discovery, the gains after the expiration of the patent, and the consumer surplus arising from the application of the new idea. The firm ignores these externalities and thus undervalues the true social benefit of the R & D. Government policy can improve matters by promoting additional research efforts.

SELF-TEST

True or False

1. Firms engage in research and development so that they can participate in competitive markets.

2. A patent confers the exclusive right to produce and market an innovation for a limited period of time.

3. Patents and copyrights are forms of intellectual property.

4. The firm that finishes second in a patent race wins nothing.

5. Holders of patents are required to set the price of the patented good equal to marginal cost.

6. Patents promote dynamic efficiency but cause short-run inefficiency.

7. The length of patents is set to balance the costs of monopoly pricing by patent holders against the incentives to innovate.

8. Defining a patent more broadly might reduce the rate of innovation by denying access to previous innovations.

9. Any firm eligible for a patent always applies for one.

10. Research and development expenditures are a variable cost of production.

11. The learning curve shows how fixed costs decline with experience.

12. Smaller firms investing in research and development have better access to capital markets.

13. Much of the research and development in new and small companies is financed by venture capital firms.

14. The market is unlikely to provide enough basic research because basic research is a public good.

15. The anti-combine laws prohibit firms from engaging in joint ventures.

Multiple Choice

1. All of the following, except one, represent research and development. Which is the odd one out?

    a. discovering new technologies
    b. discovering new ideas
    c. bringing new products to market
    d. discovering new products
    e. discovering new ways of restricting competition

2. During the life of a patent, firms competing with the patent holder:

    a. can produce the same good but cannot make use of the invention in other products.
    b. cannot produce the same good but can make use of the invention in other products.
    c. can neither produce the same good nor make use of the invention in other products.
    d. can both produce the same good and make use of the invention in other products.
    e. can pay a fee for the right to see but not use details of the invention.

3. In Canada, patents are granted for:

    a. 5 years.
    b. 10 years.
    c. 15 years.
    d. 20 years.
    e. 25 years.

4. The government's policy on patents is an example of sacrificing _____ in the interests of _____.

    a. efficiency; equity
    b. equity; efficiency
    c. short-run efficiency; dynamic efficiency
    d. short-run efficiency; equity
    e. dynamic efficiency; equity

5. The period for which a patent is granted represents a trade-off. If it were longer, it would _____; if it were shorter, it would _____.

    a. provide greater incentives for innovation; restrict the extent to which society can fully enjoy the benefits of innovation
    b. provide greater incentives for innovation; enhance the extent to which society can fully enjoy the benefits of innovation

    c. provide no incentives for innovation; eliminate the extent to which society can fully enjoy the benefits of innovation
    d. provide reduced incentives for innovation; restrict the extent to which society can fully enjoy the benefits of innovation
    e. provide reduced incentives for innovation; enhance the extent to which society can fully enjoy the benefits of innovation

6. The breadth of coverage granted in a patent represents a trade-off. If it were broader, it would _____; if it were narrower, it would _____.

    a. provide greater returns to innovation; enhance innovation by others
    b. provide reduced returns to innovation; inhibit innovation by others
    c. provide no returns to innovation; eliminate innovation by others
    d. provide reduced returns to innovation; enhance innovation by others
    e. provide greater returns to innovation; inhibit innovation by others

7. Research and development expenditures are:

    a. variable costs.
    b. fixed costs.
    c. marginal costs.
    d. recoverable costs.
    e. none of the above

8. As firms gain experience from production, costs fall. This is termed:

    a. short-run efficiency.
    b. dynamic efficiency.
    c. a trade secret.
    d. the theory of efficient markets.
    e. learning by doing.

9. Technological change and imperfect competition seem to go together. All of the following, except one, are reasons for this. Which is the odd one out?

    a. A patent to protect a technological innovation creates a monopoly.
    b. Research and development is a fixed cost; this gives large firms an advantage.
    c. Large firms have a greater incentive to undertake research and development.
    d. Large firms can often be bureaucratic; this tends to stifle innovation.
    e. Large firms have easier access to funds for research and development.

10. All of the following, except one, reflect ways in which competition affects research and development. Which is the odd one out?

    a. Firms that do not innovate are driven from the market by competition.
    b. Competition restricts innovation by eliminating profits that could be used to finance research and development.
    c. Competition is inhibited by innovation because the costs of research and development are fixed costs.

d. Competition promotes research and development because profits can be generated from successful innovations.

e. Competition inhibits innovation because it leads firms to imitate innovations, and so erodes returns.

11. Innovation yields benefits for others besides the innovator and for which the innovator is not reimbursed. These benefits are called:

a. fixed costs.

b. a patent.

c. sunk costs.

d. copyright.

e. externalities.

12. The social benefit of an innovation is:

a. the benefit to the innovator.

b. both the benefit to the innovator and the benefit to others for which the innovator is not reimbursed.

c. the benefit to others for which the innovator is not reimbursed.

d. neither the benefit to the innovator nor the benefit to others for which the innovator is not reimbursed.

e. the benefit to the innovator and any benefit to others 'for which the innovator is reimbursed.

13. A public good is characterized by:

a. the difficulty of excluding others from enjoying its benefits, and the low marginal cost of providing those benefits to others.

b. the ease with which others can be excluded from enjoying its benefits, and the low marginal cost of providing those benefits to others.

c. the impossibility of excluding others from enjoying its benefits, and the infinite cost of providing those benefits to others.

d. the ease with which others can be excluded from enjoying its benefits, and the high marginal cost of providing those benefits to others.

e. the difficulty of excluding others from enjoying its benefits, and the high marginal cost of providing those benefits to others.

14. Which of the following types of research and development is most likely to be a public good?

a. product development

b. applied research

c. basic research

d. bringing a new product to market

e. none of the above

15. Private markets:

a. will not supply even the smallest quantity of a public good.

b. produce more than the socially efficient level of a public good.

c. produce the socially efficient level of a public good.

d. produce less than the socially efficient level of a public good.

e. sometimes produce more, sometimes less than the socially efficient level of a public good.

16. Which of the following countries spends the lowest proportion of its gross domestic product on research and development?

a. the United States

b. Canada

c. the United Kingdom

d. Germany

e. Japan

17. Governments promote research and development by all of the following, except one. Which is the odd one out?

a. subsidies

b. tax credits

c. protection from foreign competition

d. patents

e. anti-combines legislation

18. Advocates of the infant industry argument argue that domestic firms:

a. with higher costs than their foreign rivals should be protected in order to save jobs.

b. should be protected if foreign labour costs are so low that the domestic firm cannot compete.

c. will only learn how to compete by being forced to do so and protection saves them from doing so.

d. with higher costs than their foreign rivals should be protected to allow them to move down the learning curve.

e. should be helped, if at all, through subsidies rather than by the hidden costs of higher prices due to protection.

19. Most economists argue that claims on behalf of infant industries are best characterized as:

a. rent seeking.

b. short-run efficiency.

c. dynamic efficiency.

d. a promotion of freer international trade.

e. an attempt to improve efficiency.

20. The Canadian government has traditionally:

a. encouraged firms to undertake joint ventures on the grounds that the joint ventures will not encourage collusion.

b. discouraged firms from undertaking joint ventures for fear that the joint ventures would encourage collusion.

c. encouraged firms to undertake joint ventures despite fears that the joint ventures will encourage collusion.

d. discouraged firms from undertaking joint ventures despite the belief that the joint ventures would discourage collusion.

e. encouraged firms to undertake joint ventures in the belief that the joint ventures will discourage collusion.

Completion

1. A good patent policy balances short-run efficiency with _____.

2. Expenditures designed to discover new ideas, products, and technologies and bring them to market are called _____.

3. The exclusive right to produce and sell an invention or innovation is a _____.

4. The winner-take-all aspect of patents encourages a so-called patent _____.

5. Rather than seek a patent, an innovator may try to hide the new knowledge as a _____.

6. _____ refers to the idea that as firms gain experience, their costs fall.

7. The curve showing how marginal costs of production decline as total experience increases is called the _____.

8. The benefits of research and development spill over to others not directly involved and generate positive _____.

9. Basic research produces knowledge from which it is difficult to exclude potential users and which can be used by others at no cost to the producers; in this sense, it is an example of a _____.

10. The hope that an industry not currently able to compete with foreign firms may in time acquire the experience to move down the learning curve is called the _____ argument for protection.

Answers to Self-Test

True or False

1. f	4. t	7. t	10. f	13. t
2. t	5. f	8. t	11. f	14. t
3. t	6. t	9. f	12. f	15. f

Multiple Choice

1. e	6. a	11. e	16. b
2. c	7. b	12. b	17. e
3. d	8. e	13. a	18. d
4. c	9. d	14. c	19. a
5. b	10. c	15. d	20. b

Completion

1 dynamic efficiency
2 research and development
3 patent
4 race
5 trade secret
6 Learning by doing
7 learning curve
8 externalities
9 public good
10 infant industry

Doing Economics: Tools and Practice Problems

Firms undertake research and development (R & D) in order to market new products or to find new and less costly ways of producing. They compete to win patents or secure trade secrets that will allow them to enjoy some protection against competition and to earn above-normal profits. In this section we study the rewards that motivate R & D. First, several problems explore the value of new product patents and trade secrets. Next, we study innovations that result in lower production costs and consider whether incumbent monopolies have as much incentive to innovate as do potential entrants.

PATENTS

A firm that is considering investment in R & D knows that a patent on a new product will allow the firm to enjoy future profits associated with the new product for 20 years, which is the duration of a patent in Canada. This is because the granting of a patent gives the firm a monopoly in the supply of the new product for the life of the patent. The value of the patent to the firm is therefore the present discounted value of the future monopoly profits. Tool Kit 15.1 shows you how to calculate this value.

Tool Kit 15.1: Calculating the Value of a Patent

Follow these steps to calculate the value of a patent, which is the present discounted value of monopoly profits over the 20-year life of a patent.

Step one: Compute monopoly profits resulting from the patent.

Step two: Find the present discounted value of 20 years of profits. This number is the value of the patent:

value of the patent = profits + $[(\text{profits})] \times 1(1 + r)^1]$
$+ [(\text{profits}) \times 1/(1 + r)^2] + \ldots$
$+ [(\text{profits}) \times 1/(1 + r)^{19}]$.

(The variable r stands for the real rate of interest. In the problems below, we will set r equal to 3 percent. A shortcut for step two is to multiply profits by 15.32.)

---

1. (Worked problem: patents) Nu Products, Inc., has come up with another winning idea—a rubberized surface for premium, no-injury waterslide parks. The company wins the patent. Demand for resurfacings is given in Table 15.1, and costs are $20,000 per park. Calculate the value of the patent.

Table 15.1

Price	Parks resurfaced
$60,000	10
$50,000	20
$40,000	30
$30,000	40
$20,000	50

Step-by-step solution

Step one: Compute the monopoly profits resulting from the patent. Table 15.2 gives the marginal revenue for resurfacings.

Table 15.2

Price	Park resurfaced	Revenue	Marginal revenue
$60,000	10	$ 600,000	$60,000
$50,000	20	$1,000,000	$40,000
$40,000	30	$1,200,000	$20,000
$30,000	40	$1,200,000	$ 0
$20,000	50	$1,000,000	−$20,000

Marginal cost equals marginal revenue when price is $40,000 and 30 parks are resurfaced. Profits then equal ($40,000 × 30) − ($20,000 × 30) = $600,000.

Step two: Find the present discounted value of 20 years of profits if the new rate of interest is 3 percent. This number is the value of the patent.

Value of the patent $= \$600,000 + [(\$600,000) \times 1/(1+r)^1]$

$$+ [(\$600,000) \times 1/(1+r)^2] + \cdots$$

$$+ [(\$600,000) \times 1/(1+r)^{19}]$$

$$= \$600,000 \times 15.32 = \$9,192,000.$$

2. (Practice problem: patents) Bugout Pesticide has discovered a new product that kills potato bugs. It wins the patent. The firm's economics department computes that it can expect to earn $100,000 per year for the length of the patent. Compute the value of the patent.

3. (Practice problem: patents) Nip and Tuck Bodyshapers have developed a new procedure for smoothing those wrinkles that trouble the after-40 generation. They have decided not to apply for a patent, but rather to keep the technique secret. They expect that others will be able to duplicate the procedure in 4 years and that the resulting competition will allow only a normal rate of return thereafter. Their costs are $5,000 per face, and they estimate that the demand curve is as given in Table 15.3.

Table 15.3

Price	Quantity
$30,000	20
$25,000	30
$20,000	40
$15,000	50
$10,000	60
$ 5,000	70

The real interest rate is expected to remain at 5 percent over the period. Find the value of the trade secret.

MONOPOLIST AND POTENTIAL ENTRANT

A firm that discovers and patents a new, lower-cost production technique will be able to earn monopoly profits for the life of the patent. If the firm is already a monopoly, it merely takes advantage of the lower costs. If the firm is a potential entrant, it can undercut the existing firm, drive it from the market, and assume its position as the monopoly supplier of the good. Tool Kit 15.2 compares the incentives for in-

novation on the part of incumbent and potential entrant firms. It shows you why an incumbent monopolist has less of an incentive to innovate.

Tool Kit 15.2: Finding Equilibrium with an Incumbent Monopolist and a Potential Entrant

Follow these steps for an illustration of how to determine who has the stronger incentive to innovate, an incumbent monopolist or a potential entrant.

Step one: Identify the incumbent's costs, the potential entrant's costs, and the demand curve.

Step two: Find the equilibrium. The incumbent sets price equal to the entrant's average cost and captures the entire market. (Actually, the price must be 1 cent less than the average cost of the entrant, but we will round up in the problems below.)

---

4. (Worked problem: monopolist and potential entrant) Dentalcomp has had the monopoly in the market for computerizing dental offices in Roseville. While other firms could set up a computer system for $20,000, Dentalcomp's costs are only $15,000. Demand is given in Table 15.4.

Table 15.4

Price	Offices computerized
$30,000	20
$25,000	30
$20,000	40
$15,000	50
$10,000	60

a. Find the equilibrium.
b. Suppose that a new innovation in programming would lower costs to $10,000. Assume that the incumbent, Dentalcomp, discovers and patents the innovation first. Find the new equilibrium and the incumbent's profits. How much is the innovation worth to Dentalcomp?
c. Now assume that a potential entrant discovers and patents the innovation first. Find the new equilibrium and the entrant's profits.
d. Who has stronger incentives to innovate?

Step-by-step solution

Step one (a): Identify the incumbent's costs, the potential entrant's costs, and the demand curve. The incumbent, Dentalcomp, has an average cost of $15,000; the entrant has an average cost of $20,000. The demand appears in Table 15.4.

Step two: Find the equilibrium. The incumbent sets price equal to the entrant's average cost, which is $20,000, and captures the entire market of 40 offices. Its profits are ($20,000 × 40) − ($15,000 × 40) = $200,000.

Step three (b): If it discovers the innovation and wins the patent, Dentalcomp is still the low-cost firm. It captures the entire market with the same price of $20,000 and earns profits of ($20,000 × 40) – ($10,000 × 40) = $400,000.

Step four (c): If a potential entrant wins the patent first, it becomes the low-price firm. It sets price equal to Dentalcomp's average cost, which is $15,000, and captures the entire market of 50 offices. Its profits are ($15,000 × 50) – ($10,000 × 50) = $250,000.

Step five (d): The gain to innovation for Dentalcomp is the difference between its profits before and after the innovation, which equals $400,000 – $200,000 = $200,000. The entrant gains $250,000 by innovating and thus has stronger incentives.

5. (Practice problem: monopolist and potential entrant) Blackdare has patented its unique process for extinguishing oil fires. It can put out a typical well fire for $150,000, but its competitors, without access to the patented process, have average costs equal to $200,000. The demand for extinguishing oil fires is given in Table 15.5.

Table 15.5

Price	Fires
$400,000	10
$350,000	12
$300,000	14
$250,000	16
$200,000	18
$150,000	20
$100,000	22

a. Find the equilibrium price and quantity and profits.
b. Suppose that a new innovation in firefighting would lower costs to $100,000. Assume that the incumbent, Blackdare, discovers and patents the innovation first. Find the new equilibrium and the incumbent's profits. How much is the innovation worth to Blackdare?
c. Now assume that a potential entrant discovers and patents the innovation first. Find the new equilibrium and the entrant's profits.
d. Who has the stronger incentives to innovate?

6. (Practice problem: monopolist and potential entrant) PhXXX Pharmaceuticals has a monopoly on the treatment of Rubinksi's Trauma, an obscure ailment of the saliva glands. The average cost of curing a patient is $2,000 for PhXXX. The only other treatment available costs $5,000. Demand for the treatment of Rubinski's Trauma is given in Table 15.6.

Table 15.6

Price	Treatments
$8,000	100
$7,000	200
$6,000	300
$5,000	400
$4,000	500
$3,000	600
$2,000	700
$1,000	800

a. Find the equilibrium price and quantity.
b. Suppose that a new genetically engineered drug would lower treatment costs to $1,000. Assume that the incumbent, PhXXX, discovers and patents the new drug first. Find the new equilibrium and the incumbent's profits. How much is the innovation worth to PhXXX?
c. Now assume that a potential entrant discovers and patents the innovation first. Find the new equilibrium and the entrant's profits.
d. Who has the stronger incentives to innovate?

Answers to Problems

2. Value of patent = $100,000 × 15.32 = $1,532,000.

3. Marginal revenue is given in Table 15.7.

Table 15.7

Price	Quantity	Revenues	Marginal revenue
$30,000	20	$600,000	—
$25,000	30	$750,000	$15,000
$20,000	40	$800,000	$ 5,000
$15,000	50	$750,000	–$ 5,000
$10,000	60	$600,000	–$15,000
$ 5,000	70	$350,000	–$25,000

Marginal revenue equals marginal cost at a price of $20,000, where 40 faces are smoothed. Profits = ($20,000 × 40) – ($5,000 × 40) = $600,000. The value of the trade secret is $600,000 + [($600,000) × 1/(1.05)] + [($600,000) × 1/(1.05)^2] + [($600,000) × 1/(1.05)^3] = $2,233,949.

5. a. Price = $200,000; quantity = 18; profits = $900,000.
   b. Price = $200,000; quantity = 18; profits = $1,800,000.
   c. Price = $150,000; quantity = 20; profits = $1,000,000.
   d. The entrant would gain $1,000,000, while Blackdare would only gain $1,800,000 – $900,000 = $900,000. The entrant has stronger incentives.

6. a. Price = $5,000; quantity = 400; profits = $1,200,000;
   b. Price = $5,000; quantity = 400; profits = $1,600,000;
   c. Price = $2,000; quantity = 700; profits = $700,000.
   d. The entrant would gain $700,000, while PhXXX would only gain $1,600,000 – $1,200,000 = $400,000. The entrant has stronger incentives.

IMPERFECT INFORMATION

Chapter Review

Chapter 16 looks at information problems in the product, capital, and labour markets. In the basic competitive model, agents have perfect information, but the real world is less kind. Consumers do not always know the quality of a good they are considering buying, lenders contemplate an uncertain future as they ponder where to invest their money, and firms know much less than they would like about the productivity of potential employees. The chapter discusses various solutions to these and other problems.

ESSENTIAL CONCEPTS

1. **Asymmetric information** exists when one side of the market knows something that the other does not. For example, the seller of a used car usually knows more about its reliability than the buyer. Asymmetric information can cause the demand curve to be upward-sloping, because buyers reason that fewer high-quality cars will be offered for sale when the price is low and this will reduce the average quality of the cars available. The changing mix of cars as the price drops is called an **adverse selection** effect. As a result, many mutually

beneficial trades do not take place. Buyers worry that sellers may exploit their informational advantage and sell them a lemon.

2. One way to send buyers a message in a market with asymmetric information is called **signalling.** For example, firms selling high-quality used cars can signal their reliability by offering warranties or by building expensive showrooms. The firms can also charge higher prices, another potentially informative signal. Buyers understand that only lemons would be sold at low prices; that is, they judge the quality according to the price.

3. When buyers observe the quality of what is sold, they can provide sellers with good incentives by linking payment to quality. For example, an employer can pay a typist according to the number of errors made. When buyers do not know the quality of goods before purchasing them, markets do not provide the incentive for firms to produce high-quality merchandise. Two possible solutions to this incentive problem are **contracts** and **reputations.**

   a. Contracts typically include **contingency clauses**, which make payment depend on the quality of the service. Spelling out contingencies provides incentives and shares the risk, but it makes contracts complicated. For this and other reasons, contracts provide only an imperfect solution to the incentive problems accompanying trade in the presence of asymmetric information.

   b. By repeatedly providing quality goods and service, a firm establishes a reputation, which enables it to earn extra profits. To preserve its valuable reputation, the firm must continue to provide quality. Reputations thus provide firms with incentives to perform well.

4. Firms try to influence customers' purchasing decisions through **informative** and **persuasive advertising.** The goal of advertising is to shift the demand curve to the right, and so enable the firm to raise prices and sell more goods. Advertising may also serve as a signal. Customers may reason that only a high-quality product with good sales would justify a large expenditure on advertising.

5. Most people are risk-averse: they prefer to reduce the uncertainty inherent in the future they face. Insurance markets have arisen to allow them to transfer some of the risk they face. But insurance companies face information problems too. They cannot accurately determine each individual's proneness to risk, but they do know that those who buy insurance tend to be those more at risk. They also know that a higher price will discourage those less at risk from buying insurance. Insurance companies too, then, face adverse selection. They also face the problem that people may behave less carefully once they have bought insurance. This is termed **moral hazard.**

6. In Chapter 7, you were introduced to **human capital theory.** This argues that individuals invest in education and training to acquire human capital, which increases their productivity and wages. An alternative view suggests that education (beyond the compulsory level) is a signal of innate productivity. Employers are imperfectly informed about the abilities of potential employees, but the employers know that only the more capable will do well in postsecondary education. The difficult courses students take at university, for example, serve as a **screen,** identifying those whom the firms would prefer to hire.

BEHIND THE ESSENTIAL CONCEPTS

1. The information problems discussed in this chapter lead the market structure away from perfect competition and create two possible situations: **barriers to entry** and firms with **downward-sloping demand curves.**

   a. Customers who cannot know the quality of goods buy from businesses with good reputations. Because a reputation is built up over time, firms that would otherwise enter an industry will not be able to justify the investment necessary to establish a good reputation. Reputation becomes a barrier to entry and results in less competition.

   b. Because customers must search to learn about price and quality, it becomes cheaper for them to shop at familiar stores. Although the goods themselves may be identical, the stores are different in the eyes of the customer because the customer knows about some stores and is ignorant of others. This means that when a store raise its price, it will not automatically lose all its customers. In other words, the store faces a downward-sloping demand curve for the products it sells; it has some market power.

2. One implication of the argument that education is a signal is that a **credentials competition** might occur. Since education identifies those who are more able, these individuals may stay in school ever longer in the hope that this will ensure they are distinguished from those who are less able. There is some indirect evidence that this has happened. For example, it is certainly the case that many jobs that once required only a high-school diploma are now open only to applicants with a degree.

SELF-TEST

True or False

1. In the market for lemons, the demand curve is upward-sloping because average quality falls as price rises.

2. When those offering high-quality products withdraw them from the market if the price falls, this is termed an adverse selection effect.

3. When consumers judge quality by price, the market clears.

4. Contingency clauses in contracts reduce incentives.

5. Reputation is a barrier to entry.

6. Firms in Canada spend as much on advertising as the government spends on foreign aid.

7. The huge amounts spent on advertising by Coke and Pepsi are an example of the Prisoner's Dilemma: if they could agree to spend less, they would both be better off.

8. All advertising is designed to be informative.

9. People who enjoy taking risks are termed risk-averse.

10. "Don't put all your eggs in one basket" advocates the principle of diversification.

11. The less risky an investment is, the higher will be its risk premium.

12. Insurance companies allow individuals to pool their risks.

13. Along the risk-incentive trade-off, more risk means a lower incentive.

14. Moral hazard refers to the tendency for those at greater risk to be the ones who are most likely to buy insurance.

15. The screening model of education argues that education merely serves as a signal of innate ability.

Multiple Choice

1. In the basic competitive model, each household is assumed to know all of the following, except one. Which is the odd one out?

   a. its opportunity set
   b. the prices of all goods and services
   c. the characteristics of all goods and services
   d. its preferences
   d. the firm's technologies

2. In the basic competitive model, each firm is assumed to know all of the following, except one. Which is the odd one out?

   a. the households' preferences
   b. the best available technology
   c. the productivity of each job applicant
   d. all input prices from every possible supplier
   e. present and future prices for its output

3. In a lemons market:

   a. buyers know the quality of the good on offer but sellers do not.
   b. sellers know the quality of the good on offer but buyers do not.
   c. neither buyers nor sellers know the quality of the good on offer.
   d. both buyers and sellers know the quality of the good on offer.
   e. both buyers and sellers infer average quality from the price.

4. In a lemons market, a higher price induces:

   a. higher quality goods into the market, and so raises average quality.
   b. lower quality goods into the market, and so lowers average quality.
   c. average quality goods into the market, with no effect on average quality.
   d. lower quality goods into the market, and so raises average quality.
   e. higher quality goods into the market, and so lowers average quality.

5. In a lemons market, once price falls below the point at which the average quality of the goods offered for sale is maximized, the demand curve:

   a. is horizontal.
   b. is negatively sloped.
   c. has an infinite price elasticity.
   d. is positively sloped.
   e. is vertical.

6. In a lemons market, changes in price alter the mix of high- and low-quality goods offered for sale. This effect is called:

   a. diminishing returns.
   b. economies of scale.
   c. adverse selection.
   d. economies of scope.
   e. moral hazard.

7. In a lemons market, excess supply:

   a. will be eliminated as firms lower their prices.
   b. may persist, because firms will not want to lower their prices, fearing this would be seen as a signal of lower quality goods.
   c. cannot persist unless the government intervenes to prevent equilibrium from being restored.
   d. may persist, because firms will not want to raise their prices, fearing this would be seen as a signal of lower quality goods.
   e. will be eliminated as firms raise their prices.

8. An incentive problem arises when there is imperfect information. The contract solution to this problem makes use of:

   a. contingency clauses.
   b. signals.
   c. adverse selection.
   d. reputations.
   e. moral hazard.

9. Reputations in the product market:

   a. promote competition.
   b. keep prices low.
   c. guarantee efficiency.
   d. help promote new products.
   e. are a barrier to entry.

10. All of the following, except one, are true of advertising. Which is the odd one out?

    a. It provides price information to potential customers.
    b. It promotes competition and efficiency.
    c. It informs customers about which products are available.
    d. It attempts to persuade customers to buy certain products.
    e. Its objective is to shift the demand curve to the right.

11. Risk-averse people:

    a. prefer uncertainty.
    b. enjoy taking risks.
    c. never buy insurance.
    d. avoid taking risks.
    e. enjoy gambling.

12. Diversification:

    a. reduces the possibility of very bad outcomes, leaving all the good outcomes still possible.
    b. increases the possibility of very good outcomes and reduces the possibility of very bad ones.
    c. reduces the possibility of very good and very bad outcomes.
    d. increases the possibility of very bad outcomes and reduces the possibility of very good ones.
    e. reduces the possibility of very good outcomes, leaving all the bad outcomes still possible.

13. Insurance markets work by:

    a. transferring risk to those without insurance.
    b. keeping options open.
    c. diversifying individuals' portfolios.

    d. making individuals more careful.

    e. pooling risk among those with insurance.

14. A risk premium occurs when the:

    a. price of an asset is high in recognition of low risk.

    b. price of an asset is high in recognition of high risk.

    c. price of, and return on, an asset are high in recognition of high risk.

    d. return on an asset is high in recognition of high risk.

    e. return on an asset is high in recognition of low risk.

15. Insurance markets face the problem that those who buy policies are typically those more likely to claim against the insurance. This is an example of:

    a. risk aversion.

    b. adverse selection.

    c. a contingency clause.

    d. moral hazard.

    e. diminishing returns.

16. Insurance markets face the problem that those who buy policies sometimes take less care once they are protected by the insurance. This is an example of:

    a. diminishing returns.

    b. risk aversion.

    c. adverse selection.

    d. moral hazard.

    e. a contingency clause.

17. All the following, except one, are strategies one would expect risk-averse individuals to adopt. Which is the odd one out?

    a. avoiding and mitigating risks

    b. keeping their options open

    c. diversification

    d. transferring and pooling risk

    e. gambling at the racetrack

18. An investor who buys mutual funds is practising:

    a. the avoidance or mitigation of risks.

    b. keeping her options open.

    c. diversification of her portfolio.

    d. the transfer of risk.

    e. the pooling of risk.

19. According to the risk-incentive trade-off:

    a. a reduction in risk also lowers incentives.

    b. people who take more risk respond better to incentives.

    c. an increase in risk also lowers incentives.

    d. people who take fewer risks respond better to incentives.

    e. a reduction in risk also increases incentives.

20. The argument advanced by some economists that a university education merely serves to identify those with innate ability could explain:

    a. adverse selection.

    b. the credentials competition.

    c. moral hazard.

    d. the efficient market theory.

    e. risk aversion.

Completion

1. In the market for _____, customers do not know the quality of the goods being sold.

2. Actions taken by sellers to convince buyers of the high quality of their goods are called _____.

3. Clauses in contracts that make the payment depend on precisely how the service is performed are called _____.

4. The reputations of existing firms act as a _____ against new competition.

5. Advertising that conveys information about price, product availability, and quality is called _____ advertising.

6. People who try to avoid risk are said to be _____.

7. If an investor splits his money among a number of different assets, he is practising _____.

8. When people take less care after buying insurance, this is called the _____ problem.

9. If someone who only has a small likelihood of claiming on insurance stops buying insurance when the price goes up, this is called the _____ problem.

10. If universities only identify those with more innate ability, we say that universities _____ individuals.

Answers to Self-Test

True or False

1. f	4. f	7. t	10. t	13. f
2. t	5. t	8. f	11. f	14. f
3. f	6. t	9. f	12. t	15. t

Multiple Choice

1. e	6. c	11. d	16. d
2. a	7. b	12. c	17. e
3. b	8. a	13. e	18. c
4. a	9. e	14. d	19. a
5. d	10. b	15. b	20. b

Completion

1. lemons
2. signals
3. contingency clauses
4. barrier to entry
5. informative
6. risk-averse
7. diversification
8. moral hazard
9. adverse selection
10. screen

Doing Economics: Tools and Practice Problems

The problems in this section address two topics related to imperfect information. First, we look at adverse selection.

The concept is applied to the market for lemons, but you should bear in mind that exactly the same principles can be applied also to the market for insurance. Second, we investigate the effect of advertising on firms' profits.

ADVERSE SELECTION

Asymmetric information refers to situations in which one party to a potential trade knows something pertinent to the trade that the other party does not know. For example, someone selling a used car typically knows more about the car than the buyer does. This allows firms that produce lemons, that is, low-quality goods, to sell their goods in the same market as producers of high-quality goods. If information were perfect, there would be two markets. As it is, there is only one.

In such situations, buyers are forced to use price as an indicator of average quality, on the assumption that high-quality goods are likely to be a larger proportion of total supply as the price rises. Buyers' demand will reach a peak at the price that delivers the highest quality per dollar spent. For higher prices, the demand curve will be negatively sloped, indicating a reduction in demand as price rises. For lower prices, the demand curve will be positively sloped, indicating that buyers will not react in the normal way to a reduction in price, because they believe the price reduction signals a lower-quality product. For a given quality-price relationship, Tool Kit 16.1 shows you how to estimate maximum quality per dollar spent.

Tool Kit 16.1: Finding the Price That Maximizes Quality per Dollar

Follow these steps to find maximum quality per dollar spent.

Step one: Identify and plot the relationship between quality and price.

Step two: For each price, find the quality-price ratio: quality-price ratio = quality/price. Select the highest.

Step three: Alternatively, you can draw a line that passes through the origin and its tangent to the quali-

---

ty-price curve. It is tangential to the curve at the point where the quality per dollar is maximized, and the value of its slope is the maximum quality-price ratio. Verify that both approaches give you the same answer.

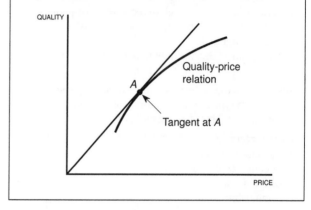

1. (Worked problem: quality and price) Consumers of 12-litre fire extinguishers care deeply about the quality of the item, but they cannot distinguish the quality until after purchase, since the quality of a fire extinguisher only matters if and when it is used. Suppose consumers believe that the relationship between quality and price is as given in Table 16.1.

Table 16.1

Price	Quality (litres of fire retardant released)
$ 5	0
$10	1.0
$15	4.5
$20	7.0
$25	10.0
$30	11.0
$35	12.0
$40	12.0

a. Find the price that maximizes quality per dollar.
b. Suppose that the market supply curve is given in Table 16.2 and that firms set a price that will allow them to sell as many extinguishers as possible. Why might the market not clear?

Table 16.2

Price	Supply
$40	28,000
$35	25,000
$30	21,000
$25	20,000
$20	19,000
$15	17,000
$10	11,000

Step-by-step solution

Step one (a): Identify and plot the relationship between quality and price. It is given in Table 16.1 and drawn in the diagram.

Step two: For each price, find the quality-price ratio. When the price is $40, the quality-price ratio is 12/40 = 0.30. Continuing, we derive Table 16.3. The maximum price-quality ratio is 0.40, which occurs at a price of $25.

Table 16.3

Price	Quality	Quality-price ratio
$ 5	0	—
$10	1.0	0.10
$15	4.5	0.30
$20	7.0	0.35
$25	10.0	0.40
$30	11.0	0.37
$35	12.0	0.34
$40	12.0	0.30

Step three: On the diagram of the quality-price relation, draw a line that passes through the origin and is tangent to the quality-price curve. The value of its slope is 10/25 = 0.40, which is the maximum quality-price ratio.

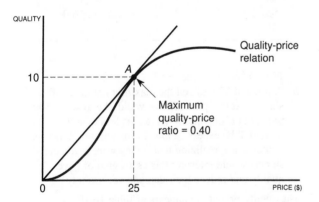

Step four (b): A price of $25 will sell the maximum number of extinguishers. At this price, firms would like to sell 20,000 units, but if maximum demand is less than this, there will be excess supply. Firms will not, however, reduce price, realizing that if they were to do so, consumers would interpret this as a signal of lower quality and reduce their demand accordingly.

2. (Practice problem: quality and price) Tourists go to San Gordo for the shrimp. Dozens of small establishments offer shrimp, but tourists have little ability to judge the quality before eating. They reason, however, that at low prices the firms cannot afford to ensure that the shrimp are tasty. Suppose consumers believe that the relationship between quality and price is as given in Table 16.4.

Table 16.4

Price (dozen shrimp)	Quality (percentage of tasty shrimp)
$1	10
$2	30
$3	60
$4	70
$5	80
$6	85

a. Find the price that maximizes quality per dollar.

b Suppose that the market supply curve is given in Table 16.5 and that firms set a price that will allow them to sell as many shrimp as possible. Why might the market not clear?

Table 16.5

Price	Supply
$6	6,000
$5	5,500
$4	5,000
$3	4,500
$2	4,000
$1	3,000

3. (Practice problem: quality and price) The boom in home exercise equipment continues, but there are many purchasers who have given up the quest for the perfect body. These purchasers offer their used equipment for sale. The market also includes those who are selling used lemons, worthless devices that do not perform as advertised. Consumers of used exercise equipment judge that the relationship between price and quality is that given in Table 16.6.

Table 16.6

Price	Quality (calories burned per hour)
$100	100
$200	500
$300	1,100
$400	1,600
$500	1,750

Find the price that maximizes quality per dollar.

ADVERTISING

The objective of advertising is to shift the demand curve to the right and thereby increase profits. To see how profits change with a successful advertising programme, simply follow the procedure outlined in Chapter 12 for deriving marginal revenue and finding the monopoly price and quantity.

4. (Practice problem: advertising) Fay's Cleaners has been advertising its new service, which offers customers the opportunity to leave and pick up their dry cleaning at the commuter train station. The demand curves before and after the advertising campaign are given in Table 16.7. Quantity measures suits cleaned and pressed. The marginal cost of each item is $1. Fixed costs equal $1,000.

Table 16.7

Before		After	
Price	Quantity	Price	Quantity
$5.00	100	$5.00	500
$4.50	200	$4.50	1,000
$4.00	300	$4.00	1,500
$3.50	400	$3.50	2,000
$3.00	500	$3.00	2,500
$2.50	600	$2.50	3,000
$2.00	700	$2.00	3,500

a. Find the profit-maximizing price and quantity and level of profits before the advertising campaign.
b. Find the profit-maximizing price and quantity and level of profits after the advertising campaign.
c. How much is the advertising campaign worth to Fay's Cleaners?

5. (Practice problem: advertising) The Vancouver Vermin, a minor league franchise in the A league, is evaluating its advertising programme. The demand curves before and after the advertising campaign are given in Table 16.8. Quantity measures the attendance. The marginal cost of another customer in the park is $.50. Fixed costs are $50,000.

a. Find the profit-maximizing price and quantity and level of profits before the advertising campaign.
b. Find the profit-maximizing price and quantity and level of profits after the advertising campaign.
c. How much is the advertising campaign worth to the Vancouver Vermin?

Table 16.8

Before		After	
Price	Quantity	Price	Quantity
$10.00	15,000	$10.00	20,000
$ 9.50	17,500	$ 9.50	30,000
$ 9.00	20,000	$ 9.00	40,000
$ 8.50	22,500	$ 8.50	50,000
$ 8.00	25,000	$ 8.00	60,000
$ 7.50	27,500	$ 7.50	70,000
$ 7.00	30,000	$ 7.00	80,000
$ 6.50	32,500	$ 6.50	90,000
$ 6.00	35,000	$ 6.00	100,000
$ 5.50	37,500	$ 5.50	110,000

Answers to Problems

2. *a.* The quality-price ratio appears in Table 16.9.

Table 16.9

Price	Quality	Quality-price ratio
$1	10	10.0
$2	30	15.0
$3	60	20.0
$4	70	17.5
$5	80	16.0
$6	85	14.2

Firms choose a price of $3.
b A price of $3 will sell the maximum number of shrimp. At this price, firms would like to sell 4,500 units, but if maximum demand is less than this, there will be excess supply. Firms will not, however, reduce price, realizing that if they were to do, consumers would interpret this as a signal of lower quality and reduce their demand accordingly.

3. The quality-price ratio appears in Table 16.10.

Table 16.10

Price	Quality	Quality-price ratio
$100	100	1.00
$200	500	2.50
$300	1,100	3.67
$400	1,600	4.00
$500	1,750	3.50

4. *a.* Price = \$3; quantity = 500;
   profits = (\$3 × 500) – (\$1 × 500) – \$1,000 – \$0.

  b. Price = \$3; quantity = 2,500; profits = (\$3 × 2,500) – (\$1 × 2,500) – \$1,000 = \$4,000.

  c. The advertising campaign increases profits by \$4,000 – \$0 = \$4,000.

5. *a.* Price = \$6; quantity = 32,500;
   profits = (\$7 × 30,000) – (\$0.50 × 30,000) – \$50,000 = \$145,000.

  b. Price = \$5.50; quantity = 110,000;
   profits = (\$5.50 × 110,000) – (\$0.50 × 110,000) – \$50,000 = \$500,000.

  c. The advertising campaign increases profits by \$500,000 – \$145,000 = \$355,000.

Chapter 17

FINANCING, CONTROLLING, AND MANAGING THE FIRM

Chapter Review

Information problems pervade the entire economy. This chapter continues the discussion of information problems in markets by extending the consideration of the market for financial capital. The same problems caused by asymmetric information in product and labour markets (Chapter 16) reappear in this chapter, when we consider how the firm is financed, how it is managed, and who owns it.

ESSENTIAL CONCEPTS

1. There are three legal forms for businesses in Canada. A single-owner firm is called a **proprietorship.** A firm with two or more owners is a **partnership.** Ownership of **corporations** is divided into shares, and each owner of a share has voting rights in management elections. The most important feature of the corporate form, however, is **limited liability**. Each owner can lose no more than his or her original investment. In contrast, if a partnership incurs large losses, each partner is fully liable for all the debts.

2. Corporations can finance their investments by borrowing, either from banks or by selling bonds, by issuing new shares of stock (equity finance), or from retained earnings, which are accounting profits not paid out as dividends to owners. If corporate managers act in the interest of the owners, they will maximize the market value of the firm. One might think that decisions corporate managers take with regard to the financing of the firm—should they rely more heavily on borrowing or on issuing new shares of stock?—would have a bearing on the value of the firm. Surprisingly, the **Modigliani-Miller theorem** states that the mix of debt and equity finance makes no difference to the market value of the firm. The Modigliani-Miller theorem is the starting point for the analysis of the financial structure of corporations. Nevertheless, certain features of real-world corporations mean that firms do care about their financial structure and watch their debt load very closely.

3. If lenders had perfect information about the default risk of borrowers, then the interest rate would adjust to clear the market for loans. In the real world, however, lenders do not know how risky each borrower is; thus, they give each borrower incentives to pay the loans back. Furthermore, charging higher interest rates attracts especially risky borrowers and motivates borrowers to take on extra risks to earn enough to repay the interest. Rather than

raise the interest rate, lenders may ration loans. This phenomenon is known as **credit rationing.**

4. Issuing new shares is one way firms can raise new capital, but this practice may also pose problems. Prospective buyers of shares may reason that managers believe that the firm is overvalued or that it has been turned down on previous loan applications. Such expectations will cause the stock price to fall when new shares are issued. When the price of a stock falls significantly in response to the issuing of new shares, economists say that the firm is **equity rationed.** Few firms raise capital through equity finance in modern economies.

5. Inefficient management lowers the market value of a firm, but shareholders often do not have good enough information to monitor the managers. Other investors may buy up a majority voting share, replace the inefficient managers, and make profits. In this way, the **market for takeovers** can promote efficient management. Some economists have reservations about the effects of hostile takeovers, but most favour leaving the control of firms to markets.

6. The **principal-agent problem** summarizes the difficulty of providing good incentives to employees. One important example is the case in which the owners of a firm are the principals and the managers are their agents. The owners (the shareholders) want managers to act in the best interest of the firm. The managers, however, may have other interests, and it is difficult for the owners to judge whether a manager takes appropriate actions. The problem for the owners is to design incentives to motivate the managers to work hard and to take the appropriate risks in order to further their own interests.

7. One approach to solving the principal-agent problem is for the agent to become a principal. If the owners of the enterprise sell a share to the manager, the manager has the appropriate incentives. Another approach involves **incentive pay.** A sales commission is one example, and a stock option, which gives the manager the right to buy a number of shares at a given price, is another. Such schemes mean that when the manager increases the market value of the firm, the manager, as an owner, will profit. The final method by which the principal-agent problem might be overcome is by direct **monitoring** of the agent.

8. Managers are not the only ones who need to be motivated. Workers do too. Piece-rate pay is a simple device when monitoring of individual performance is straightforward, though even then concerns about the quality of the work may limit its usefulness. **Efficiency wage theory** argues that an alternative motivating factor is to raise the wage above the competitive level. Advocates of this theory point to several benefits, including increased productivity, reduced labour turnover, and higher-quality work.

9. A fundamental issue in the structure of a large organization is the degree of **centralization.** A centralized, top-down structure has many layers of decision making and review. Its advantages include the approval of fewer bad projects, coordination to account for interdependen-

cies and externalitites within the organization, and a lack of duplication. A decentralized structure grants more autonomy to the individual units within the organization; it usually approves more good projects and acts more quickly with more diversity and experimentation; and it allows management to compare the performance of the units and decide how to allocate resources within the firm.

BEHIND THE ESSENTIAL CONCEPTS

1. Economists often approach a problem by first understanding a simple model and then moving on to more realistic situations. When studying corporate finance, the simple starting point is the Modigliani-Miller theorem. This theorem says that the method of corporate finance makes no difference to the market value of the firm. If the firm uses borrowing rather than new shares to finance new investment, the higher debt load makes the firm's stock riskier and lowers its price. The lower price is just enough to keep the market value of the firm the same as it would have been under equity finance.

2. What is missing from this story? In the real world of corporate finance, firms must worry about the high costs of bankruptcy, and they must consider the tax consequences of debt and equity. Managerial incentives, market perceptions of value based on these incentives, and the ultimate control of the firm's decisions may all be affected by the financial structure of the firm.

3. If a firm raises money by borrowing, the lenders receive interest payments. If it raises money through new equity, then the investors receive dividends and capital gains as the stock price rises. The Canadian tax system affects the firm's decision in several ways. It encourages borrowing and discourages equity finance because interest paid is a tax-deductible expense for the firm but dividends are not. Offsetting this to some extent is the more favourable treatment afforded individuals who receive capital gains and dividends. The net effect is that the Canadian tax system encourages borrowing to some extent.

4. Asymmetric information is also important when the firm goes to the market for loanable funds in search of capital to finance investments. Suppose you are thinking of providing some of this capital by purchasing a corporate bond. You do not know as much about the default risk as the firm issuing the bond, and you should therefore be suspicious about bonds that pay very high interest rates. After all, why would a firm pay high interest rates unless it is selling a risky bond? Other investors reason as you do, and therefore the interest rate does not rise to clear the market for bonds. Firms are credit rationed because of asymmetric information in credit markets.

5. This chapter goes a long way beyond the analysis of the firm in the basic competitive model. The competitive firm has two simple problems to solve: how much should it produce and by what means. Competitive firms hardly

need managers. The firms in this chapter are much more realistic and, naturally, more complicated. They must select employees for tasks, motivate them, monitor their efforts, and account for their outputs. Further, they must deal with uncertainty, determine the degree of centralization, and decide on the number of activities to produce in-house and contract out. It is in solving these problems that real-world managers earn their salaries.

6. As an organization grows, the level of direct control owners exercise diminishes and the problem of providing incentives arises. When incentives are the issue, the usual suspects appear: asymmetric information in that the principal (the owner) cannot observe and evaluate the activities of employees (the agents), and moral hazard in that the agents may pursue their own interests and not those of the principal. Solutions to the problem involve the risk-incentive trade-off. For example, basing pay on performance or tying pay to profitability provides stronger incentives but also subjects the agents to more risk. These are fundamental problems within any organization. An understanding of their source and nature, however, may enable you to manage better in any organization that you work for or join.

7. Efficiency wages are wages of trust. But it is not that trust is being rewarded with high wages. Rather, high wages are presumed to breed trust. The argument is that the threat of losing a wage that is higher than what can be earned elsewhere encourages moral behaviour.

SELF-TEST

True or False

1. A proprietorship is a firm owned by two or more proprietors.

2. Partnerships offer each partner limited liability in case of bankruptcy.

3. One risk of owning shares of a corporation is that should the firm go out of business, each shareholder is liable for all the debts.

4. A highly leveraged firm is one that has a high ratio of debt to equity.

5. The Modigliani-Miller theorem states that how a firm raises funds has no bearing on the firm's market value.

6. Dividends are tax deductible for firms, because individuals must pay income tax on their dividend earnings.

7. Established firms finance most of their investments through borrowing when they do not use their retained earnings.

8. If a firm cannot afford the interest rate charged by banks for loans, then it is credit rationed.

9. Credit rationing occurs because lenders know more about borrowers' default risks than the borrowers do.

10. Issuing more equity tends to lower share prices excessively.

11. The threat of a takeover may motivate managers to work hard to increase profits.

12. A simple solution to the principal-agent problem is to make the principal an agent.

13. Advocates of efficiency wages argue that they motivate workers to work more productively because the workers are concerned about the threat of losing their well-paid jobs.

14. Under centralized decision making, fewer bad projects are rejected.

15. Under decentralized decision making, fewer good projects are rejected.

Multiple Choice

1. A proprietorship is a business firm in which:
   a. there is a single owner, whose liability is limited to the amount he or she has invested in the firm.
   b. there is a single owner, who is fully liable for all debts the firm incurs.
   c. individuals have invested in the firm by buying shares of stock, and their liabilities are limited to the amounts of their investments.
   d. there are multiple owners, who are fully liable for all debts the firm incurs.
   e. there are multiple owners, whose liabilities are limited to the amounts they have invested in the firm.

2. In a partnership:
   a. the partners' liabilities are limited to the amounts they invested in the firm.
   b. each partner is liable for an equal share of any debts the firm incurs.
   c. each partner is fully liable for all debts the firm incurs.
   d. neither partner has any liability.
   e. liability is limited in precisely the way it would be if the firm were a corporation.

3. In a corporation, the owners have limited liability; this means they:
   a. are exempt from taxes on the capital gains realized on their investment.
   b. are exempt from taxes on their shares of the retained earnings of the firm.
   c. have only a limited say in how the corporation is run.
   d. can lose no more than the amounts they invest in the event of bankruptcy.
   e. receive partial reimbursement of their investments in the event of bankruptcy.

4. The owners of a corporation are its:
   a. shareholders.
   b. partners.
   c. proprietors.
   d. bondholders.
   e. executives.

5. Retained earnings equal:
   a. revenues.

b. revenues minus expenses.

c. revenues minus expenses and dividends.

d. revenues minus expenses and debt repayments.

e. revenues minus expenses, debt repayments, and dividends.

6. A firm is highly leveraged when it has a:

a. high ratio of equity to debt.

b. low ratio of retained earnings to dividends.

c. high ratio of debt to equity.

d. high ratio of retained earnings to dividends.

e. low ratio of debt to equity.

7. The Modigliani-Miller result states that as a firm's ratio of debt to equity:

a. rises, its market value falls.

b. rises, its return to equity is unaffected.

c. rises, its market value is unaffected.

d. falls, its return to equity is unaffected.

e. falls, its market value falls.

8. All of the following factors, except one, are issues that the Modigliani-Miller result regarding the equivalence of debt and equity finance ignores. Which is the odd one out?

a. Concerns about bankruptcy limit the use of debt finance.

b. Differences in tax treatment tend to favour debt finance.

c. Debt finance provides stronger incentives to management.

d. The market perceives debt finance as a signal of a healthy firm.

e. Firms often use retained earnings as a source of finance.

9. Under the Canadian tax system, a firm's:

a. interest payments are tax deductible, but its dividend payments are not; this provides an incentive to use debt finance.

b. dividend payments are tax deductible, but its interest payments are not; this provides an incentive to use debt finance.

c. interest and dividend payments are both tax deductible, so neither debt nor equity finance is favoured.

d. dividend payments are tax deductible, but its interest payments are not; this provides an incentive to use equity finance.

e. interest payments are tax deductible, but its dividend payments are not; this provides an incentive to use equity finance.

10. Under the Canadian tax system, capital gains are treated:

a. more favourably than interest payments; this provides individuals with an advantage when firms use debt finance.

b. more favourably than interest payments; this provides individuals with an advantage when firms use equity finance.

c. in the same way as interest payments, so individuals

derive no advantage from one form of finance relative to the other.

d. less favourably than interest payments; this provides individuals with an advantage when firms use debt finance.

e. less favourably than interest payments; this provides individuals with an advantage when firms use equity finance.

11. Credit rationing occurs when a bank chooses not to raise its interest rate because it is concerned that:

a. there is insufficient demand at the higher rate to justify the increase.

b. the increase will cause it to lose some of its high-risk borrowers.

c. there is already an excess supply of loans at the lower rate.

d. the increase will cause it to lose some of its low-risk borrowers.

e. those who borrow at the higher rate will be excessively cautious.

12. When an increase in the interest rate changes the mix of low-risk and high-risk borrowers, this is an example of:

a. diminishing returns.

b. economies of scale.

c. adverse selection.

d. moral hazard.

e. the principal-agent problem.

13. In the market for loanable funds, credit rationing arises because:

a. borrowers know their own default risks but lenders do not know borrowers' default risks.

b. neither borrowers nor lenders know borrowers' default risks.

c. lenders know borrowers' default risks but borrowers do not know their own default risks.

d. both borrowers and lenders know borrowers' default risks.

e. lenders know their own default risks but borrowers do not know lenders' default risks.

14. In the market for loanable funds, adverse selection means that once the rate of interest rises above the point at which the expected return from making loans is maximized, the loanable funds supply curve:

a. is horizontal.

b. is negatively sloped.

c. has an infinite price elasticity.

d. is positively sloped.

e. is vertical.

15. When banks worry that a higher interest rate on loans may induce excessive risk-taking by the borrower, this is an example of:

a. the principal-agent problem.

b. diminishing returns.

c. economies of scale.

d. adverse selection.

e. moral hazard.

16. Firms considering issuing new stock are often reluctant

to do so because they are concerned that it will have an excessively detrimental effect on the share price. This effect is termed:

a. the Modigliani-Miller result.
b. equity rationing.
c. the principal-agent problem.
d. credit rationing.
e. the risk-incentive trade-off.

17. When the firm's owners cannot easily determine whether a manager is working in the best interests of the firm, this is an example of:

a. comparative advantage.
b. diminishing returns.
c. the principal-agent problem.
d. adverse selection.
e. moral hazard.

18. The efficiency wage theory argues that, in certain circumstances, firms pay wages that are above the market level. Which of the following statements about the theory is correct?

a. The only reason firms pay the high wages is to attract workers who are more productive.
b. The only reason firms pay the high wages is to induce workers to be more productive.
c. Firms are less likely to pay efficiency wages in situations in which monitoring worker performance is more costly.
d. Firms pay the high wages to attract workers who are more productive and to induce them to be more productive.
e. Workers receiving efficiency wages know that if they leave the firm, they can always get another job paying efficiency wages.

19. All of the following, except one, are advantages of centralized decision making relative to decentralized decision making. Which is the odd one out?

a. There is more experimentation.
b. Fewer bad projects are accepted.
c. There is better coordination.
d. Fewer good projects are accepted.
e. There is less duplication.

20. All of the following, except one, are advantages of decentralized decision making relative to centralized decision making. Which is the odd one out?

a. More good projects are accepted.
b. Decisions are made and implemented more quickly.
c. Externalities within the organization are taken into account.
d. There is greater diversity and experimentation.
e. Incentives are stronger.

Completion

1. Two or more individuals owning a business together form a _____.

2. The key distinguishing characteristic of corporations is that their owners have _____.

3. According to the Modiglianai-Miller theorem, the

method of financing the corporation makes no difference to the _____ of the firm.

4. Overall the Canadian tax structure favours _____ finance.

5. When individuals or firms cannot borrow all they desire at the going interest rate, they are subject to _____.

6. There is an adverse selection effect in the credit market if higher interest rates _____ the expected return to a loan.

7. A situation in which managers of a firm may not act in the best interest of the owner is an example of the _____.

8. High wages that both reward and encourage increased productivity are called _____.

9. Fewer bad projects are accepted under _____ decision making.

10. _____ are an important determinant of whether a firm produces something itself or buys it from another firm.

Answers to Self-Test

True or False

1. f	4. t	7. t	10. t	13. t
2. f	5. t	8. f	11. t	14. f
3. f	6. f	9. f	12. f	15. t

Multiple Choice

1. b	6. c	11. d	16. b
2. c	7. c	12. c	17. c
3. d	8. e	13. a	18. d
4. a	9. a	14. b	19. a
5. e	10. b	15. e	20. c

Completion

1. partnership
2. limited liability
3. market value
4. debt
5. credit rationing
6. reduce
7. principal-agent problem
8. efficiency wages
9. centralized
10. Transactions costs

Doing Economics: Tools and Practice Problems

In the competitive model, markets clear (demand equals supply) and firms minimize costs. When information is imperfect, things are sometimes a little more complicated. In the following questions, we see how information problems can lead to rationing in the credit market and we investigate some issues surrounding the principal-agent problem.

CREDIT RATIONING

Sometimes, firms are not able to obtain loans at the going rate of interest. They are said to be credit rationed. Imperfect information is the root of the problem. As in other models with imperfect information (see Chapter 16), the price (in this case, the rate of interest) does double duty. Besides balancing demand and supply, it also serves as a signal of the average riskiness of loan applications, in the absence of direct information on default risk. Banks and other institutions that grant loans know that a higher rate of interest discourages good risks and encourages bad ones. Beyond a certain point, increasing the rate of interest further may reduce the expected return as the good risks are driven from the market. Instead, the lenders ration credit. Tool Kit 17.1 shows you how this works.

Tool Kit 17.1: Credit Rationing

Step one: Identify and plot the relationship between the interest rate and the expected rate of return on loans. Also, identify the supply and demand for loans. Note that the demand depends on the interest rate actually charged by banks, but the supply depends on the expected rate of return.

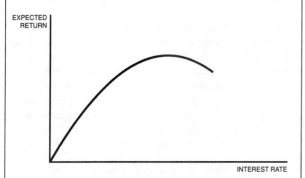

Step two: Find the interest rate that maximizes the expected rate of return. This will be the interest rate the banks charge.

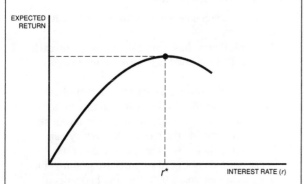

Step three: Find the quantity supplied by substituting the maximum expected rate of return into the supply curve.

Step four: Find the quantity demanded by substituting

the associated interest rate (found in step two) into the demand curve.

Step five: Find the amount of credit rationing by subtracting the loans supplied from the loans demanded:

credit rationing = loans demanded – loans supplied.

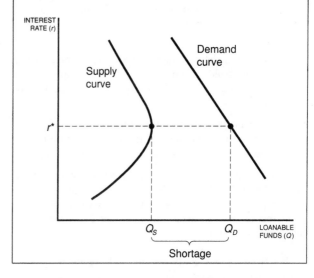

1. (Worked problem: credit rationing) Banks in North End realize that at high interest rates, the pool of loan applicants will include relatively more firms with high default rates. They calculate that the relationship between the interest rate and the expected returns is as given in Table 17.1. The table also gives the supply and demand for new loans. Note that the demand depends on the interest rate actually charged by banks, but the supply depends on the expected rate of return. Find the banks' interest rate and the level of credit rationing.

Table 17.1

Interest rate	Expected rate of return
4.0%	4.0%
4.5%	4.4%
5.0%	4.8%
5.5%	5.2%
6.0%	5.0%
6.5%	4.8%
7.0%	4.0%

Demand for loans		Supply of loans	
Interest rate	Value (thousands)	Expected rate of return	Value (thousands)
4.0%	$2,500	4.0%	$ 300
4.5%	$1,900	4.4%	$ 400
5.0%	$1,500	4.8%	$ 600
5.5%	$1,200	5.0%	$ 800
6.0%	$1,000	5.2%	$1,000
6.5%	$ 700		
7.0%	$ 400		

Step-by-step solution

Step one: Identify the relationship between the interest rate and the expected rate of return on loans, and the supply and demand for loans. They are given in Table 17.1.

Step two: Find the interest rate that maximizes the expected rate of return. The expected rate of return reaches its maximum of 5.2 percent when the interest rate is 5.5 percent.

Step three: Find the quantity supplied by substituting the maximum expected rate of return into the supply curve; $1,000,000 is supplied when the expected rate of return is 5.2 percent.

Step four: Find the quantity demanded by substituting the equilibrium interest rate into the demand curve; $1,200,000 is supplied when the interest rate is 5.5 percent.

Step five: Find the amount of credit rationing. It is $1,200,000 − $1,000,000 = $200,000. Although there is a shortage, banks will not raise the interest rate because higher interest rates bring about more defaults and a lower expected rate of return.

2. (Practice problem: credit rationing) The relationship between the interest rate and the expected rate of return is given in Table 17.2, which also gives the supply and demand curves for university loans in Gotham. Find the equilibrium interest rate and the amount of credit rationing.

Table 17.2

Interest rate	Expected rate of return
6.0%	5.8%
6.5%	6.0%
7.0%	6.2%
7.5%	6.3%
8.0%	6.2%
8.5%	6.0%
9.0%	5.0%

Demand for loans		Supply of loans	
Interest rate	Value (thousands)	Expected rate of return	Value (thousands)
6.0%	$8,000	5.0%	$1,000
6.5%	$7,000	5.8%	$1,500
7.0%	$6,000	6.0%	$2,000
7.5%	$5,000	6.2%	$2,500
8.0%	$4,000	6.3%	$3,000
8.5%	$3,000		
9.0%	$2,000		

3. (Practice problem: credit rationing) The relationship between the interest rate and the expected rate of return is given in Table 17.3, which also gives the supply and demand curves for small-business loans in Eastpointe. Find the equilibrium interest rate and the amount of credit rationing.

Table 17.3

Interest rate	Expected rate of return
6.0%	5.0%
6.5%	6.0%
7.0%	6.1%
7.5%	6.0%
8.0%	5.5%
8.5%	5.0%
9.0%	5.0%

Demand for loans		Supply of loans	
Interest rate	Value (thousands)	Expected rate of return	Value (thousands)
6.0%	$17,000	5.0%	$6,000
6.5%	$15,000	5.5%	$7,000
7.0%	$13,000	6.0%	$8,000
7.5%	$11,000	6.1%	$9,000
8.0%	$ 9,000		
8.5%	$ 7,000		
9.0%	$ 5,000		

INCENTIVES

At the heart of the principal-agent problem is the issue of incentives. How do the owners of the firm ensure that those who work for the firm have the appropriate incentives to act in the interests of the firm? The next three problems use some familiar concepts (the budget constraint and the equality between marginal benefit and marginal cost) to illustrate some aspects of the problem. First, we look at what happens when there are no prices within an organization. Second, we investigate profit-sharing agreements.

4. (Worked problem: incentives) The Add advertising agency has several creative teams in its employ, and for years each team has been given a budget of $10,000 for any services that its work requires. The teams hire outside contractors to do layouts and printing. The price of each service is $200 per day.

   a. Plot the budget constraint for the typical creative team.
   b. The typical team has spent half its budget on each service. Plot the point that corresponds to this choice.
   c. Following the recommendation of a consultant, the agency decides to do all its printing in-house. Now the creative teams purchase only layout services from outside the agency. Since they can have their printing services performed at the agency and do not need to purchase printing, their budgets are cut to $5,000. Plot the budget constraint.
   d. The agency finds that the print shop is always overcrowded. Why?

Step-by-step solution

Step one (a): Draw coordinate axes, and label the horizontal one "Printing services" and the vertical one "Layout services."

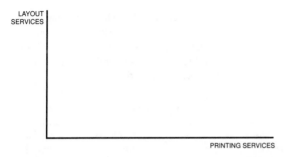

Step two: If the team spends all its budget on printing, it can purchase $10,000/$200 = 50 days. Plot this point along the horizontal axis.

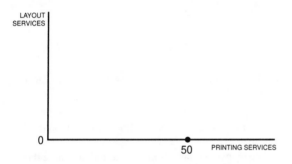

Step three: If the team spends all its budget on layouts, it can purchase $10,000/$200 = 50 days. Plot this point along the vertical axis.

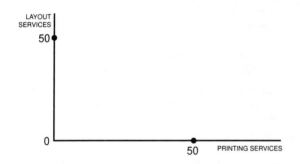

Step four (b): The team spends $5,000 on each service and buys $5,000/$200 = 25 days of each. Plot the point (25, 25) and label it *A*.

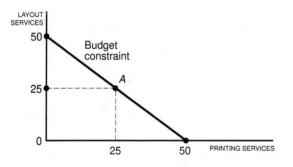

Step five (c): The team has a budget of $5,000. The price of layout service is still $200 per day, but printing is free. The team can still purchase 25 days of layout services, and it can have all of the printing that it wants. The budget constraint is a horizontal line intersecting the vertical axis at 25.

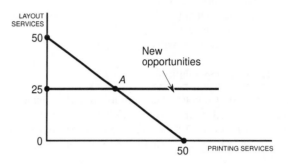

Step six (d): The new way of doing things at the agency allows teams to use printing services without paying for them. In terms of the budget constraint, the teams now can choose all the combinations to the right of point *A*. As long as printing has any value to the team, they will buy more and the shop will be overcrowded.

5. (Practice problem: incentives) Betty and Wilma are copy editors. They pore over manuscripts looking for typographical, grammatical, and other errors. Betty is self-employed and receives $2 per page. Wilma works for NTN Publishers and receives a straight salary of $800 each week. Each can edit 10 pages an hour, and each has 60 hours available every week. They both like to goof off, and they both like money.

   a. Plot Betty's budget constraint. Put income on the vertical axis and time spent goofing off on the horizontal. What is the slope of her budget constraint?
   b. Plot Wilma's budget constraint. What is its slope?
   c. Which editor has the greater incentive to goof off? Why?

6. (Worked problem: incentives) Michael and Eliot have part-time jobs as Mexway distributors; they sell soap. The amount that each can sell depends on the time that he puts in knocking on doors. The relationship is given in Table 17.4.

Table 17.4

Time (hours)	Revenue
1	$ 40
2	$ 70
3	$ 90
4	$100
5	$105
6	$106

Both Michael and Eliot place a value of $10 on 1 hour of their time.

   a. Complete the marginal benefit column.
   b. How many hours will each work? How much revenue will each earn?

c. Now suppose that Michael and Eliot form a business to sell soap. They agree to share the revenues. If Michael works 1 hour, he brings in $40, but he gives $20 to Eliot. Michael's personal reward is only $20. Revise the table above to reflect the agreement that revenues are shared.

d. Complete a marginal benefit column for the revised revenue numbers.

e. How many hours will each work now?

Step-by-step solution

Step one (a): Complete the marginal benefit column. If Michael works 1 hour, he earns $40, which is the marginal benefit. If he works 2 hours, his revenue rises from $40 to $70, which is a marginal benefit of $30. The results are given in Table 17.5.

Table 17.5

Time (hours)	Revenue	Marginal benefit
1	$ 40	$40
2	$ 70	$30
3	$ 90	$20
4	$100	$10
5	$105	$ 5
6	$106	$ 1

Step two (b): The marginal cost of an hour is $10. Setting marginal cost equal to marginal benefit implies 4 hours of work, which brings in $100.

Step three (c): Accounting for the sharing of revenues means that the relationship between time spent selling and the revenues that each gets to keep for himself are in Table 17.6.

Table 17.6

Time (hours)	Revenue
1	$20.00
2	$35.00
3	$45.00
4	$50.00
5	$52.50
6	$53.00

Step four (d): Now the marginal benefit is half what it was before, as shown in Table 17.7.

Table 17.7

Time (hours)	Revenue	Marginal benefit
1	$20.00	$20.00
2	$35.00	$15.00
3	$45.00	$10.00
4	$50.00	$ 5.00
5	$52.50	$ 2.50
6	$53.00	$ 0.50

Step five (e): Now marginal benefit equals marginal cost at 3 hours worked, which brings in only $45. Sharing the profits means that neither person receives the full benefits of his time and effort. This is the classic incentive problem. Because of bad incentives, each is led to work less.

7. (Practice problem: incentives) Mr. Davis is a sharecropper on a farm owned by Miss Tilly. He gives her one-third of his revenue from farming her 20 hectares in rural Mississauga. Table 17.8 gives the relationship between his effort and the revenue from the farm.

Table 17.8

Time (hours)	Total revenue	Mr. Davis' revenue	Marginal benefit
1	$18		
2	$33		
3	$45		
4	$54		
5	$60		
6	$63		

Mr. Davis, when not sharecropping, can work in town and make $6 per hour.

a. Complete the table.
b. How much does Mr. Davis choose to work on the farm?
c. If he owned the farm himself and did not share the revenue with Miss Tilly, how much would he work on the farm?

Answers to Problems

2. Equilibrium interest rate = 7.5%; expected return = 6.3%; credit rationing = $5,000,000 – $3,000,000 = $2,000,000.

3. Equilibrium interest rate = 7%; expected return = 6.1%; credit rationing = $13,000,000 – $9,000,000 = $4,000,000.

5. *a,b.*

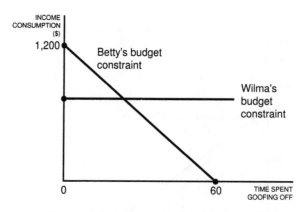

c. Wilma has more opportunities that involve less work; thus, she has more incentive to goof off.

7. *a.* The completed information is given in Table 17.9.

Table 17.9

Time (hours)	Total revenue	Mr. Davis' revenue	Marginal benefit
1	$18	$12	$12
2	$33	$22	$10
3	$45	$30	$ 8
4	$54	$36	$ 6
5	$60	$40	$ 4
6	$63	$42	$ 2

b. He works 4 hours, where the marginal benefit equals marginal cost, which is $6 per hour.

c. If he owned the farm, the marginal benefit would be as given in Table 17.10.

Table 17.10

Time (hours)	Revenue	Marginal benefit
1	$18	$18
2	$33	$15
3	$45	$12
4	$54	$ 9
5	$60	$ 6
6	$63	$ 3

Mr. Davis would work 5 hours.

Part Four

The Public Sector

GOVERNMENT AND PUBLIC DECISION MAKING

Chapter Review

To this point, the text's focus has been on private markets. Despite this, the role of government in Canada's mixed economy is pervasive, extending into all spheres of economic activity. Chapter 18 is the first of three chapters that deal with the economic analysis of government at the microeconomic level.

You might ask what economists can possibly find for government to do, given their belief that private markets work so well. Actually, economists believe that markets work well *most of the time* and that it is precisely when markets fail that the government has a role to play. This chapter describes the various reasons for government intervention. It also takes a brief look at the issue of public decision making and concludes with an analysis of Canada's federal structure and the question of the division of responsibilities between federal and provincial governments.

ESSENTIAL CONCEPTS

1. In Canada, government spending at all levels amounts to over 48 percent of gross domestic product (GDP), higher than the average for developed countries. Canadian government spending has grown dramatically in recent decades. Much of the growth of government spending is accounted for by transfers to the elderly, transfers to the provinces in the areas of health and welfare, and interest on the growing national debt.

2. The role for government arises because of concerns over market outcomes. These concerns fall into two categories. Nobody ever claimed that markets are kind, and inequality in the distribution of society's resources occupies much of the government's attention. There are also cases in which the private-market outcome is inefficient. These instances of **market failure** include an inadequate provision of **public goods** and a misallocation of resources in the presence of **externalities.**

3. The **public sector** has a variety of instruments with which to accomplish its goals. It can take direct action, by producing the good or service itself or purchasing it from private firms. It can **mandate** private sector action, **regulate** private activity, or **ban** certain behaviours altogether. Finally, with a somewhat lighter hand, the government can provide incentives to increase or decrease certain types of actions through the use of its tax and subsidy powers.

4. Markets are not the only institutions to fail. Governments fail too. They suffer from imperfect information,

there is a widespread lack of incentives for those charged with the task of administering government programmes, and policy often does not take account of behavioural responses on the part of individuals and firms in the private sector.

5. Governments are elected, of course, so one presumes the wishes of the majority are reflected in the actions governments take. The problem is that majority voting does not yield a determinate outcome when faced with multiple alternatives. This result is known as the **voting paradox.** In votes on a single issue, such as the level of spending on public schools, there is, however, a determinate outcome. In this case, a majority voting rule means that the **median voter** is the person whose preferences decide the day. Political parties, in their desire to get elected, tend to reflect the median voter's preferences; this is why, come election day, people sometimes feel there is little to choose between the parties running for office.

BEHIND THE ESSENTIAL CONCEPTS

1. **Externalities** exist whenever individuals or firms do not bear the full costs, or enjoy the full benefits of their decisions. Negative externalities are costs borne by others, such as pollution, congestion, and noise. Positive externalities are benefits enjoyed by others from such activities as basic research and innovation. Because decision makers can ignore the costs that spill over onto others, private firms overproduce negative externalities. Similarly, because they are not adequately compensated, producers of positive externalities do not create enough. Governments can improve the allocation of resources by inducing individuals to reduce negative externalities and increase positive ones.

2. **Public goods** have two important characteristics. Once they are provided, the marginal cost of another consumer's enjoyment of the good is zero. The second characteristic is that it is costly to exclude individuals from enjoying the public good. The fact that people can choose to enjoy public goods without paying for them is called the **free-rider problem.** This feature makes it difficult for private individuals to collect enough funds to provide public goods. This is why economists argue that the public sector is the appropriate institution to provide public goods.

3. Frequently, government action cannot be even remotely described as approximating the interests of the median voter. Instead, it appears to favour the interests of certain groups. This is usually a government response to what economists call **rent seeking.** The term refers to any activity designed to procure some special favour from the government. The government, through its ability to levy taxes and grant subsidies, is in a privileged position. It is not, therefore, surprising that groups will try to encourage the government to use this power to the benefit of the groups. Usually, the mythical "national interest" is invoked as the reason for the proposed intervention, but if you read about firms in an industry advocating government action in a particular area, you should always ask yourself: "what's in it for them?"

4. The debate over the appropriate division of responsibilities between federal and provincial governments in Canada's federal structure has been going on since Confederation. Decentralized decision making—power in the hands of the provinces and municipalities—ensures better provision of local public goods and services (e.g., libraries) and encourages efficient government as jurisdictions compete for residents (and their tax dollars!). But it can also exacerbate, rather than solve, problems of inappropriate market outcomes.

    One province might be encouraged to lower welfare benefits, hoping this would provide an incentive for recipients to move to other provinces. Individual provinces will behave like public citizens if asked to contribute to national public goods (e.g., defence), hoping to free-ride on other provinces. They may also impose externalities on other provinces. And, they may (and often do) practise forms of protectionism that restrict the free flow of goods and services, and labour and capital, between provinces.

SELF-TEST

True or False

1. In a federal government structure, all government activity takes place at the level of the federal government.

2. Unemployment insurance is a provincial responsibility in Canada.

3. Markets fail whenever individuals pursue their self-interest.

4. A firm generates an externality when it does not bear all the consequences of its action.

5. Private markets oversupply goods that yield positive externalities.

6. A public good is one for which the cost of production is zero.

7. The cost of excluding someone from enjoying a public good is very high.

8. Private markets undersupply public goods.

9. Governments are perfectly informed.

10. The voting paradox argues that voters favour inefficient outcomes.

11. The voting paradox suggests that only a dictator will make consistent choices.

12. The median voter is the voter with the median income.

13. When individuals or firms engage in activities designed to procure special favours from governments, this is called rent seeking.

14. Defence is a local public good.

15. The "race to the bottom" refers to competitive cuts in welfare programmes by provincial governments.

Multiple Choice

1. Which of the following is not one of the four basic questions an economy must answer?

    a. What is produced, and in what quantities?
    b. How are goods and services produced?
    c. Who makes the decisions?
    d. Which economists advise the government?
    e. For whom are the goods and services produced?

2. In Canada today, expenditures by all levels of government account for nearly _____ percent of gross domestic product.

    a. 30
    b. 35
    c. 40
    d. 45
    e. 50

3. In Canada today, interest on the federal debt accounts for about _____ percent of the federal budget.

    a. 25
    b. 20
    c. 15
    d. 10
    e. 5

4. The government's right to seize private property for public use, provided the owner is compensated adequately, is called:

    a. legal confiscation.
    b. adverse selection.
    c. eminent domain.
    d. regulation.
    e. taxation.

5. In his book *The Wealth of Nations,* Adam Smith argued that the public interest is best promoted by:

    a. government control of the economy.
    b. adherence to time-honoured traditions.
    c. the benevolence of well-meaning citizens.
    d. individuals pursuing their own self-interest.
    e. trusting to the honesty of elected officials.

6. All of the following represent cases in which government intervention is required, but in only four of the five cases is the intervention justified on the grounds of market failure. Which is the odd one out?

    a. unemployment
    b. income inequality
    c. lack of competition
    d. externalities
    e. public goods

7. If the government intervenes in the economy to deal with an instance of pollution, this represents an intervention to address:

    a. an externality.
    b. a public good.
    c. income inequality.
    d. lack of competition.
    e. unemployment.

8. Externalities can be positive or negative. In the case of a good that generates a positive externality, the private market supplies too:

    a. much of the good and sets a price that is too high.
    b. much of the good and sets a price that is too low.
    c. much of the good, though the price is neither too high nor too low.
    d. little of the good and sets a price that is too high.
    e. little of the good and sets a price that is too low.

9. Externalities can be positive or negative. In the case of a good that generates a negative externality, the costs to society are:

    a. lower than the costs to the producer, and the market price of the good is higher than the socially efficient level.
    b. lower than the costs to the producer, and the market price of the good is lower than the socially efficient level.
    c. the same as the costs to the producer, but the market price is lower than the socially efficient level.
    d. higher than the costs to the producer, and the market price is lower than the socially efficient level.
    e. higher than the costs to the producer, and the market price of the good is higher than the socially efficient level.

10. In the case of a public good, the cost of excluding someone from enjoying its benefits is _____ and the marginal cost of providing the benefits to someone is _____.

    a. high; high
    b. low; high
    c. high; low
    d. low; low
    e. zero; infinite

11. A good for which consumption is nonrivalrous and nonexcludable is:

    a. a public good.
    b. one that generates a negative externality.
    c. one that is produced by a monopoly.
    d. one that generates a positive externality.
    e. a private good.

12. The free-rider problem is a problem associated with _____ and is a consequence of their consumption being _____.

    a. private goods; nonexcludable
    b. public goods; nonexcludable
    c. private goods; excludable
    d. public goods; nonrivalrous
    e. private goods; nonrivalrous

13. The cost of excluding someone from enjoying the benefits of publicly provided health services is _____ and the marginal cost of providing the benefits to someone is _____.

    a. high; high
    b. low; low
    c. zero; zero
    d. high; low
    e. low; high

14. All of the following, except one, are potential sources of government failure. Which is the odd one out?

    a. imperfect information
    b. government waste
    c. lack of incentives
    d. market failure
    e. unforeseen consequences

15. The voting paradox demonstrates that:

    a. governments tend to reflect the preferences of the median voter.
    b. majority voting never results in a determinate outcome.
    c. majority voting sometimes results in a determinate outcome.
    d. majority voting always results in a determinate outcome.
    e. governments never reflect the preferences of the median voter.

16. The voting paradox only applies when there are:

    a. more than two people choosing among more than two options.
    b. many people choosing how much to spend on a single item.
    c. two people choosing among more than two options.
    d. more than two people choosing between two options.
    e. two people choosing between two options.

17. In a majority vote to decide how much money to spend on postsecondary education, the median voter:

    a. has a 50 percent chance of going to university.
    b. represents the dividing line between those who want to spend more and those who want to spend less.
    c. earns the median level of income.
    d. thinks that the amount of spending should be half of the amount that is currently being spent.
    e. will not represent the will of the majority.

18. All of the following, except one, are examples of rent-seeking behaviour. Which is the odd one out?

    a. owners of apartment buildings posting advertisements for tenants
    b. the textile industry arguing for tariffs to reduce imports from countries with lower-priced labour
    c. the dairy industry advocating the retention of marketing boards
    d. the automobile industry urging the government to negotiate voluntary restraints on Japanese imports
    e. the aluminum industry proposing relaxation of anti-combines legislation

19. When government bureaucrats do not work in the interests of taxpayers, this is an example of:

    a. adverse selection.
    b. the voting paradox.
    c. the free-rider problem.
    d. the median voter theory.
    e. the principal-agent problem.

20. Which of the following is an example of a local public good?

    a. defence spending
    b. publicly provided housing
    c. public libraries
    d. unemployment insurance
    e. postsecondary education

Completion

1. Selling government enterprises to the private sector is called _____.

2. The reduction or elimination of government controls on the activities of an industry is termed _____.

3. When a private market yields an inefficient outcome, this is termed _____.

4. An individual who takes an action without bearing the full costs causes an _____.

5. If the government seeks to encourage some activity, such as recycling, it can _____ the activity.

6. An individual can enjoy the benefit from a _____ at zero cost.

7. The difficulty of excluding those who do not pay for public goods from enjoying their benefits is called the _____ problem.

8. The attempt by a group to procure a special favour from the government is called _____ behaviour.

9. Political parties often take very similar positions as they all seek to approximate the interests of the _____.

10. Public libraries are an example of a _____.

Answers to Self-Test

True or False

1. f	4. t	7. t	10. f	13. t
2. f	5. f	8. t	11. t	14. f
3. f	6. f	9. f	12. f	15. t

Multiple Choice

1. d	6. b	11. a	16. a
2. e	7. a	12. b	17. b
3. a	8. e	13. e	18. a
4. c	9. d	14. d	19. e
5. d	10. c	15. c	20. c

Completion

1. privatization
2. deregulation
3. market failure
4. externality
5. subsidize
6. public good
7. free-rider
8. rent-seeking
9. median voter
10. local public good

Doing Economics: Tools and Practice Problems

When an activity generates externalities, the market, left to its own devices, will yield an inefficient outcome. An inventor, for example, knows that if her work produces an innovative new product, others will copy the idea without any payment to the inventor, so she spends less time working on her inventions than would be socially optimal. Patents are one solution to this problem, as you saw in Chapter 15. Another approach is to subsidize the activity. The first two tool kits in this chapter and the problems that follow them address aspects of this issue. The remaining tool kit looks at the voting paradox.

EFFECTS OF SUBSIDIES

In Chapter 5, you learned that taxing a product reduces the equilibrium quantity. A subsidy (which is just a negative tax) has the reverse effect. Tool Kit 18.1 shows you why. It also reveals that, as with a tax, it is irrelevant whether the subsidy is given to the producers or the consumers. The effect is the same.

1. (Worked problem: effects of subsidies) Home ownership is treated very favourably by the Canadian tax system, since capital gains earned by selling at more than the purchase price are not taxed. To see how the subsidy affects the housing market, consider the market for three-bedroom bungalows in Little Spoon. The market demand and supply curves without the subsidy are given in Table 18.1.

Table 18.1

Demand		Supply	
Price	*Quantity*	*Price*	*Quantity*
$125,000	10	$125,000	50
$100,000	14	$100,000	42
$ 90,000	25	$ 90,000	31
$ 80,000	28	$ 80,000	28
$ 70,000	31	$ 70,000	20

a. Find the equilibrium price and quantity.
b. The tax advantages accruing to the home owner amount to $20,000 over the life of the occupancy. Calculate the demand curve with the subsidy included.
c. Find the equilibrium price and quantity with the sub-

Tool Kit 18.1: Using Supply and Demand to Determine the Effects of Subsidies

Follow these steps to see how imposing a subsidy on a market influences equilibrium quantity and price.

Step one: Start with a no-subsidy equilibrium in the appropriate market.

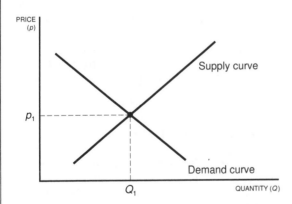

Step two: Identify the magnitude of the subsidy and whether it is paid directly to the consumers or producers.

Step three: If the subsidy is paid to consumers, shift the demand curve up (vertically) by exactly the amount of the subsidy. If the subsidy is paid to producers, shift the supply curve down by exactly the amount of the subsidy. The diagram illustrates the first case.

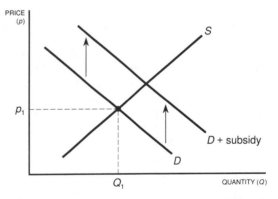

Step four: Find the new equilibrium and compare it with the original equilibrium.

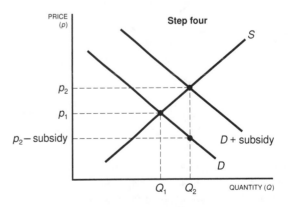

Step five: Find the new price paid by the consumers and the new price received by the producers. Verify that they differ by the amount of the tax.

sidy in place. How does the subsidy change the number of bungalows sold in Little Spoon? What happens to the price?

Step-by-step solution

Step one (a): Start with a no-subsidy equilibrium in the appropriate market. The price is $80,000; the market clears with 28 houses sold. This is the answer to part a.

Step two (b): Identify the magnitude of the subsidy and whether it is paid directly to the buyers or the sellers. The subsidy is $20,000, paid to buyers.

Step three: Because it is paid to the buyers, the subsidy causes the demand curve to shift vertically by $20,000. To calculate this, add $20,000 to each entry in the price column of the demand curve. The new demand curve is given in Table 18.2, which is the answer to part b.

Table 18.2

Demand	
Price	Quantity
$145,000	10
$120,000	14
$110,000	25
$100,000	28
$ 90,000	31

Step four (c): Find the new equilibrium and compare it with the original equilibrium. The new equilibrium price is $90,000, and the market clears at 31 houses sold. The subsidy has increased the number of home buyers in Little Spoon from 28 to 31. The price is $10,000 higher, so the $20,000 subsidy makes home buyers only $10,000 better off. Sellers share in the benefits with a $10,000 higher price. The solution is illustrated in the diagram. Buyers pay $70,000 and sellers receive $90,000. The difference is the subsidy.

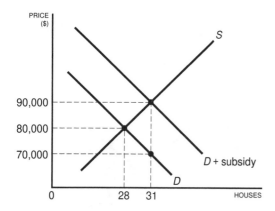

2. (Practice problem: effects of subsidies) Eyes brightening at the thought of thousands of stressed, child-raising voters, a politician has proposed child care grants of $10,000 per family. The demand and supply curves for child care services (measured in days) are given in Table 18.3.

Table 18.3

Demand		Supply	
Price (thousands)	Quantity (days)	Price (thousands)	Quantity (days)
$50	50,000	$50	100,000
$45	60,000	$45	80,000
$40	70,000	$40	70,000
$35	80,000	$35	60,000
$30	100,000	$30	50,000

a. Find the equilibrium price and quantity without the subsidy.
b. Calculate the demand with the subsidy.
c. Find the equilibrium price and quantity with the subsidy. Compare the equilibria, and explain the effects of the subsidy.

3. (Practice problem: effects of subsidies) To promote conversion to renewable sources of energy, the government has offered various tax deductions and credits for the purchase and installation of solar water heaters. The value to a typical taxpayer of the tax provisions is $3,000. The supply and demand curves for solar water heaters are given in Table 18.4.

Table 18.4

Demand		Supply	
Price	Quantity	Price	Quantity
$8,000	1,000	$8,000	10,000
$7,000	3,000	$7,000	9,000
$6,000	5,000	$6,000	8,000
$5,000	7,000	$5,000	7,000
$4,000	9,000	$4,000	6,000
$3,000	11,000	$3,000	5,000

a. Find the equilibrium price and quantity without the subsidy.
b. Calculate the demand with the subsidy.
c. Find the equilibrium price and quantity with the subsidy. Compare the equilibria, and explain the effects of the subsidy.

POSITIVE EXTERNALITIES

Individuals make decisions by balancing their private benefits and costs at the margin, but efficiency requires that all benefits and costs, not only the private ones, be included in the decision. Thus, when there are externalities, there are costs or benefits ignored by the individual making the decision, and this fact leads to inefficient decisions.

Economists distinguish between private costs and benefits, which private individuals respond to, and social costs and benefits, which incorporate the impact of the externality. In the case of a positive externality, the social marginal benefit exceeds the private marginal benefit by the marginal amount of the positive externality. Tool Kit 18.2 shows you how taking account of this distinction reveals the inefficiency of the private market outcome.

Tool Kit 18.2: Showing How Positive Externalities Lead to Inefficiencies

Follow these steps to see how balancing private marginal costs and private marginal benefits results in an inefficient outcome in the presence of an externality.

Step one: Find the private marginal benefits and costs of the relevant activity.

Step two: Find the equilibrium level of the activity, which is the level at which private marginal benefits equal marginal cost.

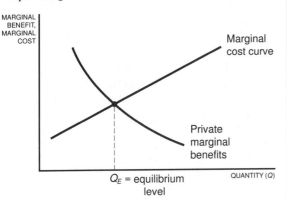

Step three: Calculate the social marginal benefits by adding the external benefit to the private marginal benefit at each level of the activity.

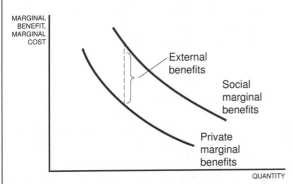

Step four: Find the efficient level of the activity, which is the level at which social marginal benefits equal marginal cost.

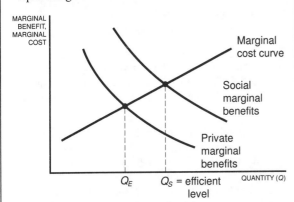

Step five: Compare the equilibrium and efficient levels of the activity.

4. (Worked problem: positive externalities) An important example of an activity that generates positive externalities is worker training. When firms train their employees, the employees not only become more productive in the job, they can also earn higher wages elsewhere. This increase in earning power is a positive externality. The QXV Corporation is considering sending some of its white-collar employees to computer school. The cost is $1,000 per week, and the private marginal benefits to QXV are given in Table 18.5. The value of the external benefit is $500 per week.

Table 18.5

Weeks at school	Private marginal benefits
1	$1,500
2	$1,250
3	$1,000
4	$ 750
5	$ 500
6	$ 250

a. How many weeks of computer schooling will the company provide?
b. Find the social marginal benefits of computer schooling.
c. What is the efficient number of weeks of schooling?

Step-by-step solution

Step one (a): Find the private marginal benefits and costs of the relevant activity. The private marginal benefits are in Table 18.5; the private marginal cost is $1,000 per week.

Step two: Find the equilibrium level of the activity. Private marginal benefits equal $1,000 at 3 weeks.

Step three (b): Calculate the social marginal benefits by adding the external benefit to the private marginal benefit at each level of the activity. The answer is in Table 18.6.

Table 18.6

Weeks at school	Private marginal benefits	Social marginal benefits
1	$1,500	$2,000
2	$1,250	$1,750
3	$1,000	$1,500
4	$ 750	$1,250
5	$ 500	$1,000
6	$ 250	$ 750

Step four (c): Find the efficient level of the activity. Social marginal benefits equal marginal cost at 5 weeks.

Step five: Compare the equilibrium and efficient levels of the activity. The equilibrium number of weeks is 3, which is less than the efficient number, which is 5. The number of weeks provided is too low because the firm ignores the externality.

5. (Practice problem: positive externalities) ZZZX Pharmaceuticals is considering how many scientists to put to work researching a new drug for Angolan flu. Each scientist, complete with equipment and assistance, costs $200,000. The research will bring profits to ZZZX, but it will also bring about advances in viral research that other companies may build on in their own research. The private benefits are given in Table 18.7. The external marginal benefits are $150,000.

Table 18.7

Scientists	Private benefits
1	$400,000
2	$600,000
3	$700,000
4	$750,000
5	$750,000

a. How many scientists will the company use? (Hint: first find the private marginal benefits.)
b. Find the social marginal benefits of research scientists.
c. What is the efficient number of scientists?

6. (Practice problem: positive externalities) Hillside County farmers have been advised to erect earthen dikes for erosion control. Each dike costs $2,000. The private marginal benefits are given in the second column of Table 18.8, but they do not include the external benefit that one farmer's erosion control efforts provide to neighbours. The external benefits appear in the third column of the table.

Table 18.8

Dikes	Private marginal benefits	External marginal benefits
1	$3,000	$8,000
2	$2,000	$7,000
3	$1,500	$6,000
4	$1,000	$5,000
5	$ 500	$4,000
6	$ 0	$3,000
7	$ 0	$2,000

a. How many dikes will each farmer erect?
b. Find the social marginal benefits of a farmer's dikes.
c. What is the efficient number of dikes?

VOTING PARADOX

The voting paradox can arise when voters are asked to choose from alternatives. There must be at least three voters and at least three alternatives. The term "voting paradox" refers to situations in which majority voting does not generate a determinate outcome. Tool Kit 18.3 shows you how to determine whether there is a determinate outcome.

Tool Kit 18.3: The Voting Paradox

Follow these steps to determine whether majority voting produces a determinate outcome.

Step one: Identify the alternatives, the voters, and their preferences.

Step two: Conduct majority votes for each pair of alternatives. For three alternatives, three votes are required; for four alternatives, six votes are needed.

Step three: Unless all the majority votes agree on the alternative that is ranked first, a voting paradox has occurred.

---

7. (Worked problem: voting paradox) Jan, Jean, and John are considering where to go for lunch. They have three alternatives. One serves Chinese food, one serves Indian food, and one serves Thai food. Their preferences across these alternatives are given in Table 18.9.

Table 18.9

	Jan	Jean	John
First choice	Indian	Thai	Chinese
Second choice	Thai	Chinese	Indian
Third choice	Chinese	Indian	Thai

a. Determine the majority choice for each pairwise comparison of two alternatives.
b. Do they reach a determinate outcome?

Step-by-step solution

Step one (a): Identify the alternatives, the voters, and their preferences. Jan, Jean, and John (the voters) are choosing from three alternative restaurants, one serving Chinese food, one serving Indian food, and one serving Thai food. The voters' preferences are given in Table 18.9.

Step two: Conduct majority votes for each pair of alternatives. Begin by comparing Chinese and Indian food. Jean and John both rank Chinese food higher than Indian, so the majority vote is for Chinese food. Now compare Indian and Thai food. Jan and John both rank Indian food higher than Thai, so the ranking so far is that Chinese beats Indian, which beats Thai. Finally, compare Thai with Chinese. Jan and Jean both prefer Thai.

Step three: The outcome of the pairwise comparisons is that Chinese beats Indian, which beats Thai, which beat Chinese. There is no unambiguous winner, so there is a voting paradox.

8. (Practice problem: voting paradox) NDP University has been left some money in a will. The deceased enjoyed watching the university football team, reading books in the library, and walking through the campus. She has therefore stipulated that the money must be spent on providing equipment for the football team, books for the library, or trees for the campus, but it cannot be split

among the alternatives. The university's three-person finance committee must decide which of the alternatives to allocate the money to. Its preferences are given in Table 18.10.

Table 18.10

	Sandy	Geraldine	Art
First choice	Library	Football	Library
Second choice	Trees	Library	Football
Third choice	Football	Trees	Trees

a. Determine the majority choice for each pairwise comparison of two alternatives.
b. Do they reach a determinate outcome?

9. (Practice problem: voting paradox) The three-person city council must decide where to raise revenue. It can impose one new tax, and the alternatives are to tax property, sales, or income. Another possibility is to raid the pension fund for retired city council members. The rankings of the members of the city council are given in Table 18.11.

Table 18.11

	Coleman	Jones	Sutherland
First choice	Property	Sales	Income
Second choice	Sales	Income	Property
Third choice	Income	Property	Sales
Fourth choice	Retirement fund	Retirement fund	Retirement fund

a. Determine the majority choice for each pairwise comparison of two alternatives.
b. Do they reach a determinate outcome?

Answers to Problems

2. a. Price = $40; quantity = 70,000.
b. The new demand curve is given in Table 18.12.

Table 18.12

Demand	
Price	Quantity
$60	50,000
$55	60,000
$50	70,000
$45	80,000
$40	100,000

c. The new equilibrium price is $45,000, and the quantity is 80,000. The subsidy increases the quantity from 70,000 to 80,000. Consumers are better off by $5,000 ($10,000 subsidy – $5,000 increase in price), and firms are better off by $5,000, which is the increase in price.

3. a. Price = $5,000; quantity = 7,000.
b. The new demand curve is given in Table 18.13.

Table 18.13

Demand	
Price	Quantity
$11,000	1,000
$10,000	3,000
$ 9,000	5,000
$ 8,000	7,000
$ 7,000	9,000
$ 6,000	11,000

c. The new equilibrium price is $7,000, and the quantity is 9,000. The subsidy increases the quantity from 7,000 to 9,000. Consumers are better off by $1,000 ($3,000 subsidy – $2,000 increase in price), and firms are better off by $2,000, which is the increase in price.

5. a. 2 scientists.
b. The social marginal benefits are given in Table 18.14.

Table 18.14

Scientists	Private benefits	Private marginal benefits	Social marginal benefits
1	$400,000	$400,000	$550,000
2	$600,000	$200,000	$350,000
3	$700,000	$100,000	$250,000
4	$750,000	$ 50,000	$200,000
5	$750,000	$ 0	$150,000

c. The efficient number is 4 scientists. The company chooses only 2 because it ignores the externality.

6. a. 2 dikes.
b. The social marginal benefits are given in Table 18.15.

Table 18.15

Dikes	Private marginal benefits	External marginal benefits	Social marginal benefits
1	$3,000	$8,000	$11,000
2	$2,000	$7,000	$ 9,000
3	$1,500	$6,000	$ 7,500
4	$1,000	$5,000	$ 6,000
5	$ 500	$4,000	$ 4,500
6	$ 0	$3,000	$ 3,000
7	$ 0	$2,000	$ 2,000

c. The efficient number of dikes is 7. Farmers only erect 2 because they ignore the external benefits.

8. *a.* Spending money on the library is preferred to spending it on trees. Spending it on the football team is preferred to spending it on trees. Spending it on the library is preferred to spending it on the football team.

   b. The majority vote is to spend the money on the library, which is preferred to spending it on either of the other alternatives. There is a determinate outcome, so there is no voting paradox.

9. *a.* First, note that taking money from the retirement fund is irrelevant. Nobody votes for that. Of the remaining three alternatives, a property tax is preferred to a sales tax, a sales tax is preferred to an income tax, and an income tax is preferred to a property tax.

   b. There is no majority winner. Since there is no determinate winner, there is a voting paradox.

EXTERNALITIES AND THE ENVIRONMENT

Chapter Review

When markets fail, government may have an economic role to play. This chapter completes the discussion of government's role in cases of market failure by taking a closer look at externalities, which were introduced in the previous chapter.

Externalities can be either positive or negative. Their distinguishing characteristic is that, if the private market is left to itself, externalities are not reflected in the market price. An important example of a negative externality is pollution, and this is the topic of Chapter 19. Pollution imposes costs on society that are not borne by the firm responsible for the pollution. As a result, the price of the good the firm produces is lower than the efficient level; this means the level of production is inefficiently high. The chapter looks at ways of correcting this inefficiency and finishes with a brief discussion of natural resource depletion.

ESSENTIAL CONCEPTS

1. A market transaction is a voluntary exchange between two parties. Any cost not reflected in the price at which the transaction takes place is a **negative externality.** The result is overproduction. A firm with a production technology that results in **pollution** generates costs to society beyond the private costs paid by the firm. Economists say that the **social costs** exceed the private costs. The extent of the externality, therefore, is measured by the excess of social costs over private costs. In the absence of the externality, the efficient outcome would be to set price equal to **private marginal cost.** The externality means that, for efficiency, price should be set equal to **social marginal cost.**

2. The **Coase theorem** says that any externality problem could be solved if the government assigned **property rights** for the externalities. For example, direct pollution of a privately owned lake would not occur unless the owner judged that the benefits exceeded the costs. In Coase's view, general environmental pollution is a serious problem because the environment is commonly, not privately, owned. Economists agree that markets require clearly defined property rights if resources are to be allocated efficiently, but most do not accept that property rights alone can always be relied upon to solve the problem of externalities.

3. Potential government solutions to the problem of externalities fall into two categories: **command and control**

regulations and marketlike devices such as taxes, subsidies, and **marketable permits.** For example, in the case of pollution, governments can issue regulations requiring pollution-control equipment or banning the use of hazardous materials. Alternatively, they can employ more market-based policies, such as taxes on pollution emissions, subsidies for pollution abatement, or even the creation of a **market for pollution permits.**

BEHIND THE ESSENTIAL CONCEPTS

1. The Coase theorem says that if property rights are clearly assigned, decisions will be efficient. The logic can best be understood with an example.

   Suppose that your neighbour likes to play the stereo very loudly each evening while you are reading this book. Clearly, there is an externality. You complain to the building manager, and there are two possible reactions. The manager might say that playing the stereo is a right of all tenants, in effect giving the property right (to make noise) to your neighbour. Or the manager may insist on quiet and give the property right (to silence) to you. According to the Coase theorem, either way of assigning property rights will do. If your neighbour has the right, then you can buy the right to silence by paying your neighbour to be quiet. If you have the right, your neighbour must buy your permission to play the music. Of course, you would prefer the latter; nevertheless, in either case, the externality is eliminated and replaced by a market transaction. (Any reader who lives in a university residence can judge how realistic it is to apply the Coase theorem to externalities.)

2. Pollution imposes costs on society that are ignored by the firm responsible for the pollution. The result is an inefficiency that can be corrected by raising the firm's marginal cost so that it equals the social marginal cost. There are three market-based methods that are typically advocated as solutions for the problem of negative externalities. A brief look at how they work reveals that two of the three achieve the desired objective of raising the firm's marginal cost. The third most definitely does not.

   a. Taxes on pollution: if the excess of social marginal cost over private marginal cost is, say, $10, a tax of $10 per unit produced will ensure that the firm sets its price and output with reference to the social marginal cost.

   b. Subsidies for pollution abatement: you learned in Chapter 18 that a subsidy lowers the price paid by the buyer. It follows that if firms' purchases of pollution abatement equipment are subsidized, more equipment will be purchased and pollution will be reduced. The problem is that this lowers the firm's costs instead of raising them. Not surprisingly, firms usually favour this solution.

   c. Marketable permits: under this scheme, firms are required to buy the right to generate a certain number of units of pollution, and the price per unit of pollution is set at the level of the externality generated per unit of pollution. In consequence, each firm takes this cost into account when determining its price and output. Furthermore, if the firm discovers a way of meeting its pollution target with fewer permits, it can sell the extra permits to firms who need them more. In other words, firms have a strong incentive to find ways of reducing pollution.

3. Whether we are using our limited natural resources efficiently and whether we are likely to run out of these resources are important economic questions. The key aspects in the answers to these questions are property rights and markets. For those resources, such as oil, minerals, and arable farmland, that are *privately owned*, markets provide good incentives for conservation. Future shortages mean high prices in the future. The profit opportunities from future sales motivate owners to conserve resources for the future. For those resources, such as the ozone layer and endangered species, that are not privately owned, there is no reason for optimism. Since there are *no markets* for these resources, there is no financial incentive to conserve.

SELF-TEST

True or False

1. Private markets always generate efficient outcomes.

2. Private markets never generate efficient outcomes.

3. Markets fail whenever individuals do not pursue their self-interest.

4. A firm generates an externality unless it bears all the consequences of its action.

5. Private markets undersupply goods that yield negative externalities.

6. The Coase theorem argues that assigning property rights appropriately solves the problem of externalities.

7. When social marginal costs exceed private marginal costs, there is a negative externality.

8. Taxes on firms that pollute can force the firms to bear the social marginal costs of their actions.

9. Subsidies on pollution abatement equipment can force firms to bear the social marginal costs of their actions.

10. Marketable pollution permits do not provide any incentive to reduce pollution because any firm that wants to pollute merely buys the right to do so.

11. Regulation of pollution is inefficient because it pays no attention to the marginal benefits and marginal costs of pollution abatement.

12. The only solution to the problem of pollution is to eliminate it.

13. Markets for natural resources pay no attention to the needs of future generations of users.

14. If future property rights are insecure, private owners of natural resources do not have the appropriate incentives to conserve them.

15. If the borrowing opportunities of private owners of natural resources are limited, the owners have too strong an incentive to conserve the natural resources.

Multiple Choice

1. Governments have an economic role to play because market outcomes are:

    a. always equitable though sometimes inefficient.
    b. always inequitable and always inefficient.
    c. sometimes inequitable and sometimes inefficient.
    d. always equitable and always efficient.
    e. sometimes inequitable though always efficient.

2. The imposition of costs on others by individuals who do not bear them and the generation of benefits for others by individuals who are not compensated for them are examples of:

    a. externalities.
    b. the voting paradox.
    c. moral hazard.
    d. the principal-agent problem.
    e. adverse selection.

3. The generation of environmental pollution by the production of a good represents an example of:

    a. a public good.
    b. a positive externality.
    c. diminishing returns.
    d. a negative externality.
    e. private costs.

4. Which of the following is not an example of a negative externality?

    a. Freon gas destroys part of the ozone layer.
    b. Carbon dioxide emissions accelerate global warming.
    c. Prices of natural resources rise as they become more scarce.
    d. Industrial smoke emissions increase lung cancer rates.
    e. The runoff of pesticides pollutes streams and rivers.

5. In the case of a _____ externality, social marginal cost _____ private marginal cost.

    a. negative; equals
    b. positive; equals
    c. negative; is less than
    d. positive; exceeds
    e. negative; exceeds

6. A negative externality occurs when an action imposes costs on society that are not reflected in the private marginal cost borne by the individual taking the action. In such a situation, social marginal cost refers to:

    a. the private marginal cost plus the marginal cost imposed on society.
    b. only the marginal cost not included in private marginal cost.
    c. only those marginal costs included in private marginal cost.

    d. the total marginal cost less the marginal cost imposed on society.
    e. the private marginal cost less the marginal cost imposed on society.

7. When the production of a good generates a negative externality, the private market supplies too:

    a. much of the good and sets a price that is too high.
    b. much of the good and sets a price that is too low.
    c. much of the good, though the price is neither too high nor too low.
    d. little of the good and sets a price that is too high.
    e. little of the good and sets a price that is too low.

8. When the production of a good generates a negative externality, social marginal cost:

    a. exceeds private marginal cost, so that price is too high and output is too low.
    b. is less than private marginal cost, so that price is too high and output is too low.
    c. exceeds private marginal cost, so that price is too low and output is too high.
    d. is less than private marginal cost, so that price is too low and output is too high.
    e. exceeds private marginal cost, so that price is too high and output is too high.

9. According to the Coase theorem, the solution to the problem of externalities can be solved by:

    a. the appropriate use of taxes.
    b. the use of marketable permits.
    c. regulation.
    d. a command and control approach.
    e. reassigning property rights.

10. The provincial government of British Columbia leases public land to private forestry firms. These firms are often accused of generating a negative externality by not using good reforestation practices. According to the Coase theorem, the solution to this problem is to:

    a. tax wood products.
    b. sell the land to the forestry firms.
    c. subsidize logging equipment.
    d. regulate how many trees can be cut.
    e. sell logging permits.

11. The government sets emission standards for new cars. This is an example of the use of _____ to deal with the problem of externalities.

    a. marketable permits
    b. property rights
    c. moral suasion
    d. command and control
    e. taxes

12. All of the following, except one, are criticisms of the command and control approach to pollution, which usually sets limits on firms' pollution. Which is the odd one out?

    a. It provides no incentive for the firms to reduce pollution below the standard.
    b. It pays no attention to the marginal benefit of reducing pollution.

c. It results in a level of pollution that is socially efficient.

d. It pays no attention to the marginal cost of reducing pollution.

e. It treats firms equally even though their marginal costs of reducing pollution may be different.

13. When social marginal cost exceeds private marginal cost, the appropriate government response is to:

a. levy a tax that will raise price and reduce production.

b. impose a subsidy that will raise price and reduce production.

c. levy a tax that will reduce price and raise production.

d. impose a subsidy that will reduce price and raise production.

e. levy a tax that will raise price and raise production.

14. All of the following, except one, are true of the marketable permits approach to pollution control. Which is the odd one out?

a. The government can control the overall level of pollution by varying the number of permits.

b. Permits define the level of pollution that a firm is allowed to emit.

c. Firms that buy permits will be ones that find pollution abatement costly.

d. There are no incentives for firms to reduce pollution voluntarily.

e. Firms that sell permits will be ones that find pollution abatement inexpensive.

15. Those who believe that the market system encourages the conservation of natural resources argue that:

a. prices send signals that encourage appropriate conservation.

b. the use of natural resources should be punished by fines or imprisonment.

c. market-based outcomes are always inefficient.

d. the government should assume ownership of natural resources.

e. natural resources are not scarce.

16. If future property rights are not secure:

a. owners of natural resources will overvalue them and the rate of extraction will be faster than is socially efficient.

b. owners of natural resources will undervalue them and the rate of extraction will be faster than is socially efficient.

c. this has no bearing on the rate of extraction of natural resources since property rights are irrelevant.

d. owners of natural resources will undervalue them and the rate of extraction will be slower than is socially efficient.

e. owners of natural resources will overvalue them and the rate of extraction will be slower than is socially efficient.

17. If owners of natural resources face limited borrowing opportunities:

a. they will undervalue the resource and the rate of extraction will be slower than is socially efficient.

b. they will overvalue the resource and the rate of extraction will be slower than is socially efficient.

c. this has no bearing on the rate of extraction of natural resources since the owners have no need to borrow money.

d. they will overvalue the resource and the rate of extraction will be faster than is socially efficient.

e. they will undervalue the resource and the rate of extraction will be faster than is socially efficient.

18. As interest rates _____, the present discounted value of future returns from natural resources _____, and so encourages faster depletion of the resource.

a. rise; rises

b. fall; rises

c. rise; falls

d. fall; falls

e. rise; is unaffected

19. Which of the following methods is the least efficient method of reducing environmental pollution?

a. taxes

b. reassigning property rights

c. marketable permits

d. command and control

e. all the above are equally inefficient.

20. Which of the following methods does not involve a balancing of marginal costs and marginal benefits of pollution control?

a. taxes on goods that generate pollution

b. command and control

c. reassigning property rights

d. marketable permits

e. subsidies for pollution abatement

Completion

1. Market _____ refers to any instance of the private market yielding an inefficient outcome.

2. An efficient solution to the problem of pollution will ensure that the price of a good equals the _____.

3. The costs and benefits not reflected in the prices of market transactions are called _____.

4. Pollution is a _____.

5. The _____ cost of pollution is borne entirely by the polluter; the _____ cost includes all costs borne by individuals in the economy.

6. The _____ claims that externality problems can be solved by the appropriate assignment of property rights.

7. Regulatory limits on pollution emissions are called the _____ approach.

8. The _____ approach to pollution control allows firms to buy and sell the right to pollute.

9. When expected future prices of natural resources are high, there is an incentive for the owners of the resources to _____ them.

10. When interest rates are _____, the incentive to conserve natural resources is reduced.

Answers to Self-Test

True or False

1. f	4. t	7. t	10. f	13. f
2. f	5. f	8. t	11. t	14. t
3. f	6. t	9. f	12. f	15. f

Multiple Choice

1. c	6. a	11. d	16. b
2. a	7. b	12. c	17. e
3. d	8. c	13. a	18. c
4. c	9. e	14. d	19. d
5. e	10. b	15. a	20. b

Completion

1. failure
2. social marginal cost
3. externalities
4. negative externality
5. private; social
6. Coase theorem
7. command and control
8. marketable permits
9. conserve
10. high

Doing Economics: Tools and Practice Problems

The first topic of this section is the use of taxes and subsidies to encourage pollution abatement. Next, we turn to situations in which market equilibrium levels are too high and investigate how taxes can be used to make the market more efficient. Finally, we focus directly on the market for pollution and the way in which the marketable permits system brings about efficient use of the environment.

POLLUTION ABATEMENT

Choosing the level of pollution abatement requires balancing marginal benefit and marginal cost. If the government taxes pollution emissions, then a firm can lower the taxes it pays by reducing emissions. If the government subsidizes pollution abatement equipment, this lowers the marginal cost of pollution abatement to the firm, and so encourages the firm to buy more equipment, which again reduces the firm's emissions. Tool Kit 19.1 shows you how a firm deter-

---

Tool Kit 19.1: Determining the Level of Pollution Abatement

Follow these steps to see how a firm will determine its optimal level of pollution abatement.

Step one: Identify the cost of pollution emission and abatement.

Step two: Calculate the marginal abatement costs:

marginal abatement cost =
change in cost/change in level of pollution abatement.

Step three: Determine the marginal benefit of abatement.

Step four: Set the marginal benefit of pollution abatement equal to its marginal cost.

---

mines its optimal level of pollution abatement, and the problems that follow assess the effect of taxes and subsidies on this optimal level.

1. (Worked problem: pollution abatement) Runoff from the Quarta Lead Mine has raised lead levels in the Maumee River. The current level of lead effluent is 10 kilograms per month. A filtering technology would enable the company to reduce its effluent. The abatement costs are given in Table 19.1.

Table 19.1

Pollution emitted (kilograms/month)	Pollution abated (kilograms/month)	Total cost	Marginal cost
10	0	$ 0	—
9	1	$ 10	
8	2	$ 25	
7	3	$ 45	
6	4	$ 70	
5	5	$100	
4	6	$135	
3	7	$175	
2	8	$225	
1	9	$290	
0	10	$400	

a. Suppose that a pollution tax (or fine) of $40 is assessed per kilogram of lead emitted. How much will the company emit? What quantity of pollution will be abated?

b. Suppose that rather than a tax, a subsidy of $40 is given per unit of pollution abated. How much will the company emit? What quantity of pollution will be abated?

c. The firm's profits from the production and sale of lead total $10,000. Compare its profits under the tax and the subsidy.

Step-by-step solution

Step one (a): The cost of pollution emission and abatement is given in Table 19.1.

Step two: Calculate the marginal abatement cost. The marginal abatement cost is the extra cost incurred in reducing pollution emissions by 1 more unit. For example, reducing pollution from 10 to 9 units raises costs from $0 to $10; therefore, the marginal abatement cost is $10 for the first unit. The remainder of the schedule is given in Table 19.2.

Table 19.2

Pollution emitted	Pollution abated	Total cost	Marginal cost
10	0	$ 0	—
9	1	$ 10	$ 10
8	2	$ 25	$ 15
7	3	$ 45	$ 20
6	4	$ 70	$ 25
5	5	$100	$ 30
4	6	$135	$ 35
3	7	$175	$ 40
2	8	$225	$ 50
1	9	$290	$ 65
0	10	$400	$110

Step three: Determine the marginal benefit of abatement. Each unit of pollution emitted incurs a tax of $40; thus, the marginal benefit of abatement is $40.

Step four: Set the marginal benefit of pollution abatement equal to its marginal cost. This results in 3 kilograms of lead emitted and 7 kilograms abated.

Step five (b): When the policy is to subsidize abatement, the marginal benefit is the subsidy, which is $40. Setting $40 equal to the marginal abatement cost again gives 3 kilograms of lead emitted and 7 kilograms abated. The answer is the same as for part a. Notice that under the subsidy scheme, each unit emitted still costs the firm $40, in the sense that any unit emitted is a unit not abated and a subsidy not received.

Step six (c): Profits under the tax equal $10,000 less the abatement cost and the tax, or

profits = $10,000 – $175 – $40 (3) = $9,705.

Under the subsidy, however,

profits = $10,000 – $175 + $40 (7) = $10,105.

Notice that the difference in profits is $10,105 – $9,705 = $400, which is the magnitude of the tax/subsidy multiplied by the number of units that the firm emits with no tax or subsidy. It is the total value of the property right to pollute.

2. (Practice problem: pollution abatement) Avenger of the Sea Tuna kills 20 dolphins during an average harvest. It has various options for reducing the dolphin kill, and the costs are given in Table 19.3.

Table 19.3

Dolphins killed	Dolphins saved	Total cost	Marginal cost
20	0	$ 0	—
18	2	$ 100	
16	4	$ 240	
14	6	$ 400	
12	8	$ 600	
10	10	$ 1,000	
8	12	$ 1,500	
6	14	$ 2,200	
4	16	$ 3,000	
2	18	$ 5,000	
0	20	$10,000	

a. Suppose that a tax (or fine) of $100 is assessed per dolphin killed. How many dolphins will be killed? What number of dolphins will be saved?

b. Suppose that rather than a tax, a subsidy of $100 per dolphin is granted for reductions in the dolphin kill. How many will the company kill? How many will be saved?

c. With no tax or subsidy, the company's profits are $10,000. Compute its profits with the tax and with the subsidy.

3. (Practice problem: pollution abatement) Flying Turkey Air Transport has its hub in Thanksgiving. Dozens of planes land and take off each night and cause considerable noise. By muffling engines or other more advanced techniques, the company can reduce its noise. The costs are given in Table 19.4.

Table 19.4

Average level of noise (decibels)	Total cost	Marginal cost
1,000	$ 0	—
900	$ 50	
800	$ 150	
700	$ 300	
600	$ 500	
500	$ 750	
400	$1,100	

a. Suppose that a pollution tax (or fine) of $2.50 is assessed per decibel of noise created. How much will the company create? What quantity of noise will be abated?

b. Suppose that rather than a tax, a subsidy of $2.50 is granted per unit of noise abated. How much will the company create? What quantity of noise will be abated?

c. With no tax or subsidy, the company's profits are $5,000. Compute its profits with the tax and with the subsidy.

NEGATIVE EXTERNALITIES

When production of a good by a firm generates a negative externality, production will be in excess of the socially efficient level, and the price will be too low. Tool Kit 19.2 shows you how to demonstrate that this is the case.

Tool Kit 19.2: Finding the Efficient Quantity in Markets with Negative Externalities

Follow these steps to see how a private market outcome is inefficient in the presence of an externality.

Step one: Determine the market equilibrium at the intersection of the supply and demand curves.

Step two: Add the marginal external cost to the supply curve, which is the private marginal cost, to determine the social marginal cost curve.

Step three: Find the efficient quantity at the intersection of the demand curve and the social marginal cost curve.

Step four: Compare the market equilibrium and socially efficient quantities.

---

4. (Worked problem: negative externalities) Runoff from local feedlots is polluting the Red Cedar River. The negative externality per steer is $100. The demand and supply curves for steer are given in Table 19.5.

Table 19.5

Demand		Supply	
Price	Quantity	Price	Quantity
$200	350	$200	1,100
$180	500	$180	1,000
$160	650	$160	900
$140	800	$140	800
$120	950	$120	700
$100	1,100	$100	600
$ 80	1,300	$ 80	500

a. Find the market equilibrium quantity and price.
b. Calculate the social marginal cost, and determine the efficient quantity of steers.

Step-by-step solution

Step one (a): Find the market equilibrium quantity and price. At a price of $140, the market clears with 800 sold.

Step two (b): Find the social marginal cost curve. We add the marginal external cost, which is $100, to the supply curve, which is the private marginal cost. Table 19.6 gives the solution.

Table 19.6

Quantity	Social marginal cost
500	$180
600	$200
700	$220
800	$240
900	$260
1,000	$280
1,100	$300

Step three: Find the socially efficient quantity at the intersection of the demand curve and the social marginal cost curve. This occurs at a quantity of 500 and a price of $180.

Step four: Compare the market equilibrium and socially efficient quantities. Notice that the socially efficient quantity is only 500, while the market produces 800. Incorporating the external cost into the supply curve would raise the price and reduce the quantity.

5. (Practice problem: negative externalities) The private flying lessons at Daredevil Airport cause noise that disturbs local residents. The residents are also uneasy about the periodic crashes. One estimate of the magnitude of the negative externalities is $15 per flight. The market supply and demand curves for flight lessons are given in Table 19.7.

Table 19.7

Demand		Supply	
Price	Quantity	Price	Quantity
$75	10	$75	100
$70	20	$70	80
$65	30	$65	60
$60	40	$60	40
$55	50	$55	20
$50	60	$50	0

a. Find the market equilibrium price and quantity.
b. Calculate the social marginal cost, and find the efficient quantity.

6. (Practice problem: negative externalities) New developments of townhouses are springing up in the once-rural community of Outland. The supply and demand curves for new townhouses are given in Table 19.8.

Table 19.8

Demand		Supply	
Price	Quantity	Price	Quantity
$140,000	100	$140,000	900
$130,000	200	$130,000	800
$120,000	300	$120,000	700
$110,000	400	$110,000	600
$100,000	500	$100,000	500
$ 90,000	600	$ 90,000	400
$ 80,000	700	$ 80,000	300

  a. Find the market equilibrium quantity of townhouses and the corresponding price.
  b. The new developments impose costs on other current residents for sewage, transportation, and congestion. An estimate of the magnitude of these negative externalities is $20,000 per townhouse. Find the socially efficient level of townhouse production and the corresponding price.

MARKETABLE PERMITS

The problem of pollution (and other negative externalities) can be attacked more directly by considering the market for pollution itself. The polluters are the demanders for pollution, and their demand curve is just the marginal abatement cost curve. If it costs a firm $40 to clean up a tonne of sludge from its emissions, then that firm is willing to pay $40 to be given the right to emit the sludge. The socially efficient level of pollution occurs where the demand curve intersects the social marginal cost curve, which is the marginal damage done by the pollution. Tool Kit 19.3 and the problems that follow explore the issue of the socially efficient level of pollution and how a marketable permit scheme can bring about this outcome.

Tool Kit 19.3: Using Marketable Permits to Bring About the Socially Efficient Level of Pollution

Follow these steps to see how a market for pollution can control pollution.

Step one: Identify the demand for pollution (the sum of all the marginal abatement cost curves) and the social marginal cost curve.

Step two: Find the socially efficient level of pollution, which is at the intersection of the demand for pollution and the marginal abatement cost curve.

Step three: Determine how many permits to sell. This quantity is the socially efficient level of pollution found in step two.

Step four: Find the market price for the permits. Read this price off the demand curve.

---

7 (Worked problem: marketable permits) Discharges from factories, runoff from farmlands, and many other activities pollute the Metatarsal Lakes. The pollution could be reduced, but any reduction would involve expensive abatement procedures. The marginal abatement cost schedule is given in Table 19.9 along with the social marginal cost of the pollution.

Table 19.9

Pollution (parts/million)	Marginal abatement cost	Social marginal cost
100	$1,200	$ 0
200	$1,000	$ 0
300	$ 900	$ 150
400	$ 800	$ 300
500	$ 700	$ 450
600	$ 600	$ 600
700	$ 500	$ 800
800	$ 300	$1,000

Find the socially efficient level of pollution, and explain how a marketable permits scheme can achieve an efficient outcome.

Step-by-step solution

Step one: Identify the demand for pollution and the social marginal cost curve. The demand is the marginal abatement cost curve given in Table 19.9, which also includes the social marginal cost curve.

Step two: Find the socially efficient level of pollution. The intersection of the demand for pollution and the marginal abatement cost curve occurs at 600 parts/million.

Step three: Determine how many permits to sell. This number is 600, and each permit entitles the holder to emit 1 part/million of pollution.

Step four: Find the market price for the permits. If 600 permits are offered for sale, their market price will be $600. This price is read off the marginal abatement cost curve at 600 units.

8. (Practice problem: marketable permits) The marginal abatement cost and social marginal cost of pollution in the Northwest Air Shed are given in Table 20.10. Find the socially efficient level of pollution, and explain how a marketable permits scheme can achieve an efficient outcome. Pollution is measured as metric tonnes of sulphur oxide.

Table 19.10

Pollution	Marginal abatement cost	Social marginal cost
10	$100	$ 0
20	$ 80	$ 0
30	$ 60	$ 5
40	$ 50	$ 10
50	$ 40	$ 20
60	$ 30	$ 30
70	$ 15	$ 50

9. (Practice problem: marketable permits) Pesticides, engine oil, chemicals, and other pollutants are finding their way into the groundwater. Abatement is possible but expensive. The marginal abatement cost and social marginal cost of this type of pollution for the Alago Aquifer are

given in Table 19.11. Find the socially efficient level of pollution, and explain how a marketable permits scheme can achieve it.

Table 19.11

Pollution	Marginal abatement cost	Social marginal cost
100	$10,000	$ 10
150	$ 8,000	$ 100
200	$ 6,000	$ 1,000
250	$ 5,000	$ 5,000
300	$ 4,000	$10,000
350	$ 3,000	$20,000

Answers to Problems

2. The marginal abatement cost for reducing the dolphin kill is given in Table 19.12.

Table 19.12

Dolphins killed	Dolphins saved	Total cost	Marginal cost
20	0	$ 0	—
18	2	$ 100	$ 50
16	4	$ 240	$ 70
14	6	$ 400	$ 80
12	8	$ 600	$ 100
10	10	$ 1,000	$ 200
8	12	$ 1,500	$ 250
6	14	$ 2,200	$ 350
4	16	$ 3,000	$ 400
2	18	$ 5,000	$ 1,000
0	20	$10,000	$ 2,500

a. The firm reduces its dolphin kill by 8 for a total of 12 killed.
b. Again, the firm reduces its dolphin kill by 8 for a total of 12 killed.
c. Profits under the tax = $10,000 − (12 × $100) = $8,800; profits under the subsidy = $10,000 + (8 × $100) = $10,800.

3. The marginal abatement cost for noise is given in Table 19.13.

Table 19.13

Average level of noise	Total cost	Marginal cost
1,000	$ 0	—
900	$ 50	$0.50
800	$ 150	$1.00
700	$ 300	$1.50
600	$ 500	$2.00
500	$ 750	$2.50
400	$ 1,100	$3.50

a. The firm will emit 500 decibels (abating 500).
b. The firm will abate 500 decibels (emitting 500).
c. Profits under tax = $5,000 − (500 × $2.50) = $3,750; profits under subsidy = $5,000 + (500 × $2.50) = $6,250.

5. a. Market equilibrium quantity = 40; price = $60;
   b. The social marginal cost is given in Table 19.14.

Table 19.14

Quantity	Social marginal cost
0	$65
20	$70
40	$75
60	$80
80	$85
100	$90

Efficient quantity = 20; price = $70.

6. a. Market equilibrium quantity = 500; price = $100,000.
   b. The social marginal cost is given in Table 19.15.

Table 19.15

Quantity	Social marginal cost
300	$100,000
400	$110,000
500	$120,000
600	$130,000
700	$140,000
800	$150,000
900	$160,000

Efficient quantity = 400; price = $110,000.

8. Efficient level = 60. If 60 permits are sold, the market price will be $30 each, 60 permits will be purchased, and the level of pollution will be 60.

9. Efficient level = 250. If 250 permits are sold, the market price will be $5,000 each, 250 permits will be purchased, and the level of pollution will be 250.

TAXATION, REDISTRIBUTION, AND SOCIAL INSURANCE

Chapter Review

So far in the text, the issue of government intervention has been couched in terms of efficiency: correcting market failures involves modifying inefficient market outcomes. But a large part of governments' time is spent addressing equity concerns. Even when the economy is completely efficient, the answer that it provides to the question "for whom are goods produced?" is not one that many find equitable. Chapter 20 therefore turns the spotlight on the methods governments use to redistribute income. It looks separately at taxes, transfers, and social insurance and asks how each promotes the goal of equity in the distribution of the economy's output. The chapter concludes with a brief examination of the fundamental trade-off between efficiency and equity.

ESSENTIAL CONCEPTS

1. The case for **redistribution** of the economy's output depends on social values relating to equity. Markets allocate too small a share of output to those at the lower end of the economic spectrum and too much to those at the upper end. In Canada, programmes such as welfare assistance and employment insurance try to redistribute income, as do many of the taxes levied by various levels of government.

2. A good tax system has four important characteristics, the first of which is **fairness**. Economists have emphasized two principles of fairness. **Horizontal equity** says that individuals in the same circumstances should pay the same tax, and **vertical equity** says that taxes should be based on ability to pay. By the standard of vertical equity, the tax system should be **progressive;** this means that the fraction of income paid in taxes—the average rate of tax—should be larger for those with more income.

3. The second characteristic of a good tax system is **efficiency**. The system should change the economy's resource allocation decisions as little as possible and also impose few extra costs on taxpayers. The Canadian tax system often encourages more consumption and production of some goods with special tax provisions called **tax subsidies**. These reduce taxes for those who engage in the favoured activity and result in lower tax revenues for the government. The lost tax revenue is called a **tax expenditure.** The other characteristics of a good tax system are **administrative simplicity** and **transparency**.

4. Government programmes for alleviating poverty target the unemployed through employment insurance, job-retraining programmes, and the overall commitment to full employment. Attempts to raise the income of the employed include minimum wage legislation and refundable tax credits. Old Age Security and the Guaranteed Income Supplement provide federal support for the aged and disabled, which is supplemented in some cases by provincial programmes. Welfare assistance programmes are operated by each province to direct money to those nonworking low-income families that are not eligible for employment insurance. These programmes are designed to provide the poor with a minimal level of basic necessities.

5. Many social insurance programmes, such as Old Age Security, employment insurance, disability insurance, and Medicare, benefit the middle class. They are financed by payroll taxes, but the ultimate burden—the economic **incidence**—is in the form of lower wages. Although they are called insurance programmes, the provisions of each cause some income to be redistributed.

6. Any programme or tax provision that promotes equality inevitably reduces efficiency. This basic **equity-efficiency trade-off** must be faced in making choices about social programmes and tax reforms. Overall, income inequality in Canada, as shown by the **Lorenz curve**, is significantly greater than in many other developed countries.

BEHIND THE ESSENTIAL CONCEPTS

1. You can judge the Canadian tax system on how well it meets the four criteria outlined in the text. The following are some arguments.

    a. Fairness: The marginal tax rate, which is the tax paid out of the extra dollar of income, is higher for higher incomes. This aspect and refundable tax credits combine to make the income tax system mildly progressive, although the progressivity is offset somewhat by a variety of special provisions that help higher-income households, such as deductions for retirement savings and capital gains exclusions. Payroll taxes and federal and provincial sales taxes are regressive, however; in sum, the total tax system is probably at best only slightly progressive.

    b. Efficiency: Although the reform of the federal tax system—the reduction of marginal income tax rates in 1988 and the introduction of the Goods and Sevices Tax (GST) in 1991—improved the efficiency of the income tax system, many special provisions remain.

    c. Administrative simplicity: An important source of administrative simplicity in the Canadian tax system is the extent to which the income taxes collected by the federal and provincial governments are harmonized. Also, the income tax reform of 1988 simplified the administration of the tax system, making it less profitable for taxpayers to search for loopholes.

The introduction of the GST in 1991, however, probably worked in the opposite direction, in part because provinces have been reluctant to harmonize their sales taxes with the GST.

    d. Transparency: For some taxes, such as the corporation income tax and sales taxes, it is difficult to determine the actual tax burden.

2. The equity-efficiency trade-off is similar to the risk-incentive trade-off you studied earlier. You learned that an employer who pays commissions, for example, will provide stronger incentives to the sales force than another who pays a straight salary. The result of the strong incentives, however, is risk for the employees. The risk is not only that incomes may be high in some months and low in others, but also that some employees may earn more than others. Just as an employer can provide strong incentives at a cost of risk for the employees, an economy can have efficiency at a cost of inequality. Social programmes that alleviate poverty also reduce the incentives to earn income. Similarly, progressive income taxation pays for social programmes, but discourages effort.

SELF-TEST

True or False

1. Redistribution is necessary to promote a more efficient allocation of resources than the market provides.

2. Horizontal equity says that upper-income individuals should pay a larger fraction of income in taxes.

3. Vertical equity says that people in similar situations should pay the same tax.

4. A tax system is progressive if upper-income individuals pay a larger fraction of income in taxes.

5. The payroll tax is an example of a progressive tax.

6. The federal government collects the provincial income tax for most provinces.

7. The 1988 tax reform reduced the administrative complexity of the Canadian tax system.

8. The corporate income tax is an example of a transparent tax.

9. Refundable tax credits increase the after-tax income of the working poor.

10. Tax expenditures refer to the lost revenue from tax subsidies, such as the deduction for retirement savings.

11. Social insurance is needs based.

12. An experience-rated employment insurance scheme charges higher premiums to workers with longer work experience.

13. The Gini coefficient is a measure of inequality.

14. The Lorenz curve illustrates the efficiency of the economy.

15. Canada has a more unequal distribution of economic goods than most other developed economies.

Multiple Choice

1. All of the following are examples of areas where government intervention is deemed appropriate by economists. Four fall into the category of correcting market failure. Which is the odd one out?

   a. unemployment
   b. income inequality
   c. lack of competition
   d. externalities
   e. public goods

2. A tax on tobacco is an example of:

   a. an excise tax.
   b. an income tax.
   c. a sales tax.
   d. a tariff.
   e. a payroll tax.

3. Which of the following taxes is levied in Canada to provide revenue for employment insurance?

   a. excise tax
   b. income tax
   c. sales tax
   d. tariff
   e. payroll tax

4. All the Canadian provinces, except one, levy provincial sales taxes. Which province is the odd one out?

   a. Nova Scotia
   b. Quebec
   c. Manitoba
   d. Alberta
   e. British Columbia

5. Which of the following taxes is levied in Canada by municipalities?

   a. excise tax
   b. property tax
   c. sales tax
   d. tariff
   e. payroll tax

6. In a tax system that satisfies the principle of horizontal equity:

   a. the marginal tax rate is the same for all individuals.
   b. the ratio of taxes to income is the same for all individuals.
   c. the ratio of taxes to income is higher for higher-income individuals.
   d. people in similar situations pay the same amount in taxes.
   e. individuals with higher incomes pay more taxes.

7. In a tax system that satisfies the principle of vertical equity:

   a. the marginal tax rate is the same for all individuals.
   b. the ratio of taxes to income is the same for all individuals.
   c. the ratio of taxes to income is higher for higher-income individuals.
   d. people in similar situations pay the same amount in taxes.
   e. individuals with higher incomes pay more taxes.

8. In a progressive tax system:

   a. the marginal tax rate is the same for all individuals.
   b. the ratio of taxes to income is the same for all individuals.
   c. the ratio of taxes to income is higher for higher-income individuals.
   d. people in similar situations pay the same amount in taxes.
   e. individuals with higher incomes pay more taxes.

9. Consider the following statements:
   I. An efficient tax system interferes as little as possible with resource allocation decisions.
   II. An efficient tax system collects its revenue at the lowest possible cost to taxpayers.

   a. Both I and II are correct.
   b. Neither I nor II is correct.
   c. I is correct; II is incorrect.
   d. I is incorrect; II is correct.
   e. Neither I nor II is incorrect, but either one is sufficient to define an efficient tax system.

10. When a reduction in taxes is allowed to an individual because she has spent money on a specific item (e.g., retirement savings), this is referred to as

    a. a lump-sum tax.
    b. tax incidence.
    c. a tax burden.
    d. tax evasion.
    e. a tax subsidy.

11. There is a cap on the amount of tax anyone is required to pay in federal payroll taxes. Because of this, these taxes are often described as:

    a. progressive.
    b. lump-sum taxes.
    c. voluntary taxes.
    d. tax evasion.
    e. a tax subsidy.

12. The burden of the corporation income tax refers to:

    a. the number of people who pay the tax.
    b. the cost of the tax subsidies built into the tax.
    c. how the tax is shifted through prices, wages, and dividends.
    d. the loss of efficiency resulting from the tax.
    e. the revenue raised by the tax.

13. All of the following, except one, are attributes of a good tax system. Which is the odd one out?

    a. efficiency
    b. fairness
    c. administrative simplicity
    d. regressivity
    e. transparency

14. When the Goods and Services Tax (GST) replaced the Manufacturers' Sales Tax (MST), the tax system improved in terms of _____ but got worse in terms of _____.

    a. fairness; efficiency
    b. efficiency; administrative simplicity
    c. administrative simplicity; transparency

d. administrative simplicity; fairness

e. transparency; fairness

15. Which of the following is social insurance, rather than a needs-based transfer programme?

    a. public provision of health services

    b. subsidized public housing

    c. welfare assistance

    d. guaranteed income supplement

    e. refundable tax credits

16. In 1950, there were _____ workers for every recipient of public pensions. Today, this number has fallen to _____.

    a. 12.5; 9

    b. 13.5; 8

    c. 14.5; 7

    d. 15.5; 6

    e. 15.5; 5

17. Raising taxes to fund expenditures aimed at the less well-off means taking money from better-off individuals whose incentives to work may be thereby adversely affected. The resulting trade-off is called the:

    a. consumption-leisure budget constraint.

    b. risk-incentive trade-off.

    c. production possibilities curve.

    d. equity-efficiency trade-off.

    e. two-period budget constraint.

18. Economists represent the degree of inequality in an economy using the:

    a. production possibilities curve.

    b. risk-incentive trade-off.

    c. Lorenz curve.

    d. equity-efficiency trade-off.

    e. consumption-leisure budget constraint.

19. The Gini coefficient is a measure of inequality derived from the Lorenz curve. When the Lorenz curve:

    a. moves closer to the 45-degree line of complete equality, the Gini coefficient increases.

    b. coincides with the 45-degree line of complete equality, the Gini coefficient equals 1.

    c. moves further from the 45-degree line of complete equality, the Gini coefficient decreases.

    d. indicates complete inequality, with all income going to one person, the Gini coefficient equals 0.

    e. moves closer to the 45-degree line of complete equality, the Gini coefficient decreases.

20. All of the following, except one, are reasons for government intervention. Which is the odd one out?

    a. abuses of market power

    b. high prices in competitive markets

    c. imperfect information

    d. undersupply of public goods

    e. negative externalities

Completion

1. The idea that individuals who are in identical situations should pay the same tax is called _____.

2. The idea that people who have more income or wealth should pay more tax is called _____.

3. A tax system in which individuals pay a larger fraction of income as income increases is called _____.

4. The term _____ refers to the revenue lost as a result of tax credits and deductions.

5. A good tax system has the characteristic of _____, which means that it is clear what each person is paying in taxes.

6. The proportion of an extra dollar of income that is paid in income tax is the _____.

7. Welfare assistance is a _____ programme.

8. The public provision of health care in Canada is an example of _____.

9. The basic trade-off that any government faces when it is designing a tax system is between efficiency and _____.

10. The _____ shows the fraction of income going to the poorest 10 percent, 20 percent, etc.

Answers to Self-Test

True or False

1. f	4. t	7. t	10. t	13. t
2. f	5. f	8. f	11. f	14. f
3. f	6. t	9. t	12. f	15. t

Multiple Choice

1. b	6. d	11. b	16. e
2. a	7. e	12. c	17. d
3. e	8. c	13. d	18. c
4. d	9. a	14. b	19. e
5. b	10. e	15. a	20. b

Completion

1. horizontal equity
2. vertical equity
3. progressive
4. tax expenditure
5. transparency
6. marginal tax rate
7. needs-based
8. social insurance
9. equity
10. Lorenz curve

Doing Economics: Tools and Practice Problems

Income taxation is an important redistributive measure. But, as with any such measure, the government has to balance its desire for equity with the need to avoid major inefficiency. The danger is that progressivity may reduce incentives to work. This trade-off between equity and efficiency is the subject of most of this section. The remainder is taken up with the use of the Lorenz curve to measure inequality.

PROGRESSIVE INCOME TAX

A progressive income tax system is one in which the average tax rate rises with income. This usually involves higher marginal rates of tax as income increases; that is, as hours worked increase, extra hours worked are remunerated at lower after-tax wage rates. This can reduce work effort. Tool Kits 20.1 and 20.2 show you why. Tool Kit 20.1 constructs the consumption-leisure budget constraint for a progressive income tax, and Tool Kit 20.2 compares this with a tax system in which the rate of tax does not vary with income.

Tool Kit 20.1: Plotting the Budget Constraint
with Progressive Income Taxes

Follow these steps to construct the consumption-leisure budget constraint when the income tax system has higher marginal rates of tax as income increases.

Step one: Identify the wage, the time available, and the tax schedule. Also, note the notches in the tax schedule, which are the income levels at which the tax rate changes.

Step two: Draw coordinate axes, labelling the horizontal one "Leisure" and the vertical one "Consumption."

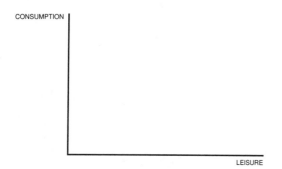

Step three: Plot the no-work point.

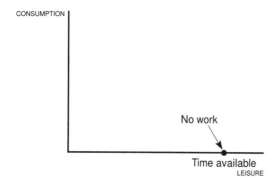

Step four: Identify the lowest level of income at which the tax rate changes. Determine how much time is needed to earn this level of income and the corresponding after-tax income:

time needed
= income at which tax rate changes/wage;
after-tax income = income − (tax rate × income).

Plot this point.

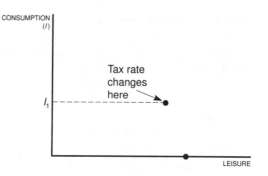

Step five: Identify the next lowest level of income at which the tax rate changes, and repeat step four. Continue.

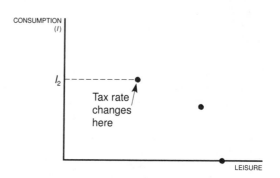

Step six: Draw line segments connecting the points. This is the budget constraint.

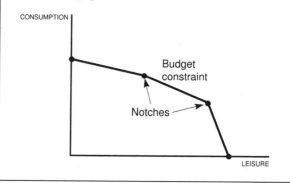

Tool Kit 20.2: Comparing Progressive and Flat
Income Tax Systems

Step one: Plot the budget constraint with the progessive tax schedule.

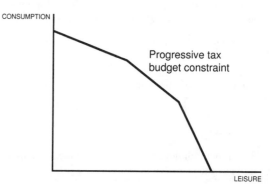

Step two: Choose a point on the budget constraint. Label it *A*.

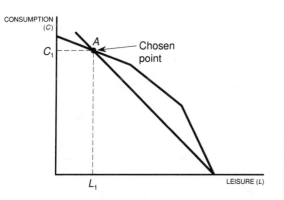

Step three: Draw a line segment from the no-work point through *A* to the vertical axis. This is the budget constraint for the proportional (flat) tax that raises the same tax revenue, at *A*, as the progressive tax.

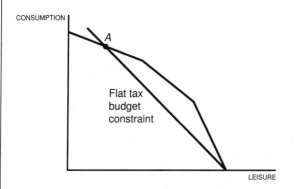

Step four: Darken the portion of the progressive tax budget constraint that lies outside the proportional tax budget constraint. These points are possible under the progressive system but not under the equivalent proportional tax system. Note that they involve less work.

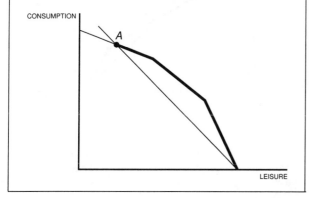

1. (Worked problem: progressive income tax) Mary Beth earns $200 per day as a design consultant and can work 300 days each year. The income tax schedule is given in the table. She has no nonwage income.

Annual income	Tax rate
$0–$10,000	0%
$10,000–$50,000	20%
$50,000 and up	40%

a. Plot her budget constraint.
b. Suppose that she chooses to work 150 days. Compute her average tax rate.
c. Compare her budget constraint drawn in part a with the budget constraint if she paid the flat tax rate computed in part b.

Step-by-step solution

Step one (a): Plot the budget constaint with the progressive tax schedule. Identify the wage, the time available, and the tax schedule. Also note the notches in the tax schedule, which are the income levels at which the tax rate changes. The wage is $200 per day. There are 300 days available, and the notches occur at $10,000 and $50,000.

Step two: Draw coordinate axes, labelling the horizontal one "Leisure" and the vertical one "Consumption."

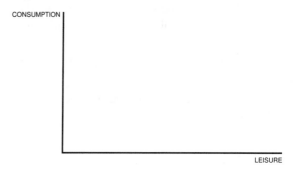

Step three: Plot the no-work point.

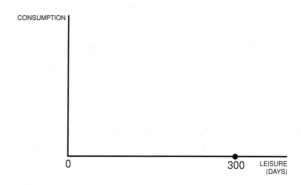

Step four: Identifty the lowest level of income at which the tax rate changes. This is $10,000. Determine how much time is needed to earn this level of income and the corresponding after-tax income:

time needed = $10,000/$200 = 50 days.
after-tax income = $10,000 - (.0 × $10,000) = $10,000.

Plot this point.

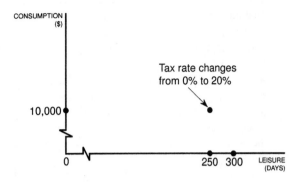

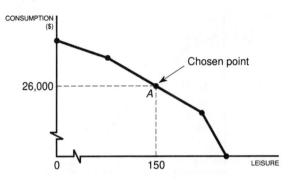

Step nine: Let *A* be Mary Beth's choice of 150 days spent working.

Step five: Identify the next lowest level of income at which the tax rate changes, and repeat step four. This point is 250 days, and $10,000 + $40,000 − (.20 × $40,000) = $42,000. Finally, if she works all 300 days, she earns $42,000 + $18,000 − (.4 × $18.000) = $52,800.

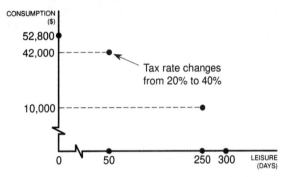

Step ten: Draw a line segment from the no-work point through *A* to the vertical axis. This is the proportional tax (flat tax = 13.3 percent) budget constraint.

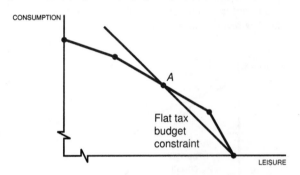

Step six: Draw line segments connecting the points. This is the budget constraint.

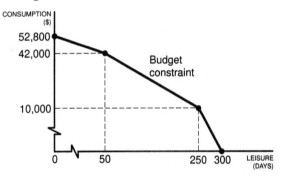

Step seven (b): Compute Mary Beth's average tax rate. She works 150 days and earns $30,000. She pays zero dollars on the first $10,000 and .20 × $20,000 = $4,000 on the remainder. Her average tax rate is $4,000/$30,000 = 13.3 percent.

Step eight (c): Compare progressive and proportional tax systems on her budget constraint. Plot the budget constraint with the progressive tax schedule.

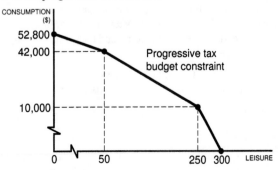

Step eleven: Darken the portion of the progressive tax budget constraint that lies outside the proportional tax budget constraint. Note that Mary Beth's incentives to work more days are weaker under the progressive tax. The two budget constraints illustrate the disincentive effects of progressive taxation.

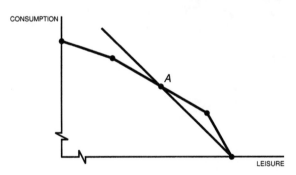

2. (Practice problem: progressive income tax) Sara earns $100 per day and can work only 200 days each year.

   a. Plot her budget constraint under the tax system given in problem 1.
   b. Suppose that she chooses to work 150 days. Compute her average tax rate.
   c. Compare her budget constraint drawn in part a with the budget constraint if she paid the flat tax rate computed in part b.

3. (Practice problem: progressive income tax) Return to problem 1 and answer parts a, b, and c under the following tax system.

Annual income	Tax rate
$0–$20,000	0%
$20,000 and up	40%

Is this tax system progressive?

LORENZ CURVE

The Lorenz curve is a convenient way to represent inequality graphically. If inequality of income is the focus, for example, the Lorenz curve shows the percentage of income received by the 10 percent of the population with the lowest incomes (the lowest 10 percent), the percentage of income received by the lowest 20 percent, and so on. Tool Kit 20.3 shows you how to construct the Lorenz curve when you know the amount of total income received by each group in the population.

Tool Kit 20.3: Plotting the Lorenz Curve

Follow these steps to construct a Lorenz curve.

Step one: Order the group from lowest income to highest.

Step two: Make a table with headings as follows.

Group	Cumulative % population	% population	% income	Cumulative % income

Step three: Compute the percentage of income for each group, and enter in the table.

Step four: Compute the percentage of the population for each group, and enter in the table.

Step five: Compute the cumulative percentage of income for each group by adding its percentage to all percentages of the lower-income groups, and enter in the table.

Step six: Compute the cumulative percentage of the population for each group by adding its percentage to all percentages of the lower-income groups, and enter in the table.

Step seven: Draw coordinate axes. Label the horizontal one "Cumulative percentage of population" and the vertical one "Cumulative percentage of income."

CUMULATIVE PERCENTAGE OF INCOME

CUMULATIVE PERCENTAGE OF POPULATION

Step eight: Plot points corresponding to each group.

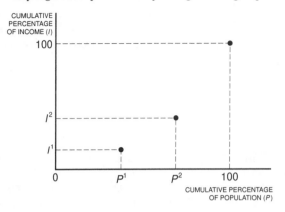

Step nine: Draw a curve connecting the points. This curve is the Lorenz curve.

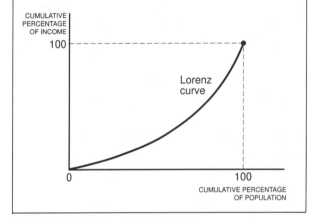

4. (Worked problem: Lorenz curve) In Costa Guano, there are four types of households: peasant farmers, ranchers, shopkeepers, and business owners. The population of each group (in millions) and the income (in Canadian dollar equivalent) of each are given in Table 20.1.

Table 20.1

	Income	Population (millions)
Peasant farmers	$ 5,000	40
Ranchers	$50,000	20
Shopkeepers	$10,000	30
Business owners	$80,000	10

Plot the Lorenz curve.

Step-by-step solution

Step one: Order the groups from lowest income to highest.

Peasant farmers	$ 5,000	40
Shopkeepers	$10,000	30
Ranchers	$50,000	20
Business owners	$80,000	10

Step two: Make a table.

Group	% population	Cumulative % population	% income	Cumulative % income
Peasant farmers				
Shopkeepers				
Ranchers				
Business owners				

Step three: Compute the percentage of income for each group, and enter in the table. For peasant farmers, it is {40 × $5,000/[(40 × $5,000) + (30 × $10,000) + (20 × $50,000) + (10 × $80,000)]} = 9 percent (this is rounded to the nearest whole percentage point). The completed column is given in Table 20.2.

Step four: Compute the percentage of the population for each group, and enter in the table. For peasant farmers, it is 40/(40 + 30 + 20 + 10) = 40 percent. Continue, and complete the column, which is given in Table 20.2.

Table 20.2

Group	% population	Cumulative % population	% income	Cumulative % income
Peasant farmers	40		9	
Shopkeepers	30		13	
Ranchers	20		43	
Business owners	10		35	

Step five: Compute the cumulative percentage of income for each group by adding its percentages to all percentages of the lower-income groups, and enter in the table. For peasant farmers, it is simply 9 percent. For shopkeepers, it is 9 + 13 = 22 percent. Continue.

Step six: Compute the cumulative percentage of the population for each group by adding its percentage to all percentages of the lower-income groups, and enter in the table. For peasant farmers, it is simply 40 percent. For shopkeepers, it is 40 + 30 = 70 percent. Continue. The complete information appears in Table 20.3.

Table 20.3

Group	% population	Cumulative % population	% income	Cumulative % income
Peasant farmers	40	40	9	9
Shopkeepers	30	70	13	22
Ranchers	20	90	43	65
Business owners	10	100	35	100

Step seven: Draw coordinate axes. Label the horizontal one "Cumulative percentage of population" and the vertical one "Cumulative percentage of the income."

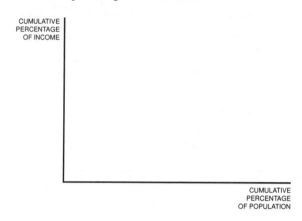

Step eight: Plot points corresponding to each group.

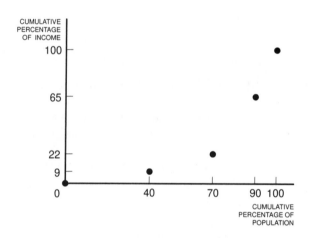

Step nine: Draw a curve connecting the points. This curve is the Lorenz curve.

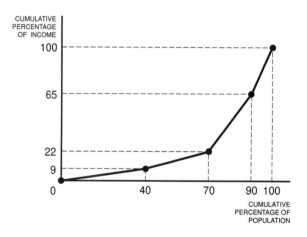

5. (Practice problem: Lorenz curve) North Dundas Provincial University is reconsidering the equity of its pay structure. All professors within a department receive the same salary, but salaries differ across departments. The number of professors in each department

and the salary of each professor in the department are given in Table 20.4.

Table 20.4

Department	Number of professors	Salary
Sociology	8	$50,000
Economics	10	$60,000
Marketing	2	$80,000
Literature	16	$30,000
Philosophy	4	$40,000

a Plot the Lorenz curve.

b An organization of faculty members proposes paying each professor $50,000. Plot the Lorenz curve for the faculty if this proposal were adopted.

c What would the Lorenz curve look like if each professor were paid $80,000?

6. (Practice problem: Lorenz curve) Exurbia, a pleasant town outside Gotham City, is populated by factory workers, bureaucrats, professionals, and retirees. All members of a particular group receive the same income and hold the same level of wealth, but incomes and levels of wealth differ across groups. The number of individuals in each group and the income and wealth of each individual in each group are given in Table 20.5.

Table 20.5

Career	Number	Income	Wealth
Factory workers	100	$30,000	$ 30,000
Bureaucrats	100	$40,000	$ 40,000
Professionals	100	$80,000	$ 80,000
Retirees	100	$50,000	$350,000

a Plot the Lorenz curve for income.

b Plot the Lorenz curve for wealth.

c Compare the two. Is there more inequality in income or in wealth?

Answers to Problems

2. *a,c.*

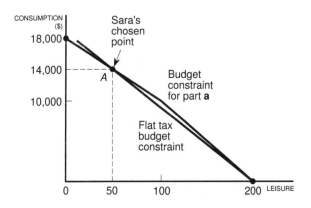

b. Tax = ($15,000 – $10,000) × .2 = $1,000; average tax rate = $1,000/$15,000 = 7 percent.

3. *a,b.*

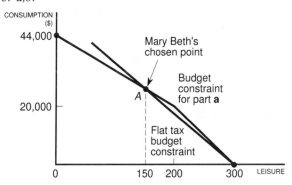

c. Tax = ($30,000 – $20,000) × .4 = $4,000; average tax rate = $4,000/$30,000 = 13.3 percent. Yes, it is progressive.

5. *a.* The Lorenz curve appears in Table 20.6 and the diagram.

Table 20.6

Department	% population	Cumulative % population	% income	Cumulative % income
Literature	40	40	27	27
Philosophy	10	50	9	36
Sociology	20	70	22	58
Economics	25	95	33	91
Marketing	5	100	9	100

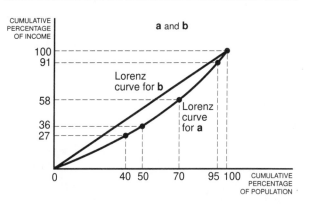

b. The complete information is given in Table 20.7. The Lorenz curve is the 45-degree line if there is equality.

Table 20.7

Department	% population	Cumulative % population	% income	Cumulative % income
Literature	40	40	40	40
Philosophy	10	50	10	50
Sociology	20	70	20	70
Economics	25	95	25	95
Marketing	5	100	5	100

c. The answer does not depend on the magnitude of income, only on its distribution. The answer is the same as for part b.

6. a. The Lorenz curve for income is given in Table 20.8 and the diagram.

Table 20.8

Career	% population	Cumulative % population	% income	Cumulative % income
Factory workers	25	25	15	15
Bureaucrats	25	50	20	35
Retirees	25	75	25	60
Professionals	25	100	40	100

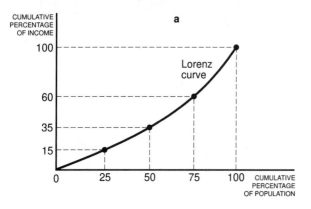

b. The Lorenz curve for wealth is given in Table 20.9 and the diagram.

Table 20.9

Career	% population	Cumulative % population	% income	Cumulative % income
Factory workers	25	25	6	6
Bureaucrats	25	50	8	14
Retirees	25	75	16	30
Professionals	25	100	70	100

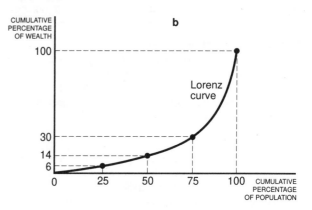

c. Wealth is distributed more unequally than income. The Lorenz curve for wealth is farther from the diagonal (45-degree line) than is the Lorenz curve for income.